lonely planet

D0395243

Discover
India

Experience the best
of India

This edition written and researched by
Daniel McCrohan,
Michael Benanav, Joe Bindloss, Lindsay Brown,
Mark Elliott, Paul Harding, Trent Holden, Amy Karafin,
Bradley Mayhew, Kate Morgan, John Noble,
Kevin Raub, Sarina Singh

Contents

Plan Your Trip

Discover India

●●●

Delhi & the
Taj Mahal   51

●●●

Mumbai
(Bombay)
& Around   109

Goa & Around

Contents

Discover India

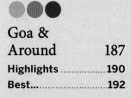

Northern Mountains & Amritsar   337

This is India

India fires the imagination and stirs the soul like no other place on earth, bristling with a mind-stirring mix of landscapes and cultural traditions. Your journey through India, no matter how fleeting, will blaze in your memory long after you've left its shores.

Famously chaotic, India doesn't have to be intimidating. True, the big cities can be bedlam, and the markets border on feverish, but there's a bounty of laid-back charms to explore too, from idyllic palm-fringed beaches and tranquil backwaters to sweeping deserts, snow-brushed mountains and lush green tea plantations.

Natural beauty abounds, but man-made gems also the dot the land. India's history is one of the world's most epic tales, and it has carved its incredible, indelible mark throughout the sub-continent. Temples hide in forests, fortresses rise from the desert, and palaces, mausoleums and more line the banks of the holy rivers that feed India's deeply sacred essence.

Spirituality is the common thread that weaves its way through India. Religion is alive, and thriving. It's woven into almost every aspect of daily life and it enriches your experiences at every turn. Follow pilgrims on a temple trail, place an offering on a roadside shrine, smell wafts of incense and feel the well-worn stone of the temple floor beneath your bare feet.

Nourishment of a different nature awaits you at restaurant tables everywhere. You're about to jump on board one of the wildest culinary trips of your travelling life. Frying, simmering, sizzling, kneading, roasting and flipping a deliciously diverse repertoire of dishes, feasting your way through the subcontinent is a tongue-teasing ride to remember.

India is indeed a feast of opportunities. And even on a short trip you can go surprisingly in-depth and experience a remarkable range of wonders. Just try not to fit too much onto your plate. It's more rewarding to experience a small amount more fully; so slow down, relax and above all enjoy the phenomenon that is India.

> " Fiery India will blaze in your memory long after you've left its shores. "

Priest at a Jain temple in Ranakpur (p166), Rajasthan

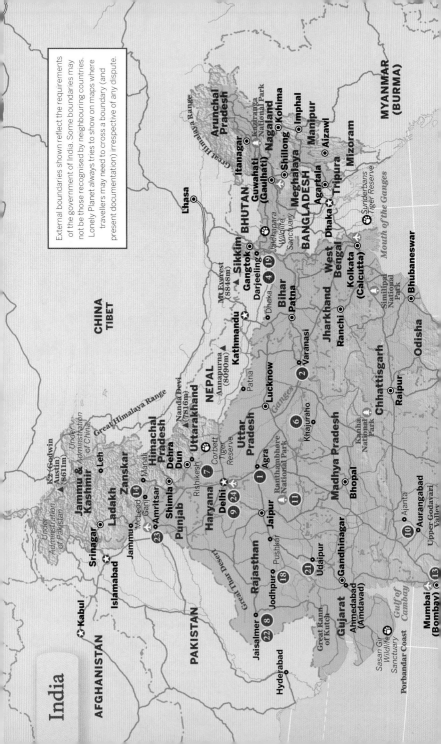

India

External boundaries shown reflect the requirements of the government of India. Some boundaries may not be those recognised by neighbouring countries. Lonely Planet always tries to show on maps where travellers may need to cross a boundary (and present documentation) irrespective of any dispute.

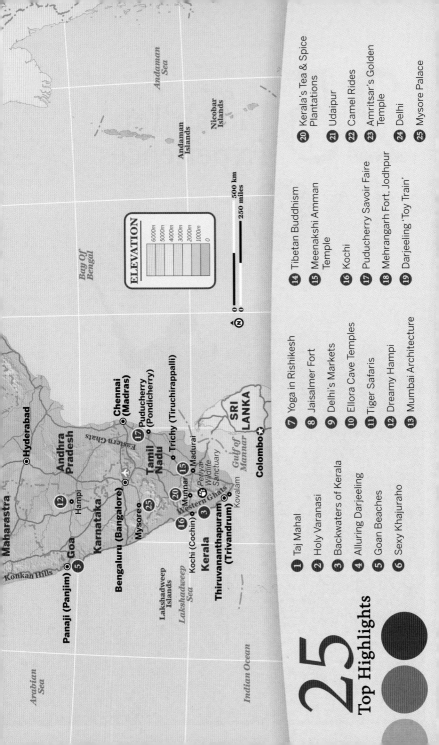

25
Top Highlights

1 Taj Mahal
2 Holy Varanasi
3 Backwaters of Kerala
4 Alluring Darjeeling
5 Goan Beaches
6 Sexy Khajuraho
7 Yoga in Rishikesh
8 Jaisalmer Fort
9 Delhi's Markets
10 Ellora Cave Temples
11 Tiger Safaris
12 Dreamy Hampi
13 Mumbai Architecture
14 Tibetan Buddhism
15 Meenakshi Amman Temple
16 Kochi
17 Puducherry Savoir Faire
18 Mehrangarh Fort, Jodhpur
19 Darjeeling 'Toy Train'
20 Kerala's Tea & Spice Plantations
21 Udaipur
22 Camel Rides
23 Amritsar's Golden Temple
24 Delhi
25 Mysore Palace

ELEVATION

| 6000m |
| 5000m |
| 4000m |
| 3000m |
| 2000m |
| 1000m |
| 0 |

500 km
250 miles

Arabian Sea

Andaman Sea

Bay Of Bengal

Andaman Islands

Nicobar Islands

Maharastra

Hyderabad

Andhra Pradesh

Eastern Ghats

Chennai (Madras)
Puducherry (Pondicherry)
Trichy (Tiruchirappalli)

Konkan Hills

Panaji (Panjim)
Goa

Karnataka

Hampi

Bengaluru (Bangalore)

Mysore

Kochi (Cochin)

Kerala

Munnar
Western Ghats
Periyar Wildlife Sanctuary

Tamil Nadu

Madurai

Lakshadweep Islands

Lakshadweep Sea

Thiruvananthapuram (Trivandrum)

Kovalam

Gulf of Mannar

SRI LANKA

Colombo

Indian Ocean

25 India's Top Experiences

Taj Mahal

The Taj Mahal (p94) rises from the beaten earth of Uttar Pradesh as it does in dreams, but even the wildest imaginings leave travellers underprepared for that breath-stealing moment when its gates are traversed and this magnificent world wonder comes into focus. It is the embodiment of architectural perfection; the ultimate monument to love. Don't let fears of tour buses or hordes of visitors make you think you can skip the Taj – you can't.

SEAN CAFFREY/GETTY IMAGES ©

② Holy Varanasi

Everyone in Varanasi (p316) seems to be dying or praying or hustling or cremating someone, or swimming or laundering or washing buffaloes in the sewage-saturated Ganges. The goddess river will clean away your sins and help you escape from that tedious life-and-death cycle – and Varanasi is *the* place to take a sacred dip. So take a deep breath, put on a big smile for the ever-present touts, go to the holy water and get your karma in order.

Backwaters of Kerala

It's unusual in India to find a place as vast and tranquil as the backwaters (p240): 900km of interconnected rivers, lakes and lagoons lined with tropical flora. Even if you do, there won't be a way to experience it that's as peaceful and intimate as a few days on a teak-and-palm-thatch houseboat. Float along the water – as the sun sets behind the palms, or while eating to-die-for Keralan seafood, or as you sleep under a twinkling sky – and forget about life on land for a while.

The Best...
Quiet Retreats

BACKWATERS, KERALA
There are few things more relaxing than travelling through the 900km network of waterways fringing Kerala's coast. (p241)

SHIMLA, HIMACHAL PRADESH
An engaging blend of hilltop holiday town and Indian city, surrounded by rolling landscapes of green, reached via the 'toy train'. (p354)

MUNNAR, KERALA
Relax in a homestay at a remote tea plantation near this Kerala hill station. (p246)

SUNDERBANS TIGER RESERVE
Escape the city chaos of nearby Kolkata with a boat trip through part of the world's largest mangrove forest. (p306)

13

The Best...
Beaches

PALOLEM
Nodding palms, beach huts on stilts and white sands – this is one of Goa's loveliest spots. (p214)

VARKALA
Dramatic russet sea cliffs drop down to a broad sandy beach that hosts a mix of Hindu priests, backpackers and local volleyball enthusiasts. (p236)

GIRGAUM CHOWPATTY
Mumbai's jostling, colourful city beach is a favoured spot for an evening stroll and a serve of *bhelpuri* (fried dough with rice, lentils and spices). (p119)

CHERAI BEACH
Kochin's best-kept secret, this long stretch of undeveloped white sand on nearby Vypeen Island also comes with miles of lazy backwaters just a few hundred metres from the seafront. (p250)

Alluring Darjeeling

④

Up in a tippy-top nook of India's far northeast is storied Darjeeling (p309). It's no longer a romantic mountain hideaway, but the allure remains. Undulating hills of bulbous tea shrubs are pruned by women in colourful dresses; the majestic Himalaya peek through puffy clouds as the sun climbs out from behind the mountains; and little alleys wend their way through mountain mist, past clotheslines and monasteries. Ride the 'toy train' and drink it all in – the tea and the town's legendary enchantment.

Goan Beaches

⑤

There's no better place in India to be lazy than on one of Goa's spectacular beaches (p197). With palm groves on one side of the white sands and gently lapping waves on the other, the best beaches live up to your image of a tropical paradise. But it's not an undiscovered one: the sands are also peppered with fellow travellers and beach-shack restaurants. Goa's treasures are for fans of creature comforts who like their seafood fresh and their holidays easy. Palolem beach

Sexy Khajuraho

Are the sensuous statues on the temples of Khajuraho (p328) the Kamasutra, Tantric examples for initiates or allegories for the faithful? They're definitely naughty fun, with hot nymphs, a nine-person orgy and even men getting it on with horses. Once the titillation passes, you'll be pleasantly absorbed by the exquisite carving of these thousand-year-old temples and the magical feeling of 11th-century India

Yoga in Rishikesh

Where better to do the downward dog than in the self-styled 'Yoga Capital of the World'? Rishikesh (p348) has a beautiful setting, surrounded by forested hills and cut through by the fast-flowing Ganges. There are masses of ashrams and all kinds of yoga, meditation classes and alternative therapies, from laughing yoga to crystal healing.

Jaisalmer Fort

Rising up from the deserts of Rajasthan, Jaisalmer's 12th-century citadel (p179) looks like something from a dream. The enormous golden sandstone fort, with its crenellated ramparts and undulating towers, is a fantastical structure, even while camouflaged against the desert sand. Inside, an ornate royal palace, fairy-tale mansions, intricately carved temples and narrow lanes conspire to create one of the world's best places to get lost.

The Best...
Forts

JAISALMER FORT
A grand sandcastle of a fort, rearing out of the desert; once a stop on the ancient camel trade routes. (p179)

MEHRANGARH
Formidable fortress protruding out of a great rocky escarpment, which towers over the old city of Jodhpur. (p173)

AGRA FORT
With the Taj Mahal overshadowing it, it's easy to overlook one of the finest Mughal forts in India. (p93)

AMBER FORT
Mighty fortress of pale yellow and pink sandstone and white marble, just outside Jaipur. (p147)

KUMBALGARH
A vast, isolated fortress in the forested hills near Udaipur. The journey here is almost as amazing as the sight itself. (p166)

17

Delhi's Markets

Shopaholics: be careful not to lose control. No interest in shopping? Get in touch with your consumerist side. Delhi (p86) is one of the world's finest places to shop, and its markets – Old Delhi, Khan Market or the specialty bazaars – have something you want, guaranteed (though you may not have known this beforehand). The range of technicolour saris, glittering gold and silver bling, mounds of rainbow vermilion, aromatic fresh spices, stainless-steel head massagers, bangles and bobby pins, heaping piles of fruit and marigold and coconut offerings is simply astounding. Paharganj bazaar

9

The Best...
Places for Food

DELHI
Dine on almost any international flavour in India's capital, with remarkably good food ranging from streetside stalls to creative-cuisine restaurants. (p77)

KERALA
With a long coastline, endless spice plantations and coconut groves, the fragrant cuisine of Kerala is refreshingly delicious. (p230)

GOA
Famous for fresh fish curries, often served on a banana leaf, Goan cuisine is perfumed with many influences brought by traders from overseas. (p196)

MUMBAI
One of India's great food centres, where a cornucopia of flavours from all over the country collides with international trends and tastebuds. (p123)

10 Ellora Cave Temples

The pinnacle of ancient Indian rock-cut architecture, these astounding cave temples (p134) were chipped out laboriously through five centuries by generations of Buddhist, Hindu and Jain monks. The caves here are younger than those at nearby Ajanta, but are embellished with a profusion of remarkably detailed sculptures, and the location, strung along a 2km-long escarpment, allowed for more monumental designs, with elaborate courtyards carved in front of the shrines themselves.

Tiger Safaris

You have to be lucky to spot a tiger in India, but it can be done. Try Ranthambhore National Park (p161), in Rajasthan. It's one of India's most exciting experiences to steal through the undergrowth, surrounded by birds and butterflies, in search of a tiger. And even if you don't catch sight of one, the other wildlife, and the deep-forest setting of most tiger reserves, will prove a breathtaking distraction.

11

JOHN HAY/GETTY IMAGES ©

12

Dreamy Hampi

The surreal rockscape of Hampi (p217) was once the cosmopolitan capital of a powerful Hindu empire. The glorious ruins of its temples and royal structures join sublimely with the terrain: giant rocks balance on pedestals near an ancient elephant stable; temples tuck into crevices between boulders; boats float by rice paddies near a giant bathtub fit for a queen. Watching the sunset's rosy glow over the dreamy landscape, you might just forget what planet you're on.

13

Mumbai Architecture

Mumbai (p118) has always absorbed everything in her midst and made it her own. The result is a heady mix of buildings with countless influences. The art deco and modern towers are flashy, but it's the Victorian-era structures, the neo-Gothic, Indo-Saracenic and Venetian Gothic, that have come to define Mumbai. All the spires, gables, arches and onion domes make for a pleasant walk through the city's past.

Chhatrapati Shivaji Terminus

GAVIN HELLIER/GETTY IMAGES ©

Tibetan Buddhism

Up north, in places such as McLeod Ganj (p364), where the air is cooler and crisper, quaint hill settlements give way to snow-topped peaks. Here, the cultural influences came not by coasts but via mountain passes. Tibetan Buddhism thrives, and multilayered monasteries emerge from the forest or steep cliffs as vividly and poetically as the sun rises over mountain peaks. Weathered prayer flags on forest paths blow in the wind, the sound of monks chanting reverberates in meditation halls, and locals bring offerings and make merit, all in the shadow of the mighty Himalaya.

The Best...
Unesco World Heritage Sites

TAJ MAHAL
Just one of a trio of Unesco sites in Agra, so spare time for Agra Fort and Fatehpur Sikri too. (p94)

ELLORA CAVES
The epitome of ancient Indian rock-cut architecture, chipped out laboriously over five centuries. (p134)

AJANTA CAVES
Ancient caverns guarding a hoard of unparalleled artistic treasures. (p135)

KHAJURAHO
Famed temples carved with exquisite skill and erotic detail. (p328)

QUTB MINAR
Architecture reflecting different building styles over hundreds of years. (p74)

HAMPI
An incredible collection of 15th- and 16th-century temples just a short trip from Goa. (p217)

The Best...
Temples

**MEENAKSHI AMMAN
TEMPLE, MADURAI**
Abode of a triple-breasted,
fish-eyed goddess, a pinnacle of South Indian temple
architecture. (p282)

KHAJURAHO
The erotic carvings of these
temples are among the
finest sacred art in the
world. (p328)

**SHORE TEMPLE,
MAMALLAPURAM**
A magnificent masterpiece
of rock-cut elegance overlooking the sea. (p272)

VITTALA TEMPLE, HAMPI
Never finished, nor
consecrated, this 16th-
century structure in
boulder-strewn Hampi
remains the pinnacle of
Vijayanagar art. (p218)

**GOLDEN TEMPLE,
AMRITSAR**
Gorgeous to look at and
atmospheric to visit,
this is Sikhism's holiest
shrine. (p371)

KAILASA TEMPLE, ELLORA
The centrepiece of the
Ellora caves took 150
years to carve from a
rock face. (p134)

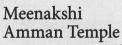

Meenakshi Amman Temple

A six-hectare complex (p282) enclosed by 12 tall *gopurams* (gateway towers), covered in a multicoloured stucco frenzy of thousands of deities, mythical creatures and monsters, Meenakshi Amman is the pinnacle of South Indian temple architecture. It's an inspirational dedication to Shiva, a work of utmost splendour that's an onslaught on the senses. Within is a hive of activity, with tranquil tanks and dramatic halls; it's one of India's key places to experience the vibrant wonder of religious life.

ABOVE: SUYOG GAIDHANI/GETTY IMAGES © LEFT: NEIL MCALLISTER/GETTY IMAGES ©

Kochi

It's easy to be beguiled in the ancient Keralan port of Kochi (p248). Its most charming district, Fort Cochin, displays a tantalising cocktail of influences, from the rambling Dutch, British and Portuguese villas to the cantilevered Chinese fishing nets still in use off the promenade, from the overgrown foreign cemeteries to the ancient synagogue, decorated with hand-painted Cantonese tiles. It's a laid-back place to wander and breathe in the living history of this wonderfully atmospheric spice port.

Puducherry Savoir Faire

In this former French colony (p277), yellow houses line cobbleston streets, grand cathedra are adorned with archi-tectural frou-frou and t croissants are the real deal. But Puducherry's also a Tamil town – with all the history, temples and bustle tha go along with that – and a classic retreat town, too, with the Sri Aurob-indo Ashram at its hear Turns out that yoga, *pain au chocolat*, Hindu gods and colonial-era architecture make for a atmospheric melange.

Notre Dame des Anges

PAUL HARDING/GETTY IMAGES ©

Mehrangarh Fort, Jodhpur

India is full of incredible, fantastical forts, but one of the most memorable you will see is Mehrangarh (p173), which towers over the blue city of Jodhpur like an illustration from the Brothers Grimm. It seems to grow out of the rock face, with imposing walls shooting skywards from the cliff on which it stands. The architecture is half solid fortress, half delicate palace. The blue-city views are enchanting.

18

The Best...
Views

TIGER HILL, DARJEELING
A stunning 250km panorama of Himalayan horizon, including Everest (8848m), Lhotse (8501m), and Makalu (8475m). (p309)

TOP STATION, MUNNAR
On the Kerala–Tamil Nadu border, Top Station has spectacular views over the Western Ghats. (p246)

GUN HILL, MUSSOORIE
Take a cable car up to Gun Hill (2530m) on a clear day for views of several peaks. (p346)

TAJ MAHAL, AGRA
From the north bank of the Yamuna River, from a rooftop cafe in Taj Ganj, or from one of the towers in Agra Fort. (p95)

JAISALMER FORT
Your first glimpse of this sandcastle-like fortress is unforgettable. But don't miss climbing it for sweeping views of the Thar Desert. (p179)

The Best...
Places for Walks & Hikes

MANALI
Take a stroll along the Beas River, or hire a guide and hike into the mountains. (p359)

RISHIKESH
Walk to a waterfall or a riverside beach, or follow pilgrims on a temple trail. (p348)

DARJEELING
Trek into the hills, or just saunter around the tea plantations. (p309)

MUSSOORIE
Easy walks with great views, as well as longer guided treks. (p346)

MCLEOD GANJ
Short walks with fine mountain views. (p364)

UDAIPUR
Take a city walking tour, explore the surrounding countryside or walk the fort walls at nearby Khumbhalgarh. (p166)

Darjeeling 'Toy Train'

19

India's quintessential journey is still the train ride, and one of the prettiest and quaintest journeys is the narrow-gauge train trip on the Darjeeling Himalayan Railway, aka the toy train (p310). This hilltop treasure made its first journey in 1881 and is one of the few hill railways still operating in India (there's another good one serving Shimla). Parts of the line are still served by steam locomotives, the views are often stunning, and such is the romantically slow speed of the train that you'll find locals hopping on and off as your chug your way up the mountain.

TOM COCKREM/GETTY IMAGES ©

20 Kerala's Tea & Spice Plantations

The southern state of Kerala is famous for its beaches and backwaters, but one of the region's highlights is its lush plantations in the hills, such as those around Munnar (p246). Travel inland and you'll discover more shades of green than you thought could possibly exist, with endless rolling clumps of tea, brilliantly bright rice paddies, spiky ginger plantations, and field after field of coffee, cardamom and pepper.

BARTOSZ HADYNIAK/GETTY IMAGES ©

Udaipur

On your honeymoon? No? Well, make as if you are and indulge in the storybook romance of Udaipur (p163), a town seemingly sculpted from faded lace and built around several beautiful lakes, framed by pale blue hills. It's a great place to laze on sun-bleached rooftops, kick back and read some good books, browse the city's stalls and shops and explore its labyrinthine lakeside palace. Jagdish Temple

Camel Rides

Live out a maharaja fantasy and take a desert 'safari' around Jaisalmer (p182). You'll lollop through the rocky terrain atop the tall, goofy creatures, camp out among sand dunes under star-packed skies and visit remote villages where desert dwellers' clothes flicker like flames against the landscape, gaggles of children run out to see you and musicians sing about local life.

Amritsar's Golden Temple

The Sikhs' holiest shrine (p372) is a magical place for people of all religions to worship. Seeming to float atop a pool named for the 'nectar of immortality', the temple is a gorgeous structure, made even more so by its extreme goldness (the lotus-shaped dome is gilded with the real thing). Even when crowded with happy pilgrims, the temple is peaceful, with birds singing outside and the lake gently lapping against the godly abode.

23

The Best...
Places for Outdoor Activities

MANALI
Himalayan foothills form a backdrop for hiking, mountain biking, paragliding, rafting and more. (p359)

RISHIKESH
If yoga isn't your thing, try hiking, rafting, kayaking or just lazing around on a riverside beach. (p348)

PALOLEM, GOA
Kayak out to sea on dolphin-spotting trips, or take a guided hike into the surrounding jungle. (p214)

AROUND JAIPUR
Take a spectacular balloon ride above Amber Fort, or spend a day with the elephants at stables nearby. (p146)

Delhi

India's capital (p60) has had several incarnations over the past few thousand years, which partly explains why there' much going on here. Dust, noise and chaos aside, Delhi is of stunning architecture, culture (its residents come from over the country), good food and even better shopping. T Mughal legacy is one of its biggest attractions: Old Delhi i crumbling splendour, with the majestic Jama Masjid, the sive Red Fort and other monuments of the historic Mugha capital adorning the old city like royal jewels. Jama Masjid

The Best...
Places for Wildlife

RANTHAMBHORE NATIONAL PARK
With 1334 sq km of wild jungle hemmed in by rocky ridges, and the amazing 10th-century Ranthambhore Fort, this is a fantastic place for spotting tigers. (p161)

CORBETT TIGER RESERVE
This legendary park has around 200 tigers, and 200 to 300 wild elephants. (p352)

SUNDERBANS TIGER RESERVE
This 2585-sq-km reserve forms part of the world's largest mangrove forest, home to the largest single population of tigers on earth. (p306)

PERIYAR WILDLIFE SANCTUARY
Kerala's most popular wildlife reserve is home to around 1000 wild elephants. (p242)

Mysore Palace

Undoubtedly over the top, this 100-year-old Indo-Sarcenic marvel (p259) is a kaleidoscope of stained glass, mirrors and gaudy colours, and is among the grandest of India's royal buildings. Illuminated majestically on weekends, the palace's magnificent exterior houses sculptures, paintings, carved doorways, mosaic floors and numerous collections of artefacts, including an intriguing armoury containing more than 700 weapons.

India's
Top Itineraries

Delhi to Jaipur The Golden Triangle

5 DAYS

This is the classic, awe-inspiring route: you can discover the many different sides of Delhi before visiting India's most famous monument, the Taj Mahal, taking a side trip to the deserted former capital of Fatehpur Sikri, then heading to the pink city of Jaipur, before returning to Delhi.

PAKISTAN

CHINA

Bhakra Dam

NEPAL

DELHI ❶

Sambhar Salt Lake

❹ **JAIPUR**   ❸   ❷ **AGRA**

FATEHPUR SIKRI

---

❶ Delhi (p60)

Explore the capital's highlights, from its buzzing restaurants and astounding shops to the medieval old city with its imposing **Red Fort** and huge **Jama Masjid**. Try to include trips to **Qutb Minar** and **Humayun's tomb**.

DELHI ➲ AGRA

🚃 **Two to three hours** The 6am Bhopal Shatabdi Express from New Delhi station takes two hours; other trains (there are many) take three.
🚗 **Three hours** If taking the new expressway; otherwise, four to five hours.

❷ Taj Mahal, Agra (p93)

Rabindranath Tagore described it as 'a teardrop on the cheek of eternity', Rudyard Kipling as 'the embodiment of all things pure'. And somehow this epic monument to love really does live up to all the hype. Try to visit in the early morning and leave room for a side trip to **Agra Fort**. But don't forget, the Taj is closed on Fridays!

AGRA ➲ FATEHPUR SIKRI

🚌 **One hour** From Agra's Idgah bus stand, every 30 minutes. 🚗 **One hour** 40km southwest by road.

❸ Fatehpur Sikri (p101)

The short-lived capital of the Mughal empire in the 16th century, the magnificent fortified ancient city of **Fatehpur Sikri**, 40km southwest of Agra, is a well-preserved and atmospheric Unesco World Heritage Site. The city was an Indo-Islamic masterpiece, but was erected in an area that suffered from water shortages and so was abandoned shortly after Emperor Akbar's death.

AGRA ➲ JAIPUR

🚃 **3½ hours** The Shatabdi Express leaves every afternoon (except Thursdays) from Agra Fort train station. 🚗 **Six hours** It's around 230km from Agra to Jaipur.

❹ Jaipur (p146)

The dusky, grubby pink city glitters with bazaars and centres around its sprawling **City Palace** as well as the **Hawa Mahal** – a honeycomb-like palace. Outside the city is the majestic **Amber Fort**, which you can reach on the back of a painted elephant.

Mumbai to Palolem
A Taste of Goa

This trip will immerse you in the mixed-up rhythms of Mumbai before you head south to relax on the white-sand beaches of Goa, eat delicious seafood and explore this fascinating region's culture.

ARABIAN SEA

1 MUMBAI (BOMBAY)

2 PANAJI (PANJIM)

3 PALOLEM

① Mumbai (Bombay) (p118)

Enjoy eating in some of India's best restaurants, browsing in some of its most atmospheric bazaars, admiring the grandiose frilliness of Mumbai's colonial-era architecture, strolling on **Girgaum Chowpatty** eating *kulfi* (ice cream) and taking the boat out to **Elephanta Island**.

MUMBAI ➡ PANAJI

✈ **One hour** Fly to Goa's Dabolim Airport, 29km south of Panaji, then take a taxi. 🚆 **10½ hours** Take the 11.05pm Konkan Kanya Express from Mumbai's CST station, and get off the following morning at Karmali (Old Goa), a short taxi ride from Panaji.

② Panaji (Panjim) (p196)

Discover the Portuguese-flavoured old quarters of the Goan capital, **Panaji**, lingering over lunch at one of its ravishing restaurants and enjoying a tranquil boat trip on the Mandovi River. Take a day trip to **Old Goa** for elegantly crumbling grand cathedrals; vestiges of its former splendour.

PANAJI ➡ PALOLEM

🚗 **Two hours** It's a short drive south to Palolem. 🚆 **One hour** The daily train from Karmali (Old Goa) to Cancona leaves you with a short taxi ride to Palolem, but it departs Old Goa at an awkwardly late 10.20pm.

③ Palolem (p214)

Formerly Goa's best-kept secret, Palolem is the perfect place to end your trip and relax for a couple of days, with a stunning crescent **beach**. There's not much nightlife, but it's ideal for chilling out, basking in the sunshine and swimming in limpid seas. There's also yoga, **massage therapies** and even **kayaking** on offer.

Girgaum Chowpatty (Chowpatty Beach; p119), Mumbai
CHRISTER FREDRIKSSON/GETTY IMAGES ©

10 DAYS

Delhi to Jaisalmer
The Land of the Kings

This royal journey includes Delhi and the Taj Mahal before it ventures across Rajasthan, the 'Land of the Kings'. Search for tigers in the jungles of Ranthambhore, then explore the forts and palaces of the 'Lake City' (Udaipur), the 'Blue City' (Jodhpur) and the 'Golden City' (Jaisalmer).

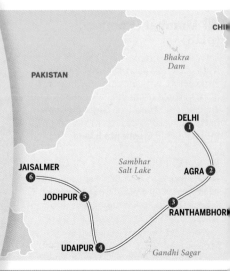

1. Delhi (p60)

Starting your trip in Delhi, be sure to visit some of its major sights, including the **Qutb Minar**, **Humayun's tomb** and the **Red Fort**. Also, don't miss out on eating at some of best restaurants in India.

DELHI ➡ AGRA

🚆 **Two to three hours** The 6am Bhopal Shatabdi Express from New Delhi station takes just two hours. Other trains (there are many) take three.
🚗 **Three hours** If taking the new expressway; otherwise, four to five hours.

2. Agra (p93)

Make an early start to see the **Taj Mahal**, one of the wonders of the world, followed by a lazy lunch in Agra before visiting the magnificent Mughal **Agra Fort**.

AGRA ➡ RANTHAMBHORE

🚗 **Five to six hours** It's around 250km drive from Agra to Ranthambhore. 🚆 **Five hours** There's only one daily train to Sawai Madhopur (for Ranthambhore); the 6.15am PNBE Kota Express from Agra Cant station, although others run on selected days from Agra Fort station.

3. Ranthambhore (p161)

Visit **Ranthambhore National Park** to see wild jungle scrub, hemmed in by rocky ridges and dotted by ruined *chhatris* domed kiosks), temples and a spectacularly overgrown **10th-century fort**, all the while keeping your eyes peeled for tigers.

RANTHAMBHORE ➡ UDAIPUR

🚆 **7½ hours** The overnight Mewar Express leaves Sawai Madhopur for Udaipur at 11.50pm, arriving at 7.20am. 🚗 **Six to seven hours** It's 380km by road.

4. Udaipur (p163)

Relax in what is perhaps India's most romantic city, framed by ancient Aravalli hills and ranged around the glassy waters of **Lake Pichola**. Visit the impressive **City Palace**, go **boating** on the lake then watch the sun set from a rooftop restaurant.

UDAIPUR ➡ JODHPUR

🚗 **Six to seven hours** There are no trains to Jodhpur, so hire a car and driver. 🚆 **Eight hours** There are hourly buses until 10pm, but it's a long slog.

5. Jodhpur (p172)

Towered over by the mighty fortress of **Mehrangarh**, the 'Blue City' of Jodhpur stretches out, a jumble of pale-painted houses – from the bird's-eye viewpoint of the fort, it looks like a fantastical, cubist painting.

JODHPUR ➡ JAISALMER

🚆 **Six hours** There's a 5.10am train, but the better option is the overnight Jodhpur-Jaisalmer Express, which leaves Jodhpur at 11.45pm.
🚗 **Five hours** Your hotel can help arrange a car and driver, or else negotiate with drivers at the taxi stand outside the train station.

6. Jaisalmer (p178)

Romantically remote, this desert citadel is home to India's most remarkable **fort**; a still-inhabited, 12th-century bastion that seems to rise, mirage-like from the surrounding desert. Wander the narrow streets of the old city and take a **camel safari** if you have time, before you board the 5.15pm Jaisalmer-Delhi Express back to Delhi, arriving at 11.10am the following day.

Mehrangarh fort (p173), overlooking Jodhpur
MARJI LANG/GETTY IMAGES ©

10 DAYS

Chennai to Mumbai
Sun, Sea & Temples

Laid-back Kerala is the highlight of this southern tour, which begins in Tamil Nadu and ends in Mumbai. From Chennai, head south to the incredible Meenakshi Amman Temple before crossing into Kerala where you'll enjoy the beach, the backwaters and a charming ancient spice port before ending your trip in massive Mumbai.

MUMBAI (BOMBAY) 6

CHENNAI (MADRAS) 1

LAKSHADWEEP SEA

KOCHI (COCHIN) 5

ALAPPUZHA (ALLEPPEY) 4

MADURAI 2

VARKALA 3

Thiruvananthapuram (Trivandrum)

SRI LANKA

1 Chennai (Madras) (p266)

Take it easy in Chennai on your first day; visit a museum or two; perhaps hook up with one of the city's walking tours; certainly take a sunset stroll along **Marina Beach**.

CHENNAI ➲ MADURAI

🚃 **Nine hours** The most convenient of the daily trains to Madurai Junction is the overnight Pandian Express, which leaves Chennai Central at 9.20pm. ✈ **One hour** Spice Jet flies daily to Madurai.

2 Madurai (p281)

The heart and soul of Tamil Nadu, Madurai is one of India's oldest cities and home to the remarkable **Meenakshi Amman Temple**. Covering six hectares and including 12 tall *gopurams* (gateway towers), each encrusted with a staggering array of gods, goddesses, demons and heroes, this is one of India's greatest temple complexes.

MADURAI ➲ VARKALA

🚃 **Nine hours** The 11.05pm Quilon Passenger is the best of three daily trains to Trivandrum. It arrives at 6.40am, giving you plenty of time to reach the beach at Varkala, by train (40 minutes), bus (1½ hours) or taxi (one hour)

3 Varkala (p236)

Hindu place of pilgrimage and laid-back **beach resort**, Varkala stretches out along the coast on the edge of some stunningly dramatic, russet-streaked sea cliffs. It's a great place to kick back for a day or two, resting up at its small-scale resorts and guesthouses and indulging in some **ayurvedic treatments**.

Kathakali dancer, Kochi (p248)
KIMBERLEY COOLE/GETTY IMAGES ©

VARKALA ➲ ALAPPUZHA

🚃 **Two hours** There are six daily trains to Alappuzha (Alleppey), although only the 10.25am, 6pm and 8pm are at convenient times. 🚗 **Three hours** Your hotel should be able to help arrange a taxi.

4 Alappuzha (Alleppey) (p238)

Alappuzha is the gateway to Kerala's fabled **backwaters**, a network of lakes and canals, lined by lush vegetation and waterside villages. It's one of India's most magical experiences to take an overnight **houseboat** and sleep on the water under the stars. Inquire about the possibility of taking a houseboat all the way to Kochi.

ALAPPUZHA ➲ KOCHI

🚃 **1½ hours** Regular trains run from Alappuzha (Alleppey) to Ernakulam (Kochi). 🚗 **1½ hours** Ask your hotel to help arrange a taxi.

5 Kochi (Cochin) (p248)

Soak in 500 years of colonial history and stay in one of Fort Cochin's beautiful heritage hotels. See **giant fishing nets** from China, a 400-year-old **synagogue**, ancient mosques and charming Portuguese-era mansions.

KOCHI ➲ MUMBAI

✈ **Two hours** The train takes 40 hours, but there are daily flights.

6 Mumbai (Bombay) (p118)

End your trip in cosmopolitan Mumbai, with its **colonial architecture**, great **shopping**, classy **cafes** and some of the best **restaurants** in India. Consider a side trip to the rock-cut temples on **Elephanta Island** and don't miss a sunset stroll along **Girgaum Chowpatty**.

Mumbai to Varanasi
The Best of India

Taking two weeks, you can see a surprising amount via a few canny domestic flights. This tour mixes the nation's best cities and most breathtaking sights with some of India's more laid-back natural charms.

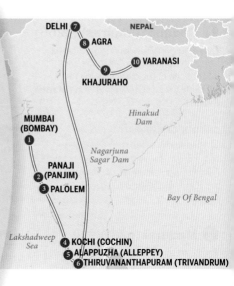

❶ Mumbai (Bombay) (p118)

Book yourself onto one of the excellent **heritage walking tours**; a hassle-free way of getting your bearings on your first day in India.

. . . .

MUMBAI ⭢ PANAJI

✈ **One hour** Fly into Dabolim Airport and take a taxi to Panaji or Palolem. 🚃 **10½ hours** The 11.05pm Konkan Kanya Express from Mumbai arrives the following morning at Karmali, a short ride from Panaji.

. . . .

❷ Panaji (Panjim) (p196)

Spend a day soaking up the Portuguese-flavoured charm of the Goan capital, including a trip to the crumbling remains of **Old Goa**.

. . . .

PANAJI ⭢ PALOLEM

🚗 **Two hours**. 🚃 **One hour** The daily train from Karmali (Old Goa) to Cancona leaves you with a short autorickshaw or taxi ride to Palolem, but it departs Old Goa at an awkwardly late 10.20pm.

. . . .

❸ Palolem (p214)

Arguably India's best **beach**, Palolem is a wonderfully easygoing place in which to relax while you're still getting used to the

whole India thing. Chill out, enjoy a massage and go **dolphin spotting** in a kayak.

. . . .

PALOLEM ⭢ KOCHI

✈ **5½ hours** Take a taxi (two hours) to Dabolin Airport, from where there are daily flights to Kochi. 🚃 **18 hours** Take a taxi (two hours) to Karmali (Old Goa) train station, then take the 10.20pm Netravati Express; it arrives at Ernakulam 2.10pm the next day.

. . . .

❹ Kochi (Cochin) (p248)

Head for **Fort Cochin**, where you can stay in a heritage property, visit the ancient **Pardesi Synagogue** and eat some splendid **seafood**.

. . . .

KOCHI ⭢ ALAPPUZHA

🚃 **1½ hours** There are regular trains from Kochi to Alappuzha. 🚗 **1½ hours** Around 50km by road.

. . . .

❺ Alappuzha (Alleppey) (p238)

The gateway to the famed Keralan **backwaters**. Book yourself onto a houseboat and explore this network of waterways.

. . . .

ALAPPUZHA ⭢ THIRUVANANTHAPURAM

🚃 **Three hours** To connect with the afternoon flight to Delhi, catch the 7am Trivandrum Express.

Backwaters (p240) near Thiruvananthapuram
MARK DAFFEY/GETTY IMAGES ©

DELHI ➲ AGRA
🚃 **Two to three hours** The 6am Bhopal Shatabdi Express from New Delhi station takes just two hours. Other trains (there are many) take three.
🚗 **Three hours** If taking the new expressway; otherwise, four to five hours.

⑧ Agra (p93)

Visit the **Taj Mahal**, India's most iconic sight. It will not disappoint. Leave time to also see nearby **Agra Fort** and, if possible, the equally impressive **Fatephur Sikri**.

AGRA ➲ KHAJURAHO
🚃 **Seven to eight hours** The 11.20pm UP SMPRK KRNTI takes seven hours and leaves every evening except Wednesday. The 11.05am UDZ KURJ Express runs daily and takes 8½ hours. Both leave from Agra Cantonment station.

⑨ Khajuraho (p328)

With exquisitely fine carvings, the **Word Heritage temples** of Khajuraho are one of India's most extraordinary sights, swathed as they are in ancient erotica.

KHAJURAHO ➲ VARANASI
✈ **50 minutes** Air India has a 3.05pm flight on Monday, Wednesday and Saturday. 🚃 **11 hours** The 11.40pm Khajuraho-Varanasi Link Express leaves for Varanasi Junction every Tuesday, Friday and Sunday.

⑩ Varanasi (p316)

Varanasi makes a unique final stop on your tour of India. One of Hinduism's holiest cities, this is where pilgrims come to wash away a lifetime of sins in the sacred waters of the **Ganges**. It's a remarkable place to experience, particularly on an early-morning **boat trip** along the river. From here you can fly daily to Delhi, Mumbai or Kolkata to connect with your flight home.

There are also daily trains at 3.30pm, 5.43pm and 6.15pm. 🚃 **3½ hours** Buses for Trivandrum depart every 20 minutes. 🚗 **3½ hours** Your guesthouse can help arrange a taxi.

⑥ Thiruvananthapuram (Trivandrum) (p230)

If you can't leave Alappuzha early enough to connect with a flight to Delhi, lay up in Trivandrum for a day. The **zoological gardens** and **museums** are worth a visit, and it's only 15km to the beach at **Kovalam**.

THIRUVANANTHAPURAM ➲ DELHI
✈ **Four to five hours** Most flights include a short stop in either Mumbai or Bengaluru (Bangalore).

⑦ Delhi (p60)

Naturally, the nation's capital has tons for you see: magnificent **historical sights**, fabulous **restaurants** and super **shopping**. For best use of your short time, consider one of the many guided tours.

India Month by Month

Top Events

- **Carnival**, January or February
- **Holi**, February or March
- **Ganesh Chaturthi**, August or September
- **Navratri**, September or October
- **Diwali (Festival of Lights)**, October or November

January

Republic Day (Free India)
Commemorates the founding of the Republic of India on 26 January 1950; the biggest celebrations are in Delhi, which holds a military parade along Rajpath and the Beating of the Retreat ceremony three days later.

Kite Festival (Sankranti)
This Hindu festival, marking the sun's passage into Capricorn, is celebrated in many ways – from banana-giving to cockfights. But it's the mass kite-flying in Uttar Pradesh and Maharashtra that steals the show.

Pongal (Southern Harvest)
The Tamil festival of Pongal marks the end of the harvest season. Southern families prepare pots of *pongal* (rice, sugar, dhal and milk), symbolic of prosperity and abundance, then feed it to decorated cows.

Vasant Panchami
Hindus dress in yellow and place books, musical instruments and other educational objects in front of idols of Saraswati, the goddess of learning, to receive her blessing. As it follows the Indian lunar calendar, it can also fall in February.

February

The Prophet Mohammed's Birthday
The Islamic festival of Eid-Milad-un-Nabi celebrates the birth of the Prophet Mohammed with prayers and processions, especially in Jammu and Kashmir.

Losar (Tibetan New Year)
Tantric Buddhists all over India – particularly in Himachal Pradesh and Ladakh – celebrate for 15 days,

(left) September Ganesh Chaturthi, Mumbai
WIN INITIATIVE/GETTY IMAGES ©

with the most important festivities during the first three. Losar is usually in February or March, though dates can vary between regions.

Skiing the Northern Slopes

Jammu and Kashmir (when peaceful), Himachal Pradesh and Uttarakhand have fine skiing and snowboarding for all levels (at some of the ski world's lowest costs). Snow season tends to be January to March, with February a safe bet.

Carnival in Goa

The four-day party kicking off Lent is particularly big in Goa. Sabado Gordo, Fat Saturday, starts it off with parades of elaborate floats and costumed dancers, and the revelry continues with street parties, concerts and general merrymaking.

March

Holi

One of North India's most ecstatic festivals; Hindus celebrate the beginning of spring according to the lunar calendar (either February or March) by throwing coloured water and *gulal* (powder) at anyone within range. Bonfires held the night before symbolise the death of the demoness Holika.

Wildlife-watching

When the weather warms up, water sources dry out and animals have to venture into the open to find refreshment – your chance to spot elephants, deer and, if you're lucky, tigers and leopards. Visit www.sanctuaryasia.com for detailed info.

Rama's Birthday

During Ramanavami, which lasts from one to nine days, Hindus celebrate with processions, music, fasting and feasting, enactments of scenes from the Ramayana and, at some temples, ceremonial weddings of Rama and Sita idols.

April

Mahavir's Birthday

Mahavir Jayanti commemorates the birth of Jainism's 24th and most important *tirthankar* (teacher and enlightened being). Temples are decorated and visited, Mahavir statues are given ritual baths, processions are held and offerings are given to the poor. It can also fall in March.

May

Buddha's Birthday

Commemorating Buddha's birth, nirvana (enlightenment) and parinirvana (total liberation from the cycle of existence, or passing away), Buddha Jayanti is quiet but moving: devotees dress simply, eat vegetarian food, listen to dharma talks and visit monasteries or temples.

Trekking

May and June, the months preceding the rains in the northern mountains, are surprisingly good times for trekking, with sunshine and temperate weather. Try trekking tour operators in Himachal Pradesh, Jammu and Kashmir and Uttarakhand.

July

Snake Festival

The Hindu festival Naag Panchami is dedicated to Ananta, the coiled serpent Vishnu rested upon between universes. Women return to their family homes to fast, while snakes are venerated as totems against flooding and other evils. Falls in July or August.

Brothers & Sisters

On Raksha Bandhan (Narial Purnima) girls fix amulets known as *rakhis* to the wrists of brothers and close male friends

cleaned and decorated with flowers and *rangoli* (chalk pictures), families dress up and eat special fish dishes and sweets, and offerings are made at the Fire Temple.

🎇 Eid al-Fitr

Muslims celebrate the end of Ramadan with three days of festivities, beginning 30 days after the start of the fast. Prayers, shopping, gift-giving and, for women and girls, *mehndi* (henna designs) may all be part of the celebrations.

September

🎇 Ganesh Chaturthi

Hindus celebrate the birthday of Ganesh, the elephant-headed god, with verve, particularly in Mumbai. Clay idols of Ganesh are paraded through the streets before being ceremonially immersed in rivers, tanks (reservoirs) or the sea. Ganesh Chaturthi may also be in August.

October

🎇 Gandhi's Birthday (2 October)

A solemn national celebration of Mohandas Gandhi's birth, with prayer meetings at his cremation site in Delhi. Schools and businesses close for the day.

🎇 Durga Puja

The conquest of good over evil, exemplified by the goddess Durga's victory over the buffalo-headed demon Mahishasura, is celebrated, particularly in Kolkata, where images of Durga are displayed then ritually immersed in rivers and water tanks.

🎇 Navratri

The Hindu 'Festival of Nine Nights' leading up to Dussehra, the following day, celebrates the goddess Durga in all her incarnations. Festivities, in

to protect them in the coming year. Brothers reciprocate with gifts and promises to take care of their sisters.

🎇 Ramadan (Ramazan)

Thirty days of dawn-to-dusk fasting mark the ninth month of the Islamic calendar. Muslims turn their attention to Allah, with a focus on prayer and purification.

August

🎇 Independence Day (15 August)

This public holiday marks the anniversary of India's independence from Britain in 1947. Celebrations are a countrywide expression of patriotism, with flag-hoisting ceremonies (the biggest one is in Delhi), parades and patriotic cultural programs.

🎇 Pateti (Parsi New Year)

Parsis celebrate Pateti, the Zoroastrian new year, especially in Mumbai. Houses are

September or October, are particularly vibrant in West Bengal, Gujarat and Maharashtra; in Kolkata, Durga images are ritually immersed in rivers and tanks.

Dussehra

The nine-day festival of Navratri culminates in colourful Dussehra, which celebrates the victory of the Hindu god Rama over the demon-king Ravana. Dussehra is big in Kullu, where effigies of Ravana are ritually burned, and Mysore, which hosts one of India's grandest parades.

Diwali (Festival of Lights)

In October or November, Hindus celebrate Diwali for five days, giving gifts, lighting fireworks, and burning oil lamps or hanging lanterns to lead Lord Rama home from exile. One of India's prettiest festivals.

Eid al-Adha

Muslims commemorate Ibrahim's readiness to sacrifice his son by slaughtering a goat or sheep and sharing it with family, the community and the poor.

November

Pushkar Camel Fair

This famous event attracts up to 200,000 people, who bring with them 50,000 camels, horses and cattle. The town becomes a extraordinary swirl of colour, thronged with musicians, mystics, tourists, traders, animals, devotees and camera crews.

Muharram

A month of remembrance when Shiite Muslims commemorate the martyrdom of the Prophet Mohammed's grandson Imam with beautiful processions.

December

Christmas Day (25 December)

The festivities are especially big in Goa and Kerala, with musical events, elaborate decorations and special Masses, while Mumbai's Catholic neighbourhoods become festivals of lights.

Far left: October Diwali **Left: March** Holi

Get Inspired

📖 Books

○ **Ramayana** (1973) RK Narayan's condensed, novelistic retelling of the ancient classic.

○ **India's Struggle for Independence** (1989) Bipan Chandra expertly chronicles the history of India from 1857 to 1947.

○ **A Fine Balance** (1995) A moving and tragic Mumbai story by Rohinton Mistry.

○ **The God of Small Things** (1997) Vibrant, beautiful novel by Arundhati Roy, set in Kerala.

○ **Nine Lives** (2011) William Dalrymple's fascinating insight into the enduring nature of traditional culture in contemporary India.

🎞 Films

○ **Gandhi** (1982) Hugely popular biographical film about the Great Soul.

○ **Fire** (1996) **Earth** (1998) **Water** (2005) Deepa Mehta's acclaimed trilogy.

○ **Lagaan** (2001) Critically acclaimed historical drama (with songs).

○ **Devdas** (2002) Lush Bollywood treat starring Aishwarya Rai.

○ **Slumdog Millionaire** (2008) Oscar-winning drama about a young man from the slums of Mumbai who is accused of cheating on *Who Wants to be a Millionaire?*.

🎵 Music

○ **Hare Rama Hare Krishna** (1971) Film soundtrack with fantastic 'Dum Maro Dum'.

○ **The Sounds of India** (1968) Legendary sitar player Ravi Shankar's finest.

○ **A Morning Raga/An Evening Raga** (1968) Beautiful raga played by virtuoso Ravi Shankar and tabla player Alla Rakha.

○ **Chaudhvin Ka Chand** (1960) Film music by Shankar with vocals by Asha Bhosle.

○ **Pakeezah** (1972) Sumptuous film soundtrack by Ghulam Mohammed and Naushad Ali.

🔖 Websites

○ **Lonely Planet** (www.lonelyplanet.com) Country profile, accommodation information and traveller forums.

○ **Times of India** (www.timesofindia.com) India's largest English-language newspaper.

○ **Incredible India** (www.incredibleindia.org) Official India Tourism site.

○ **Saavn** (www.saavn.com) Free, legal streaming of Indian music, including Bollywood soundtracks and traditional classics.

⏱ Short on time?

This list will give you an instant insight into the country.

Read RK Narayan's novel *Ramayana* gives the lowdown on the great epic.

Watch *Gandhi*, directed by Richard Attenborough, about the nation's favourite son.

Listen Ravi Shankar's *The Sounds of India* is a seminal sitar album.

Log on Incredible India (www.incredibleindia.org) is the tourist board's useful site.

Hawa Mahal (Palace of the Winds; p149), Jaipur

Need to Know

Currency
Indian rupees (₹)

Language
Hindi and English
(plus local languages)

ATMs
Most urban centres have foreign-friendly ATMs; carry cash as back-up.

Credit Cards
MasterCard and Visa widely accepted.

Visas
Six-month tourist visa valid from date of issue (not date of arrival).

Mobile Phones
Use local networks to avoid expensive roaming costs.

Wi-Fi
In most upmarket hotels and many hostels nationwide, and in some cafes and restaurants in major cities.

Internet Access
Internet cafes in cities and towns; few in rural areas.

Driving
Affordable car-with-driver hire lets you avoid dealing with hair-raising road conditions.

Tipping
Restaurants usually add service charges (tipping more is optional). Tip drivers for long trips, plus hotel porters and cycle-rickshaw riders.

When to Go

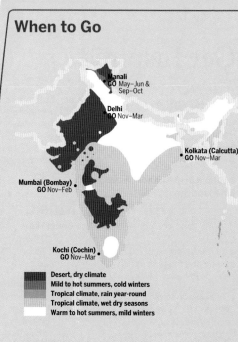

Manali
GO May–Jun & Sep–Oct

Delhi
GO Nov–Mar

Kolkata (Calcutta)
GO Nov–Mar

Mumbai (Bombay)
GO Nov–Feb

Kochi (Cochin)
GO Nov–Mar

Desert, dry climate
Mild to hot summers, cold winters
Tropical climate, rain year-round
Tropical climate, wet dry seasons
Warm to hot summers, mild winters

High Season
(Dec-Mar)

○ Pleasant weather, mostly. Peak crowds and prices. Pre-book flights and accommodation.

○ In December and January northern cities can get cold, bitterly so in the far north.

Shoulder Season
(Jul-Nov)

○ July to early September is the prime time to visit Ladakh.

○ Southeast coast (and southern Kerala) experiences heavy rain any time from October to early December.

Low Season
(Apr-Jun)

○ April to June can be unbearably hot. Hotels prices competitive.

○ June's southern monsoons sweep up north (except Ladakh) by July. Fatiguing humidity.

○ Beat the heat by fleeing to the hills.

Advance Planning

○ **One to two months before** Check your passport is valid for at least six months, and apply for a visa.

○ **Six weeks before** Seek advice regarding the necessary vaccinations, and obtain malaria tablets if necessary.

○ **One week before** Get travel insurance and ensure it will cover you for any activities you want to do.

Your Daily Budget

Budget less than ₹1000

o Stay at cheap guesthouses with shared bathrooms, or in hostels.

o Eat at roadside stalls or basic restaurants.

o Travel by train and bus, and occasionally autorickshaw.

Midrange ₹1000 to ₹5000

o Good accommodation (with private bathrooms) and restaurants.

o Travel by train, autorickshaw and taxi.

Top End more than ₹5000

o Sleep and dine like royalty in a restored palace.

o Hire a car and driver, but take the train for romance and an autorickshaw for adventure!

Exchange Rates

Australia	A$1	₹56
Canada	C$1	₹53
Euro zone	€1	₹71
Japan	¥100	₹55
New Zealand	NZ$1	₹46
UK	UK£1	₹84
US	US$1	₹54

For current exchange rates see www.xe.com

What to Bring

o **Non-revealing clothes** Covering up will win locals' respect; essential when visiting holy sites.

o **Money belt** A well-concealed belt for valuables.

o **Sunscreen & sunglasses** To be sure of good UV protection, bring them from home.

o **Tampons** Usually found only in big (or touristy) towns, though sanitary pads are widely available.

o **Mosquito repellent** Especially for malarial areas.

o **Water bottle** Use water-purification tablets or filters.

o **Sleeping sheet** If you're unsure about hotel linen or taking overnight train journeys.

Arriving in India

Ask if your hotel can arrange an airport pickup.

Delhi

Taxi Prepaid taxi booths at the airport

Metro Airport Express Metro Train (5.15am to 11.30pm) links up with metro system

Mumbai

Taxi Prepaid taxi booths at the airport

Chennai

Train MRTS train is cheapest way to the centre

Taxi & Autorickshaw Catch from prepaid booths

Kolkata

Taxi Prepaid fixed-price taxis available from the airport; very few after 10pm (when it costs more)

Bus Half-hourly AC buses from the airport

Getting Around

o **Rail** Reliable; especially recommended for overnight journeys.

o **Car** Easiest and safest to hire a car and driver. Advisable not to travel on the roads at night.

o **Air** Quick and efficient for long distances; numerous airlines have competitive prices.

o **Bus** From sleek AC coaches to decrepit vehicles. Take only if most convenient.

o **Rickshaws** The easiest way to zip around towns; mostly motorised.

Accommodation

o **Government-owned & tourist bungalows** Usually mid-priced, some heritage properties.

o **Homestays/B&Bs** Family-run, small-scale places, from basic village huts to comfortable middle-class city homes.

o **Top-end & heritage hotels** From modern five-star chains to glorious palaces and forts.

Be Forewarned

o **Touts** Use recommended guides – ask other travellers or the official local tourist office.

o **Taxi & rickshaw drivers** Disregard 'it's no good/closed/burnt down': they'll try to take you to places that pay them a commission.

o **Gem scams** If a gem deal seems too good to be true, *it is.*

o **Clean water** Drink bottled or purify your own.

Delhi & the Taj Mahal

Mystery, magic, mayhem.

Welcome to Delhi, City of Djinns, home to 16.7 million people, where the ruins of Mughal forts and medieval bazaars are scattered between the office blocks, shopping malls and tangled expressways. Like an eastern Rome, India's capital is littered with the relics of lost empires. A succession of armies stormed across the Indo-Gangetic plain and imprinted their identity onto the vanquished city, before vanishing into rubble and ruin like the conquerors who preceded them.

Modern Delhi, with its stellar restaurants and eclectic emporiums, is a chaotic tapestry of medieval fortifications, dusty bazaars and colonial-era town planning. And it's all just a short hop from the city of Agra, another former Mughal capital and home to India's most celebrated landmark of all: the Taj Mahal.

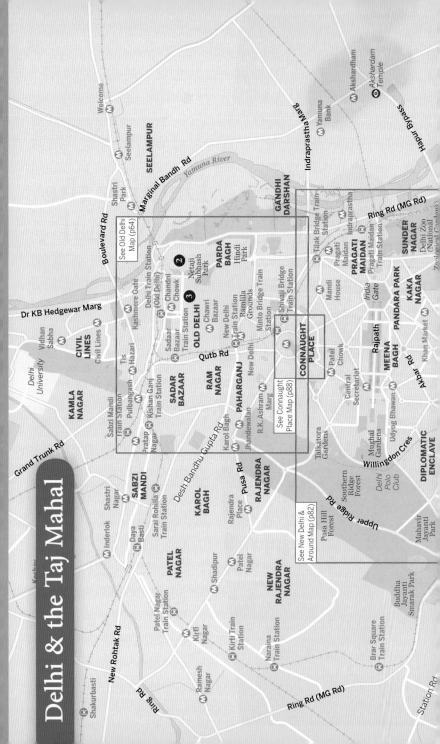

Delhi & the Taj Mahal

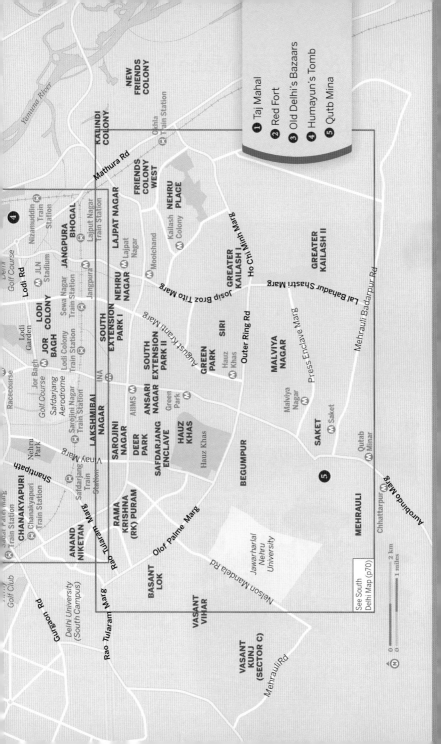

Delhi & the Taj Mahal's Highlights

Taj Mahal

A building that gleams, its perfection like something from a dream, the Taj Mahal (p95) will exceed all your expectations, however high they are. This was the pinnacle of Mughal architecture, and the building has not been diminished by age or any of the surrounding commercialism. If you don't make time to come here, you'll regret it.

1

Red Fort

2

The Red Fort (p60) is awash with splendour, a sandstone queen bee overlookin the Old Delhi hive. Surrounded by magnificent red walls, the remaining buildings might be a shadow of their former selves, but it's still possible to imagine the glories of the imperial court; the battered structures and grounds dotte with British-built barracks resonate wit Delhi's tumultuous history.

DAMIEN SIMONIS/GETTY IMAGES ©

Old Delhi's Bazaars

3

Losing yourself in the madness of Old Delhi's bazaars (p86) is more than just a manic shopping experience – it's a head-spinning assault on the senses. Aromatic incense and pungent spices mix with car fumes, body odour and worse, while the soundtrack is a constant barrage of shouts, barks, music and car horns. It's not so much retail therapy as heightened reality; intense, but unforgettable.

4

Humayun's Tomb

Desperate for a little piece of tranquillity amid the hubbub and traffic of Delhi? This great Mughal tomb (p69), built for the second Mughal emperor, was the inspiration for and forerunner of the Taj Mahal. Surrounded by manicured gardens, it is also one of the most serene places in the capital.

5

Qutb Minar

One of Delhi's most spectacular sights, the ruins of Qutb Minar (p75) date from the onset of Islamic rule in India. Not only is the site a beautiful place to wander, but it's fascinating to see the political and religious historical developments of the time through the adaptations of its architecture.

Delhi & the Taj Mahal's Best...

Wining & Dining

○ **Bukhara** Small menu, big reputation: regarded as Delhi's finest. (p81)

○ **Indian Accent** Creative new Indian cuisine at its best. (p84)

○ **Olive** A delightful slice of the Mediterranean tucked away in the suburbs. (p83)

○ **Karim's** Sumptuous kebabs and other meaty treats, in the heart of the Old City. (p78)

○ **Hotel Saravana Bhavan** Down-to-earth atmosphere serving the best south-Indian thali in town. (p79)

○ **Esphahan** Agra's finest restaurant and a stone's throw from the Taj Mahal. (p99)

Shopping

○ **Old Delhi's Bazaars** Sights, sounds and smells like no other shopping experience – an assault on the senses.

○ **Central Cottage Industries Emporium** Aladdin's cave of handicrafts. (p87)

○ **State Emporiums** Handicraft centres from regions across the country – a retail tour of India. (p86)

○ **Khan Market** Exclusive enclave for clothes, homewares and books. An expat favourite. (p87)

○ **Kamala** Crafts and curios with a touch of class. (p86)

Rooms with Panache

○ **Imperial** Raj-era class through and through; don't miss high tea! (p73)

○ **Devna** Charming hosts run Delhi's most charismatic guesthouse. (p76)

○ **Manor** Intimate and elegant, this is South Delhi's best boutique hotel. (p76)

○ **Hotel Palace Heights** The capital's coolest place to rest your head. (p76)

○ **Oberoi Amarvilas** View the Taj Mahal from your bathtub in Agra's finest hotel. (p99)

Places to Chill

○ **Sunset at Delhi's India Gate** Everyone gathers to wander and eat ice cream.

○ **Humayun's Tomb** Graceful Mughal tomb set in serene symmetrical gardens. (p69)

○ **Lodi Garden** Delhi's loveliest escape, dotted by crumbling tombs. (p68)

○ **Bahai House of Worship** Designed for quiet meditation, the petal-shaped 'Lotus Temple' welcomes people of all religions. (p68)

○ **Amatrra Spa** Where the A-list come to be pampered. (p70)

Left: India Gate (p69)
Above: Spice market, Old Delhi

Need to Know

ADVANCE PLANNING

○ **Two months before** Get your visa.

○ **Six weeks before** Have any vaccinations.

○ **One month before** Book hotel rooms and long train journeys online.

○ **A few days before** Put your name down for city tours you wish to take.

RESOURCES

○ **Delhi Tourism** Free-advertising city maps are widely available; for street-by-street detail, seek out the excellent 245-page Eicher City Map (₹340).

○ **Delhi Tourism** (www.delhitourism.nic.in) Official government tourism website

○ **The Delhi Walla** (www.thedelhiwalla.com) An offbeat view of Delhi by local journalist Mayank Austen Soofi.

○ **Times City** (www.timescity.com/delhi) Restaurant and bar reviews from the *India Times*.

○ **Lonely Planet** (www.lonelyplanet.com/india/delhi) For planning advice, author recommendations, traveller reviews and insider tips.

GETTING AROUND

○ **Airport Pick-up** Save yourself heaps of hassle by getting your hotel to pick you up when you arrive.

○ **Delhi Metro** The quickest way to get around the city.

○ **Taxis & Autorickshaws** They have meters, but they rarely use them, so agree on your fare beforehand.

○ **Taxi Tours** Arrange them at prepaid taxi booths or through your hotel. Prices start at ₹850 per day without a guide.

○ **To Agra** The fastest trains from Delhi take only two hours. Expect at least three hours and ₹3000 by car.

BE FOREWARNED

○ **Commission** Ensure your taxi or autorickshaw driver takes you where to want to go, rather than a hotel, souvenir shop or unscrupulous travel agent masquerading as a tourist office.

○ **'English Students'** Be dubious of chatty young men claiming to be students wanting to improve their English – the conversation is usually the preamble to a scam.

○ **Tourist Office** Don't believe anyone who tries to direct you to a 'tourist office' around Connaught Place. There is only one Government of India tourist office, at 88 Janpath.

○ **Small Change** Carry small denomination bills (below ₹50), as rickshaw drivers rarely have change.

(LEFT) PHOTOSINDIA/GETTY IMAGES ©
(ABOVE) CORMAC MCCREESH/GETTY IMAGES ©

57

Old Delhi Walking Tour

This loop visits Old Delhi's major bazaars and monuments. It's hectic walking through the crowds: if it gets too much, hail a cycle-rickshaw to glide through the mayhem.

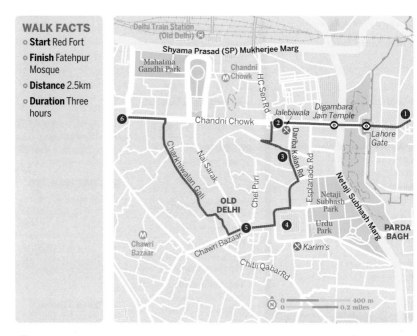

WALK FACTS
- **Start** Red Fort
- **Finish** Fatehpur Mosque
- **Distance** 2.5km
- **Duration** Three hours

① Red Fort

Start your walk outside the Red Fort, looking up at Lahore Gate, with the walls of the Red Fort stretching out on either side of you. Then, turn your back on the fort and start down Chandni Chowk. Crossing the frantic road, the first thing you will see on your left is Digambara Jain Temple. It contains a bird hospital, reflecting the Jain philosophy of the preservation of all life.

② Sisganj Gurdwara

Continuing to walk down Chandni Chowk, you'll next pass the Jalebiwala on your left, where there's always a crowd of people waiting for the next freshly fried batch of sweet squiggles. Also on your left you'll see the Sisganj Gurdwara, a permanently thronged Sikh temple. It commemorates the martyrdom of Sikh Guru Tegh Bahadur, who was beheaded by the Mughals on this spot in 1675.

③ Kinari Bazaar

Just after the temple, dive left into one of the narrow lanes that snake off the main drag (the one just before the famous sweet shop of Ghantewala). First you'll find a delicious cluster of hole-in-the-wall restaurants, where you can eat a freshly fried *paratha* (bread) stuffed with vegetables and cheese, the perfect snack. Soon the lane meets busy Kinari Bazaar – turn left onto the bazaar. This market stocks everything you might need for a wedding: garlands, grooms' turbans, bridal jewellery and decorations.

④ Jama Masjid

Follow Kinari Bazaar until the junction with Dariba Kalan Rd, then turn right, following it until you meet another junction. Turn right again and follow the lane round a short distance until it opens out to look onto Jama Masjid. It's a surprise to see the imposing building, reached via tall flights of steps. For a bird's-eye view over where you've been walking, enter and climb the minaret.

⑤ Chawri Bazaar

If you haven't eaten lunch yet, you might want to stop at Karim's on the south side of the Jama Masjid, famous for its delicious Mughlai cuisine. Otherwise, take the street leading west from the great mosque to Chawri Bazaar. The stalls here are piled high with paper products, from greeting cards to wallpaper, and also specialise in brass and copper items. After about 200m take the lane on the right, Charkhiwalan Gali, and follow the bazaar lane straight until you hit the junction with Chandni Chowk.

⑥ Fatehpur Mosque

The western end of Chandni Chowk is marked by the mid-17th-century Fatehpuri Masjid, named after one of Shah Jahan's wives. It offers a striking tranquillity after the craziness of the streets. After the 1857 First War of Independence the mosque was sold to a Hindu merchant, who used it as a warehouse, but it was later returned to local Muslims.

Delhi in...

TWO DAYS

On day one, acclimatise gently at tranquil sites such as the **National Museum** (p69), **Gandhi Smriti** (p80) and **Humayun's tomb** (p69). In the evening head to **Hazrat Nizam-ud-din Dargah** (p78) to hear the Sufis sing *qawwalis*.

On day two, follow our Old Delhi Walking Tour, launching into the Old City's action-packed **bazaars** (p86).

FOUR DAYS

The first day, wander around **Qutb Minar** (p75) and **Mehrauli** (p81) before some meditation at the **Bahai House of Worship** (p68). In the evening, watch the mesmerising **Dances of India** (p85), then kick back at a bar.

Day two visit Old Delhi's **Red Fort** (p60), then launch into the Old City's **bazaars** (p86) and visit the **Jama Masjid** (p61). Day three, visit some sights of New and South Delhi, including **Humayun's Tomb** (p69), then take an autorickshaw to **Connaught Place** (p67) to eat.

Day four, visit the laid-back **Crafts Museum** (p80) and finish off around **Connaught Place** (p67) to explore the government **emporiums** (p86).

Painting inside Gandhi Smriti
ANDERS BLOMQVIST /GETTY IMAGES ©

Discover Delhi & the Taj Mahal

DELHI

◎ Sights

Most sights in Delhi are easily accessible via metro. Note that many places are closed on Monday.

Old Delhi

Sprawling around the Red Fort, medieval-era Old Delhi is a constant barrage of noise, colour and smells that bombard the senses.

Red Fort   Fort
(Map p64; Indian/foreigner ₹10/250, video ₹25, combined museum ticket ₹5, audio tour in Hindi/English ₹60/100; ⊙9am-6pm Tue-Sun; Ⓜ Chandni Chowk) Converted to a barracks by the British, this massive fort is a sandstone carcass of its former self, but it still conjures up memories of the splendour of Mughal Delhi. Protected by a dramatic 18m-high wall, the marble and sandstone monuments here were constructed at the peak of the dynasty's power, when the empire was flush with gold and precious stones. Shah Jahan founded the fortress between 1638 and 1648 to protect his new capital city of Shahjahanabad, but he never took up full residence, after his disloyal son, Aurangzeb, imprisoned him in Agra Fort.

The last Mughal emperor of Delhi, Bahadur Shah Zafar, was flushed from the Red Fort in 1857 and exiled to Burma for his role in the First War of Independence. The new conquerors cleared out most of the buildings inside the fortress walls and replaced them with ugly barrack blocks for the colonial army.

Cycle rickshaws, Chandi Chowk (p67)
PETER ADAMS/GETTY IMAGES ©

Don't Miss
Jama Masjid

Towering over Old Delhi, the 'Friday Mosque' was Shah Jahan's final architectural opus, built between 1644 and 1658. India's largest mosque has room for 25,000 of the faithful in its central courtyard, and it remains an animated place of worship. Perfectly proportioned, the mosque is crowned by three onion domes, constructed of alternating vertical strips of red sandstone and white marble, and guarded by towering 40m-high minarets.

For an extra charge you can climb the narrow southern minaret (notices say that unaccompanied women are not permitted) for mesmerising views over the jumbled rooftops of the old city, with tiny paper kites flitting over the cityscape. On a clear day, you can see one of the key features of Lutyens' design for New Delhi – the Jama Masjid, Connaught Place and Sansad Bhavan (Parliament House) are in a direct line.

Entry is through gate 1 or 3 – remove your shoes at the top of the stairs. Women are asked to wear the scarves and robes provided. You'll be expected to pay the camera fee, even if the only camera is inside your mobile phone, and additional requests for money are not unheard of.

NEED TO KNOW

Map p64; camera, video each ₹300, tower ₹100; ⊙non-Muslims 8am to half-hour before sunset, minaret 9am-5.30pm; Ⓜ Chawri Bazaar

The ticket for foreigners covers the museums inside the fort. The audio tour is worthwhile to bring the site to life.

Lahore Gate. the main gate to the fort looks towards Lahore in Pakistan, the second most important city in the

Continued on p66

●●●
Red Fort

Highlights

The main entrance to the Red Fort is through Láhore Gate ❶ – the bastion in front of it was built by Aurangzeb for increased security. You can still see bullet marks from 1857 on the gate.

Walk through the Chatta Chowk (Covered Bazaar), which once sold silks and jewellery to the nobility; beyond it lies Naubat Khana ❷, a russet-red building, which houses Hathi Pol (Elephant Gate), so called because visitors used to dismount from their elephants or horses here as a sign of respect. From here it's straight on to the Diwan-i-Am ❸, the Hall of Public Audiences. Behind this are the private palaces, the Khas Mahal ❹ and the Diwan-i-Khas ❺. Entry to this Hall of Private Audiences, the fort's most expensive building, was only permitted to the highest official of state. Nearby is the Moti Masjid (Pearl Mosque) ❻ and south is the Mumtaz Mahal ❼, housing the Museum of Archaeology, or you can head north, where the Red Fort gardens are dotted by palatial pavilions and old British barracks. Here you'll find the *baoli* ❽, a spookily deserted water tank. Another five minutes' walk – across a road, then a railway bridge – brings you to the island fortress of Salimgarh ❾.

Salimgarh
Salimgarh is the 16th-century fort built by Salim Shah Sur. It was constructed on an island of the Yamuna River and only recently opened to the public. It is still partly used by the Indian army.

Museum on India's Struggle for Freedom

Chatta Chowk

Lahore Gate
Lahore Gate is particularly significant, as it was here that Jawaharlal Nehru raised the first tricolour flag of independent India in 1947.

Naubat Khana
The Naubat Khana (Drum House) is carved in floral designs and once featured musicians playing in the upper gallery. It housed Hathi Pol (Elephant Gate), where visitors dismounted from their horse or elephant.

Baoli

The Red Fort step well is seldom visited and is a hauntingly deserted place, even more so when you consider its chambers were used as cells by the British from August 1942.

Moti Masjid

The Moti Masjid (Pearl Mosque) was built by Aurangzeb in 1662 for his personal use. The domes were originally covered in copper, but the copper was removed and sold by the British.

Diwan-i-Khas

This was the most expensive building in the fort, consisting of white marble decorated with inlay work of cornelian and other stones. The screens overlooking what was once the river (now the ring road) were filled with coloured glass.

Baidon Pavilion

Zafar Mahal

Hammam

6

5

Rang Mahal

Mumtaz Mahal

4

7

3

2

Pit Stop

To refuel, head to Paratha Gali Wali, a food-stall-lined lane off Chandni Chowk noted for its many varieties of freshly made *paratha* (traditional flat bread).

←NORTH

Delhi Gate

Diwan-i-Am

These red sandstone columns were once covered in shell plaster, as polished and smooth as ivory, and in hot weather heavy red curtains were hung around the columns to block out the sun. It's believed the panels behind the marble throne were created by Florentine jeweller Austin de Bordeaux.

Khas Mahal

Most spectacular in the Emperor's private apartments is a beautiful marble screen at the northern end of the rooms; the 'Scales of Justice' are carved above it, suspended over a crescent, surrounded by stars and clouds.

Old Delhi

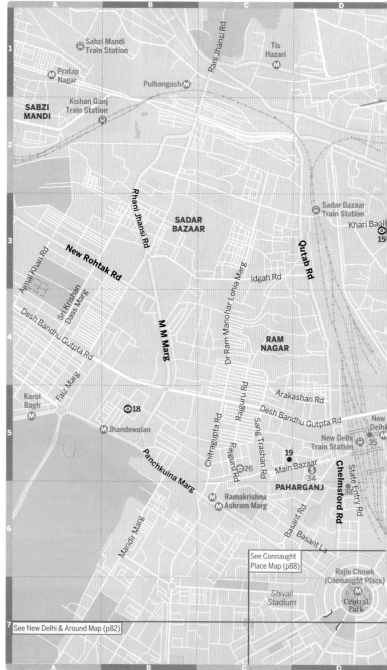

Sabzi Mandi Train Station

Pratap Nagar

Pulbangash Ⓜ

Rani Jhansi Rd

Tis Hazari Ⓜ

SABZI MANDI

Kishan Ganj Train Station

Sadar Bazaar Train Station

Khari Baoli

Ajmal Khan Rd

New Rohtak Rd

Rhani Jhansi Rd

SADAR BAZAAR

Qutab Rd

15

Sri Krishan Dass Marg

Desh Bandhu Gutpta Rd

Dr Ram Manohar Lohia Marg

Idgah Rd

M M Marg

RAM NAGAR

Karol Bagh Ⓜ

Faiz Marg

Ⓞ18

Ⓜ Jhandewalan

Chitragupta Rd

Ralguru Rd

Raiguru Rd

Sang Trashan Rd

Arakashan Rd

Desh Bandhu Gutpta Rd

19

Main Bazaar

New Delhi Ⓜ

New Delhi Train Station

35

State Entry Rd

Panchkuina Marg

Ⓞ26

$ 34

PAHARGANJ

Chelmsford Rd

38

Mandir Marg

Ⓜ Ramakrishna Ⓜ Ashram Marg

Basant Rd

Basant La

See Connaught Place Map (p88)

Shivaji Stadium

Rajiv Chowk (Connaught Place)

Ⓜ Central Park

See New Delhi & Around Map (p82)

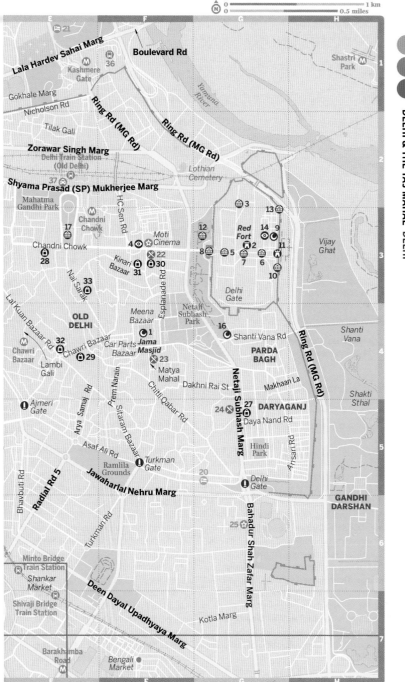

0 _____ 1 km
0 _____ 0.5 miles

Shastri Park

Lala Hardev Sahai Marg

Boulevard Rd

Kashmere Gate

Gokhale Marg

Nicholson Rd

Ring Rd (MG Rd)

Tilak Gali

Ring Rd (MG Rd)

Yamuna River

Zorawar Singh Marg

Delhi Train Station (Old Delhi)

Lothian Cemetery

Shyama Prasad (SP) Mukherjee Marg

Mahatma Gandhi Park

HC Sen Rd

Chandni Chowk

Moti Cinema

Red Fort

Vijay Ghat

Chandni Chowk

Chandni Chowk

Kinari Bazaar

Nai Sarak

Esplanade Rd

Delhi Gate

OLD DELHI

Meena Bazaar

Netaji Subhash Park

Shanti Vana Rd

Shanti Vana

Lal Kuan Bazaar Rd

Chawri Bazaar

Car Parts Bazaar

Jama Masjid

Matya Mahal

PARDA BAGH

Makhaan La

Shakti Sthal

Chawri Bazaar

Lambi Gali

Prem Narain

Sitaram Bazaar

Chitli Qabar Rd

Dakhni Rai St

Netaji Subhash Marg

DARYAGANJ

Daya Nand Rd

Ajmeri Gate

Arya Samaj Rd

Asaf Ali Rd

Turkman Gate

Ramlila Grounds

Hindi Park

Ansari Rd

Bhavbuti Rd

Radial Rd 5

Jawaharlal Nehru Marg

Delhi Gate

GANDHI DARSHAN

Turkman Rd

Bahadur Shah Zafar Marg

Minto Bridge Train Station

Shankar Market

Shivaji Bridge Train Station

Deen Dayal Upadhyaya Marg

Kotla Marg

Barakhamba Road

Bengali Market

Old Delhi

Continued from p61

Mughal empire. During the struggle for Independence, nationalists promised to raise the Indian flag over the gate, an ambition that became a reality on 15 August 1947.

Immediately beyond the gate is the regal **Chatta Chowk (Covered Bazaar)**, which once sold silk and jewels, but now mainly sells souvenirs. At the eastern end of the bazaar, the arched **Naubat Khana (Drum House)** once accommodated royal musicians and served as a parking lot for royal horses and elephants. Upstairs is the **Indian War Memorial Museum** (◷8am-5pm Tue-Sun), with a fearsome-looking collection of historic weaponry.

Beyond the Naubat Khana, a monumental arcade of sandstone columns marks the entrance to the **Diwan-i-Am**, the 'hall of public audiences', where the emperor greeted guests and dignitaries from a pietra-dura covered balcony.

Those in favour with the emperor, or conquered rivals begging for peace, were admitted to the **Diwan-i-Khas**, the white marble hall of private audiences. This delicate, wedding cake–like pavilion features some outstanding carving and inlay work. The legendary gold and jewel-studded Peacock Throne was looted from the pavilion by Nadir Shah in 1739.

South of the Diwan-i-Khas is the dainty **Khas Mahal**, containing the emperor's private apartments, and shielded from prying eyes by lace-like carved marble screens. An artificial stream, the **nahr-i-bihisht** (river of paradise) once flowed through theapartments to the adjacent **Rang Mahal** (Palace of Colour), home to the emperor's chief wife. The exterior of the palace was once lavishly painted; inside is an elegant lotus-shaped fountain.

South of the Rang Mahal, the **Mumtaz Mahal** is a pavilion that once contained the quarters for other women of the royal household. Today, it houses the **Museum of Archaeology** (⊙9am-5pm Tue-Sun), with royal vestments, miniature paintings, astrolabes, Mughal scrolls and a shirt inscribed with verses from the Quran to protect the emperor from assassins.

North of the Diwan-i-Khas are the **royal hammams** (baths), which once contained a sauna and hot baths for the royal family, and the **Moti Masjid** (Pearl Mosque), an elegant private place of worship for the emperor. The outer walls align with the fort walls, while the inner walls are slightly askew to correctly align with Mecca. Both are closed to visitors, but you can peer through the screen windows.

North of the royal baths is the **Shahi Burj**, a three-storey octagonal tower, where Shah Jahan planned the running of his empire. In front of the tower is what remains of an elegant formal garden, centred on the Zafar Mahal, a sandstone pavilion surrounded by a deep, empty water tank.

Sound & Light Show
Show

(Map p64; Tue-Fri ₹60, Sat & Sun ₹80; ⊙in English 8.30pm, 9pm May-Aug, 7.30pm Nov-Jan) Every evening, except Mon-day, the Red Fort is the setting for a bombastic sound and light show,

with coloured spotlights and a portentous voiceover, highlighting key events in the history of the Red Fort.

Chandni Chowk
Area

(Map p64; Ⓜ Chandni Chowk) Old Delhi's main thoroughfare is a chaotic shopping street, mobbed by hawkers, motorcycles, stray dogs and porters, and offering the full medieval bazaar experience. In the time of Shah Jahan, a tree-lined canal ran down its centre, reflecting the moon, hence the name Chandni Chowk, or 'moonlight place'.

Connaught Place Area

Connaught Place
Area

(Map p88; Ⓜ Rajiv Chowk) New Delhi's colonial heart is Connaught Place, named after George V's paternal uncle. Its white, colonnaded streets radiate out from the central circle of Rajiv Chowk, lined with swanky stores and restaurants. The outer circle (divided into blocks G to N) is technically called Connaught Circus, and

Moti Masjid (Pearl Mosque)
PATRICK HORTON/GETTY IMAGES ©

If You Like…
Quiet Retreats

If you're attracted to tranquil places such as Humayun's Tomb, then try these calm oases.

1 LODI GARDENS

(Map p82; Lodi Rd; ⊙6am-8pm Oct-Mar, 5am-8pm Apr-Sep; Ⓜ Khan Market/Jor Bagh) This peaceful park is Delhi's favourite escape, popular with everyone from power-walking politicians to amorous teens. The gardens are dotted with the crumbling tombs of Sayyid and Lodi rulers, including the impressive 15th-century **Bara Gumbad tomb** and mosque, and the strikingly different tombs of **Mohammed Shah** and **Sikander Lodi**. It's a haven for birds and butterflies but mobbed by picnickers on Sundays.

2 BAHAI HOUSE OF WORSHIP

(Lotus Temple; Map p70; 📞26444029; www.bahaihouseofworship.in; Kalkaji; ⊙9am-7pm Tue-Sun, to 6pm winter; 📶; Ⓜ Kalkaji Mandir) Designed by Iranian-Canadian architect Fariburz Sahba in 1986, Delhi's Bahai temple is a wonderful place to enjoy silence – a rare experience in Delhi. Styled after a lotus flower, with 27 immaculate white-marble petals, the temple was created to bring faiths together; visitors are invited to pray or meditate silently according to their own beliefs. The attached visitor centre tells the story of the Bahai faith. Photography is prohibited inside the temple. Nearby is Delhi's flamboyant ISKCON temple, operated by the Hare Krishna movement.

the inner circle (divided into blocks A to F) is Connaught Place, but locals call the whole area 'CP'. Almost every visitor to Delhi comes here, which partly explains the rampant touts.

Jantar Mantar   Historic Site

(Map p88; Sansad Marg; Indian/foreigner ₹5/100, video ₹25; ⊙9am-dusk; Ⓜ Patel Chowk) The most eccentric of Delhi's historic sites, Jantar Mantar (equivalent to 'abracadabra' in Hindi) looks like an enormous abstract sculpture, but this odd

collection of curving geometric buildings has a purpose – the monuments are carefully calibrated to monitor the movement of the stars and planets. Maharaja Jai Singh II constructed the observatory in 1725 – it's an extremely popular place to pose for a portrait.

Agrasen ki Baoli   Monument

(Map p88; Hailey Rd; ⊙dawn-dusk; Ⓜ Barakhamba Rd) A remarkable thing to discover among the office towers southeast of Connaught Place, this atmospheric step-well was erected in the 14th century; 103 steps descend to the bottom, flanked by arched niches.

New Delhi & Around

Rajpath   Area

(Map p82; Ⓜ Khan Market) The focal point of Edwin Lutyens' plan for New Delhi was Rajpath (Kingsway), a grand parade linking India Gate to the offices of the Indian government. Constructed between 1914 and 1931, these grand civic buildings were intended to spell out in stone the might of the British empire – just 16 years later, the British were out on their ear and Indian politicians were pacing the corridors of power.

Shielded by a wrought-iron fence at the western end of Rajpath, the 340-room **Rashtrapati Bhavan** (President's House; 📞23012960; dmsp@rb.nic.in; ⊙9.30-11.30am & 2.30-4pm Mon, Wed, Fri & Sat), is the official residence of the president of India, and former home to the British viceroy. Mountbatten, India's last viceroy, was said to have employed 418 gardeners to care for the Mughal-style **gardens**.

Rashtrapati Bhavan is flanked by the mirror-image, dome-crowned **North Secretariat** and **South Secretariat**, housing government ministries. The Indian parliament meets nearby in the **Sansad Bhavan** (Parliament House), a circular, colonnaded edifice at the end of Sansad Marg.

TIM MAKINS/GETTY IMAGES ©

⭐ Don't Miss
Humayun's Tomb

The most perfectly proportioned and captivating of Delhi's mausoleums, Humayun's Tomb seems to float above the gardens that surround it. Built in the mid-16th century by Haji Begum, the Persian-born senior wife of the Mughal emperor Humayun, the tomb brings together Persian and Mughal elements, creating a template that strongly influenced the Taj Mahal.

The arched facade is inlaid with bands of white marble and red sandstone, and the building follows strict rules of Islamic geometry, with an emphasis on the number eight. The surrounding gardens, alive with green parakeets, contain further tombs, including that of Haji Begum.

NEED TO KNOW

Map p82; Indian/foreigner ₹10/250, video ₹25; ☾dawn-dusk; Ⓜ JLN Stadium

At Rajpath's eastern end, and constantly thronged by tourists, is **India Gate**. This 42m-high stone memorial arch, designed by Lutyens, pays tribute to around 90,000 Indian army soldiers who died in WWI, the Northwest Frontier operations, and the 1919 Anglo-Afghan War.

National Museum   Museum
(Map p82; ☎ 23019272; www.nationalmuseum india.gov.in; Janpath; Indian/foreigner ₹10/300, audio guide English, French or German ₹400, audio guide Hindi ₹150, camera Indian/foreigner ₹20/300; ☾10am-5pm Tue-Sun; Ⓜ Central Secretariat) Offering a compelling snapshot of India's last 5000 years, this splendid museum is perfect for a rainy day and not so large that it overwhelms. Exhibits include rare relics from the Harappan Civilisation, antiquities from the Silk Route, a mesmerising collection of miniature paintings (look out for the handpainted playing cards), woodcarvings, textiles, statues and musical instruments, and

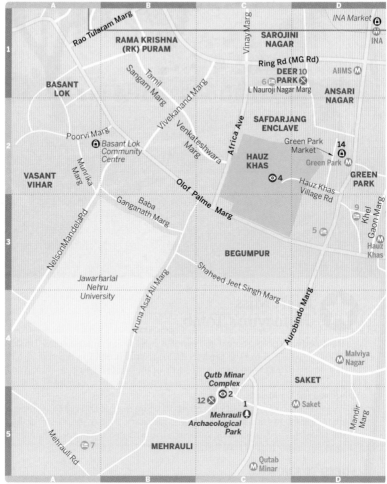

an armoury with gruesomely practical weapons and a suit of armour for an elephant.

Activities

Amatrra Spa
Spa

(Map p82; ☏24122921; www.amatrraspa.com; Ashok Hotel, Chanakyapuri; ⊗9am-10pm; Ⓜ Racecourse) Amatrra is where the A-list come to be pampered. There's a cover charge of ₹1000 for nonguests; treatments range from conventional massages to ayurvedic treatments such as *njavarak-*

izhi (massage with bundles of heated rice; ₹4800 per hour).

Courses

Tannie Baig
Cooking

(Map p70; ☏9899555704; tanniebaig13@gmail.com; 2hr lesson ₹3200; Ⓜ Hauz Khas) Recommended two-hour cooking lessons (the fee covers up to five participants) run by food writer Tannie Baig, who runs the Treetops guesthouse (p76; guests get 50% discount).

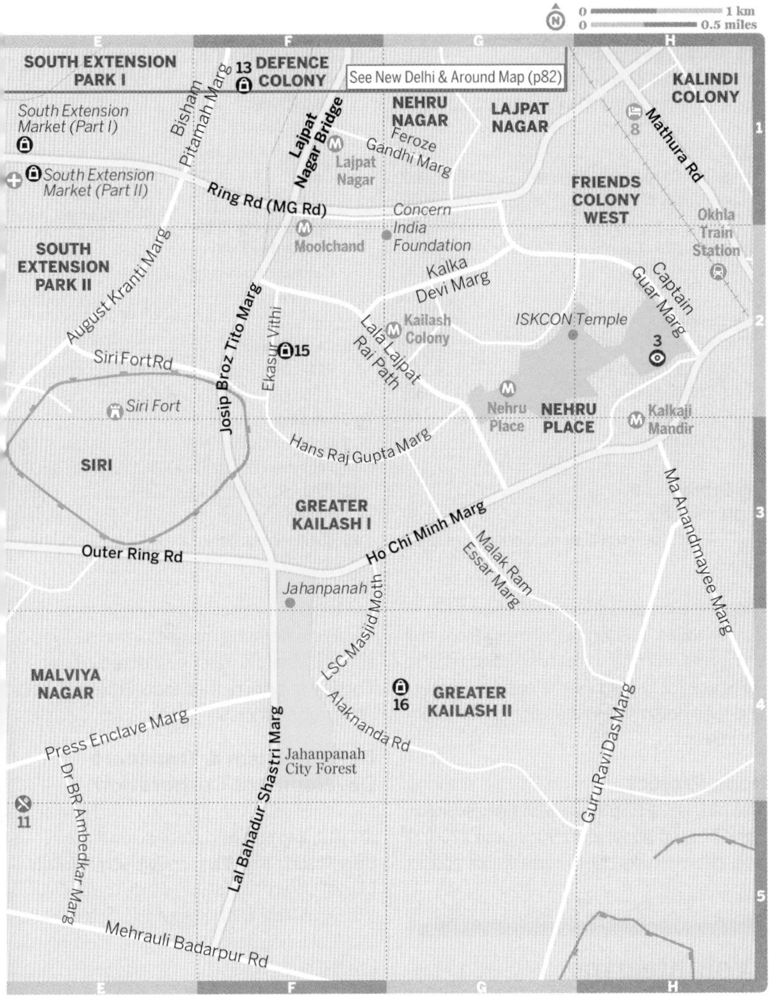

Tours

Tours are a good way to see Delhi without being overwhelmed, but avoid Monday when many sites are shut. Admission fees and camera/video charges aren't included in tour prices below, and rates are per person. Book several days in advance. For a bespoke tour, India Tourism Delhi can arrange multilingual, government-approved guides.

DelhiByCycle Cycling
(**☎9811723720; www.delhibycycle.com; ₹1600; ⏰6.30-10am)** Run by a Dutch journalist, this is a fantastic way to see Delhi. Tours focus on specific neighbourhoods – Old Delhi, New Delhi, Nizamuddin and Lodi Rd, and the banks of the Yamuna. The price includes chai and a Mughal breakfast.

Salaam Balaak Trust Walking
(**Map p64; ☎23584164; www.salaambaalaktrust.com; Gali Chandiwali, Paharganj; suggested donation ₹200; Ⓜ Ramakrishna Ashram Marg)** This

South Delhi

charitable organisation offers two-hour 'street walks' guided by former street children, who will show you first-hand what life is like for Delhi's homeless youngsters. The fees help the trust assist children on the streets.

Hope Project　　　　　　　Walking
(Map p82; ☏24353006; www.hopeprojectindia. org; 127 Hazrat Nizamuddin; 90min walk ₹200) ☙ This charity runs 90-minute walks around the basti (slum) of Nizamuddin, providing some challenging insights into the lives of some of Delhi's most neglected citizens. The fee supports the Hope Project's work. Wear modest clothing.

Delhi Tourism & Transport Development Corporation
　　　　　　　　　　　　　Bus Tours
(DTTDC; Map p88; http://delhitourism.nic.in; Baba Kharak Singh Marg; ⊙7am-9pm; Ⓜ Rajiv Chowk) Offers zip-around bus tours (AC ₹310) of New Delhi (9am to 1.30pm) and Old Delhi (2.15pm to 5.45pm), visiting all the big sights.

Delhi Transport Corporation Tours　　　　　Tour
(Map p88; ☏23752774; www.dtc.nic.in; Scindia House; tour ₹200; ⊙Tue-Sun; Ⓜ Rajiv Chowk) Inexpensive full-day air-con bus tours to the top sights from Connaught Place, leaving 9.15am and returning at 5.45pm.

Volunteering

There plenty of ways to assist Delhi's less fortunate residents. The Salaam Balaak Trust (p71) in Paharganj and the Hope Project (above) in Nizamuddin often have openings for volunteers – contact them directly for opportunities. Mother Teresa's Missionaries of Charity run projects in Delhi which may accept volunteers – contact their **Kolkata office** (☏22172277; www.motherteresa. org; 54A AJC Bose Rd; ⊙8am-noon & 3-6pm Fri-Wed) for information.

🛏 Sleeping

It's wise to book in advance, as popular places can fill up in a flash, leaving new arrivals easy prey for commission sharks. Call or email ahead to confirm your booking 24 hours before you arrive. Most hotels offer pick-up from the airport with advance notice. Homestays are becoming an attractive alternative to hotels. For details of government-approved places contact India Tourism Delhi, or check www.incredibleindianhomes.com and www.mahindrahomestays.com.

Hotels with a minimum tariff of ₹1000 charge luxury tax (10% at the time of research) and service tax (7.42% at the time of research), and some also add a service charge (up to 10%). Room rates in this chapter include taxes; all rooms have private bathrooms unless otherwise stated. Most hotels have a noon checkout and luggage storage is usually possible.

Old Delhi

Most hotels in the old town see few foreign visitors.

Hotel Broadway   Hotel $$
(Map p64; ☎43663600; www.hotelbroadwaydelhi.com; 4/15 Asaf Ali Rd; s/d incl breakfast ₹3060/5000; ✴@; Ⓜ New Delhi) A surprising find in a commercial part of the old city, Broadway is smarter inside than out. Some rooms have old-fashioned wood panelling while others have been elegantly kitted out by French designer Catherine Lévy. For refreshments, head to the curio-filled Chor Bizarre restaurant or the atmospheric 'Thugs' bar upstairs.

Maidens Hotel   Hotel $$$
(Map p64; ☎23975464; www.maidenshotel.com; 7 Sham Nath Marg; r from ₹9980; ✴@🛜🛋; Ⓜ Civil Lines) Set in immaculate gardens, Maidens is a graceful wedding cake of a hotel, built in 1903. Lutyens stayed here while supervising the building of New Delhi,

and the enormous high-ceilinged rooms still have a certain colonial-era charm. There are two restaurants, a pool and a bar.

Connaught Place & Around

The following places are close to Rajiv Chowk metro station.

Prem Sagar Guest House   Guesthouse $$
(Map p88; ☎23345263; www.premsagarguesthouse.com; 1st fl, 11 P-Block; s/d from ₹3523/4110; ✴@) A reliable choice, with 12 snug rooms that aren't flash, but are clean, with TVs and fridges. There's a pot plant–filled rear terrace, and internet in reception.

Imperial   Hotel $$$
(Map p88; ☎23341234; www.theimperialindia.com; Janpath; s/d from ₹18,166/20,868; ✴@🛜🛋) The inimitable Raj-era Imperial marries colonial classicism with gilded

Jantar Mantar observatory (p68)
UNIQUELY INDIA/GETTY IMAGES ©

Don't Miss
Qutb Minar

In a city awash with ancient ruins, the Qutb Minar complex is something special. The first monuments here were erected by the sultans of Mehrauli, and subsequent rulers expanded on their work, hiring the finest craftsmen and artisans to create an exclamation mark in stone to record the triumph of Muslim rule.

Map p70

☎ 26643856

Indian/foreigner ₹10/250, video ₹25, decorative light show Indian/foreigner ₹20/250, audio guide ₹100

🕙 dawn-dusk

Ⓜ Qutab Minar

The complex, which is studded with ruined tombs and monuments, is dominated by the spectaclular Qutb Minar, a soaring Afghan-style victory tower and minaret, erected by Sultan Qutb-ud-din in 1193 to proclaim his supremacy over the vanquished Hindu rulers of Qila Rai Pithora. The tower has five distinct storeys with projecting balconies, but Qutb-ud-din only completed the first level before being unfortunately impaled on his saddle while playing polo. His successors completed the job.

Quwwat-ul-Islam Masjid

At the foot of the Qutb Minar stands the Quwwat-ul-Islam Masjid, the first mosque to be built in India. Its design shows a clear fusion of Islamic and pre-Islamic styles. Altamish, Qutb-ud-din's son-in-law, expanded the original mosque with a cloistered court between 1210 and 1220, and Ala-ud-din's added the exquisite marble-and-sandstone Alai Darwaza gatehouse in 1310.

Iron Pillar

Standing in the courtyard of the Quwwat-ul-Islam mosque is a 7m-high iron pillar that vastly predates the surrounding monuments. A six-line Sanskrit inscription indicates that it was initially erected outside a Vishnu temple, possibly in Bihar, in memory of Chandragupta II, who ruled from AD 375 to 413. What the inscription does not tell is how it was made – scientists have never discovered how the iron, which has not rusted after 1600 years, could be cast using the technology of the time.

Alai Minar

When the Sultan Ala-ud-din made additions to the complex in the 14th century, he also conceived an ambitious plan to erect a second tower of victory, exactly like the Qutb Minar, but twice as high! Construction of the Alai Minar got as far as the first level before the sultan died; none of his successors saw fit to bankroll this extravagant piece of showboating. The 27m-high plinth can be seen just north of the Qutb Minar.

Qutb Minar Don't Miss List

DILLIWALA SUREKHA NARAIN PROVIDES WALKING TOURS AROUND DELHI SIGHTS, INCLUDING QUTB MINAR, WITH DELHI METRO WALKS

1 **QUWWAT-UL-ISLAM MOSQUE**
In 1192 AD, Muhammad Ghori from Afghanistan defeated Prithviraj Chauhan, a Hindu and Rajput ruler, and left his slave, Qutbuddin Aibak, to establish the Qutb complex. Aibak demolished around 27 Hindu temples and built a mosque (known as Quwwat-ul-Islam or Might of Islam), using the remains. The result is an intriguing blend of Hindu and Islamic elements. The Hindu elements include conical domes with supporting pillars and beams. At the far end, you will see Islamic ideas in the form of corbelled arches.

2 **QUTB MINAR**
This victory tower was established in 1199, and is the tallest stone tower in India: 72.5m high with 379 steps. On each floor you can see stalactite corbelling and arabesque Islamic decoration with floral and geometric patterns and calligraphy of Quranic verses.

3 **ALAI DARWAZA & ALAI MINAR**
Alauddin Khilji, who founded the second city of Delhi, added the Alai Darwaza – a stunning gateway in arabesque decoration – in 1311, creating a southern entrance to the Qutb Minar.

4 **TOMB OF IMAM ZAMIM**
Next to the Alai Darwaza, this Lodhi-style square tomb has 12 pillars with red sandstone lattice work. Inside you see how a circle has been converted to a dome (circular structure) with the help of squinches. The marble sculpture of a small pen box on the lid of the tomb shows that this is the tomb of a man.

5 **TOMB OF ALTAMISH**
At the far end of the complex is the square tomb of Iltutmish, which has no Hindu features, and combines the Islamic practices of arabesque floral and geometrical patterns in sandstone and marble with a large sculpture on a male tomb, decorative prayer niche, and calligraphy from the Quran.

art deco. In terms of style, service and luxury, it leaves other hotels in the cold. Rooms boast high ceilings, flowing drapes, French linen, marble baths and finely crafted furniture, and the hallways and atriums are lined with 18th- and 19th-century paintings and prints. The 1911 bar and Spice Route restaurant are highly recommended, and the Atrium cafe serves the perfect high tea (see boxed text, p85).

Hotel Palace Heights   Hotel $$$
(Map p88; ☎43582610; www.hotelpalaceheights. com; 26-28 D-Block; s/d ₹7632/8219; ✷@☎) This boutique hotel is cool enough to wear shades, offering sleek rooms with gleaming white linen, black lampshades and caramel and amber tones. There's an excellent restaurant, **Zāffrān** (mains ₹435-500; ◷11am-3.30pm & 7-11pm), and 24-hour room service.

Corus   Hotel $$$
(Map p88; ☎43652222; www.hotelcorus.com; 49 B-Block; s/d from ₹7045/7632; ✷@☎) As well as a prime location, you get spotless tiled floors and dazzling white sheets at the Corus. More money gets you more floor space. There's an attractive restaurant, **Bonsai**, with a white-pebbled courtyard.

New Delhi

Taj Mahal Hotel   Hotel $$$
(Map p82; ☎23026162; www.tajhotels.com; 1 Mansingh Rd; s/d ₹24,071/28,181; ✷@☎⛱) The Taj pulls out all the stops, with a lobby full of Indian artworks and painted Mughal domes, lavish restaurants and a pool surrounded by manicured gardens. The luxuriously appointed rooms have all the five-star frills.

South Delhi

Treetops   Guesthouse $$
(Map p70; ☎9899555704; tanniebaug13@gmail. com; R-8b Hauz Khas Enclave; d incl breakfast ₹2500/3500; ✷@☎; Ⓜ Hauz Khas) The elegant home of a charming and hospitable couple, journalist Murad Baig and

food writer Tannie, Treetops offers lovely large rooms opening onto a leafy roof terrace overlooking the park. It's minutes from the metro, and Tannie gives cookery lessons. Evening meals are available.

K-One One   Guesthouse $$
(Map p82; ☎43592583; www.parigold.com; K-11 Jangpura Extn; s/d incl breakfast ₹4000/4500; ✷@☎; Ⓜ Jangpura) Set in a tidy and peaceful enclave, and handy for the metro, this family-run guesthouse offers four en suite rooms painted in jewel-bright hues, and there's a roof terrace dotted with pot plants. The owner runs the Parul Puri cooking classes.

Devna   Guesthouse $$$
(Map p82; ☎41507176; www.tensundernagar. com; 10 Sunder Nagar; d ₹4500-5500; ✷@☎) Fronted by a pretty courtyard garden, and run with panache by the charming Atul and Devna, this one of Delhi's most charismatic guesthouses. The walls are lined with photos of maharajas and works of art (yes, those are original Jamini Roys) and the rooms are decked out with quirky antiques. The upstairs rooms front onto tiny terraces.

Manor   Hotel $$$
(Map p70; ☎26925151; www.themanordelhi.com; 77 Friends Colony (West); d incl breakfast from ₹8760; ✷@) A more intimate alternative to Delhi's five-star chains, this 16-room boutique hotel oozes privacy and elegance. Set amid lush lawns off Mathura Rd, the Manor offers the kind of designer touches normally found in the homes of Bollywood stars. There's a colonial air to the opulent rooms and the restaurant, Indian Accent (p84), is one of Delhi's finest.

Bnineteen   Guesthouse $$$
(Map p82; ☎41825500; www.bnineteen. com; B-19 Nizamuddin East; d incl breakfast from ₹8500; ✷@) Located in posh and peaceful Nizamuddin East, with views over Humayun's Tomb from the rooftop, this gorgeous place shows an architect's touch. Rooms are modern and refined, and there is a state-of-the-art shared kitchen on each floor.

Food hawker, Chandni Chowk (p67)

GREG ELMS/GETTY IMAGES ©

Amarya Villa
Guesthouse $$$

(Map p70; ☎41759267; www.amaryagroup.com; a-2/20 Safdarjang Enclave; s/d ₹4725/5203; ❄@🔊; Ⓜ Hauz Khas) The European owners of Amarya Villa have created a stylish haven straight out of an interior-design magazine. It's boutique all the way, with scattered artefacts, lavish fabrics and colour themes for every room. The same owners run the similarly chic **Amarya Haveli** (Map p70; ☎41759268; P5 Hauz Khas; Ⓜ Lajpat Nagar) in Hauz Khas, with similar prices.

....

Airport Area

Chhoti Haveli
Homestay $$

(Map p70; ☎26124880; http://chhotihaveli.com; A1006, Pocket A, Vasant Kunj; s/d ₹3300/3800; ❄@🔊) Set in a block of low-rise apartments in a quiet, leafy area near the airport, this well-kept place offers tastefully decorated rooms. Potted plants and scattered petals on the doorstep show a personal touch.

Radisson Blu Plaza
Hotel $$$

(☎26779191; www.radissonblu.com; National Hwy 8; s/d from ₹10,624/11,804; ❄@🔊♒) Airport-facing Radisson is your typical business-class hotel. But oh, what a joy to lie down on soft linen and orthopaedic beds after a long-haul flight. On-site are Chinese, Indian and Italian restaurants.

🍴 Eating

Delhi is a foodie paradise, and locals graze throughout the day, whether munching the city's famous *dilli ki chaat* (street-food snacks and salads) at stalls in the old town, or sitting down to indulgent feasts at Delhi's fine-dining restaurants.

Midrange and upmarket restaurants charge a service tax of around 10%; drinks taxes can suck a further 20% (alcoholic) or 12.5% (nonalcoholic) from your wallet. Taxes haven't been included unless indicated. Many restaurants also levy a 10% service charge, in lieu of a tip.

Telephone numbers have been provided for restaurants where reservations are recommended.

/GETTY IMAGES ©

⭐ **Don't Miss**
Hazrat Nizam-ud-din Dargah

Hidden away in a tangle of bazaars selling rose petals, attars (perfumes) and offerings, the marble shrine of the Muslim Sufi saint Nizam-ud-din Auliya offers a window through the centuries. Brightly painted, full of music and crowded with devotees, this is how Delhi's historic tombs and shrines must have been in life. The ascetic Nizam-ud-din died in 1325 at the ripe old age of 92, and his mausoleum became a point of pilgrimage for Muslims from across the empire.

It's one of Delhi's most extraordinary pleasures to take a seat on the marble floor and listen to Sufis singing rousing *qawwali* (devotional hymns) at sunset. Scattered around the surrounding alleyways are more tombs and a huge *baoli* (step well). Entry is free, but visitors may be asked to make a donation.

NEED TO KNOW
Map p82; off Lodi Rd; ⏰24hr; Ⓜ JLN Stadium

Old Delhi

Karim's
Mughlai $

(Map p64; Gali Kababyan; mains ₹37-340; ⏰7am-midnight; Ⓜ Chawri Bazaar) Just off the lane leading south from the Jama Masjid, Karim's has been delighting carnivores since 1913. The menu is dominated by meaty Mughlai treats such as mutton *burrah* (marinated chops), *seekh* kebabs and tandoori chicken. There's a **branch** (Map p82) in Nizamuddin West.

Jalebiwala
Sweets $

(Map p64; Dariba Corner, Chandni Chowk; jalebis per 100g ₹25; ⏰8.30am-9.45pm; Ⓜ Chandni Chowk) Century-old Jalebiwala does Delhi's – if not India's – finest *jalebis* (deep-fried, syrupy fried dough), so pig out and worry about the calories tomorrow.

Ghantewala
Sweets $

(1862A Chandni Chowk; mithai per 100g from ₹20; ⊙8am-10pm; Ⓜ Chandni Chowk) Delhi's most famous sweetery, 'the bell ringer' has been churning out *mithai* (Indian sweets) since 1790. Try some *sohan halwa* (ghee-dipped gram-flour biscuits).

Chor Bizarre
Kashmiri $$

(Map p64; ⌗23273821; Hotel Broadway, 4/15 Asaf Ali Rd; mains ₹305-500; ⊙7.30-10.30am, noon-3.30pm & 7.30-11.30pm; Ⓜ New Delhi) A dimly lit cavern, filled with antiques and bric-a-brac, Chor Bizarre (meaning 'thieves market') offers delicious and authentic Kashmiri cuisine, including *wazwan*, the traditional Kashmiri feast. They offer an old-town walking tour combined with lunch for ₹1800.

Moti Mahal
Mughlai $$

(Map p64; ⌗23273661; 3704 Netaji Subhash Marg; mains ₹200-380; ⊙11am-midnight) The original, much-copied Moti Mahal has been open for six generations – the food is much more impressive than the faded surroundings. Delhi-ites rate the place for its superior butter chicken and *dhal makhani*. There's live *qawwali* (Islamic devotional singing) Wednesday to Monday (8pm to midnight).

Connaught Place

The following eateries are all close to the Rajiv Chowk metro stop.

Hotel Saravana Bhavan
South Indian $

(Map p88; 15-P Block; mains ₹65-165; ⊙8am-10pm) Delhi's best thali (₹165) is served up in unassuming surroundings – a simple Tamil canteen on the edge of Connaught Place. There are queues every meal time to sample the splendid array of richly spiced veg curries, dips, breads and condiments that make it onto every thali plate. There's a second **branch** (Map p88; 46 Janpath).

Detour:
Akshardham Temple

Rising dramatically over the eastern suburbs, the Hindu Swaminarayan Group's controversially ostentatious **Akshardham Temple** (⌗22016688; www.akshardham.com; National Hwy 24, Noida turning; admission free, exhibitions ₹170, fountains ₹30; ⊙9.30am-6.30pm Tue-Sun; Ⓜ Akshardham) is a wedding-cake confection of salmon-coloured sandstone and white marble, drawing elements from traditional Orissan, Gujarati, Mughal and Rajasthani architecture. The interior offers an almost psychedelic journey through Hindu mythology, with 20,000 carved deities, saints and mythical beings.

Surrounding this spiritual showpiece is a series of Disneyesque exhibitions, including a boat ride through 10,000 years of Indian history, animatronics telling stories from the life of Swaminarayan, and musical fountains. Allow at least half a day to do it justice (weekdays are less crowded).

Wenger's
Bakery $

(Map p88; 16 A-Block; snacks ₹30-90; ⊙10.45am-7.45pm) Legendary Wenger's has been baking since 1926; come for cakes, sandwiches, biscuits, savoury patties and other snacks to eat on the trot.

Nirula's
Ice Cream $

(Map p88; 14 K-Block Connaught Place; ice cream from ₹50; ⊙10am-midnight) A decades-old ice-cream parlour serving a rainbow of flavours, from workaday strawberry to exotic *badam pista* (almond and pistachio with cardamom).

If You Like...
Museums

If you like the National Museum (p69), Delhi has many other facinating museums that will pique your interest.

1 **GANDHI SMRITI**
(Map p82; ☏23012843; 5 Tees January Marg; camera free, video prohibited; ⊙10am-5pm Tue-Sun, closed every 2nd Sat of month; Ⓜ Racecourse) This poignant memorial is where Mahatma Gandhi was shot dead by a Hindu zealot on 30 January 1948, after campaigning against intercommunal violence. Concrete footsteps lead to the spot where Gandhi died, marked by a small pavilion.

2 **NATIONAL GALLERY OF MODERN ART**
(Map p82; ☏23382835; http://ngmaindia.gov. in; Jaipur House; Indian/foreigner ₹10/150; ⊙10am-5pm Tue-Sun; Ⓜ Khan Market) Delhi's flagship art gallery displays a remarkable collection of paintings, including primitive-inspired artworks of Nobel Prize winner Rabindranath Tagore.

3 **CRAFTS MUSEUM**
(Map p82; ☏23371641; Bhairon Marg; ⊙10am-5pm Tue-Sun; Ⓜ Pragati Maidan) Set up like a traditional village, this captivating museum aims to preserve the traditional crafts of India, from handloom weaving to Mithila wall painting.

4 **NATIONAL RAIL MUSEUM**
(Map p82; ☏26881816; Service Rd, Chanakyapuri; adult/child ₹20/10, video ₹100; ⊙9.30am-5.30pm Tue-Sun) Trainspotters and kids will adore this one, with its decaying collection of old steam locos and carriages, and a toy train (adult/child ₹20/10) that chuffs around the grounds.

5 **SULABH INTERNATIONAL MUSEUM OF TOILETS**
(☏25031518; www.sulabhtoiletmuseum.org; Sulabh Complex, Mahavir Enclave, Palam Dabri Rd; ⊙10am-5pm Mon-Sat) Run by a pioneering charity that has done extraordinary work bringing sanitation to the poor of Delhi, this quirky museum displays toilet-related paraphernalia dating from 2500 BC to modern times. A guided tour (free) brings the loos to life.

Véda Indian $$$
(Map p88; ☏41513535; 27 H-Block; mains ₹300-700; ⊙12.30pm-11.30pm) Fashion designer Rohit Baal created Véda's sumptuous interior – a dark boudoir with swirling neo-Murano chandeliers and shimmering mirror mosaics. The menu puts a modern spin on classic Mughlai dishes, and chefs make liberal use of fresh herbs and spices. It's great for a date.

Spice Route Asian $$$
(Map p88; ☏23341234; Imperial Hotel, Janpath; mains ₹500-2050) It took seven years to create the extravagant interior at Spice Route, with its murals, temple columns and wood carvings. The menu spans South India, Sri Lanka and Southeast Asia, and the food offers substance to match the style. Reservations recommended.

United Coffee House Multicuisine $$$
(Map p88; ☏23416075; 15 E-Block; mains ₹250-490; ⊙10am-11pm) Not a coffee shop, but an upscale restaurant, with an old-world dining room full of characters who look as elderly as the fixtures and fittings. The menu covers everything from pizza to butter chicken.

New Delhi & Around
Alkauser Street Food $$
(Map p82; www.alkausermughlaifood. com; Kautilya Marg; kebabs from ₹110; ⊙6-10.30pm) The family behind this hole-in-the-wall takeaway earned their stripes cooking kebabs for the Nawabs of Lucknow in the 1890s. The house speciality is the *kakori* kebab, a pâté-smooth combination of lamb and spices, but other treats include biryani (cooked *dum puhkt* style in a *handi* pot sealed with pastry) and perfectly prepared lamb *burra* (marinated chops) and *murg malai tikka* (chicken marinated with spices and paneer). There are several branches, including one in the Safdarjang Enclave market (Map p70).

Bukhara Indian $$$
(Map p82; ☎26112233; ITC Maurya, Sadar Patel Marg; mains ₹1475-2550; ⊙12.30-2.45pm & 7-11.45pm) Widely considered Delhi's best restaurant, this glam hotel eatery serves Northwest Frontier–style cuisine at low tables, with delectable kebabs that you won't find in cheaper kebab houses. Reservations are essential.

Eau de Monsoon Indian $$$
(Map p82; ☎23710101; Le Meridien, Janpath; mains ₹1200-2495; ⊙12.30-3pm & 7-11.30pm; ⓂPatel Chowk) Behind waterfall windows, the Meridien's top restaurant works magic with globally sourced ingredients. The fusion menu runs to morel mushroom and pea curry and lobster combined with char-grilled prawns. Smart dress is the way to go.

Amici Italian $$$
(Map p82; ☎43587191; 47 Khan Market; pizza ₹300-400; ⊙11am-11pm) Calm and unpretentious, Amici actually pays some attention to the way they make pizzas in Italy. There are branches in the **Select Citywalk Mall** (Map p70; Saket), **Defence Colony Market** (Map p70) and **Hauz Khas Village** (Map p70).

....

South Delhi

Gunpowder South Indian $$
(Map p70; ☎26535700; 3rd fl, 22 Hauz Khas Village; mains ₹100-400; ⊙noon-3pm & 7.30-11pm Tue-Sun; ⓂGreen Park) Tucked away on the 3rd floor at the end of the last alley in Hauz Khas, Gunpowder serves up Keralan treats like toddy-shop *meen* (fish) curry, sweet-and-sour pumpkin and blistering stir-fried buffalo with coconut and chilli. It's small and informal; bookings are advised.

Mehrauli Archaeological Park

Bordering the Qutb Minar complex, but overlooked by most of the tourist hordes, the **Mehrauli Archaeological Park** (Map p70; ⊙dawn-dusk; ⓂQutab Minar) FREE preserves some of the most atmospheric relics of the second city of Delhi. Scattered around a forest park that spills into a chaotic basti (slum) are the ruins of dozens of tombs and palace buildings and several colonial follies. The most impressive structure is the Jamali Khamali mosque, attached to the tomb of the Sufi poet Jamali. Ask the caretaker to open the doors so you can see the intricate incised plaster ceiling. Nearby are the Rajon ki Baoli, a majestic 16th-century step-well with a monumental flight of steps, and the time-ravaged tombs of Balban and Quli Khan.

Lasagna at Olive restaurant (p83)
GRAHAM CROUCH/GETTY IMAGES ©

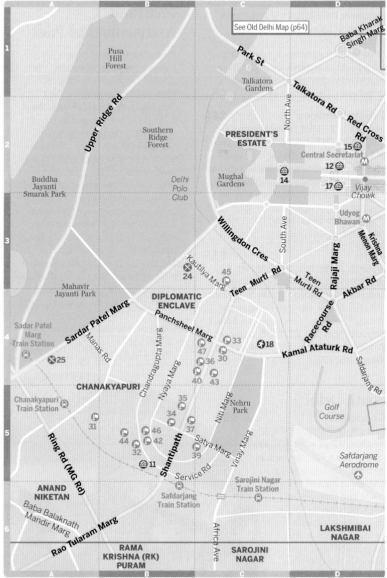

See Old Delhi Map (p64)

Baba Kharak Singh Marg

Park St

Pusa Hill Forest

Talkatora Gardens

Talkatora Rd

Red Cross Rd

North Ave

Upper Ridge Rd

Southern Ridge Forest

PRESIDENT'S ESTATE

Central Secretariat

15

12

Buddha Jayanti Smarak Park

Delhi Polo Club

Mughal Gardens

14

17

Vijay Chowk

Udyog Bhawan

Krishna Menon Marg

Willingdon Cres

South Ave

Rajaji Marg

Akbar Rd

Mahavir Jayanti Park

Kautilya Marg

24

45

Teen Murti Rd

Teen Murti Rd

Racecourse Rd

DIPLOMATIC ENCLAVE

Sardar Patel Marg

Panchsheel Marg

Kamal Ataturk Rd

Sadar Patel Marg Train Station

Manas Rd

Chandragupta Marg

33

47

30

18

Safdarjang Rd

25

36

40

43

CHANAKYAPURI

Nyaya Marg

35

Niti Marg

Golf Course

Chanakyapuri Train Station

31

34

Nehru Park

Safdarjang Aerodrome

Ring Rd (MG Rd)

44

32

46

42

Shantipath

37

Satya Marg

39

Vinay Marg

11

Service Rd

Sarojini Nagar Train Station

ANAND NIKETAN

Baba Balaknath Mandir Marg

Safdarjang Train Station

LAKSHMIBAI NAGAR

Rao Tularam Marg

RAMA KRISHNA (RK) PURAM

Africa Ave

SAROJINI NAGAR

Not Just Parathas   Indian $$

(Map p70; 84 M-Block, Great Kailash II; dishes ₹64-395; ☺noon-midnight) They don't just serve *parathas*, they serve 120 types of *paratha!* Try them stuffed with kebabs, veg curries, shredded chicken and untold other fillings.

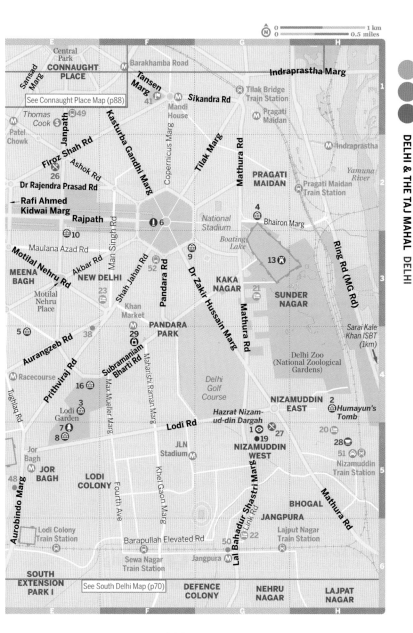

Olive Mediterranean **$$$**
(Map p70; ☏ 29574443; One Style Mile, Mehrauli;
tasting lunch menu from ₹495, dinner mains from
₹575; ☺noon-midnight; Ⓜ Qutab Minar) Uber-
chic Olive creates a little piece of
the Mediterranean in the suburbs. The
haveli setting, combined with beach-
house colours, is unlike anywhere else in
Delhi. Come for inventive Mediterranean
dishes – asparagus and walnut pizza,
seasonal vegetables in filo pastry – as
tasty as the clientele.

New Delhi & Around

Indian Accent   Indian **$$$**
(Map p70; ☏ 26925151; Manor, 77 Friends
Colony; tasting menu veg/nonveg ₹2375/2575)
Overlooking lush lawns at the Manor
hotel, this exclusive restaurant serves
inspired modern Indian cuisine. Familiar
and unfamiliar ingredients are thrown
together in surprising combinations – try
the silken tofu with quinoa pulao and goji
berry curry.

🍷 Drinking

CAFES

Chain coffeeshops abound – Café Coffee
Day is the most prolific (you'll rarely have
to walk more than a hundred yards to find
a branch), but there are also abundant
branches of Costa and Barista, particu-
larly around Connaught Place.

Café Turtle
Cafe

(Map p82; Full Circle Bookstore, Khan Market; Khan Market) Allied to the Full Circle Bookstore, this boho cafe ticks all the boxes when you're in the mood for coffee, cakes and calm reading space. There are branches in **N-Block Market** (Map p70; N-Block, Greater Kailash Part I) and **Nizamuddin East** (Map p82).

Kunzum Travel Cafe
Cafe

(Map p70; www.kunzum.com; Hauz Khas Village; ⏱11am-7.30pm Tue-Sun; 📶; Ⓜ Green Park) Run by the team of travel writers behind the informative *Delhi 101* guidebook, Kunzum has a pay-what-you-like policy for the self-service French-press coffee and tea. There's free wi-fi and travel books and magazines to browse. They also run heritage walks.

Indian Coffee House
Cafe

(Map p88; Mohan Singh Place, Baba Kharak Singh Marg; ⏱9am-9pm; Ⓜ Rajiv Chowk) Stuck-in-time Indian Coffee House looks poised to go under, but the roof terrace is a popular hang-out thanks to the staggeringly cheap menu of snacks (₹9 to ₹40) and South Indian coffee (₹14).

BARS

1911
Bar

(Map p88; Imperial Hotel, Janpath; drinks from ₹650 ; ⏱6am-1am; Ⓜ Rajiv Chowk) The elegant bar at the Imperial is the ultimate neocolonial extravagence. Sip perfectly prepared cocktails in front of murals of cavorting maharajas.

Q'BA
Bar

(Map p88; 📞45173333; 1st fl, 42 E-Block; ⏱noon-1am; Ⓜ Rajiv Chowk) Connaught Place's swishest watering hole has a Q-shaped bar, sultry lighting and sumptuous leather upholstery. Upstairs is for fine dining and there's a cool roof terrace, a great place to spend a sticky summer evening.

Shalom
Bar

(Map p70; www.shalomexperience.com; 18-N Block Market, Greater Kailash I; ⏱11am-1am)

This lounge-bar and restaurant, with wooden furniture and moody lighting, is one of the doyennes of the Delhi bar scene. As well as wine, beer, cocktails and nightly DJs, there's top-notch Mediterranean fare.

Entertainment

To access Delhi's dynamic arts scene, check local listings. October and March is the 'season', with shows and concerts (often free) happening nightly.

TLR
Live Music

(Map p70; www.tlrcafe.com; Hauz Khas Village; ⏱noon-1am; Ⓜ Green Park) Delhi's prime boho hang-out, TLR (The Living Room) more than justifies the trek to Hauz Khas. Come for groovy people, live music, jam sessions, DJ sets and other streetwise events from 9pm most evenings.

Dances of India
Dance

(Map p64; 📞26234689; Parsi Anjuman Hall, Bahadur Shah Zafar Marg; show ₹400; ⏱6.45pm; Ⓜ Chawri Bazaar) A one-hour performance of regional dances that includes Bharata Natyam (Tamil dance), Kathakali, bhangra and Manipuri.

High Tea at the Imperial

Raise your pinkie finger! High tea at the Imperial (p73) is perhaps the most refined way to while away an afternoon in Delhi. Sip tea from bone-china cups and pluck dainty sandwiches and cakes from tiered stands, while discussing the latest goings-on in Shimla and Dalhousie. High tea is served in the Atrium from 3pm to 6pm daily (weekday/weekend ₹750/1050). For ₹2500, you can add a 1½-hour tour of the Imperial's fantastic collection of Indian and colonial art.

Old Delhi's Bazaars

Old Delhi's bazaars are a head-spinning assault on the senses: an aromatic barrage of incense, spices, car fumes, body odour and worse, with a constant soundtrack of shouts, barks, music and car horns. This is less retail therapy, more heightened reality. The best time to come is mid-morning, when you actually move through the streets.

Whole districts here are devoted to individual items. **Chandni Chowk** (Map p88; Old Delhi; ⏰10am-7pm Mon-Sat; Ⓜ Chandni Chowk) is all clothing, electronics and break-as-soon-as-you-buy-them novelties. For silver jewellery, head for **Dariba Kalan** (Map p64), the alley near the Sisganj Gurdwara. Off this lane, the **Kinari Bazaar** (Map p64) (literally 'trimmings market') is famous for *zardozi* (gold embroidery), temple trim and wedding turbans. Running south from the old Town Hall, **Nai Sarak** (Map p64) is lined with stalls selling saris, shawls, chiffon and *lehanga* (long skirts), while nearby **Ballimaran** (Map p64) has sequinned slippers and fancy, curly-toed jootis.

Beside the Fatehpuri Masjid, on Khari Baoli, is the nose-numbing **Spice Market** (Gadodia Market; Map p64), ablaze with piles of scarlet-red chillis, knobbly ginger and turmeric roots, peppercorns, cumin, coriander seed, cardamoms, dried fruit and nuts. For gorgeous wrapping paper and wedding cards, head to **Chawri Bazaar** (Map p64), leading west from the Jama Masjid. For steel cookpots and cheap-as-chapatis paper kites, continue northwest to **Lal Kuan Main Bazaar** (Map p64).

🔒 Shopping

Away from government-run emporiums and other fixed-price shops, haggle like you mean it. Many taxi and autorickshaw drivers earn commissions (via your in-flated purchase price) by taking travellers to dubious, overpriced emporiums – don't fall for it.

Old Delhi

Aap Ki Pasand (San Cha)   Food & Drink
(Map p64; 15 Netaji Subhash Marg; ⏰9.30am-7pm Mon-Sat) An elegant tea shop selling a full range of Indian teas, from Darjeeling and Assam to Nilgiri and Kangra. You can try before you buy, and teas come lovingly packaged in drawstring bags.

Connaught Place

State Emporiums   Handicrafts, Clothing
(Map p88; Baba Kharak Singh Marg; ⏰11am-7pm Mon-Sat; Ⓜ Rajiv Chowk) Strung out along Baba Kharak Sing Marg are the official emporiums of the different Indian states, showcasing state-produced goods and handicrafts. Shopping here is like taking a tour around India – top stops include Kashmir, for papier mâché and carpets; Rajasthan, for miniature paintings and puppets; Uttar Pradesh for marble inlaywork; Karnataka for sandalwood sculptures; Tamil Nadu for metal statues; and Odisha for stone carvings.

Kamala   Handicrafts
(Map p88; Baba Kharak Singh Marg; ⏰10am-7pm Mon-Sat; Ⓜ Rajiv Chowk) Upscale crafts and curios, designed with real panache, from the Crafts Council of India.

Central Cottage Industries Emporium
Handicrafts

(Map p88; ☏ 23326790; Janpath; ⊙ 10am-7pm; Ⓜ Rajiv Chowk) This government-run, fixed-price multilevel Aladdin's cave of India-wide handicrafts is a great place to browse. Prices are higher than in the state emporiums, but the selection of woodcarvings, jewellery, pottery, papier mâché, jootis, brassware, textiles, beauty products and miniature paintings is superb.

Fabindia
Clothing, Homewares

(Map p88; www.fabindia.com; 28 B-Block, Connaught Place; ⊙ 11am-8pm) Readymade clothes in funky Indian fabrics, from elegant kurtas and dupattas to Western-style shirts, plus stylish homewares. There are branches in **Green Park** (Map p70), **Khan Market** (Map p82), **N-Block Market** (Map p70; N-Block, Greater Kailash I) and **Select Citywalk** (Map p70) in Saket.

···

New Delhi

Khan Market
Market

(Map p82; ⊙ around 10.30am-8pm Mon-Sat; Ⓜ Khan Market) Favoured by expats and Delhi's elite, the boutiques in this enclave are devoted to fashion, books and home-wares. For handmade paper, check out **Anand Stationers** (Map p82), or try **Mehra Bros** (Map p82) for cool papier mâché ornaments and Christmas decorations. Literature lovers should head to **Full Circle Bookstore** and **Bahrisons**. For ethnic-inspired fashions and homeware, hit **Fabindia**, **Anokhi** and **Good Earth**, and for elegantly packaged ayurvedic remedies, browse **Kama**.

🛈 Information

Dangers & Annoyances

Shop & Hotel Touts Taxi-wallahs at the international airport and around tourist areas frequently act as touts for hotels, claiming that your chosen hotel is full, poor value, overbooked, dangerous, burned down or closed, or that there are riots in Delhi, as part of a ruse to steer you to a hotel where they'll get a commission. Insist on being taken to where you want to go – making a show of writing down the registration plate number may help. Drivers at Connaught Place run a similar scam for private souvenir emporiums.

Travel Agent Touts Many travel agencies in Delhi claim to be tourist offices, even branding themselves with official tourist agency logos. There is only one tourist office – at 88 Janpath – and any other 'tourist office' is just a travel agency. Should you legitimately need the services of a travel agent, ask for a list of recommended agents from the bona-fide tourist office. Be wary of booking a multistop trip out of Delhi, particularly to Kashmir. Travellers are often hit for extra charges, or find out the class of travel and accommodation is less than they paid for.

Train Station Touts Touts at New Delhi train station endeavour to steer travellers away from the legitimate International Tourist Bureau (on level 1 in the main building on the Paharganj side) and into private travel agencies where they earn a commission. Don't believe any claims about the station booking office until you have seen it with your own eyes.

Internet Access

Most hotels offer internet access (often with wi-fi), but internet cafes can be found everywhere, including in Khan Market, Paharganj and Connaught Place. Rates start at ₹35 per hour.

Medical Services

Pharmacies are found on most shopping streets and in most suburban markets. Reputable hospitals:

All India Institute of Medical Sciences (IIMS; Map p70; ☏ 26588500; www.aiims.edu; Ansari Nagar; Ⓜ AIIMS)

Apollo Hospital (☏ 26925858; www.apollohospdelhi.com; Mathura Rd, Sarita Vihar)

Money

There are banks with ATMs everywhere you look in Delhi. Forex offices are concentrated around Connaught Place, particularly along Radial Rd 7. Travel agents and moneychangers offer international money transfers.

Baluja Forex (Map p64; 4596 Main Bazaar, Paharganj; ⊙ 9am-7.30pm; Ⓜ New Delhi)

Connaught Place

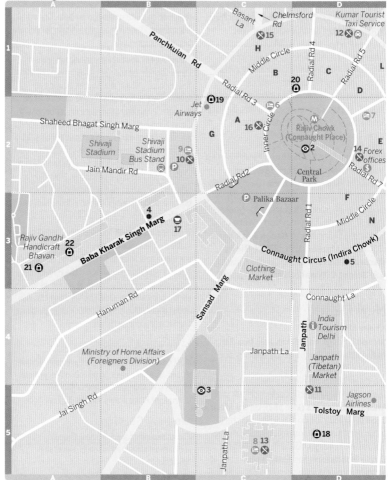

Thomas Cook (Map p82; Hotel Janpath, Janpath; ⏱9.30am-7pm Mon-Sat; Ⓜ Patel Chowk)

Tourist Information

The only official tourist information centre is India Tourism Delhi. Ignore touts who (falsely) claim to be associated with this office. Most states around India have their own regional tourist offices in Delhi – ask at India Tourism Delhi for contact details.

India Tourism Delhi (Government of India; Map p88; ☏ 23320008, 23320005; www.incredibleindia.org; 88 Janpath; ⏱9am-6pm Mon-Fri, to 2pm Sat; Ⓜ Rajiv Chowk) A useful source of advice on Delhi, getting out of Delhi, and visiting surrounding states. Has a free Delhi map and brochures, and publishes a list of recommended agencies and B&Bs. Come here to report tourism-related complaints.

❶ Getting There & Away

Delhi's airport can be prone to thick fog in December and January (often disrupting airline schedules) – it's wise to allow a day between connecting flights during this period.

Air

Indira Gandhi International Airport (✆ 0124-3376000; www.newdelhiairport.in) is about 14km southwest of the centre. International and domestic flights use the gleaming new Terminal 3. Ageing Terminal 1 is reserved for low-cost carriers. Free shuttle buses run between the two terminals every 20 minutes.

The arrivals hall at Terminal 3 has 24-hour forex, ATMs, prepaid taxi and car-hire counters, tourist information, bookshops, cafes and a **Premium Lounge** (✆ 61233922; 3hr s/d ₹2348/3522) with short-stay rooms.

For comprehensive details of domestic routes, pick up *Excel's Timetable of Air Services Within India* (₹55) from newsstands. Note that prices fluctuate and seats can be much cheaper if you book online with low-cost carriers.

Air India/Indian Airlines (Map p82; ✆ 24622220; www.airindia.in; Aurobindo Marg; ☉ 9.30am-5.30pm) Also has an office at Safdarjung Airport.

Jagson Airlines (Map p88; ✆ 23721593; Vandana Bldg, 11 Tolstoy Marg; ☉ 10am-6pm Mon-Sat)

Jet Airways (Map p88; ☎39893333; www.jetairways.com; 11/12 G-Block, Connaught Place; ⏱9am-6pm Mon-Sat) Also has information on JetKonnect flights.

Spicejet (☎1800 1803333; www.spicejet.com)

Bus

Most travellers enter and leave Delhi by train, but buses are a useful option if the trains are booked up.

Services to destinations north and west of Delhi leave from the Kashmere Gate Inter State Bus Terminal (ISBT; Map p64; ☎23860290) in Old Delhi, accessible by metro. For buses to destinations east of Delhi, including Dehra Dun, Haridwar and Rishikesh, head to the Anand Vihar ISBT in the eastern suburbs, accessible on the blue Metro line. Services to destinations south of Delhi leave from the Sarai Kale Khan ISBT on the ring road near Nizamuddin train station.

All the bus stands are chaotic so arrive at least 30 minutes ahead of your departure time. You can avoid the hassle by paying a little more for private

Major Trains from Delhi

DESTINATION	TRAIN NO & NAME	FARE (₹)	DURATION (HR)	FREQUENCY	DEPARTURES & TRAIN STATION
Agra	12280 Taj Exp	74/273 (A)	3	1 daily	7.10am NZM
	12002 Bhopal Shatabdi	384/805 (B)	2	1 daily	6.15am NDLS
Amritsar	12013/12031 Shatabdi Exp	591/1305 (B)	6	2 daily	7.20am
Chennai	12434 Chennai Rajdhani	2152/3150/ 5380 (C)	28	2 weekly	4pm NZM
	12622 Tamil Nadu Exp	528/1482/ 2375 (D)	33	1 daily	10.30pm NDLS
Goa (Madgaon)	12432 Trivandrum Rajdhani	1991/ 2960/ 5075 (C)	26	2 weekly	11am NZM
Jaipur	12958 ADI Swama Jayanti Rajdani	617/ 835/ 1400 (C)	5	1 daily	7.55pm NDLS
	12916 Ashram Exp	175/ 450/ 655 (D)	6	1 daily	
	12015 Ajmer Shatabdi	482/ 1040 (B)	4½	6 weekly	6.05am NDLS
Kalka (for Shimla)	12011 Kalka Shatabdi	482/1040 (B)	4½	1 daily	7.40am NDLS
Khajuraho	12448 UP Sampark Kranti Exp	269/728/ 1085 (D)	10½	daily except Wed	daily
Mumbai	12952 Mumbai Rajdhani	1550/2270/ 3870 (C)	16	1 daily	4.30pm NDLS
	12954 August Kranti Rajdani	1550/2270/ 3870 (C)	17½	1 daily	4.55pm NZM
Udaipur	12963 Mewar Exp	305/831/ 1245 (D)	12½	1 daily	7.05pm NZM
Varanasi	12560 Shivganga Exp	306/836/ 1255 (D)	13	1 daily	6.55pm NDLS

Train stations: NDLS – New Delhi, DLI – Old Delhi, NZM – Hazrat Nizamuddin
Fares: (A) 2nd class/chair car; (B) chair car/1st-class AC; (C) 3AC/2AC/1st-class AC; (D) sleeper/3AC/2AC

A Muslim cleric reads at a Delhi mosque

DAMIEN SIMONIS/GETTY IMAGES ©

deluxe buses that leave from locations in central Delhi – enquire at travel agencies or your hotel for details.

Considering the traffic situation at either end, the train is your best bet for Agra. **Himachal Pradesh Tourism Development Corporation** (HPTDC; Map p82) runs a bus for Dharamsala (₹1100, 12 hours) from Chanderlok House on Janpath. For Rishikesh, the luxury Royal Cruiser leaves from the Anand Vihar ISBT at 10am, 9pm and 11pm daily (₹643, six hours). Rajasthan Tourism runs deluxe buses from **Bikaner House** (Map p82; ☏ 23381884; www.rtdc.com; Bikaner House, Pandara Rd), near India Gate, to the following destinations:

Ajmer (Volvo; ₹923, nine hours, one daily)

Jaipur (super deluxe/Volvo ₹500/780, six hours, hourly)

Jodhpur (super deluxe/Volvo ₹965/1256, 11 hours, two daily)

Udaipur (Volvo; ₹1375, 15 hours, one daily)

Train

There are three main stations in Delhi – (Old) Delhi train station (aka Delhi Junction) in Old Delhi, New Delhi train station near Paharganj, and Nizamuddin train station, south of Sunder Nagar. Make sure you know which station your train is leaving from.

There are two options for foreign travellers – you can brave the queues at the main **reservation office** (Map p64; Chelmsford Rd; ⊙ 8am-8pm, to 2pm Sun), or visit the helpful **International Tourist Bureau** (Map p64; ☏ 23405156; ⊙ 8am-8pm Mon-Sat, to 2pm Sun) on the 1st floor in the main building at New Delhi railway station. Do not believe anyone who tells you it has shifted, closed or burnt down!

When making reservations here, you can pay in foreign currency, in travellers cheques (Thomas Cook cheques in US dollars, euros or pounds sterling, Amex cheques in US dollars and euros, or Barclays cheques in US dollars) or in rupees, backed up by money-exchange certificates (or ATM receipts). Bring your passport.

When you arrive, complete a reservation form, then queue to check availability, before paying for your booking at the relevant counter. This is the best place to get last-minute bookings for quota seats to popular destinations, but the queues can be outrageous.

If you prefer to brave the standard reservation office, check the details for your journey (including the train number) in advance on the Indian Railways website (www.indianrail.gov.in) or Erail (http://erail.in), or in the invaluable publication *Trains at a Glance* (₹45), available at newsstands. You'll need to fill out a reservation form and queue – after 7pm is the quietest time to book.

ℹ️ Getting Around

The metro system has transformed getting around the city, making it incredibly easy to whizz out to the remotest suburbs. Keep small change handy for rickshaw fares.

To/From the Airport

International flights often arrive at ghastly hours, so it pays to book a hotel in advance and notify staff of your arrival time. Organised city transport runs to/from Terminal 3; a free shuttle bus runs every 20 minutes between Terminal 3 and Terminal 1.

Pre-arranged pick-ups Hotels offer pre-arranged airport pick-up, but you'll pay extra to cover the airport parking fee (up to ₹140) and ₹80 charge to enter the arrivals hall. To avoid the entry fee, drivers may wait outside Gates 4–6.

Metro The Airport Express line (www.delhiairportexpress.com) runs every 13 minutes from 5.15am to 11.30pm, completing the journey from Terminal 3 to New Delhi train station in around 40 minutes (₹150).

Bus Air-conditioned buses run from outside Terminal 3 to Kashmere Gate ISBT every 20 minutes, via the Red Fort, LNJP Hospital, New Delhi Station Gate 2, Connaught Place, Parliament St and Ashoka Rd (₹50).

Taxi In front of the arrivals buildings at Terminal 3 and Terminal 1 are Delhi Traffic Police prepaid taxi counters (📞23010101; www.delhitrafficpolice.nic.in) offering fixed-price taxi services. You'll pay about ₹350 to New or Old Delhi, and ₹450 to the southern suburbs, plus a 25% surcharge between 11pm and 5am. Insist that the driver takes you to your chosen destination and only surrender your voucher when you arrive.

You can also book a prepaid taxi at the Megacabs (p93) counter outside the arrivals building at both the international and domestic terminals. It costs ₹600 to ₹700 to the centre, but you get a cleaner car with air-con.

Autorickshaw & Taxi

Local taxis (recognisable by their black and yellow livery) and autorickshaws have meters but these are effectively ornamental as most drivers refuse to use them. Delhi Traffic Police runs a network of prepaid autorickshaw booths (see www.delhitrafficpolice.nic.in/prepaid-booths.htm) where you can pay a fixed fare, including 24-hour stands at the New Delhi, Old Delhi and Nizamuddin train stations; elsewhere, you'll need to negotiate a fare before you set off.

Fares are invariably elevated for foreigners so haggle hard, and if the fare sounds too

School children in cycle-rickshaw

RICK GERHARTER/GETTY IMAGES ©

outrageous, find another cab. For an autorickshaw ride from Connaught Place, expect to pay around ₹30 to Paharganj, ₹40 to India Gate, ₹60 to the Red Fort, ₹70 to Humayan's Tomb and ₹100 to Hauz Khas. The website www.taxiautofare.com can provide suggested fares for other journeys.

Taxis typically charge twice the autorickshaw fare. Note that fares may vary as fuel prices go up and down. From 11pm to 5am there's a 25% surcharge for autorickshaws and taxis.

Car

Numerous operators will rent out a car with a driver, or you can negotiate directly with taxi drivers at taxi stands around the city. Note that some taxis can only operate inside the city limits, or in certain surrounding states. For a day of local sightseeing, there is normally an eight-hour, 80km limit – anything over this costs extra. The following companies get positive reports from travellers.

Kumar Tourist Taxi Service (Map p88; ✆23415930; www.kumarindiatours.com; 14/1 K-Block, Connaught Place; ◷9am-9pm) Rates are among Delhi's lowest – a day of Delhi sightseeing costs from ₹1000 (the eight hours and 80km limit applies).

Metropole Tourist Service (Map p82; ✆24310313; www.metrovista.co.in; 224 Defence Colony Flyover Market; ◷7am-7pm) Under the Defence Flyover Bridge (on the Jangpura side).

Cycle-Rickshaw

Cycle-rickshaws are useful for navigating Old Delhi and the suburbs, but are banned from many parts of New Delhi, including Connaught Place, and from the clogged main artery of Chandni Chowk. Negotiate a fare before you set off – expect to pay about ₹30 for the trip from Paharganj to Connaught Place.

Metro

Delhi's magnificent metro (✆23417910; www.delhimetrorail.com) is fast and efficient, with signs and arrival/departure announcements in Hindi and English. Trains run from around 6am to 11pm and the first carriage in the direction of travel is reserved for women only. Note that trains can get insanely busy at peak commuting times (around 9am to 10am and 5pm to 6pm) – avoid travelling with luggage during rush hour if at all possible.

Radiocab

You'll need a local mobile number to order a radiocab, or ask a shop or hotel to assist. These air-conditioned cars are clean, efficient, and use reliable meters, charging ₹20 at flagfall then ₹20 per km.

Some reliable companies:

Easycabs (✆43434343; www.easycabs.com)

Megacabs (✆41414141; www.megacabs.com)

Quickcabs (✆45333333; www.quickcabs.in)

UTTAR PRADESH & THE TAJ MAHAL

....

Agra

✆0562 / POP 1.7 MILLION

◉ Sights & Activities

Agra Fort   Fort
(Indian/foreigner ₹20/300, video ₹25; ◷dawn-dusk) With the Taj Mahal overshadowing it, one can easily forget that Agra has one of the finest Mughal forts in India. Construction of the massive red-sandstone fort, on the bank of the Yamuna River, was begun by Emperor Akbar in 1565. Further additions were made, particularly by his grandson Shah Jahan, using his favourite building material – white marble. The fort was built primarily as a military structure, but Shah Jahan transformed it into a palace, and later it became his gilded prison for eight years after his son Aurangzeb seized power in 1658.

The ear-shaped fort's colossal double walls rise over 20m in height and measure 2.5km in circumference. The Yamuna River originally flowed along the straight eastern edge of the fort, and the emperors had their own bathing ghats here. It contains a maze of buildings, forming a city within a city, including vast underground sections, though many of the structures were destroyed over the years by Nadir Shah, the Marathas, the Jats and finally the British, who used the fort as a garrison. Even today, much of the fort is used by the military and so is off-limits to the general public.

The **Amar Singh Gate** to the south is the sole entry point to the fort these days and where you buy your entrance ticket.

Continued on p98

★ Don't Miss
Taj Mahal

Rabindranath Tagore described it as 'a teardrop on the cheek of eternity', while its creator, Emperor Shah Jahan, said it made 'the sun and the moon shed tears from their eyes'. Every year, tourists numbering more than twice the population of Agra pass through its gates to catch a once-in-a-lifetime glimpse of what is widely considered the most beautiful building in the world. Few leave disappointed.

Indian/foreigner ₹20/750, video ₹25

🕐 dawn-dusk Sat-Thu

Closed Fri to those not attending prayers at the mosque

Entry & Information

The Taj can be accessed through the west, south and east gates; the south gate is nearest to Taj Ganj. There are separate queues for men and women at all three gates. Cameras and videos are permitted but you cannot take photographs inside the mausoleum itself.

A 500ml bottle of water and shoe covers are included with your ticket. If you keep your ticket you get small entry-fee reductions when visiting Agra Fort, Fatehpur Sikri, Akbar's Tomb or the Itimad-ud-Daulah on the same day. You can also store your luggage for free beside the ticket offices. The Taj is arguably at its most atmospheric at sunrise, which is also the most comfortable time to visit, with far fewer crowds. Sunset is another magical viewing time. You can also view the Taj for five nights around full moon; entry numbers are limited, and tickets must be bought a day in advance from the **Archaeological Survey of India office** (Map p82; ☎011-23010822; www.asi.nic.in; Janpath; ⊙9.30am-1pm & 2-6pm Mon-Fri).

Inside the Grounds

The Taj stands on a raised marble platform at the northern end of the classical Mughal *charbagh* (ornamental gardens), with its back to the Yamuna River. Its raised position means that the backdrop is only sky – a masterstroke of design. Decorative 40m-high white minarets grace each corner of the platform. The sandstone **mosque** to the west is an important gathering place for Agra's Muslims. The identical building to the east, the **jawab**, was built for symmetry.

The central Taj structure is made of semitranslucent white marble, carved with flowers and inlaid with thousands of semiprecious stones in beautiful patterns. Inside, directly below the main dome is the Cenotaph of Mumtaz Mahal, an elaborate false tomb surrounded by a perforated marble screen inlaid with dozens of different types of semiprecious stones. Beside it, offsetting the symmetry of the Taj, is the Cenotaph of Shah Jahan, who was interred here with little ceremony by his usurping son Aurangzeb in 1666. The real tombs are in a locked basement room below.

Taj Mahal Don't Miss List

HISTORIAN AND WRITER DR NEVILLE SMITH'S FAMILY HAS LIVED IN AGRA FOR OVER FOUR GENERATIONS

1 PERFECT SYMMETRY
There is a perfect balance of structures to the left and right of an imaginary middle line cut through the building's centre. You see the same number of turrets, cupolas and pavilions on the left and right of the central dome, as well as on the main structure.

2 MATHEMATICAL ACCURACY
If you stand in front of the main tomb in the Cenotaph Chamber and look straight towards the main gateway due south, you will find that the tomb aligns exactly with the middle of the gateway. That such accuracy was achieved, without the technical instruments of today, says much about the architectural and engineering skills of the builders.

3 OPTICAL ILLUSION
The Quranic verses on the mausoleum do not appear to decrease in size as they go up to the base of the main dome, which would be the case if they were chiselled in equal size and placed in their grooves. The letters were increased in size along with the grooves in which they were to be inserted, so that a person looking at them from the ground would see them as equal in size and the optical effect of their tapering to the top would be avoided.

4 ARCHITECTURAL SYMBOLISM
The Taj can be seen as conceptualising the feminine grace of Mumtaz Mahal. The dome has been likened to the head of a woman and its base as her neck, around which the marble inlay gives the appearance of Mumtaz Mahal arrayed in all her finery.

5 LANDSCAPING INNOVATION
Unlike other Mughal and, indeed, Muslim garden tombs, which all have a tomb set in the centre of a garden with waterways radiating from it, the Taj has been placed at the northen end of a garden. Shah Jahan broke away from the typical Muslim garden tomb for better scenic effect, so the edifice dominates the garden.

Taj Mahal

Timeline

1631 Emperor Shah Jahan's beloved third wife, Mumtaz Mahal, dies in Buhanpur while giving birth to their 14th child. Her body is initially interred in Buhanpur itself, where Shah Jahan is fighting a military campaign, but is later moved, in a golden casket, to a small building on the banks of the Yamuna River in Agra.

1632 Construction of a permanent mausoleum for Mumtaz Mahal begins.

1633 Mumtaz Mahal is interred in her final resting place, an underground tomb beneath a marble plinth, on top of which the Taj Mahal will be built.

1640 The white-marble mausoleum is completed.

1653 The rest of the Taj Mahal complex is completed.

1658 Emperor Shah Jahan is overthrown by his son Aurangzeb and imprisoned in Agra Fort.

1666 Shah Jahan dies. His body is transported along the Yamuna River and buried underneath the Taj, alongside the tomb of his wife.

1908 Repeatedly damaged and looted after the fall of the Mughal empire, the Taj receives some long-overdue attention as part of a major restoration project ordered by British viceroy Lord Curzon.

1983 The Taj is awarded Unesco World Heritage Site status.

2002 Having been discoloured by pollution in more recent years, the Taj is spruced up with an ancient recipe known as *multani mitti* – a blend of soil, cereal, milk and lime once used by Indian women to beautify their skin.

Today More than three million tourists visit the Taj Mahal each year. That's more than twice the current population of Agra.

Go Barefoot
Help the environment by entering the mausoleum barefoot instead of using the free disposable shoe covers.

Pishtaqs
These huge arched recesses are set into each side of the Taj. They provide depth to the building while their central, latticed marble screens allow patterned light to illuminate the inside of the mausoleum.

Minaret

Plinth

Entranc

Marble Relief Work
Flowering plants, thought to be representations of paradise, are a common theme among the beautifully decorative panels carved onto the white marble.

Be Enlightened
Bring a small torch into the mausoleum to fully appreciate the translucency of the white marble and semiprecious stones.

Filigree Screen
This stunning screen was carved out of a single piece of marble. It surrounds both cenotaphs, allowing patterned light to fall onto them through its intricately carved *jali* (latticework).

Central Dome
The Taj's famous central dome, topped by a brass finial, represents the vault of heaven, a stark contrast to the material world, which is represented by the square shape of the main structure.

Yamuna River

NORTH →

Pietra Dura
It's believed that 35 different precious and semi-precious stones were used to create the exquisite pietra dura (marble inlay work) found on the inside and outside of the mausoleum walls. Again, floral designs are common.

Calligraphy
The strips of calligraphy surrounding each of the four pishtaqs get larger as they get higher, giving the impression of uniform size when viewed from the ground. There's also calligraphy inside the mausoleum, including on Mumtaz Mahal's cenotaph.

Cenotaphs
The cenotaphs of Mumtaz Mahal and Shah Jahan, decorated with pietra dura inlay work, are actually fake tombs. The real ones are located in an underground vault closed to the public.

Taj Mahal History

The Taj was built by Shah Jahan as a memorial for his third wife, Mumtaz Mahal, who died giving birth to their 14th child in 1631. The death of Mumtaz left the emperor so heartbroken that his hair is said to have turned grey virtually overnight. Construction of the Taj began the following year and, although the main building is thought to have been built in eight years, the whole complex was not completed until 1653. Not long after it was finished Shah Jahan was overthrown by his son Aurangzeb and imprisoned in Agra Fort where, for the rest of his days, he could only gaze out at his creation through a window. Following his death in 1666, Shah Jahan was buried here alongside Mumtaz.

In total, some 20,000 people from India and Central Asia worked on the building. Specialists were brought in from as far away as Europe to produce the exquisite marble screens and pietra dura (marble inlay work) made with thousands of semiprecious stones.

The Taj was designated a World Heritage Site in 1983 and looks as immaculate today as when it was first constructed – though it underwent a huge restoration project in the early 20th century.

Continued from p93

Its dogleg design was meant to confuse attackers who made it past the first line of defence – the crocodile-infested moat.

You can walk here from Taj Ganj, or it's ₹25 in a cycle-rickshaw.

Taj Museum   Museum
(admission ₹5; ⊙10am-5pm Sat-Thu) Within the Taj complex, on the western side of the gardens, this small but excellent museum houses a number of original Mughal miniature paintings, including 17th-century ivory portraits of Emperor Shah Jahan and Mumtaz Mahal. Also here aresome very well preserved gold and silver coins dating from the same period, plus architectural drawings of the Taj and some nifty celadon plates, said to break or change colour if the food served on them contains poison.

Tours

Amin Tours   Cultural Tours
(🖉9837411144; www.daytourtajmahal.com) If you can't be bothered handling the logistics, look no further than this recommended agency for all-inclusive private

Agra day trips from Delhi by car (₹6250) or train (₹6000).

UP Tourism   Coach Tours
(www.up-tourism.com; incl entry fees Indian/foreigner ₹400/1700) Agra Cantonment train station (🖉2421204; ⊙7am-10pm) Taj Rd (🖉2226431; 64 Taj Rd; ⊙10am-5pm Mon-Sat) UP Tourism runs daily coach tours that leave Agra Cantonment train station at 10.30am, after picking up passengers arriving from Delhi on the Taj Express. The tour includes the Taj Mahal, Agra Fort and Fatehpur Sikri with a 1¼-hour stop in each place. Tours return to the station so that day trippers can catch the Taj Express back to Delhi at 6.55pm. Contact either of the UP Tourism offices to book a seat, or just turn up at the train station tourist office at 9.45am to sign up for that day.

Sleeping

It's possible to see Agra on a day trip from Delhi, but it's a rush. If you want to see more than just the Taj, or just fancy a change of scene, consider booking a night or two at one of the following.

Oberoi Amarvilas
Hotel $$$

(📞2231515; www.oberoihotels.com; Taj East Gate Rd; d with/without balcony ₹56,210/48,901; ❄@🛜🏊) The ultimate in luxury.

N Homestay
B&B $$

(📞9690107860; www.nhomestay.com; 15 Ajanta Colony, Vibhav Nagar; s/d incl breakfast ₹1200/1500; ❄@🛜) Hugely welcoming homestay 15 minutes' walk from the Taj.

Hotel Sheela
Hotel $

(📞2333074; www.hotelsheelaagra.com; Taj East Gate Rd; d with fan ₹600-800, with AC ₹1000; ❄) Popular budget option with a pleasant garden; close to the Taj Mahal's east gate.

✖ Eating

Saniya Palace Hotel
Multicuisine $$

(mains ₹30-180; ⏰6am-11pm) With cute tablecloths, dozens of potted plants and a bamboo pergola for shade, this is the most pleasant rooftop restaurant in Taj Ganj. It also has the best rooftop view of the Taj bar none. The kitchen isn't the cleanest in town, but its usual mix of Western dishes and Western-friendly Indian dishes usually go down without complaints.

Dasaprakash
South Indian $$

(www.dasaprakashgroup.com; 1 Gwalior Rd; meals ₹110-150; ⏰noon-11pm) Fabulously tasty and religiously clean, Dasaprakash whips up consistently great South Indian vegetarian food, including spectacular thalis (₹125 to ₹300), dosa and a few token Continental dishes. The ice-cream desserts (₹70 to ₹145) are another speciality. Comfortable booth seating and woodlattice screens make for intimate dining.

Pinch of Spice
North Indian $$$

(www.pinchofspice.in; 1076/2 Fatahabad Rd; mains ₹190-350; ⏰noon-11pm) This modern North Indian superstar at the beginning of Fatahabad Rd is the best spot outside of a five-star hotel to indulge yourself in rich curries and succulent tandoori kebabs. The *murg boti masala* (chicken tikka swimming in a rich and spicy country gravy) and the *paneer lababdar* (fresh cheese cubes in a spicy red gravy with sauteed onions) are outstanding.

Esphahan
North Indian $$$

(📞2231515; Taj East Gate Rd, Oberoi Amarvilas Hotel; mains ₹775-1250; ⏰dinner) There are only two sittings each evening at Agra's finest restaurant (6.30pm and 9.30pm) so booking a table is essential. Highlights of the small but exquisite menu include succulent North Indian tandoor preparations (anything is good), a lamb *raan* steeped in chocolate and coffee undertones that packs a wallop of velvety spice, and some memorable unpolished rice topped with decadent Kerala shrimp curry. It's all set to a romantic background soundtrack of a

Mughal-era inlay work in a mosque
AYAN82/GETTY IMAGES ©

live *santoor* (Kashmiri stringed instrument) player. Skip the espresso.

ⓘ Information

Agra is wired, even in restaurants. Taj Ganj is riddled with internet cafes, most charging between ₹30 and ₹40 per hour. ATMs are all over the city; there's one near each gate of the Taj.

Medical Services

Amit Jaggi Memorial Hospital (www.ajmh. in; Vibhav Nagar, off Minto Rd) If you're sick, Dr Jaggi, who runs this private clinic, is the man to see. He accepts most health insurance plans from abroad; otherwise a visit runs ₹1000 (day) or ₹2000 (night). He'll even do house calls.

ⓘ Getting There & Away

Air

Commercial flights to Agra's Kheria Airport began again in late 2012 after a long absence. **Air India** (www.airindia.com) now flies Monday, Wednesday and Saturday to Varanasi (1.50pm) via Khajuraho. A new international airport, something Delhi lobbyists have fought against for years, was also greenlighted at time of research, but don't expect to see it in this edition's lifespan.

To access the airport, part of Indian Air Force territory, your name must be on the list of those with booked flights that day. Tickets must be purchased online or by phone.

Train

Most trains leave from **Agra Cantonment (Cantt) train station**, although some go from Agra Fort station. A few trains, such as Marudhar Exp, run slightly different numbers on different days than those listed, but timings remain the same.

Express trains are well set up for day trippers to/from Delhi but trains run to Delhi all day. If you can't reserve a seat, just buy a 'general ticket' for the next train (about ₹62), find a seat in Sleeper class then upgrade when the ticket collector comes along. Most of the time, he won't even make you pay any more.

ⓘ Getting Around

Autorickshaw

Agra's green-and-yellow autorickshaws run on CNG (compressed natural gas) and are less environmentally destructive. Just outside Agra Cantt station is the prepaid autorickshaw booth, which gives you a good guide for haggling elsewhere. Note, autos aren't allowed to go to Fatehpur Sikri.

Sample prices from Agra Cantt station: Fatahabad Rd ₹100; Sadar Bazaar ₹60; Taj Mahal ₹100; Shilpgrarm (Taj East Gate) ₹120; half-day (four-hour) tour ₹400; full-day (10-hour) tour ₹500. Prices do not include a ₹5 booking fee.

Cycle-Rickshaw

Agree on fares beforehand. Price estimates from the Taj Mahal include: Agra Cantt train station ₹40; Agra Fort ₹30; Fatahabad Rd ₹20; Sadar Bazaar ₹30; half-day tour ₹200.

Taxi

Outside Agra Cantt the prepaid taxi booth gives a good idea of what taxis should cost. Non-AC prices include:

Agra Fort (p93)
DAMIEN SIMONIS/GETTY IMAGES ©

Delhi ₹3000; Fatahabad Rd ₹150; Sadar Bazaar ₹100; Taj Mahal ₹150; half-day (four-hour) tour ₹650; full-day (eight-hour) tour ₹850. Prices do not include a ₹10 booking fee.

Fatehpur Sikri

☎ 05613 / POP 29,000

This magnificent fortified ancient city, 40km west of Agra, was the short-lived capital of the Mughal empire between 1571 and 1585, during the reign of Emperor Akbar. Akbar visited the village of Sikri to consult the Sufi saint Shaikh Salim Chishti, who predicted the birth of an heir to the Mughal throne. When the prophecy came true, Akbar built his new capital here, including a stunning mosque –

still in use today – and three palaces for each of his favourite wives, one a Hindu, one a Muslim and one a Christian (though Hindu villagers in Sikri dispute a few of these claims). The city was an Indo-Islamic masterpiece, but erected in an area that supposedly suffered from water shortages and so was abandoned shortly after Akbar's death.

◎ Sights

Jama Masjid　　　　　　Mosque

This beautiful, immense mosque was completed in 1571 and contains elements of Persian and Indian design. The main entrance, at the top of a flight of stone steps, is through the spectacular 54m-high **Buland Darwaza** (Victory Gate),

Agra Train Services

DELHI–AGRA TRAINS FOR DAY TRIPPERS

TRIP	TRAIN NO & NAME	FARE (₹)	DURATION (HR)	DEPARTURES
New Delhi-Agra	12002 Shatabdi Exp	384/805 (A)	2	6am (except Fri)
Agra-New Delhi	12001 Shatabdi Exp	415/850 (A)	2	8.35pm (except Fri)
Hazrat Nizamuddin-Agra	12280 Taj Exp	75/273 (B)	3	7.10am
Agra-Hazrat Nizamuddin	12279 Taj Exp	75/273 (B)	3	6.55pm

Fares: (A) AC chair/1AC; (B) 2nd-class/AC chair

OTHER TRAINS FROM AGRA (AGC/AF)

DESTINATION	TRAIN NO & NAME	FARE (₹)	DURATION (HR)	DEPARTURES
Jaipur*	12036 Shatabdi Exp	415/890 (C)	3½	4.20pm (except Thu)
Khajuraho	12448 UP SMPRK KRNTI	207/546/ 805 (A)	8	11.20pm (except Wed)
Mumbai (CST)	12138/12137 Punjab Mail	410/1139/ 1770 (A)	23	8.55am
Varanasi	93238/13237 Kota PNBE Exp	262/733/ 1110 (A)	12	11.30pm

Fares: (A) sleeper/3AC/2AC; (B) sleeper/3AC only; (C) AC chair/1AC only,
*leaves from Agra Fort station

Fatehpur Sikri

A WALKING TOUR OF FATEHPUR SIKRI

You can enter this fortified ancient city from two entrances, but the northeast entrance at Diwan-i-Am (Hall of Public Audiences) offers the most logical approach to this remarkable Unesco World Heritage site. This large courtyard (now a garden) is where Emperor Akbar presided over the trials of accused criminals. Once through the ticket gate, you are in the northern end of the **Pachisi Courtyard 1**. The first building you see is **Diwan-i-Khas 2** (Hall of Private Audiences), the interior of which is dominated by a magnificently carved central stone column. Pitch south and enter **Rumi Sultana 3**, a small but elegant palace built for Akbar's Turkish Muslim wife. It's hard to miss the **Ornamental Pool 4** nearby – its southwest corner provides Fatehpur Sikri's most photogenic angle, perfectly framing its most striking building, the five-storey Panch Mahal, one of the gateways to the Imperial Harem Complex, where the **Lower Haramsara 5** once housed more than 200 female servants. Wander around the Palace of Jodh Bai and take notice of the towering ode to an elephant, the 21m-high **Hiran Minar 6**, in the distance to the northwest. Leave the palaces and pavilions area via Shahi Darwaza (King's Gate), which spills into India's second-largest mosque courtyard at **Jama Masjid 7**. Inside this immense and gorgeous mosque is the sacred **Tomb of Shaikh Salim Chishti 8**. Exit through the spectacular **Buland Darwaza 9** (Victory Gate), one of the world's most magnificent gateways.

Buland Darwaza
Most tours end with an exit through Jama Masjid's Victory Gate. Walk out and take a look behind you: Behold! The magnificent 15-storey sandstone gate, 54m high, is a menacing monolith to Akbar's reign.

Shahi Darwaza (King's Gate)

Tomb of Shaikh Salim Chishti
Each knot in the strings tied to the 56 carved white marble designs of the interior walls of Shaikh Salim Chishti's tomb represents one wish of a maximum three.

Jama Masjid
The elaborate marble inlay work at the Badshahi Gate and throughout the Jama Masjid complex is said to have inspired similar work 82 years later at the Taj Mahal in Agra.

Hiran Minar

This bizarre, seldom-visited tower off the north-west corner of Fatehpur Sikri is decorated with hundreds of stone representations of elephant tusks. It is said to be the place where Minar, Akbar's favourite execution elephant, died.

Pachisi Courtyard

Under your feet just past Rumi Sultana is the Pachisi Courtyard where Akbar is said to have played the game *pachisi* (an ancient version of ludo) using slave girls in colourful dress as pieces.

Diwan-i-Khas

Emperor Akbar modified the central stone column inside Diwan-i-Khas to call attention to a new religion he called Din-i-Ilahi (God is One). The intricately carved column features a fusion of Hindu, Muslim, Christian and Buddhist imagery.

Panch Mahal

Diwan-i-Am (Hall of Public Audiences)

Rumi Sultana

Don't miss the headless creatures carved into Rumi Sultana's palace interiors: a lion, deer, an eagle and a few peacocks were beheaded by jewel thieves who swiped the precious jewels that originally formed their heads.

Ornamental Pool

Tansen, said to be the most gifted Indian vocalist of all time and one of Akbar's treasured nine *Navaratnas* (Gems), would be showered with coins during performances from the central platform of the Ornamental Pool.

Lower Haramsara

Akbar reportedly kept more than 5000 concubines, but the 200 or so female servants housed in the Lower Haramsara were strictly business. Knots were tied to these sandstone rings to support partitions between their individual quarters.

built to commemorate Akbar's military victory in Gujarat.

Inside the courtyard of the mosque is the stunning white-marble **tomb of Shaikh Salim Chishti**, which was completed in 1581 and is entered through an original door made of ebony. Inside it are brightly coloured flower murals while the sandlewood canopy is decorated with mother-of-pearl shell. Just as Akbar came to the saint four centuries ago hoping for a son, childless women visit his tomb today and tie a thread to the *jali,* which are among the finest in India. To the right of the tomb lie the gravestones of family members of Shaikh Salim Chishti and nearby is the entrance to an underground tunnel (barred by a locked gate) that reputedly goes all the way to Agra Fort! Behind the entrance to the tunnel, on the far wall, are three holes, part of the ancient ventilation system. You can still feel the rush of cool air forcing its way through them. Just east of Shaikh Salim Chishti's tomb is the red-sandstone **tomb of**

Islam Khan, the final resting place of Shaikh Salim Chishti's grandson and one-time governor of Bengal.

On the east wall of the courtyard is a smaller entrance to the mosque – the **Shahi Darwaza** (King's Gate), which leads to the palace complex.

Palaces & Pavilions

Palaces

(Indian/foreigner ₹20/260, video ₹25; ☼ dawn-dusk) A large courtyard dominates the northeast entrance at **Diwan-i-Am** (Hall of Public Audiences). Now a pristinely manicured garden, this is where Akbar presided over the courts from the middle seat of the five equal seatings along the western wall, flanked by his advisors. It was built to utilise an echo sound system, so Akbar could hear anything at any time from anywhere in the open space. Justice was dealt with swiftly if legends are to be believed, with public executions said to have been carried out here by elephants trampling to death convicted criminals.

The **Diwan-i-Khas** (Hall of Private Audiences), found at the northern end of the Pachisi Courtyard, looks nothing special from the outside, but the interior is dominated by a magnificently carved stone central column. This pillar flares to create a flat-topped plinth linked to the four corners of the room by narrow stone bridges. From this plinth Akbar is believed to have debated with scholars and ministers who stood at the ends of the four bridges.

Next to Diwan-i-Khas is the **Treasury**, which houses secret stone safes in some corners (one has been left with its stone lid open for visitors to see). Sea monsters carved on the ceiling struts were

Diwan-i-Khas
PREMIUM UIG/GETTY IMAGES ©

Tomb of Shaikh Salim Chishti

HUW JONES/GETTY IMAGES ©

there to protect the fabulous wealth once stored here. The so-called **Astrologer's Kiosk** in front has roof supports carved in a serpentine Jain style.

Just south of the Astrologer's Kiosk is **Pachisi Courtyard**, named after the ancient game known in India today as ludo. The large, plus-shaped gameboard is visible surrounding the block in the middle of the courtyard. In the southeast corner is the most intricately carved structure in the whole complex, the tiny but elegant **Rumi Sultana**, which was said to be the palace built for Akbar's Turkish Muslim wife, but other theories say it was used by Akbar himself as a R&R/powder room during court sessions. On one corner of the **Ladies Garden** just west of Pachisi is the impressive **Panch Mahal**, a pavilion whose five storeys decrease in size until the top one consists of only a tiny kiosk. The lower floor has 84 columns, all different, and total colums clock in at 176.

Continuing anticlockwise will bring you to the **Ornamental Pool**. Here, singers and musicians would perform on the platform above the water while Akbar watched from the pavilion in his private quarters, known as **Daulat Khana** (Abode of Fortune). Behind the pavilion is the **Khwabgah** (Dream House), a sleeping area with a huge stone bunk bed. Nowadays the only sleeping done here is by bats, hanging from the ceiling. The small room in the far corner is full of them!

Heading west from the Ornamental Pool is the **Palace of Jodh Bai**, and the one-time home of Akbar's Hindu wife, said to be his favourite. Set around an enormous courtyard, it blends traditional Indian columns, Islamic cupolas and turquoise-blue Persian roof tiles. Just outside, to the left of Jodh Bai's former kitchen, is the **Palace of the Christian Wife**. This was used by Akbar's Goan wife Mariam, who gave birth to Jehangir here in 1569, though some believe Akbar never had a Christian wife at all, and that Mariam was short for Mariam-Ut-Zamani, a title he gave to Jodh Bai meaning 'Beautiful like a Rose', or 'Most Beautiful Woman on Earth'. Like many of the buildings in the palace complex, it contains elements of different religions,

105

DELHI & THE TAJ MAHAL FATEHPUR SIKRI

as befitted Akbar's tolerant religious beliefs. The domed ceiling is Islamic in style, while remnants of a wall painting of the Hindu god Shiva can also be found.

Walking past the Palace of the Christian Wife once more will take you west to **Birbal Bhavan**, ornately carved inside and out, and thought to have been the living quarters of one of Akbar's most senior ministers. The **Lower Haramsara**, just to the south, housed Akbar's large inventory of live-in female servants.

Plenty of ruins are scattered behind the whole complex, including the **Caravanserai**, a vast courtyard surrounded by rooms where visiting merchants stayed. Badly defaced carvings of elephants still guard **Hathi**

Pol (Elephant Gate), while the remains of the small **Stonecutters' Mosque** and a **hammam** (bath) are also a short stroll away. Other unnamed ruins can be explored north of what is known as the **Mint** but is thought to have in fact been stables, including some in the interesting village of Sikri to the north.

Tours

Official Archaeological Society of India guides can be hired from the ticket office for ₹300 (English), but they aren't always the most knowledgeable (some have been birthrighted in). Official Uttar Pradesh Tourism guides have gone through more rigorous training and can be hired for ₹750. Our favorite is **Pankaj Bhatnagar** (☏8126995552; www.tajinvitation.com).

Eating

Fatehpur Sikri's culinary speciality is *khataie,* the biscuits you can see piled high in the bazaar below Jama Masjid.

If you want to stop for lunch, try the basic but friendly guesthouse **Hotel Ajay Palace** (282950; Agra Rd; mains ₹40-120), where you can sit on the rooftop at the large, elongated marble table and enjoy a view of the village streets with the Jama Masjid towering above you. Note it is not 'Ajay Restaurant By Near Palace' at the bus stand – it's 50m down the road, back towards Agra.

Getting There & Away

Tours and taxis all arrive at the Gulistan Tourist Complex parking lot; from here shuttle buses (₹5) depart for Fatehpur Sikri's Diwan-i-Am entrance (right side of the street) and Jodh Bai entrance (left side of the street). Note that if you have hired an unauthorised guide, you will not be allowed to enter at Diwan-i-Am.

Buses run to Agra's Idgah bus stand from the bazaar every half-hour (₹34), from 6am to 7pm.

Mumbai (Bombay) & Around

Mumbai is big. It's full of dreamers and hard-labourers, starlets and gangsters, stray dogs and exotic birds, artists and servants, fisherfolk and *crorepatis* (millionaires) and lots and lots of other people. It has a prolific film industry, some of Asia's biggest slums, the world's most expensive home, and the largest tropical forest in an urban zone. It's India's financial powerhouse and fashion epicentre,and a pulse point of religious tension. It has even evolved its own language, Bambaiyya Hindi, which is a mix of...everything.
But Mumbai does not have to be overwhelming: it just has its own rhythm, which takes a little while to find – give yourself some time. And while you're here, seize the chance to visit the nearby Unesco sites of Ellora and Ajanta, epic cave temples containing some astounding religious art.

Mumbai & Around

① Colonial-era architecture

② Eating in Mumbai

③ Girgaum Chowpatty (Chowpatty Beach)

④ Cave Temples at Ellora and Ajanta

⑤ Elephanta Island

Esselworld & Water Kingdom

Global Pagoda

Gorai Ferry

Borivali

Gorai Island

Manori Creek

Marve Jetty

Kandivali

Malad

Sanjay Gandhi National Park

Kanheri Caves

Tulsi Lake

Nasik (160km)

ARABIAN SEA

Malad Creek

Western Express Hwy

Goregaon

Aarey Milk Colony

Vihar Lake

Jogeshwari

Powai Lake

Andheri

JUHU

Domestic Terminal

International Terminal

Eastern Express Hwy

Thane Creek

Vile Parle

Santa Cruz

KHAR

Khar Rd

LOKMANYA TILAK (KURLA)

BANDRA

Bandra

Kurla

DHARAVI

Thane Creek

Mahim

CHEMBUR

Karjat (80km); Pune (140km)

Matunga Rd

Wadala

Dadar

Sewri

WORLI

Lower Parel

Elephanta Island

Haji Ali's Mosque

Mumbai City Museum

Butcher Island

⑤

Mumbai Central

③

FORT ①

Churchgate

See Fort Area & Churchgate Map (p126)

②

See Colaba Map (p120)

Gateway of India

Mumbai Harbour

Mandwa (20km)

URAN

Ferry

0 ___ 5 km
0 ___ 2 miles

Mumbai & Around's Highlights

Mumbai's Colonial-Era Architecture

The grandiose frilliness of Mumbai's fabulous 19th-century colonial-era architecture is epito-mised by the crazy Gothic facade of the famous train station, Chhatrapati Shivaji Terminus (p119), and marries well with the larger-than-life feel of the city itself – a place of Bollywood dreams, tumults of people, slick business operations, fashionistas, tycoons and endless-seeming slums. Chhatrapati Shivaji Terminus

Eating in Mumbai

Mumbai is a city shaped by flavours from over India and the world. You can dine like a maharaja at high-end restaurants (try Indigo for starters), but the street food here also shouldn't be missed. The most famous is *bhelpuri*, readily available at Girgaum Chowpatty (p119). These crisp-fried thin rounds of dough, mixed with puffed rice, lentils, lemon juice, onions, herbs, chilli and tamarind chutne and piled high onto takeaway paper plate are perfect street-snack material.

Girgaum Chowpatty (Chowpatty Beach) 3

The favoured place for a late-afternoon amble (p119) is this swathe of sand edged by sparkling (if toxic) sea and backed by the Mumbai skyline. It's fantastic for people-watching while munching on the famous Mumbai *bhelpuri*. During the Ganesh Chaturthi festival (in August/September) you'll see glorious colour and mayhem as huge effigies of the elephant god are dunked in the sea.

Cave Temples at Ellora and Ajanta 4

These ancient sites, 100km to 150km from Mumbai, represent some of the finest rock carvings in India. Ajanta (p135), the older site, dates back around 2000 years and includes exquisite Buddhist wall paintings. Ellora (p134) contains the standout Kailasa Temple, one of the world's largest rock-cut sculptures, hewn against a rocky slope by 7000 labourers over a 150-year period; it's one of the finest pieces of ancient architecture on the subcontinent.

Elephanta Island 5

If you don't have time to make it all the way out to Ellora or Ajanta then Elephanta Island (p123), just a short boat ride from the city centre, makes a great half-day trip. This tranquil island and Unesco World Heritage Site is home to a labyrinth of cave temples carved into the basalt rock, and the artwork here also represents some of the most impressive temple carving in all of India. There's a classical music festival in February.

113

Mumbai & Around's Best...

Wining & Dining

○ **Indigo** A gourmet haven serving inventive European cuisine. (p124)

○ **Koh** Mumbai's outstanding Thai restaurant. (p125)

○ **Culture Curry** Exquisite dishes from all over Asia. (p126)

○ **Samrat** Strap yourself in for the Gujurati thali of your life. (p124)

○ **Pradeep Gomantak Bhojanalaya** Unpretentious home-style Malvani cuisine. (p124)

Places for a Drink

○ **Aer** You may have to remortgage the house to afford the cocktails, but the city views are out of this world. (p128)

○ **Bluefrog** Best place in Mumbai to check out local bands. (p128)

○ **Cafe Mondegar** Good people, good vibe...and a jukebox! (p128)

○ **Leopold's Café** Wobbly fans and a lively atmosphere: a Mumbai travellers' institution. (p128)

○ **Harbour Bar** Affordable drinks, fabulous views. (p128)

Shopping

○ **Crawford Market** Bas-reliefs by Rudyard Kipling's father adorn the Norman Gothic exterior to this British-Bombay fruit and veg market. (p129)

○ **Mangaldas Market** Like a mini town, complete with its own lanes, this is one of the city's prime clothing and fabrics market. (p129)

○ **Contemporary Arts & Crafts** Inventive takes on traditional crafts. (p129)

○ **Phillips** 150-year-old antiques shop containing a multitude of things you never knew you wanted. (p129)

Pockets of Tranquillity

- **Global Pagoda** A haven for *vipassana* meditation, built to promote peace. (p121)

- **Cruises** A boat around Mumbai Harbour is a good way to escape the city. (p121)

- **Jijamata Udyan** Home of the City Museum and lush 19th-century gardens. (p120)

- **Elephanta Island** A peaceful place with ancient rock-cut temples. (p123)

Need to Know

- **One month before** Book your accommodation; start even earlier if you're travelling over Christmas and New Year.

- **One week before** Book any domestic flights and long-distance train tickets.

- **On arrival** Arrange any long-distance taxi rides via a recommended local agency or your hotel.

BE FOREWARNED

- **Bring directions** Print a map or detailed landmark directions for your hotel – many airport taxi drivers don't speak English.

- **Touts** Tend to hang around the Gateway of India – keep your wits about you here.

- **Taxis and autorickshaws** They have a combination of mechanical and electronic meters, which are not calibrated to display current fares. Drivers by law should keep the most current conversion chart in their vehicle; don't hesitate to ask to see it, or print out copies from the **Mumbai Traffic Police** (www. trafficpolicemumbai. org/Tariffcard_Auto_ taxi_form.htm).

GETTING AROUND

- **Premier taxi** The black-and-yellow cabs are the easiest way to get around the city, and in South Mumbai drivers usually use the meter without prompting.

- **Autorickshaw** Confined to the suburbs from Bandra north.

- **Car hire** Cars with driver are generally hired for an eight-hour day and an 80km maximum, with additional charges if you go over. For a non-air-conditioned car, the going rate is about ₹1200.

RESOURCES

- **Mumbai Magic** (www. mumbai-magic.blogspot. com) An excellent blog on the city's hidden corners.

- **Mumbai Boss** (www. mumbaiboss.com) Seriously the boss of what's on in Mumbai.

- **Maharashtra Tourism Development Corporation** (www. maharashtratourism.gov. in) Official tourism site.

- **Lonely Planet** (www. lonelyplanet.com/ india/mumbai) For planning advice, author recommendations, traveller reviews and insider tips.

Left: Fruit at Crawford Market (p129) **Above:** Sunset at Girgaum Chowpatty (Chowpatty Beach; p119)

Mumbai's Colonial-era Architecture Walking Tour

The grandiose colonial-era architecture of Mumbai is a remarkable feature of the cityscape. Take this stroll to see its most spectacular 19th-century hits.

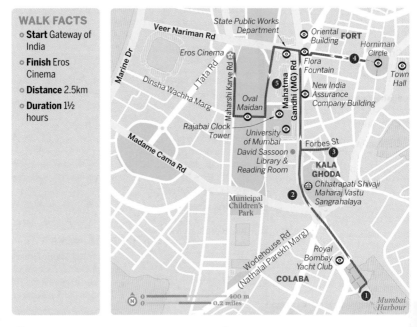

WALK FACTS

- **Start** Gateway of India
- **Finish** Eros Cinema
- **Distance** 2.5km
- **Duration** 1½ hours

① Gateway of India

Starting from the Gateway of India walk up Chhatrapati Shivaji Marg, past the members-only colonial relic Royal Bombay Yacht Club on one side and the art deco complex Dhunraj Mahal on the other, towards Regal Circle. The car park in the middle of the circle has the best view of the surrounding buildings, including the old Sailors Home which dates from 1876 and is now the Maharashtra Police Headquarters, as well as the art deco cinema Regal and the old Majestic Hotel, now the Sahakari Bhandar cooperative store.

② National Gallery of Modern Art

Continue up MG Rd, past the restored facade of the National Gallery of Modern Art. Opposite is the Chhatrapati Shivaji Maharaj Vastu Sangrahalaya; step into the front gardens to admire this grand building. Back across the road is the 'Romanesque Transitional' Elphinstone College and the David Sassoon Library & Reading Room, where members escape the afternoon heat lazing on planters' chairs on the upper balcony.

❸ Keneseth Eliyahoo Synagogue

Cross back over to Forbes St to visit the synagogue before returning to MG Rd and continuing north along the left-hand side of the road, to admire the art deco stylings of the New India Assurance Company Building. In a traffic island ahead lies the pretty Flora Fountain, erected in 1869 in honour of Sir Bartle Frere, the Bombay governor responsible for dismantling the fort. From here, there's a nice view of the 1885 Oriental Building to the north.

❹ St Thomas' Cathedral

Turn east down Veer Nariman Rd, walking towards St Thomas' Cathedral. Ahead lies the stately Horniman Circle, an arcaded ring of buildings laid out in the 1860s around a botanical garden. The circle is overlooked from the east by the neoclassical town hall, which contains the regally decorated members-only Asiatic Society of Bombay Library and Mumbai's State Central Library.

❺ High Court

As you retrace your steps back to Flora Fountain, glance to the north at the striking red Bombay Samachar building, home to the oldest continuously published newspaper in India, before continuing west past the Venetian Gothic-style State Public Works Department, now the entrance to the High Court. Turn south on to Bhaurao Patil Marg to see the High Court in full glory and the equally venerable and ornately decorated University of Mumbai. The university's 80m-high Rajabai Clock Tower and the facade of the High Court are best observed from within the Oval Maidan. Turn around to compare the colonial edifices with the row of art deco beauties lining Maharshi Karve (MK) Rd, culminating in the wedding-cake tower of the Eros Cinema.

Mumbai in...

TWO DAYS

In the morning, follow part or all of our walking tour, before having lunch in the Fort area. Dive into the maze of bazaars just to the north; colourful **Crawford Market** (p129) is a good place to start.

The next day, visit the ornate **Dr Bhau Daji Lad Mumbai City Museum** (p120), then take in a beach sunset at **Girgaum Chowpatty** (p119) before heading for dinner at one of Mumbai's stand-out restaurants.

FOUR DAYS

Follow the two-day itinerary above, then on day three hop on a ferry to nearby **Elephanta Island** (p123). Finish the day with a meal in Colaba before swapping tales with fellow travellers at **Leopoald's Café** (p128).

Head out to **Global Pagoda** (p121) on your final day, returning in the afternoon to visit the museums and galleries of **Kala Ghoda** (p119). Dine in style in the evening, but leave enough time to take in a show; either a concert at the **National Centre for the Performing Arts** (p128) or a gig at **Bluefrog** (p128).

St Thomas' Cathedral (p122)

Discover Mumbai (Bombay) & Around

MUMBAI (BOMBAY)

◎ Sights

Mumbai is an island connected by bridges to the mainland. The southernmost peninsula is Colaba, traditionally the travellers' nerve centre, with many of the major attractions, and directly north of Colaba is the busy commercial area known as Fort, where the British fort once stood.

Colaba

Taj Mahal Palace, Mumbai Landmark

(Map p120) This stunning hotel is a fairy-tale blend of Islamic and Renaissance styles jostling for prime position among Mumbai's famous landmarks. Facing the harbour, it was built in 1903 by the Parsi industrialist JN Tata, supposedly after he was refused entry to one of the European hotels on account of being 'a native'.

Gateway of India Monument

(Map p120) This bold basalt arch of colonial triumph faces out to Mumbai Harbour from the tip of Apollo Bunder. Incorporating Islamic styles of 16th-century Gujarat, it was built to commemorate the 1911 royal visit of King George V, but not completed until 1924. These days, the gateway is a favourite gathering spot for locals and a top spot for people-watching.

Fort & Churchgate

Lined up in a row and vying for your attention with aristocratic pomp, many of Mumbai's majestic Victorian buildings pose on

Gateway of India
EURASIA/GETTY IMAGES ©

the edge of **Oval Maidan**. This land, and the **Cross** and **Azad Maidans** immediately to the north, was on the oceanfront in those days, and this series of grandiose structures faced west directly out to the Arabian Sea.

Kala Ghoda, or 'Black Horse', is a sub-neighbourhood of Fort just north of Colaba and contains many of Mumbai's museums and galleries alongside a wealth of colonial-era buildings.

Chhatrapati Shivaji Terminus (Victoria Terminus)   Historic Building

(Map p126) Imposing, exuberant and overflowing with people, this famous train station, built in 1887, is the city's most extravagant Gothic building, the beating heart of its railway network, and an aphorism for colonial India. Today it is Asia's busiest train station. Officially renamed Chhatrapati Shivaji Terminus (CST) in 1998, it's still better known locally as VT. It was added to the Unesco World Heritage list in 2004.

Chhatrapati Shivaji Maharaj Vastu Sangrahalaya (Prince of Wales Museum)   Museum

(Map p126; www.themuseummumbai.com; K Dubash Marg; Indian/foreigner ₹50/300, camera/video ₹200/1000; ⏲10.15am-6pm Tue-Sun) Mumbai's biggest and best museum displays a mix of exhibits from all over India. The domed behemoth, an intriguing hodgepodge of Islamic, Hindu and British architecture, was opened in 1923 to commemorate King George V's first visit to India (back in 1905, while he was still Prince of Wales). There's an outdoor cafeteria here, and the museum shop is excellent.

··

Kalbadevi to Mahalaxmi

Marine Drive & Girgaum Chowpatty   Beach

(Map p126; Netaji Subhashchandra Bose Rd) Built on land reclaimed from Back Bay in 1920, Marine Dr arcs along the shore of the Arabian Sea from Nariman Point past Girgaum Chowpatty (where it's known as

Local Knowledge

Mumbai Don't Miss List

ARCHITECT ABHA BAHL IS
CO-FOUNDER OF THE BOMBAY HERITAGE WALKS GROUP

1 ST THOMAS' CATHEDRAL, FORT
Standing witness to almost the entire history of the British in Bombay, this was the city's first Anglican church. A 44m Gothic-style clock tower dominates, along with the distinctive stone flying buttresses. Stepping into the large airy cathedral, with its striking stained-glass windows, you are transported back into the 19th century.

2 TOWN HALL
The Town Hall on Horniman Circle is also one of Mumbai's oldest surviving colonial buildings. Built in 1833 to serve the burgeoning port, its grand scale and key location were designed to flaunt British might. Today it houses the members-only Asiatic Library.

3 KENESETH ELIYAHOO SYNAGOGUE
On VB Gandhi Marg is an unmistakable blue-painted building, the KE Synagogue, built in 1884 by Jacob Sassoon. Its beautifully maintained ornate interior has wooden balconies resting on carved brackets, the *tebah* (raised platform in the centre of the main prayer room) and a fine *hekhal* (wall niche where the Torah is kept) that faces west, towards Jerusalem.

4 CHHATRAPATI SHIVAJI (VICTORIA) TERMINUS
Perhaps the world's finest railway station, and Mumbai's largest public building. An architectural gem and symbol of the city's prosperity, it's also an engineering marvel with an astounding ensemble of statues, carvings, stained glass and embellishments that took 10 years to complete.

Chowpatty Seaface) and continues to the foot of Malabar Hill. Lined with flaking art deco apartments, it's one of Mumbai's

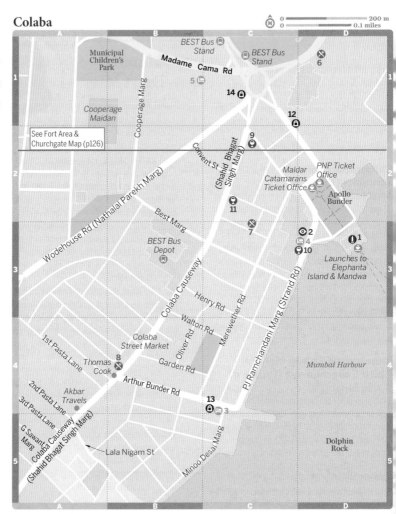

N
0 ——————— 200 m
0 ——————— 0.1 miles

Municipal Children's Park

Madame Cama Rd

BEST Bus Stand

BEST Bus Stand

8
6

Cooperage Marg

5

14

Cooperage Maidan

See Fort Area & Churchgate Map (p126)

Convent St (Shahid Bhagat Singh Marg)

12

9

Wodehouse Rd (Nathalal Parekh Marg)

Best Marg

BEST Bus Depot

Maldar Catamarans Ticket Office

PNP Ticket Office

Apollo Bunder

11

7

2
4
10

1

Launches to Elephanta Island & Mandwa

Colaba Causeway

Henry Rd

Walton Rd

Oliver Rd

Merewether Rd

PJ Ramchandani Marg (Strand Rd)

Mumbai Harbour

1st Pasta Lane

Colaba Street Market

Thomas Cook

8

Garden Rd

Arthur Bunder Rd

Akbar Travels

2nd Pasta Lane

3rd Pasta Lane

G Sawant Marg

Colaba Causeway (Shahid Bhagat Singh Marg)

Lala Nigam St

Minoo Desai Marg

13

3

Dolphin Rock

MUMBAI (BOMBAY) & AROUND MUMBAI

most popular promenades and sunset-watching spots.

Girgaum Chowpatty (the beach often referred to as just 'Chowpatty') remains a favourite evening spot for courting couples, families, political rallies and anyone out to enjoy what passes for fresh air. Evening *bhelpuri* at the throng of stalls at the beach's southern end is an essential part of the Mumbai experience. Forget about taking a dip: the water's toxic.

Dr Bhau Daji Lad Mumbai City Museum
Museum

(www.bdlmuseum.org; Dr Babasaheb Ambedkar Rd; Indian/foreigner ₹10/100; ⏰10am-5.30pm Thu-Tue) Jijamata Udyan – formerly named Victoria Gardens – is a lush and sprawling mid-19th-century garden and zoo. It's home to this gorgeous museum, built in Renaissance revival style in 1872 as the Victoria & Albert Museum. It reopened in 2007 after an impressive and sensitive four-year renovation. In addition to

Colaba

extensive structural work, the building's Minton tile floors, gilt ceiling mouldings, and ornate columns, chandeliers and staircases were restored to their former historically accurate glory. Skip the zoo.

Gorai Island

Global Pagoda
Landmark

(www.globalpagoda.org; Gorai; ⏰9am-7pm, meditation classes 11am & 4pm) FREE Rising up like a mirage from polluted Gorai Creek and the lush but noisy grounds of the Esselworld and Water Kingdom amusement parks, this breathtaking, golden 96m-high stupa was modelled after Burma's Shwedagon Pagoda. The dome, which houses relics of the Buddha, was built entirely without supports using an ancient technique of interlocking stones. To get here, take a train from Churchgate to Borivali (exit the station the 'West' side), then an autorickshaw (₹40) to the ferry landing, where Esselworld ferries (return

₹35) come and go every 30 minutes. The last ferry to the pPagoda is 5.25pm.

🎟 Tours

Fiona Fernandez's *Ten Heritage Walks of Mumbai* (₹395) contains walking tours in the city, with fascinating historical background.

The Government of India tourist office (p130) can provide a list of approved multilingual guides; most charge ₹750/950 per half/full day.

Bombay Heritage Walks
Walking

(📞23690992, 9821887321; www.bombay heritagewalks.com) Run by two enthusiastic architects, BHW has the best city tours in heritage neighbourhoods. Two-hour guided tours are ₹2000 for up to four people; longer tours are ₹3000 for three people; both include a 'handy keepsake'.

Mumbai Magic Tours
City Tour

(📞9867707414; www.mumbaimagic.com; 2hr tours from ₹1500 per person) City tours, designed by the authors of the fabulous Mumbai Magic blog (www.mumbai-magic.blogspot.com), focus on food markets, traditional dance and music, and Jewish heritage, among others, and cover many places you would never find on your own.

Cruises
Cruise

(📞22026364; ⏰8am-8pm) A cruise on Mumbai Harbour is a good way to escape the city and see the Gateway of India as it was intended. Half-hour ferry rides (₹70) depart from the Gateway of India; tickets are sold on-site.

🛏 Sleeping

You'll need to recalibrate your budget here: Mumbai has the most expensive accommodation in India.

To stay with a local family, contact **Indiatourism** (www.incredibleindia. com) for a list of homes across the city participating in Mumbai's **paying-guest and B&B program** (s/d from ₹400/800).

If You Like...
Colonial-Era Architecture

If you love Mumbai's sumptuous colonial-era buildings such as Chhatrapati Shivaji, seek out the following fantastic examples in the Fort area.

1 HIGH COURT

(Map p126; Eldon Rd) A hive of daily activity, packed with judges, barristers and other cogs in the Indian justice system, the High Court is an elegant 1848 neo-Gothic building. You are permitted (and it is highly recommended) to walk around inside the building and check out the pandemonium and pageantry of public cases that are in progress – just walk right in! You'll have to surrender your camera to the guards, then make your way through the maze-like building to the original building's courtyard opposite Court 6.

2 ST THOMAS' CATHEDRAL

(Map p126; Veer Nariman Rd; ◷7am-6pm) This charming cathedral, begun in 1672 and finished in 1718, is the oldest English building standing in Mumbai. It's a marriage of Byzantine and colonial-era architecture, and its airy interior is full of exhibitionist colonial memorials.

Colaba

Sea Shore Hotel   Guesthouse $

(Map p120; ☑ 22874237; 4th fl, Kamal Mansion, Arthur Bunder Rd; s/d without bathroom from ₹624/988) The Sea Shore's shoebox-size rooms are simple but nearly hotel-quality, with incongruously high-design communal bathrooms. Interior rooms have no window, but front-facing rooms have (through dingy, tiny screens) million-dollar views of Mumbai Harbour. The same owners run **India Guest House** (Map p120; ☑ 22833769; s/d without bathroom ₹416/520) downstairs, with similar bathrooms but not-as-nice rooms.

YWCA   Guesthouse $$

(Map p120; ☑ 22025053; www.ywcaic.info; 18 Madame Cama Rd, Colaba; s/d/t/q incl breakfast & dinner ₹2126/3150/4462/6301; ❄@ ☞) The YWCA is immaculate – your room is scrubbed down every single day – and ridiculously good value: rates, which are a good ₹1000 cheaper than most in its class, include breakfast, dinner, early-morning tea, free wi-fi...*and a newspaper*. But there's a trade-off here with the long list of borderline-monastic rules, which some find off-putting.

Taj Mahal Palace, Mumbai   Heritage Hotel $$$

(Map p120; ☑ 66653366; www.tajhotels.com; Apollo Bunder; s/d tower from ₹27,887/29,649, palace from ₹38,162/39,923; ❄@ ☞ ☎) With its sweeping arches, staircases and domes, the Taj really does feel like a palace. Following the 2008 terrorist attacks here, some 285 rooms were lavishly restored in fuchsia, saffron and willow-green colour schemes (and security is Fort Knox level). Rooms in the tower wing lack the period details of the palace wing, but some have spectacular full-on views of the Gateway. The hotel's Harbour Bar (p128), Mumbai's first licensed bar, is legendary.

Fort & Churchgate

Sea Green Hotel   Hotel $$

(Map p126; ☑ 66336525; www.seagreenhotel.com; 145 Marine Dr; s/d from ₹3974/5063; ❄) This excellent art deco hotel, and its twin, **Sea Green South** (Map p126; ☑ 22821613; www.seagreensouth.com; 145A Marine Dr; s/d from ₹3974/5063; ❄), have spacious but spartan rooms, originally built in the 1940s to house British soldiers. Ask for one of the sea-view rooms: they're the same price.

Residency Hotel   Hotel $$

(Map p126; ☑ 22625525; www.residencyhotel.com; 26 Rustom Sidhwa Marg; s/d incl breakfast from ₹3640/3875; ❄@ ☞) Recent renova-

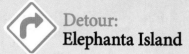

Detour:
Elephanta Island

Nine kilometres northeast of the Gateway of India in Mumbai Harbour, the rock-cut temples on Gharapuri, better known as **Elephanta Island** (http://asi.nic. in/; Indian/foreigner ₹10/250; ⏱caves 9am-5pm Tue-Sun), are a Unesco World Heritage Site and worth crossing the waters for.

The temples are thought to have been created between AD 450 and 750, when the island was known as Gharapuri (Place of Caves). The Portuguese called it Elephanta because of a large stone elephant near the shore, which collapsed in 1814 and was moved by the British to Mumbai's Jijamata Udyan.

Aggressive, expensive guides will meet you at the jetty and try to convince you to employ their services; you don't really need one. Opt instead for Pramod Chandra's *A Guide to the Elephanta Caves*, for sale at the stalls lining the stairway.

Launches (economy/deluxe ₹120/150) head to Gharapuri from the Gateway of India every half-hour from 9am to 3.30pm. Buy tickets at the booths lining Apollo Bunder. The voyage takes just over an hour.

The ferries dock at the end of a concrete pier, from where you can walk or take the **miniature train** (₹10) to the **stairway** (admission ₹10) leading up to the caves.

:ions have transformed the friendly Residency into a contemporary design–style hotel, with mood lighting, rain showers and leather-walled elevators. Rooms also have fridges, flatscreens, slippers and wi-fi (free in the pricier rooms). But there are odd oversights (why only a single towel in double rooms?) that shouldn't happen in this price range.

Western Suburbs

Anand Hotel
Hotel $$
📞26203372; anandhote@yahoo.co.in; Gandhigram Rd, Juhu; s/d from ₹2348/3875; ❄) The rooms here are so clean, homey and old-fashioned – think embroidered artwork in the rooms, steel clothes-drying rods on the balconies and images of Ganesh everywhere – that they feel like they're in someone's Bombay apartment. It's around the corner from the ISKCON temple and upstairs from the excellent Dakshinayan restaurant, so the location couldn't be any better either.

🍴 Eating

Colaba

Hotel OCH
Indian $
(Map p120; Shahid Bhagat Singh Rd; mains ₹65-110, thalis ₹65-105; ⏱7am-10.30pm) The best of the Colaba cheapies, with decent lunch thalis and evening *pav bhaji* in a cafeteria-like setting. Popular with families and cops working next door.

Theobroma
Cafe $$
(Map p120; Colaba Causeway; confections ₹40-95, light meals ₹180-200; ⏱7am-midnight) Perfectly executed cakes, tarts and brownies, as well as sandwiches and breads, go well with the coffee here. The pastries change regularly; if you're lucky, you'll find the Portuguese vanilla cinnamon custard tart (₹70). For brunch, have the *akoori* – Parsi-style scrambled eggs – with green mango. The **Bandra branch** (33rd Rd, near Linking Rd; ⏱8am-11.30pm) is big and airy, with the same menu.

Indigo
Fusion $$$

(Map p120; ☎66368980; www.foodindigo.com; 4 Mandlik Marg; mains ₹750-1100; ⏰12-3pm & 6.30pm-midnight) Colaba's finest eating option is a gourmet haven offering inventive European cuisine, a long wine list, sleek ambience and a gorgeous roof deck lit with fairy lights. Favourites include the kiwi margaritas (₹465), Cochin oysters (₹765) and zucchini-wrapped prawns with polenta and saffron butter (₹1100). Reserve on weekends.

Fort & Churchgate

Pradeep Gomantak Bhojanalaya
Maharashtrian $

(Map p126; Sheri House, Rustom Sidhwa Marg; mains ₹60-130; ⏰11am-4pm Mon-Sat) The *surmai* (seer) rice plate here looks plain – a fried piece of fish, some dhal, rice and chutneys on a stainless steel plate – but the meal will transport you. The food is home-style Malvani cuisine, from coastal Maharashtra, and so fresh you can taste the individual flavours dancing with one another. Savour the sublime, pink *sol kadhi*, a soothing, spicy drink of coconut milk and kokum.

Samrat
Gujarati $$

(Map p126; ☎42135401; www.prashantcaterers. com; Prem Ct, J Tata Rd; thalis lunch/dinner & Sun ₹265/330, mains ₹170-250; ⏰noon-11pm)

Mumbai For Children

Little tykes with energy to burn will love the Gorai Island amusement parks, **Esselworld** (www.esselworld. in; adult/child ₹690/490; ⏰11am-7pm, from 10am Sat & Sun) and **Water Kingdom** (www.waterkingdom.in; adult/ child ₹690/490; ⏰11am-7pm, from 10am Sat & Sun). Both have lots of rides, slides and shade. Combined tickets are ₹890/690 adult/child. It's a ₹35 ferry ride from Borivali jetty.

Left: The bar at Indigo **Below:** Gujarati food in Colaba
(LEFT) RICHARD I'ANSON/GETTY IMAGES ©; (BELOW) GRAHAM CROUCH/GETTY IMAGES ©

If this is your first thali, strap yourself in: the cavalcade of taste and texture (and sweetness – this is Gujarati food) will leave you wondering what just happened. Come hungry. Samrat is also the king of a pure-veg empire that includes **210°C** (Map p126), an outdoor cafe and bakery, and **Relish** (Map p126), with Asian-Mexican-Lebanese fusion, at the same location.

Kala Ghoda Café   Cafe $$

(Map p126; www.kgcafe.in; 10 Ropewalk Lane, Kala Ghoda; light meals ₹100-275, dinners ₹375-525; ☺8.30am-11.45pm; 🛜) 🍴 An artsy, modern and miniscule cafe that's a favourite among journalists and other creative types, who come for the organic coffee sourced from sustainable plantations, organic teas, excellent sandwiches and salads, and charming breakfasts – after fighting for one of the few tables.

Koh   Thai $$$

(Map p126; ☎39879999; InterContinental, Marine Dr; mains ₹495-1395; ☺12.30-3pm & 7.30pm-midnight) India's first signature Thai restaurant is Mumbai's hottest and most beautifully designed dining destination. Celebrity chef Ian Kittichai works his native cuisine into an international frenzy of flavour with revelatory dishes like wok-tossed black-pepper tenderloin, and oven-roasted aubergine sprinkled with nori (paired with hot-stone garlic rice), throwing preconceived notions about Thai food to the curb.

Kalbadevi to Mahalaxmi

New Kulfi Centre   Sweets $

(cnr Chowpatty Seaface & Sardar V Patel Rd; kulfi per 100gm ₹35-50; ☺10am-1am) Serves the best *kulfi* (firm-textured ice cream) you'll have anywhere, which means it's pretty much the best thing in the world. Killer flavours include pistachio, *malai* (cream) and saffron.

125

Western Suburbs

Culture Curry South Indian $$$
(Kataria Rd, Matunga West; mains ₹319-499;
⊙noon-3.45pm & 7pm-12.30am) There's a
lot more to southern food than *idli* and
dosas. Exquisite dishes from all over the
south, ranging from Andhra and Coorg to
Kerala, are the specialty here. Vegetarians
are particularly well served: the *rajma*

Fort Area & Churchgate

◉ Sights
1. Chhatrapati Shivaji Maharaj
   Vastu Sangrahalaya (Prince
   of Wales Museum) E6
2. Chhatrapati Shivaji Terminus
   (Victoria Terminus) F1
3. High Court D4
4. Marine Drive & Girgaum
   Chowpatty B4
5. St Thomas' Cathedral E4

⌂ Sleeping
6. Residency Hotel E3
7. Sea Green Hotel B4
   Sea Green South Hotel .... (see 7)

✦ Eating
   210°C .... (see 11)
8. Kala Ghoda Café E5
9. Koh B3
10. Pradeep Gomantak Bhojanalaya E3
    Relish .... (see 11)
11. Samrat C4

♦ Drinking & Nightlife
12. Café Universal F3
13. Mocha Bar C3

✧ Entertainment
14. National Centre for the
    Performing Arts A6
15. NCPA Box Office A6

◉ Shopping
16. Contemporary Arts & Crafts E2

ℹ Information
17. Anita CyberCafé E4
18. Dutch Consulate E2
19. German Consulate B6
20. Indiatourism D3
    Israeli Consulate .... (see 23)
21. Singaporean Consulate B6
22. Sri Lankan Consulate E4
23. Thai Consulate B6

⊕ Transport
24. Central Railways Reservation
    Centre F1
    Western Railways Reservation
    Centre .... (see 20)

curry (kidney and green beans in coconut gravy; ₹259) is extraordinary. The same owners run **Goa Portuguesa**, specialising in fiery Goan dishes, and the Maharashtrian **Diva Maharashtracha**, on the same block. From Matunga station, they're about 750m west along Kataria Rd.

🍷 Drinking & Nightlife

Colaba

Cafe Mondegar
Bar

(Map p120; 📞 22020591; Metro House, 5A Shahid Bhagat Singh Rd; ⏰ 7am-12.30am) 'Mondys' draws a healthy foreign crowd, but with a mix of locals, who all cosy up together in the small space, bonding over the excellent jukebox, one of Mumbai's few. Good music, good people.

Harbour Bar
Bar

(Map p120; Taj Mahal Palace. Apollo Bunder; ⏰ 11am-11.45pm) The views here – of the Gateway of India and boats in the harbour – are spectacular, and the drinks are reasonably priced (for Mumbai; from ₹350/750 for a beer/wine). Snuggle up in a booth beside one of the big picture windows as the day's winding down on Apollo Bunder.

Leopold's Café
Bar

(Map p120; cnr Colaba Causeway & Nawroji F Rd; ⏰ 7.30am-12.30am) Love it or hate it, most tourists end up at this Mumbai travellers' institution at one time or another. Around since 1871, Leopold's has wobbly ceiling fans, crap service and a rambunctious atmosphere conducive to swapping tales with strangers. There's food, but the lazy evening beers, especially the 3L yards, are the real draw.

Fort & Churchgate

Mocha Bar
Cafe

(Map p126; 82 Veer Nariman Rd, Churchgate; coffees ₹60-150; ⏰ 10am-1.30am; 📶) This atmospheric Arabian-styled cafe is often filled to the brim with students deep in esoteric conversation or gossip. Cosy, low-cushioned seating (including some old cinema seats), exotic coffees, shakes and teas, and global comfort cuisine promote an intellectually chillaxed vibe. Sometimes the wi-fi works.

Café Universal
Bar

(Map p126; 299 Shahid Bhagat Singh Rd, Fort; ⏰ 9am-11pm Mon-Sat, 4-11pm Sun) A little bit of France near CST. The Universal has an art nouveau look to it, with butterscotch-colour walls, a wood-beam ceiling and marble chandeliers, and is a cosy place for happy hour and Kingfisher draughts (₹160).

Western Suburbs

Aer
Lounge

(Four Seasons Hotel, 34th fl, 114 Dr E Moses Rd, Worli; cover ₹2000-2500 Wed-Sat after 8pm; ⏰ 5.30pm-1.30pm) With astounding city views on one side and equally impressive sea and sunset views on the other, rooftop Aer is India's tallest and most stunning lounge. You'll need to remortgage your home for a cocktail (₹850), but the ₹350 Kingfishers are a steal at these views. A DJ spins low-key house and techno nightly from 9pm, but Aer is more about the eye candy, both near and far.

✪ Entertainment

Mumbai Mirror, an insert of the *Times of India*, lists Mumbai happenings, as do *Time Out Mumbai* (www.timeoutmumbai.net; ₹50), www.nh7.in (live-music listings) and Mumbai Boss (www.mumbaiboss.com).

Bluefrog
Live Music

(📞 61586158; www.bluefrog.co.in; D/2 Mathuradas Mills Compound, Senapati Bapat Marg, Lower Parel; admission after 9pm Sun & Tue-Thu ₹350, Fri & Sat ₹600; ⏰ 6.30pm-1.30am Tue-Sat, from 11.30am Sun) Bluefrog is a concert space, production studio, restaurant and one of Mumbai's most happening spaces. It hosts exceptional local and international acts, and has space-age booth seating in the intimate main room. Happy hour – also known as 'one on the Frog' – is buy one, get one free 6.30pm to 9pm.

National Centre for the Performing Arts
Theatre, Live Music

(NCPA; Map p126; 📞 66223737, box office 22824567; www.ncpamumbai.com; Marine Dr & Sri V Saha Rd, Nariman Point; tickets ₹200-800; ⏰ box office 9am-7pm) Spanning 800 sq metres, this cultural centre is the hub of Mumbai's music, theatre and dance scene. In any given week, it might host experimental plays, poetry readings, art exhibitions, Bihari dance troupes, ensembles from Europe or Indian classical music, as well as the occasional dance workshop open to the public. Many performances are free. The **box office** (Map p126) is at the end of NCPA Marg.

🔒 Shopping

Colaba

Phillips   Antiques
(Map p120; www.phillipsantiques.com; Wodehouse Rd; ⊙10am-7pm Mon-Sat) The 150-year-old Phillips has nizam-era royal silver, wooden ceremonial masks, Victorian glass and various other gorgeous things that you never knew you wanted. It also has high-quality reproductions of old photos, maps and paintings, and a warehouse shop of big antiques.

Central Cottage Industries Emporium   Handicrafts, Souvenirs
(Map p120; 📞22027537; www.cottageemporium. in; Chhatrapati Shivaji Marg; ⊙10am-6pm) Fair-trade souvenirs. Now has a second **Colaba branch** (Map p120; Kamal Mansion, Arthur Bunder Rd; ⊙11am-7pm Mon-Sat).

Fort & Churchgate

Contemporary Arts & Crafts   Handicrafts
(Map p126; www.cac.co.in; 210 DN Rd; ⊙10.30am-7.30pm) The CAC stocks contemporary, inventive takes on traditional crafts: these are not your usual handmade souvenirs. Home goods fill much of the store, but plenty of pieces will fit in a suitcase.

Kalbadevi to Mahalaxmi

Markets   Market
You can buy just about anything in the dense bazaars north of CST, which tumble one into the next in a mass of people and stuff. **Crawford Market (Mahatma Phule market; cnr DN & Lokmanya Tilak Rds)**, with fruit and vegetables, is the last outpost of British Bombay before the tumult of the central bazaars begins. Bas-reliefs by Rudyard Kipling's father, Lockwood Kipling, adorn the Norman Gothic exterior.

Mangaldas Market, traditionally home to traders from Gujarat, is a mini town, complete with lanes, of fabrics. Even if you're not the type to have your clothes tailored, drop by **DD Dupattawala (Shop No 217, 4th Lane)** for pretty scarves and dupattas at fixed prices. **Zaveri Bazaar** for jewellery and **Bhuleshwar Market (cnr Sheikh Menon St & M Devi Marg)** for fruit and vegetables are just north of here.

Cafe Mondegar
ORIEN HARVEY/GETTY IMAGES ©

Chor Bazaar is known for its antiques, though nowadays much of it is reproductions; the main area of activity is Mutton St, where shops specialise in 'antiques' and miscellaneous junk. Dhabu St, to the east, is lined with fine leather goods.

Information

Internet Access

Anita CyberCafé (Map p126; Cowasji Patel Rd, Fort; per hr ₹30; ⊙9.30am-10pm Mon-Sat, from 2pm Sun) Opposite one of Mumbai's best chai stalls (open evenings).

Medical Services

Breach Candy Hospital (⌥23672888, emergency 23667809; www.breachcandyhospital.org; 60 Bhulabhai Desai Marg, Breach Candy) Best in Mumbai, if not India.

Money

ATMs are everywhere, and foreign-exchange offices changing cash and travellers cheques – including Akbar Travels (below) and Thomas Cook beanches in Fort (below) and Colaba (Map p120; ⌥66092608; Colaba Causeway; ⊙9.30am-6pm) – are also plentiful.

Tourist Information

Indiatourism (Government of India Tourist Office; Map p126; ⌥22074333; www.incredibleindia.com; Western Railways Reservation Complex, 123 Maharshi Karve Rd; ⊙8.30am-6pm Mon-Fri, to 2pm Sat) Provides information for the entire country, as well as contacts for Mumbai guides and homestays.

Travel Agencies

Akbar Travels (www.akbartravelsonline.com; ⊙10am-7pm Mon-Fri, to 6pm Sat) Colaba (Map p120; ⌥22823434; 30 Alipur Trust Bldg, Shahid Bhagat Singh Rd); Fort (Map p126; ⌥22633434; 167/169 Dr Dadabhai Naoroji Rd) Extremely helpful, with good exchange rates.

Thomas Cook (Map p126; ⌥61603333; 324 Dr Dadabhai Naoroji Rd, Fort; ⊙9.30am-6pm Mon-Sat)

Getting There & Away

Air

Airports

Chhatrapati Shivaji International Airport (BOM; ⌥66851010; www.csia.in), about 30km from the city centre, has been undergoing a $2 billion modernisation since its privatisation in

Crawford Market (p129)

PETER ADAMS/GETTY IMAGES ©

Selected Trains from Mumbai

DESTINATION	TRAIN NO & NAME	SAMPLE FARE (₹)	DURATION (HR)	DEPARTURE
Agra	12137 Punjab Mail	410/1139/1770/3050 (A)	22	7.40pm CST
Aurangabad	11401 Nandigram Exp	176/480/715 (B)	7	4.35pm CST
Chennai	12163 Chennai Exp	403/1116/1730/2980 (A)	23½	8.30pm CST
Delhi	12951 Rajdhani Exp	1550/2270/3870 (C)	16	4.40pm BCT
	12137 Punjab Mail	442/1231/1925/3330 (A)	25½	7.40pm CST
Margao	10103 Mandovi Exp	288/811/1235/2105 (A)	12	6.55am CST
	12133 Mangalore Exp	308/842/1265 (B)	9	11.05pm CST
Jaipur	12955 Jaipur Exp	383/1059/1630/2805 (A)	18	6.50pm BCT
Kochi	16345 Netravati Exp	430/1222/1935 (B)	26½	11.40am LTT

Station abbreviations: CST (Chhatrapati Shivaji Terminus); BCT (Mumbai Central); LTT (Lokmanya Tilak)
Fares: (A) sleeper/3AC/2AC/1AC; (B) sleeper/3AC/2AC; (C) 3AC/2AC/1AC

2006. At press time, the shiny new terminal T2, serving both domestic and international flights, was expected to open in 2014 and the existing domestic terminals converted to cargo.

At time of writing, the airport comprised three domestic terminals (1A, 1B and 1C) and two international terminals (2B and 2C). The domestic side was known locally as Santa Cruz airport, the international as Sahar. A free shuttle bus ran between the two every 30 minutes for ticket-holders.

Bus

Long-distance government-run buses depart from the well-organised Mumbai Central bus terminal (☎ inquiry 23024075) right by Mumbai Central train station. They're cheaper and more frequent than private services, but the quality and crowd levels vary.

Private buses depart from Dr Anadrao Nair Rd near Mumbai Central train station, or from Paltan Rd, near Crawford Market. To check on departure times and current prices, visit Citizen Travels (☎23459695; D Block, Sitaram Bldg, Paltan Rd) or National CTC (☎23015652; Dr Anadrao Nair Rd).

More convenient for Goa and southern destinations are the private buses run by Chandni Travels (Map p126; ☎22713901, 22676840), which depart six times a day from in front of Azad Maidan.

Train

Three train systems operate out of Mumbai, but the most important services for travellers are Central Railways and Western Railways. Tickets for either system can be bought from any station in South Mumbai or the suburbs that has computerised ticketing.

Central Railways (☎139), handling services to the east and south, plus a few trains to the north, operates from CST. The reservation centre (Map p126; ☺8am-8pm Mon-Sat, to 2pm Sun) is on the southern side of CST. Foreign tourist quota tickets can be bought at Counter 52. You can buy nonquota tickets with a credit card (₹90 fee) at counters 10 and 11.

Some Central Railways trains depart from Dadar (D), a few stations north of CST, or Lokmanya Tilak (LTT), 16km north of CST.

Western Railways (☎139) has services to the north from Mumbai Central train station, usually called Bombay Central (BCT). The reservation centre (Map p126; ☉8am-8pm Mon-Sat, to 2pm Sun), opposite Churchgate station, has foreign tourist quota tickets at counter 14.

ⓘ Getting Around

To/From the Airports

International

The international airport has a **prepaid-taxi booth**, with set fares for every neighbourhood, outside arrivals. Taxis are ₹650/750 (non-AC/AC) to Colaba or Fort, plus a ₹10 service charge and ₹10 per bag. The journey to Colaba takes about 45 minutes at night and 1½ to two hours during the day. Tips are not required.

Meru Cabs (🖉44224422; www.merucabs. com) has a counter in arrivals. The air-conditioned metered taxis charge ₹27 for the first kilometre and ₹20 per kilometre thereafter (25% more at night). Routes are tracked by GPS, so no rip-offs!

A taxi from South Mumbai to the international airport should be around ₹500; negotiate a fare beforehand. Add ₹10 per bag and 25% to the meter charge at night, and add an hour onto the journey time between 4pm and 8pm.

Domestic

There's a **prepaid taxi counter** in the arrivals hall. A non-AC/AC taxi costs ₹380/465 to Colaba or Fort, plus ₹10/15 service charge, ₹10 per bag and 25% extra at night.

Car

Cars with driver are generally hired for an eight-hour day and an 80km maximum, with additional charges if you go over. For a non-air-conditioned car, the going rate is about ₹1200.

Taxi & Autorickshaw

Mumbai's black-and-yellow taxis are the most convenient way to get around southern Mumbai, and drivers *almost* always use the meter without prompting. The minimum fare is ₹19; after the first 1.6km, it's ₹12 per additional kilometre.

Autorickshaws are the name of the game from Bandra going north. The minimum fare is ₹15, up to 1.6km, and ₹10 per additional kilometre.

Both taxis and autorickshaws tack 25% onto the fare from midnight to 5am.

Tip: Mumbaikars tend to navigate by landmarks, not street names.

MAHARASHTRA

Aurangabad

🕿0240 / POP 1,171,330 / ELEV 515M

Aurangabad lay low through most of the tumultuous history of medieval India and only hit the spotlight when the last Mughal emperor, Aurangzeb, made the city his capital from 1653 to 1707. With the emperor's death came the city's rapid decline, but the brief period of glory saw the building of some fascinating monuments, including a Taj Mahal replica (Bibi-qa-Maqbara), that continue to draw a steady trickle of visitors. But the real reason for traipsing all the way here is because the town is an excellent base for exploring the World Heritage Sites of Ellora and Ajanta.

◉ Sights

Bibi-qa-Maqbara   Monument

(Indian/foreigner ₹5/100; ☉dawn-10pm) Built by Aurangzeb's son Azam Khan in 1679 as a mausoleum for his mother Rabia-ud-Daurani, Bibi-qa-Maqbara is widely known as the 'poor man's Taj'. With its four minarets flanking a central onion-domed mausoleum, the white structure bears striking resemblance to Agra's Taj Mahal. It is much less grand, however, and apart from having a few marble adornments, namely the plinth and dome, much of the structure is finished in lime mortar.

ⓕ Tours

Classic Tours (🖉2337788; www.classictours. info; Station Rd East, MTDC Holiday Resort) and the **Indian Tourism Development Corporation** (ITDC; 🖉2331143) both run daily bus tours to the Ajanta and Ellora Caves. The trip to Ajanta Caves costs ₹450 and the tour to Ellora Caves, ₹300; prices include a guide but don't cover admission fees.

For private tours, try **Ashoka Tours & Travels** (🖉2359102, 9890340816; atkadam88@gmail.com; Station Rd West, Hotel Panchavati), which owns a decent fleet of taxis and can personalise your trip around Aurangabad and to Ajanta (₹1600 for up to four people) and Ellora (₹1100 for up to four people).

🛏️ Sleeping

Hotel Panchavati Hotel **$**
(☎2328755; www.hotelpanchavati.com; Station
Rd West; s/d ₹525/625, with AC ₹775/900;
❄️) Panchavati is popular with budget
travellers, and for good reason. On offer
are a range of compact, colour-themed
and thoughtfully appointed rooms, with
comfortable beds and balconies. Choose
between front-facing, park-view rooms, or
the much quieter, tree-view rooms at the
rear. There are two restaurants and a bar.
The managers are efficient and friendly
and the hotel sits easily at the top of the
value-for-money class.

Lemon Tree Hotel **$$$**
(☎6603030; www.lemontreehotels.com; Airport
Rd, R7/2 Chikalthana; s/d incl breakfast from
₹7345/8815; ❄️@🛜🏊) Fresh as lemon-
ade, this swish hotel encircles what we
thought was the best swimming pool
in the Deccan. The standard rooms,
although not large, are brightened by vivid
tropical tones offset against snow-white
walls. Adding a dash of class is the prim
Citrus Café, and the Slounge bar, where
you can down a drink while hustling a
fellow traveller in a game of pool. It's one
place you're sure to have a nice stay.

🍴 Eating

Tandoor North Indian **$$**
(Station Rd East, Shyam Cham-
bers; mains ₹160-290) Offering
fine tandoori dishes and
flavoursome North
Indian veg and non-veg
options in a weirdly
Pharaonic atmos-
phere, Tandoor is one
of Aurangabad's top
stand-alone restau-
rants. A few Chinese
dishes are also on
offer, but patrons
clearly prefer the dishes
coming out of, well, the
tandoor.

ℹ️ Getting There & Away

Air

The airport is 10km east of town. En route are the
offices of Indian Airlines (☎2485241; Jalna Rd)
and Jet Airways (☎2441392; www.jetairways.
com; Jalna Rd). There are direct daily flights to Delhi
(around ₹7000) and Mumbai (around ₹4000).

Bus

Ordinary buses head to Ellora from the MSRTC
bus stand (Station Rd West) every half-hour
(₹25, 45 minutes), and hourly to Jalgaon (₹140,
four hours) via Fardapur (₹95, two hours). The
T-junction near Fardapur is the drop-off point for
Ajanta.

Private bus agents are located around the
corner from the MSRTC bus stand, where Dr
Rajendra Prasad Marg becomes Court Rd; a few
sit closer to the bus stand. Deluxe overnight bus
destinations include Mumbai (with/without AC
₹550/400, sleeper ₹750, eight hours).

Train

Aurangabad's train station (Station Rd East) is
not on a main line, but two heavily booked trains
run direct to/from Mumbai. The Tapovan Express
(2nd class/chair ₹112/476, 7½ hours) departs

Bibi-qa-Maqbara
BODY PHILIPPE/HEMIS.FR/GETTY IMAGES ©

Aurangabad at 2.35pm, and departs Mumbai at 6.10am. The Janshatabdi Express (2nd class/chair ₹142/555, 6½ hours) departs Aurangabad at 6am and Mumbai at 1.50pm.

Getting Around

Autorickshaws are as common here as mosquitoes in a summer swamp. The taxi stand is next to the MSRTC bus stand; share jeeps also depart from here for destinations around Aurangabad, including Ellora and Daulatabad. Expect to pay ₹600 for a full-day tour in a rickshaw, or ₹1100 in a taxi.

Ellora

02437

Give a man a hammer and chisel, and he'll create art for posterity. Come to the World Heritage Site **Ellora cave temples** (Indian/foreigner ₹10/250; ☉dawn-dusk Wed-Mon), located 30km from Aurangabad, and you'll know exactly what we mean. The epitome of ancient Indian rock-cut architecture, these caves were chipped out laboriously over five centuries by generations of Buddhist, Hindu and Jain monks. Monasteries, chapels, temples – the caves served every purpose, and they were stylishly embellished with a profusion of remarkably detailed sculptures. Unlike the caves at Ajanta, which are carved into a sheer rock face, the Ellora caves line a 2km-long escarpment, the gentle slope of which allowed architects to build elaborate courtyards in front of the shrines, and render them with sculptures of a surreal quality.

Ellora has 34 caves in all: 12 Buddhist (AD 600–800), 17 Hindu (AD 600–900) and five Jain (AD 800–1000). The grandest, however, is the awesome Kailasa Temple (Cave 16), the world's largest monolithic sculpture, hewn top to bottom against a rocky slope by 7000 labourers over a 150-year period. Dedicated to Lord Shiva, it is clearly among the best that ancient Indian architecture has to offer.

Official guides can be hired at the ticket office in front of the Kailasa Temple for ₹750. Most guides have an extensive knowledge of cave architecture, so try not to skimp. If your tight itinerary forces you to choose between Ellora or Ajanta, Ellora wins hands down.

Sights

Kailasa Temple Hindu Temple
This rock-cut temple, built by King Krishna I of the Rashtrakuta dynasty in AD 760, was built to represent Mt Kailasa (Kailash), Shiva's Himalayan abode. To say that the assignment was daring would be an understatement. Three huge trenches were bored into the sheer cliff face with hammers and chisels, following which the shape was 'released', a process that entailed removing 200,000 tonnes of rock, while taking care to leave

Kailasa Temple
PAUL HARDING/GETTY IMAGES ©

behind those sections that would later be used for sculpting. Covering twice the area of the Parthenon in Athens and being half as high again, Kailasa is an engineering marvel that was executed straight from the head with zero margin for error.

Buddhist Caves
Caves

The southernmost 12 caves are Buddhist *viharas* (monasteries), except Cave 10, which is a *chaitya* (assembly hall). While the earliest caves are simple, Caves 11 and 12 are more ambitious, and on par with the more impressive Hindu temples.

Hindu Caves
Caves

Where calm and contemplation infuse the Buddhist caves, drama and excitement characterise the Hindu group (Caves 13 to 29). In terms of scale, creative vision and skill of execution, these caves are in a league of their own.

All these temples were cut from the top down, so it was never necessary to use scaffolding – the builders began with the roof and moved down to the floor.

Jain Caves
Caves

The five Jain caves may lack the artistic vigour and ambitious size of the best Hindu temples, but they are exceptionally detailed. The caves are 1km north of the last Hindu temple (Cave 29) at the end of the bitumen road.

✖ Eating

MTDC Ellora Restaurant & Beer Bar
Indian $

(mains ₹80-130, thali ₹80-130; ⊙8am-5pm) Located within the temple complex, this is a good place to settle in for lunch, or pack takeaways in case you want to picnic beside the caves.

❶ Getting There & Away

Do note that the temples are closed on Tuesday! Buses regularly ply the road between Aurangabad and Ellora (₹25); the last bus departs from Ellora at 8pm. Share jeeps leave when they're full, with drop-off outside the bus stand in Aurangabad (₹60). A full-day autorickshaw tour to Ellora, with stops en route, costs ₹600; taxis charge around ₹1100.

Ajanta
☏02438

Fiercely guarding its horde of priceless artistic treasures from another era, these Buddhist caves, 105km northeast of Aurangabad, could well be called the Louvre of ancient India. Much older than Ellora, its twin in the World Heritage Sites listings, these secluded caves date from around the 2nd century BC to the 6th century AD and were among the earliest monastic institutions to be constructed in the country.

Authorised guides are available to show you around for ₹600.

◎ Sights

Ajanta Caves
Caves

(Indian/foreigner ₹10/250, video ₹25; ⊙9am-5.30pm Tue-Sun) The 30 caves of Ajanta line the steep face of a horseshoe-shaped gorge bordering the Waghore River. Five of the caves are *chaityas* while the other 25 are *viharas*. Caves 8, 9, 10, 12, 13 and part of 15 are early Buddhist caves, while the others date from around the 5th century AD (Mahayana period).

✖ Eating

Ajanta Restaurant & Beer Bar
Fast Food $

(mains ₹100-150, thali from ₹120; ⊙9am-5.30pm Tue-Sun) A restaurant and refreshment centre, right by the main ticket office at the caves, that serves a decent vegetarian thali, and cold drinks including beer.

❶ Getting There & Away

The caves are closed on Monday. Buses from Aurangabad or Jalgaon will drop you at the T-junction (where the highway meets the road to the caves), 4km from the site. Pay an 'amenities' fee (₹10) here, and walk to the departure point for the green-coloured buses (with/without AC ₹20/10) that zoom up to the caves. Buses return on a half-hourly basis (last bus at 5pm) to the T-junction.

MSRTC buses passing through Fardapur stop at the T-junction. After the caves close you can board buses to Aurangabad or Jalgaon outside MTDC Holiday Resort in Fardapur, 1km down the main road towards Jalgaon. Taxis are available in Fardapur.

Rajasthan

It is said that there is more history in Rajasthan than the rest of India put together.
Welcome to the Land of the Kings; a fabled realm of maharajas, majestic forts and lavish palaces.

India is littered with splendid ruined bastions but nowhere will you find fortresses quite as magnificent as those in Rajasthan, which rise imperiously from the desert landscape like fairy-tale mirages of a bygone era. As enchanting as they are, though, there is more to this most royal of regions than its seemingly timeless architectural wonders.

This is also a land of sand dunes and jungle, of camel trains and wild tigers, of glittering jewels, vivid colours and vibrant culture. There are festivals galore, and the shopping and cuisine are nothing short of spectacular. In truth, Rajasthan just about has it all. It is the must-see state of this must-see country; brimming with startling, thought-provoking and, ultimately, unforgettable attractions.

Elephant and keeper in Jaipur (p146)
HUW JONES/GETTY IMAGES ©

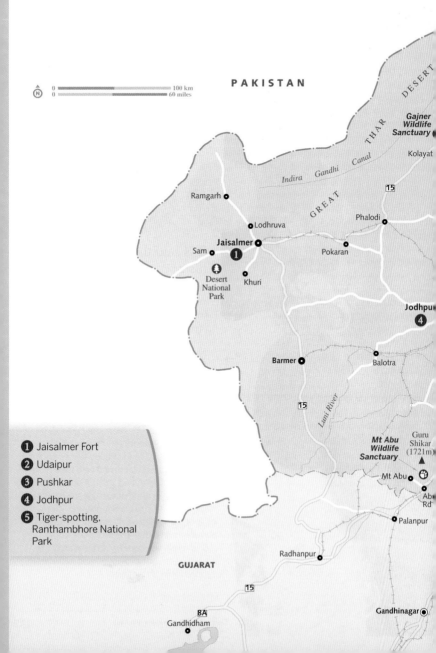

Rajasthan

PAKISTAN

0 ————————— 100 km
0 ————————— 60 miles

THAR DESERT

Gajner Wildlife Sanctuary

Kolayat

Indira Gandhi Canal

GREAT

15

Ramgarh

Lodhruva

Phalodi

Jaisalmer ❶

Sam

Pokaran

❷ Desert National Park

Khuri

Jodhpur ❹

Barmer

Balotra

15

Luni River

Mt Abu Wildlife Sanctuary

Guru Shikar (1721m) ▲

Mt Abu

Abu Rd

Palanpur

❶ Jaisalmer Fort
❷ Udaipur
❸ Pushkar
❹ Jodhpur
❺ Tiger-spotting, Ranthambhore National Park

GUJARAT

Radhanpur

15

8A
Gandhidham

Gandhinagar

Rajasthan's Highlights

Jaisalmer Fort

Rising from the desert scrub like a beautiful, oversized sandcastle, surrounded by 99 bastions, the city of Jaisalmer resonates with its history. Despite today's commercialism, it retains a sense of epic romance. Visiting the ancient citadel (p179) and exploring the desert on camelback are mirage-like, otherworldly experiences that will stay with you long after you leave.

Udaipur

Surrounded by the wooded ridges of the Aravalli Hills and centred on two glimmering, mirror-calm lakes, Udaipur (p163) is Rajasthan's most romantic city, home to serene views on sunny rooftops; fantastical, lace-like, cupola-topped palaces, temples and *havelis* (noble houses); and narrow, crooked, colourful streets.

Pushkar

3

The pastel-hued pilgrimage destination of Pushkar (p158) is a mystical small town set around a holy lake. Although it's a popular travellers' stop, the town feels essentially spiritual, and there's always something going on at one of the temples around the lake. The diminutive town also hosts one of India's most famous fairs, the Pushkar Camel Fair.

4

Jodhpur

The blue city (p172) really is blue, as you'll see when you climb up to its majestic fortress, Mehrangarh, which rears out of its rocky escarpment like a vision from a fairy tale. Listen to the city's secrets from its soaring ramparts, and get lost in its glittering bazaars, where you can buy polished tubas and trumpets, heaped spices, jewellery and shimmering temple decorations.

5

Tiger-spotting, Ranthambhore National Park

Ranthambhore (p161) is one of India's most spectacular national parks, an area of lush, tangled jungle dotted by ruined *chhatris* (cenotaphs) and temples, topped by a magical cliff-top fortress, and inhabited by exotic birds and wild animals, including, of course, tigers. The big cats are used to visitors and you have a good chance of spotting one here.

Rajasthan's Best...

Heritage Hotels

- **Taj Lake Palace** The icon of Udaipur. (p167)
- **Rohet Garh** Countryside manor with literary connections. (p175)
- **Narain Niwas Palace Hotel** Ramshackle splendour set among tree-shaded gardens in Jaipur. (p152)
- **Pal Haveli** Jodhpur's most charming *haveli*. (p174)
- **Hotel Nachana Haveli** 280-year-old Jaisalmer *haveli*, set around three courtyards. (p181)
- **Alsisar Haveli** Beautifully renovated *haveli* in the heart of Jaipur. (p152)

Wining & Dining

- **Indique** Jodhpur's candle-lit rooftop restaurant, with old-city views. (p176)
- **Ambrai** Udaipur's loveliest waterfront restaurant. (p170)
- **Millets of Mewar** Healthy, friendly, delicious: another Udaipur gem. (p169)
- **Saffron** Sublime Indian cuisine in an open-air Jaisalmer setting. (p184)
- **Out of the Blue** Best pizza in Pushkar...and great coffee to boot. (p160)
- **Handi Restaurant** Top-notch but down-to-earth vegetarian restaurant in Jaipur. (p154)

Forts

- **Jaisalmer** Mirage-like sandstone fortress rising up from the Thar Desert. (p179)
- **Mehrangarh** Mighty rock fort overlooking Jodhpur's 'Blue City'. (p173)
- **Amber** Magnificent fort in a village outside Jaipur. (p147)
- **Ranthambhore** Jungle fort secreted away inside a tiger-inhabited national park. (p161)
- **Kumbhalgarh** Vast yet remote; in the Aravali Hills beyond Udaipur. (p166)

Adventures

o **Ranthambhore National Park** The best place to spot tigers in the wild. (p161)

o **Jaisalmer** Camel safaris in the desert. (p178)

o **Amber Fort** Take a balloon ride over Jaipur's famous citadel. (p153)

o **Udaipur** Head to Krishna Ranch for countryside horse treks. (p163)

o **Amber Fort** Sign up with Elefantastic to wash, ride, swim with, paint and feed elephants. (p147)

Need to Know

ADVANCE PLANNING

o **Two months before** Book any particularly special palace hotels, especially if you're travelling in the high season (October to March).

o **One week before** Book train tickets for longer journeys.

o **One day before** Call your hotel to confirm your booking.

RESOURCES

o **Festivals of India** (www.festivalsofindia.in) All about Indian festivals.

o **Incredible India** (www.incredibleindia.org) Official India tourism site.

o **Rajasthan Tourism** (www.rajasthantourism.gov.in) Rajasthan government tourism site.

o **Lonely Planet** (www.lonelyplanet.com/india/rajasthan) Destination information, accommodation reviews and travellers' forum.

GETTING AROUND

o **Car & driver** Between ₹7 and ₹12 per kilometre, with a minimum of 250km per day and ₹150 extra for overnight stays. Note, you'll have to pay for the driver's return trip even if you only travel one way.

o **Train** Jaipur, Sawai Madohpur (for Ranthambhore), Jaipur, Udaipur, Jodhpur and Jaisalmer are all served by rail. Pushkar's nearest rail hub is Ajmer, 30 minutes' drive away.

o **Bus** All destinations are served by bus; AC Volvo buses tend to be the most comfortable.

BE FOREWARNED

o **Gem scams** Don't get smooth-talked into buying gems with an eye to making a profit.

o **Camel safaris** Ask other travellers for recommendations of the best operators.

o **Hotel touts** Prepare to be besieged in Jaipur and Jodhpur. Pre-arrange hotel pick-up if possible.

t: Traditional dancers inside Mehrangarh fort (p173) **Above:** Amber Fort (p147)

(LEFT) AMAR GROVER/GETTY IMAGES ©;
(ABOVE) TIM MAKINS/GETTY IMAGES ©

Rajasthan Itineraries

The first of these itineraries covers the eastern highlights of Rajasthan, while the second takes in several of the most spectacular desert cities of the western part of the region. For a longer stay you could combine the two journeys.

5 DAYS

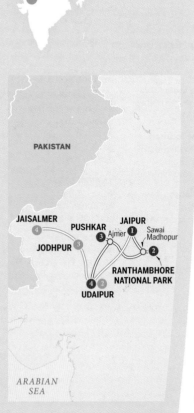

JAIPUR TO UDAIPUR
EASTERN PROMISE

Start your trip in the pink city of ❶ **Jaipur**, visiting its colourful bazaars, City Palace, Amber Fort and Hawa Mahal. Next, take a train from here to Sawai Madhopur, the nearest station to ❷ **Ranthambhore National Park**, to explore the lush jungle landscape of the park with its myriad wildlife, see its ancient, overgrown fort, and go tiger-spotting.

Returning from Sawai Madhopur, take the train to Ajmer, from where it's a short hop by taxi or bus to the magical small town of ❸ **Pushkar**. Spend a day chilling out in this beguilingly pretty pilgrim and traveller centre, lazing in rooftop cafes and seeing the sunset from the Monsoon Palace.

You can either hire a taxi for the next leg of the journey, or return to Ajmer to travel to ❹ **Udaipur** by train. The milk-white city, built across several lakes, is the ideal place to end your journey on a high, exploring its impressive City Palace and spending your last day boating on beautiful Lake Pichola, before taking the train back to Jaipur or flying to Delhi or Mumbai.

Top Left: City Palace (p147), Jaipur
Top Right: Backstreet, Jodhpur (p172)
(TOP LEFT) GETTY IMAGES ©; (TOP RIGHT) INDIA PHOTOGRAPHY/GETTY IMAGES ©

JAIPUR TO JAISALMER

WESTERN DESERT

Again start your trip in the Rajasthani capital, ❶ **Jaipur**, visiting the sights of the pink city, including the City Palace and Amber Fort, and seeing a blockbuster Bollywood film at the sumptuous, meringue-like Rajmandir Cinema. Next, make your way via train or taxi to the laid-back town of ❷ **Udaipur** to visit its City Palace, indulge in some lakeside lazing, and take boats across Lake Pichola against a backdrop of misty blue hills.

The easiest and quickest way to reach ❸ **Jodhpur** from Udaipur is to hire a taxi. Known as the blue city, Jodhpur features an amazing impressionistic cityscape overlooked by the magnificent fortifications of Mehrangarh. Spend your time here visiting the fort itself, for wonderful views over the city, and don't miss the old city's glittering bazaars. Make sure you book ahead for the overnight train to (and back from) the desert city of ❹ **Jaisalmer**, where you can explore the golden sandstone fort, see its beautifully carved *havelis* and Jain temples, and take an overnight trip into the desert on camelback, spending the night under a firmament of stars.

Discover Rajasthan

Ajmeri Gate, Old City (Pink City)
HUW JONES/GETTY IMAGES ©

EASTERN RAJASTHAN

Jaipur

📞0141 / POP 3 MILLION

Jaipur, Rajasthan's capital, is an enthralling historical city and the gateway to India's most flamboyant state.

The city's colourful, chaotic streets ebb and flow with a heady brew of old and new. Careering buses dodge dawdling camels, leisurely cycle-rickshaws frustrate swarms of motorbikes, and everywhere buzzing autorickshaws watch for easy prey. In the midst of this mayhem, the splendours of Jaipur's majestic past are islands of relative calm evoking a different pace and another world. At the city's heart, the City Palace continues to house the former royal family, while the Jantar Mantar (the royal observatory) maintains a heavenly aspect, and the honeycomb Hawa Mahal gazes on the bazaar below. And just out of sight, in the arid hill country surrounding the city, is the fairy-tale grandeur of Amber Fort, Jaipur's star attraction.

◎ Sights

Consider buying a **composite ticket** (Indian/foreigner/foreign student ₹50/300/150), which gives you entry to Amber Fort, Central Museum, Jantar Mantar, Hawa Mahal and Narhargarh, and is valid for two days from time of purchase.

OLD CITY (PINK CITY)

The Old City (known as the Pink City by some) is partially encircled by a crenellated wall punctuated at intervals by grand gateways. The major gates are Chandpol

BRENT WINEBRENNER/GETTY IMAGES ©

⭐ Don't Miss
Amber Fort

The magnificent, honey-hued 17th-century **Amber Fort** (Indian/foreigner ₹25/200, guide ₹200, audio guide Hindi/other ₹100/150; ⏰8am-6pm, last entry 5.30pm), an ethereal example of Rajput architecture, rises from a rocky mountainside about 11km northeast of Jaipur, and is the city's must-see sight.

It is made up largely of a royal palace, built from pale yellow and pink sandstone and white marble, and divided into four main sections, each with its own courtyard.

You can trudge up to the fort from the road in about 10 minutes. Cold drinks are available at the top. The ticket office is also here. Alternatively, ride up to the entrance on an **elephant** (₹900 one way for two people).

Hiring a guide (₹200) at the ticket office, or grabbing an audio guide (₹150), is highly recommended as there are very few signs and many blind alleys.

There are frequent buses (non-AC/AC ₹10/20, 15 minutes) to Amber from near the Hawa Mahal in Jaipur city centre. They drop you opposite where you start your climb up to the entrance of Amber Fort. The elephant rides start 100m further down the hill from the bus drop-off. An autorickshaw/taxi will cost at least ₹200/600 for the return trip from Jaipur city centre. RTDC city tours include Amber Fort.

(*pol* means 'gate'), Ajmeri Gate and Sanganeri Gate.

City Palace   Palace
(Indian/foreigner incl camera ₹75/300, video ₹200, audio guide ₹80, human guide from ₹300, Chandra Mahal tour ₹2500; ⏰9.30am-5pm)
A complex of courtyards, gardens and buildings, the impressive City Palace is right in the centre of the Old City. The outer wall was built by Jai Singh, but within it the palace has been enlarged and adapted over the centuries. Despite the gradual development, the whole is a striking blend of Rajasthani and Mughal architecture.

Jaipur

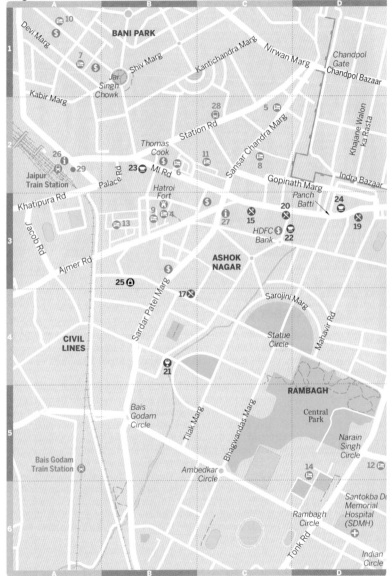

Jantar Mantar Historic Site
(Indian/foreigner ₹40/200, audio guide ₹150,
human guide ₹200; ⊙9am-4.30pm) Adjacent
to the City Palace is Jantar Mantar, an
observatory begun by Jai Singh in 1728
that resembles a collection of bizarre
sculptures. The name is derived from the
Sanskrit *yanta mantr*, meaning 'instrument of calculation', and in 2010 it was
added to India's list of Unesco World
Heritage Sites.

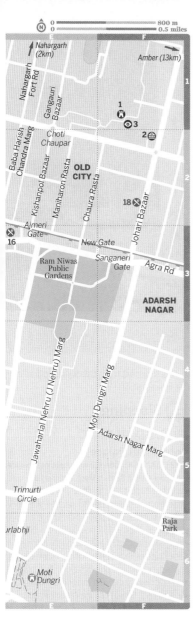

Jaipur

Hawa Mahal Historic Building
(Indian/foreigner incl camera ₹10/50, audio guide Hindi/English ₹80/110, human guide ₹200; ⊙9am-5pm) Jaipur's most distinctive landmark, the Hawa Mahal, or Palace of the Winds, is an extraordinary,

pink-sandstone, delicately honeycombed hive that rises a dizzying five storeys. It was constructed in 1799 by Maharaja Sawai Pratap Singh to enable ladies of the royal household to watch the life and processions of the city. The top offers stunning views over Jantar Mantar and the City Palace one way, and over Siredeori Bazaar the other.

Tours

RTDC
Sightseeing

(☏ 2200778; tours@rtdc.in; RTDC tourist information bureau, Platform 1, Jaipur train station; half-/full-day tours ₹250/300; ⏰ 8am-6.30pm Mon-Sat) Rajasthan Tourism Development Corporation offers tours of Jaipur's main sights, including Amber Fort. Fees don't include admission charges. Tours include a shopping stop.

The **Pink City by Night tour** (₹375; 6.30pm to 10.30pm) explores several well-known sights, again including Amber Fort, and includes dinner at Nahargarh fort.

Tours depart from the tourist office at the train station.

Sleeping

AROUND MI ROAD

Hotel Pearl Palace Hotel **$**
(☏ 2373700, 9414066311; www.hotelpearlpalace.com; Hari Kishan Somani Marg, Hathroi Fort; dm ₹175, r ₹400-1250; ❄ @ 🛜) Great-value Pearl Palace continues to set the standard for budget digs in Jaipur. There's quite a range of rooms to choose from – small, large, shared bath, private bath, dorms, some balconied, some with air-con or fan cooled, but all are thoughtfully decorated and spotlessly clean. Congenial hosts Mr and Mrs Singh offer all manner of services including free pick-up from bus and train stations (8am to 11pm only), moneychanging and travel advice. The rooftop restaurant is also excellent. The only disappointment is that wi-fi isn't free (₹150 per day), but this place is rightfully popular. Advance booking highly recommended.

Left: Jantar Mantar observatory (p148) **Below:** Hawa Mahal (Palace of the Winds; p149)

(LEFT) HUW JONES/GETTY IMAGES ©; (BELOW) DOUG PEARSON/GETTY IMAGES ©

Karni Niwas   Guesthouse $$

(☏ 2365433; www.hotelkarniniwas. com; C-5 Motilal Atal Marg; without/with AC from ₹700/850; ✱ @ 🛜) Welcoming and trustworthy management running a simple but comfortable guesthouse with large, clean rooms. There's no restaurant, but there is an all-day menu, and tables and chairs are dotted around the place, in alcoves and on shared balconies and terraces, so there are plenty of nice spots to eat and drink. Free pick-up from the train or bus station is available. Free wi-fi throughout.

Atithi Guest House   Guesthouse $$

(☏ 2378679; atithijaipur@hotmail.com; 1 Park House Scheme Rd; s/d from ₹750/850, with AC ₹1300/1400; ✱ @ 🛜) With slightly less character than its rivals, this spotlessly clean hotel can feel a little sterile, but it's the perfect antidote to Jaipur's dusty streets. It's central but peaceful, and the service is friendly and helpful. There's a immaculate kitchen and restaurant (guests only), and you can also dine on the very pleasant rooftop terrace. Wi-fi is ₹75 per day.

Hotel Arya Niwas   Hotel $$

(☏ 4073456; www.aryaniwas.com; Sansar Chandra Marg; r from ₹1050, s/d from ₹1150/1600; ✱ @ 🛜) Housed in a nicely renovated mansion hidden behind a scruffy four-storey block, this is a popular travellers' haunt, with a travel desk, bookshop, yoga lessons (₹100) and good-value massage treatments (from ₹350). The clean rooms face an inner courtyard and vary in layout and size so check out a few. It's a little drab in general, but there's a certain charm, not least because of the extensive colonial-style terrace overlooking a soothing expanse of lawn in front of the hotel's excellent **Chitra Cafe**.

All Seasons Homestay
Homestay $$

(☏9460387055; www.allseasonshomestayjaipur.com; 63 Hathroi Fort; s ₹1150-1550, d ₹1250-1650; @) Ranjana and her husband Dinesh run this welcoming homestay in their lovely garden bungalow on a quiet back street behind deserted Hathroi Fort. There are only four guestrooms but each is lovingly cared for and one or two have basic kitchen facilities. There's a pleasant lawn area, home-cooked meals and free internet.

Pearl Palace Heritage
Hotel $$$

(☏9414066311, 2375242; www.pearlpalaceheritage.com; 54 Gopal Bari, Lane 2; r ₹2000-2500; ✷@🛜) The second hotel for the successful Pearl Palace team is a more upmarket, heritage-style property. As we've come to expect from Mr Singh, the attention to detail is fabulous, with privately commissioned hand-carved panels in the corridors and hand-painted murals in the rooms, which are wonderfully spacious and individually themed (Jaisalmer, Kutch, Indus etc). Each room has its own computer plus free wi-fi, tea/coffee makers, wall-mounted TV and beautifully designed bathrooms.

Alsisar Haveli
Heritage Hotel $$$

(☏2368290; www.alsisar.com; Sansar Chandra Marg; s/d from ₹4680/6160; ✷@🛜🏊) Beautifully renovated 19th-century *haveli* (this one really is a genuine *haveli*, unlike many namesakes) with immaculate high-ceilinged rooms, elegant Rajput arches and antique furnishings. If you can't afford to stay here, sample its atmosphere by coming for a dip in the lovely garden pool (nonguests ₹250 per hour).

BANI PARK

Upmarket Bani Park is a relatively peaceful area (away from the main roads, at least), about 2km west of the Old City (₹50 in a cycle-rickshaw).

Hotel Anuraag Villa
Hotel $$

(☏2201679; www.anuraagvilla.com; D249 Devi Marg; s ₹600-1850, d ₹790-1850; ✷@🛜) This quiet and comfortable option has no-fuss, spacious rooms and a large tree-shaded lawn where you can find some quiet respite from the hassles of sightseeing. It has a recommended restaurant with garden seating and open kitchen. Staff members are efficient and helpful.

Jas Vilas
Guesthouse $$$

(☏2204638; www.jasvilas.com; C9 Sawai Jai Singh Hwy; s/d ₹3700/4000; ✷@🛜🏊) This small but impressive hotel was built in 1950 and is still run by the same charming family. It offers 11 spacious rooms, most of which face the sparkling courtyard pool. Three garden-facing rooms are wheelchair accessible. In addition to the relaxing courtyard and lawn, there's a cosy dining room. Management will help with all onward travel planning.

RAMBAGH ENVIRONS

Narain Niwas Palace Hotel
Heritage Hotel $$$

(☏2561291; www.hotelnarain-niwas.com; Narain Singh Rd; r incl breakfast from ₹7400; ✷@🛜🏊) Built in 1928 by

Jaipur street food
GREENLIN/GETTY IMAGES ©

General Amar Singh, this genuine heritage hotel has a wonderful ramshackle splendour. There's a lavish dining room with liveried staff, a veranda on which to drink tea, and antiques galore. The high-ceilinged rooms are varyingly atmospheric and the bathrooms also vary greatly – so inspect before committing. The large secluded garden pool (nonguests ₹200) is heavenly, as is the spa, and the sprawling gardens come complete with wandering peacocks. The restaurant (7.30am to 10.30pm; mains ₹150 to 3₹00) and bar (3pm to 11pm) are also open to nonguests. Wi-fi costs ₹500 a day!

Rambagh Palace
Heritage Hotel $$$

(☏ 2211919; www.tajhotels.com; Bhawan Singh Marg; r from ₹27,500; ✿@🛜🏊) This splendid palace was once the Jaipur pad of Maharaja Man Singh II and, until recently, his glamorous wife Gayatri Devi. Veiled in 19 hectares of gardens, there are fantastic views across the immaculate lawns, and the rooms and facilities are top notch. Nonguests are only made to feel welcome if they dress to impress and flash the cash. Minimum spend in the bar for nonguests: ₹1500 per person. In the restaurants: ₹2500.

AMBER FORT AREA

Mosaics Guesthouse
Guesthouse $$$

(☏ 8875430000, 2530031; www.mosaics-guesthouse.com; Siyaram Ki Doongri, Amber; s/d incl breakfast ₹3200/3500; ✿@🛜) The decidedly untouristy village of Amber, with its colourful food market and scattering of temples and palace ruins, all nestled in the shadow of the magnificent Amber Fort, makes a low-key alternative to hectic Jaipur as a possible place to stay. There are a couple of cheap guesthouses in the village, but for something more comfortable, try the gorgeous French-run Mosaics Guesthouse, with four lovely rooms and a roof terrace with beautiful fort views. Meals cost a set-price ₹500. It's about 1km past the fort. Keep going along the main road towards Kunda Village, then, just before you reach the Delhi Hwy, turn sharp right towards Narad Ka Bagh, then turn immediately right to Siyaram Ki Doongri.

Hot-Air Ballooning

For something a little bit special, consider treating yourself to a sunrise balloon ride above Amber Fort with India's leading hot-air balloon company, **Sky Waltz** (☏ 9717295801; www.skywaltz.com; US$240). Run by Aussie expat Paul Macpherson, and with a team of highly experienced foreign pilots, Sky Waltz offers spectacular early-morning balloon flights over the fort and surrounding countryside.

The package includes pick-up from your hotel in Jaipur (at around 6am), tea, coffee and cookies, watching the balloon inflation, the flight itself and drop-off at your hotel afterwards. The whole thing lasts around three hours, including the one-hour flight.

Balloon-flight season is September to March.

🍴 Eating

AROUND MI ROAD

Indian Coffee House
South Indian $

(MI Rd; mains ₹20-45; ⏰8am-9.30pm) Jaipur's tucked-away branch of the South Indian institution, this 50-year-old, fan-cooled coffee house not only does the cheapest filter coffee in town (₹12), it also whips up a selection of tasty dishes – dosa (wafer-thin savoury crepes), *uttapam* (thick savoury rice pancake), *idly* (spongy round fermented rice cake), *vada* (doughnut-shaped deep-fried lentil cake) – as well as toast, omelettes and sandwiches. A great spot for a cheap breakfast or lunch.

Old Takeaway The Kebab Shop
Kebabs $

(151 MI Road; kebabs ₹80-120; ⏰6-11pm) One of a few similarly named road-side kebab shops that open up each evening on this stretch of MI Road. This one (at No 151) is the original (so we're told) and the best (we

A Day with the Elephants

The hugely popular elephant rides up to the entrance at Amber Fort are fine for a quick bit of fun, but if you want to spend some quality time with elephants and their handlers, treat yourself to an afternoon with **Elefantastic** (☑8094253150; www.elefantastic.in; 90 Chandra Mahal Colony, Delhi Rd, Amber; 'day with the elephants' afternoon package per person ₹5100).

Set up by Rahul, a former elephant rider, this new, well-run company looks after around two dozen elephants at its stables, 2km northeast of Amber Fort. The 'day with the elephants' package gives you the opportunity to meet, feed, ride, wash and even swim with elephants. It's a particularly incredible experience for young children, who can come along for a negligible price if they are accompanied by paying adults.

The standard package is an afternoon thing, and includes a late-afternoon Rajasthani meal at a family home. You can stay the night too, allowing you to join in with the elephants' early-morning routines.

agree). It knocks up outstanding tandoori kebabs, including paneer sheesh, mutton sheesh and the mouthwatering tandoori chicken. Pull up a stool and tuck in.

Chitra Cafe
Cafe **$**

(Hotel Arya Niwas, Sansar Chandra Rd; mains ₹40-110; ☺7am-9.45pm) Hotel Arya Niwas' charming Chitra Cafe conjures up images of a bygone colonial era, with its rattan tables and chairs scattered along a covered terrace overlooking the hotel's cooling front lawn. It's great value too, especially if you plump for the thali (₹125). Also does homemade cakes and cookies, plus shakes and safe-to-eat ice creams.

Peacock Rooftop Restaurant
Multicuisine **$$**

(☑2373700; Hari Kishan Somani Marg, Hotel Pearl Palace; mains ₹70-180; ☺7am-11pm) Hotel Pearl Palace's pride and joy, Peacock is one of the best hotel rooftop restaurants you'll find. The traveller-friendly atmosphere is relaxed, the view towards Hathroi Fort is romantic and the beer is ice cold. Most importantly, though, the food is mouthwatering. A number of world cuisines are on offer; all are prepared well, but it's the Indian dishes that truly hit the spot, particularly the tandoori kebabs. They also do fresh juices, filter coffee and breakfast croissants.

Handi Restaurant
North Indian **$$**

(MI Rd; mains ₹140-300; ☺noon-3.30pm & 6pm-11pm) The Indian food here is as good as at any top restaurant in town, but the atmosphere is far less stuffy. Popular with local families, Handi is decked out like a large traditional village eatery, with a dried-mud floor, bamboo-lined walls and wicker roofing. It offers scrumptious tandoori and barbecued dishes as well as rich Mughlai curries. In the evenings it sets up a smoky kebab stall at the entrance to the restaurant. No beer.

Copper Chimney
Indian **$$**

(☑2372275; MI Rd, Maya Mansions; mains ₹150-400; ☺noon-3.30pm & 6.30-11pm) Copper Chimney is casual, almost elegant, and definitely welcoming, with the requisite waiter army and a fridge of cold beer (from ₹100). It offers excellent veg and nonveg Indian cuisine, including aromatic Rajasthani specials. There is also Continental and Chinese food and a small selection of Indian wine, but the curry and beer combos are hard to beat.

Niro's
Indian **$$$**

(☑2374493; MI Rd; mains ₹200-500; ☺10am-11pm) Established in 1949, Niro's is a long-standing favourite on MI Road. It's very plush these days – and has prices to match – but the quality of food is as good as ever, with plenty of Rajasthani specialities among its extensive Indian menu. Also does some Chinese and international cuisine, but the Indian dishes are definitely the pick. Beer from ₹160.

Little Italy
Italian **$$$**

(☏4022444; Prithviraj Marg, 3rd fl, KK Sq; mains ₹300-500; ⊙noon-11pm) Arguably the best Italian restaurant in town, this is part of a small national chain that offers excellent vegetarian pasta, risotto and wood-fired pizzas in cool, contemporary surroundings. The menu is extensive and includes some Mexican items and first-rate Italian desserts. Also has a decent wine list.

OLD CITY

LMB
Vegetarian **$$**

(☏2560845; Johari Bazaar; mains ₹150-250; ⊙8am-11pm) Laxmi Misthan Bhandar (LMB), is an upmarket *sattvik* (vegetarian) restaurant in the Old City that's been going strong since 1954. A welcoming air-conditioned refuge from frenzied Johari Bazaar, LMB is a bit of an institution with its singular decor, attentive waiters and extensive sweet counter. It's also very popular with tourists these days. The Rajasthan thali is excellent, as is its signature *kulfa*, a fusion of *kulfi* and *falooda* with dry fruits and saffron.

🍷 Drinking

Lassiwala
Cafe

(MI Rd; ⊙7.30am till sold out) This famous, much-imitated lassi institution is a simple place that whips up fabulous, creamy lassis in a clay cup (small/large ₹17/34). Get here early to avoid disappointment; they usually sell out by 4pm. Will the real Lassiwala please stand up? Imitators abound, it's the one that says 'Shop 312' and 'Since 1944', directly next to an alleyway.

100% Rock
Bar

(Hotel Shikha, Yudhishthir Mar, C-Scheme; beer from ₹160; ⊙10am-11.30pm) Attached to, but separate from Hotel Shikha (and formerly known as TC Bar), this is the closest thing there is to a beer garden in Jaipur, with plenty of outdoor seating as well as air-conditioned side rooms and a clubby main room with a small dance floor. Two-for-one beer offers are common, making this popular with local youngsters.

Brewberry's
Cafe

(G-2 Fortune Heights, opp ICICI Bank; coffee from ₹40; ⊙8am-midnight) Modern wi-fi-enabled cafe with fresh coffee and a good mix of Indian and Western food and snacks. Has some patio seating.

Café Coffee Day
Cafe

(Country Inn Hotel, MI Rd; coffee ₹60-90; ⊙10am-10pm) Dependable, air-conditioned branch of India's most popular coffee-shop chain. There's another one on the way to Bani Park.

Elephant ride, Amber Fort (p147)
CHRISTER FREDRIKSSON/GETTY IMAGES ©

🔒 Shopping

Jaipur is a shopper's paradise. Commercial buyers come here from all over the world to stock up on the amazing range of jewellery, gems, artefacts and crafts that come from all over Rajasthan. You'll have to bargain hard though – shops have seen too many cash-rich, time-poor tourists.

The old city is still loosely divided into traditional artisans quarters:

Bapu Bazaar is lined with saris and fabrics, and is a good place to buy trinkets. **Johari Bazaar** is where many jewellery shops are concentrated, selling gold, silver and highly glazed enamelwork known as *meenakari*, a Jaipur speciality.

Kishanpol Bazaar is famous for textiles, particularly *bandhani* (tie-dye). **Nehru Bazaar** also sells fabric, as well as jootis, trinkets and perfume. MI Rd is another good place to buy jootis. The best place for bangles is the old-city alleyway called **Maniharon ka Rasta**.

Mojari   Clothing
(Shiv Heera Marg; shoes ₹500-750; ⏰10am-6.30pm Mon-Sat) Named after the traditional decorated shoes of Rajasthan, Mojari is a UN-supported project that helps rural leatherworkers, traditionally among the poorest members of society. There is a small range of wonderful handmade footwear on display (and loads more out the back), including embroidered, appliquéd and open-toed shoes, mules and sandals. There's a particularly good choice for women, and there's a small selection of handmade leather bags and purses too.

ℹ️ Information

Medical Services

Most hotels can arrange a doctor on-site.

Santokba Durlabhji Memorial Hospital (SDMH) (☎2566251; www.sdmh.in; Bhawan Singh Marg) Private hospital, with 24-hour emergency department, helpful staff and clear bilingual signage. Consultancy fee ₹400.

Money

There are plenty of places to change money, including numerous hotels and masses of ATMs (especially around MI Road), most of which accept foreign cards. We've marked a selection on our map.

Thomas Cook (☎2360940; MI Rd, Jaipur Towers; ⏰9.30am-6pm) Changes cash and travellers cheques (Amex only), and does advances on credit cards.

Tourist Information

RTDC Tourist Reception Centre (☎5155137; www.rajasthantourism.gov.in; Room 21, former RTDC Tourist Hotel; ⏰9.30am-6pm Mon-Fri) Has free maps and brochures on Jaipur and Rajasthan, organises city tours, private taxis and government-registered guides. There are also branches at the **airport** (☎2722647); **Amber Fort** (☎2530264); **Jaipur train station** (☎2200778; Platform 1; ⏰24hr); and

Decorative window, Hawa Mahal
(Palace of the Winds; p149)
GLENN BEANLAND/GETTY IMAGES ©

the main bus station (☎5064102; Platform 3; ☺10am-5pm Mon-Fri).

ⓘ Getting There & Away

Air

Air India, IndiGo and Jet Airways all fly daily between Jaipur and various other Indian cities.

Bus

Rajasthan State Road Transport Corporation (RSRTC) buses all leave from the main bus stand (Station Rd), where there's a left-luggage cloakroom' (₹10 per bag for 24 hours), as well as a prepaid autorickshaw stand.

Deluxe buses leave from Platform 3, tucked away in the right-hand corner of the bus station, and can be booked in advance from the reservation office (☎5116032) here.

Car

Most hotels can arrange car and driver hire, or else go to the RTDC Tourist Reception Centre (p156) at the train station.

Train

The efficient railway reservation office (☎135; ☺8am-9pm Mon-Sat, to 2pm Sun) is to your left as you enter Jaipur train station. It's open for advance reservations only (more than five hours before departure).

For same-day travel, buy your ticket at the northern end of the train station on Platform 1, window 10.

Nine daily trains go to Delhi, three to Agra, four to Jodhpur and three to Udaipur. Eleven daily trains go to Ajmer (for Pushkar), while six go to Sawai Madhopur (for Ranthambhore National Park). Only one daily train (11.45pm) goes to Jaisalmer.

ⓘ Getting Around

To/From the Airport

An autorickshaw/taxi costs at least ₹200/400. There's a prepaid taxi booth inside the airport.

Autorickshaw

There are prepaid autorickshaw stands at the bus and train stations. Rates are fixed by the government, which means you don't have to haggle. Keep hold of your docket, though, until you reach your destination. Your driver won't get paid without it.

In other cases you should be prepared to bargain hard. Expect to pay at least ₹50 from the train or bus station to the Old City.

Cycle-Rickshaw

Slightly cheaper than autorickshaws, but not much. Tips appreciated.

Taxi

There are unmetered taxis available which will require negotiating a fare, or you can try Mericar

Major Trains from Jaipur

DESTINATION	TRAIN	DEPARTURE TIME	ARRIVAL TIME	FARE (₹)
Agra (Cantonment)	19666 Udaipur-Kurj Exp	6.15am	11am	135/362 (A)
Ajmer	12195 Intercity Express	9.40am	11.45am	65/230 (B)
Bikaner	12307 Howrah Jodhpur Exp	12.15am	8am	198/521 (A)
Delhi (New Delhi)	12016 Ajmer Shatabdi	5.50pm	10.40pm	555/1150 (D)
Delhi (S Rohilla)	12985 Dee Double Decker	6am	10.30am	360 (C)
Jaisalmer	14659 Delhi-Jaisalmer Exp	11.45pm	11am	252/703 (A)
Jodhpur	12307 Howrah-Jodhpur Exp	12.15am	6am	178/459 (A)
Sawai Madhoper	12466 Intercity Exp	11.05am	1.15pm	65/140/230 (E)
Udaipur	19665 Kurj-Udaipur Exp	10.30pm	6.10am	194/533 (A)

Fares: (A) sleeper/3AC; (B) 2nd-class seat/AC chair; (C) AC chair; (D) AC chair/1AC; (E) 2nd-class seat/sleeper/AC chair

(☎4188888; www.mericar.in; flagfall incl 2km ₹50, afterwards per km ₹13, 25% night surcharge 10pm-5am). It's a 24-hour service and taxis can also be hired for sightseeing for four-/six-/eight-hour blocks, costing ₹650/1000/1300.

Pushkar

☎0145 / POP 15,000

Pushkar has a magnetism all of its own, and is quite unlike anywhere else in Rajasthan. It's a prominent Hindu pilgrimage town and devout Hindus should visit at least once in their lifetime. The town curls around a holy lake, said to have appeared when Brahma dropped a lotus flower. It also has one of the world's few Brahma temples. With 52 bathing ghats and 400 milky-blue temples, the town often hums with *puja*s (prayers) generating an episodic soundtrack of chanting, drums and gongs, and devotional songs.

The result is a muddle of religious and tourist scenes. The main street is one long bazaar, selling anything to tickle a traveller's fancy, from hippie-chic tie-dye to didgeridoos. Despite the commercialism and banana pancakes, the town remains enchantingly small and authentically mystic.

◉ Sights

Temples   Hindu Temple

Pushkar boasts hundreds of temples, though few are particularly ancient as

Camel Rides

Plenty of people in Pushkar offer short **camel rides** (around ₹200 per hour), which are a good way to explore the starkly beautiful landscape – a mixture of desert and the rocky hills – around town. Sunset rides are most popular. It's best to ask at your hotel. Inn Seventh Heaven is reliable.

they were mostly desecrated by Aurangzeb and subsequently rebuilt.

Most famous is the **Brahma Temple**, said to be one of the few such temples in the world as a result of a curse by Brahma's consort, Saraswati. The temple is marked by a red spire, and over the entrance gateway is the *hans* (goose symbol) of Brahma. Inside, the floor and walls are engraved with dedications to the dead.

Ghats   Ghat

Fifty-two bathing ghats surround the lake, where pilgrims bathe in the sacred waters. If you wish to join them, do it with respect. Remember, this is a holy place: remove your shoes, and don't smoke, kid around or take photographs.

Some ghats have particular importance: Vishnu appeared at **Varah Ghat** in the form of a boar, Brahma bathed at **Brahma Ghat**, and Gandhi's ashes were sprinkled at **Gandhi Ghat** (formerly Gau Ghat).

🏃 Activities

Nonguests can use the pool at **Hotel Navaratan Palace** (☎2772145; www.pushkar navaratanpalace.co.in) for ₹100.

Shannu's Riding School   Horse Riding

(☎2772043; www.shannus.weebly.com; Panch Kund Marg; ride/lessons per hr ₹400) French-Canadian and long-time Pushkar resident Marc Dansereau can organise riding lessons and horse safaris on his graceful Marwari steeds. You can stay here too (single/double ₹500/600).

🛏 Sleeping

Shri Shyam Krishna Guesthouse   Guesthouse $

(☎2772461; skguesthouse@yahoo.com; Sadar Bazaar; s/d ₹300/500, without bathroom ₹150/350; 🖳) Housed in a lovely old blue-washed building, and sharing lawns and gardens with a still-active Krishna temple, this sprawling guesthouse has ashram austerity, genuine friendly management

BARTOSZ HADYNIAK/GETTY IMAGES ©

⭐ Don't Miss
Pushkar Camel Fair

Come the month of Kartika, the eighth lunar month of the Hindu calendar and one of the holiest, Thar camel drivers spruce up their ships of the desert and start the long walk to Pushkar in time for Kartik Purnima (Full Moon). Each year around 200,000 people converge here, bringing with them some 50,000 camels, horses and cattle. The place becomes an extraordinary swirl of colour, sound and movement, thronging with musicians, mystics, tourists, traders, animals, devotees and camera crews.

It's hard to believe, but this seething mass is all just a sideshow. Kartik Purnima is when Hindu pilgrims come to bathe in Pushkar's sacred waters. The religious event builds in tandem with the camel fair in a wild, magical crescendo of incense, chanting and processions to dousing day, the last night of the fair, when thousands of devotees wash away their sins and set candles afloat on the holy lake.

and makes a great budget choice for families. Some of the cheaper rooms are cell-like, and there's only hot water in the private bathrooms, but all rooms share the simple, authentic ambience.

Inn Seventh Heaven Heritage Hotel **$$**
📞 5105455; www.inn-seventh-heaven.com; Chotti Basti; r ₹950-2800; ❄️ @ 📶) You enter this lovingly converted *haveli* through heavy wooden doors into an incense-perfumed courtyard, centred with a marble fountain. There are 12 individually decorated rooms on three levels, with traditionally crafted furniture and comfortable beds. On the roof you'll find the excellent Sixth Sense restaurant as well as sofas and swing chairs for relaxing with a book. Early booking (two-night minimum, no credit cards) is recommended.

Hotel Kanhaia Haveli   Hotel $$

(☎2772146; www.pushkarhotelkanhaia.com; Chotti Basti; r ₹300-1750; ❄@📶) With a vast range of rooms, from cheap budget digs to smart air-conditioned doubles and suites, you are sure to find a room and price that suits at this converted court-yard hotel. As you spend more the rooms get bigger and lighter with more windows and even balconies.

Hotel Pushkar
Palace   Heritage Hotel $$$

(☎2772001; www.hotelpushkarpalace.com; r incl breakfast ₹7000; ❄@) Once belonging to the Maharaja of Kishangarh, this top-end hotel boasts a romantic lakeside setting. Beautifully appointed rooms have carved wooden furniture and separate dressing areas leading into exquisite bathrooms. Rooms open onto a shared veranda which overlooks the central garden and has views of the lake. No internet and no swimming pool, but rooms do have coffee makers and flatscreen TVs. Expect 40% discounts when it's quiet.

🍴 Eating

Honey & Spice   Multicuisine $

(Laxmi Market, off Sadar Bazaar; mains ₹90-150; ⏰7.30am-6.45pm) 🍃 This unassuming cafe-restaurant is pretty much unique in Pushkar, with its emphasis on super-healthy food rather than lake views. It's tucked away behind shops on Sadar Bazar so that nothing can distract you from the fabulous menu, which is small but outstanding. Offerings such as 'exotic stir fry in ginger and honey sauce' share space with a selection of imaginative salads, pastas, juices and herbal teas. There are vegan options too and the breakfast menu – brown toasts, fresh fruits, por-ridge, muesli – is equally healthy, while the fresh coffee (from ₹50) includes blends infused with spices such as carda-mon and cinnamon.

Sunset Café   Multicuisine $

(mains ₹75-200; ⏰7.30am-midnight; 📶) Right on the eastern ghats, this cafe has un-interrupted lake views. It offers the usual traveller menu, including well-priced Indi-an dishes, pizza and pasta, plus there's a German bakery serving OK cakes. As the name suggests, the lakeshore setting is perfect at sunset, but this is also a pleas-ant spot for breakfast (espresso ₹60).

Out of the Blue   Italian $$

(mains ₹100-200; ⏰8am-11pm; 📶) Arguably the best restaurant in Pushkar, Out of the Blue does decent Indian, Israeli and even Tibetan dishes, but it's the Italian food that steals the show, with excellent thin-crust pizzas sharing the menu with some delicious pasta options. It also does the best coffee in town (from ₹40), making this a smart choice for breakfast too.

Sixth Sense   Multicuisine $$

(Inn Seventh Heaven; mains ₹120-200; ⏰8.30am-4pm & 6-10pm; 📶) This chilled rooftop restaurant is a great place to head even if you didn't score a room in its popular hotel. Seasonal Indian vegeta-bles and rice, vegetable sizzlers, pasta and pizzas are all excellent, as are the filter coffee and fresh juice blends. Its ambience is immediately relaxing and the pulley apparatus that delivers the deli-cious food from the ground-floor kitchen is enthralling.

🔒 Shopping

Pushkar's Sadar Bazaar is lined with enchanting little shops and is a good place for picking up gifts. Many of the vibrant textiles come from the Barmer district south of Jaisalmer. There's plenty of silver and beaded jewellery catering to foreign tastes, and some old tribal pieces too.

Lala International   Clothing

(Sadar Bazaar; ⏰9.30am-8pm) Brilliantly col-ourful women's clothing. Modern designs but Indian in theme. Dresses and skirts start from around ₹500. Prices are clearly labelled and fixed.

❶ Getting There & Away

The nearest major train station is Ajmer, 11km away. Frequent buses link Pushkar with Ajmer (₹10 to ₹12, 30 minutes, every 10 minutes).

A taxi to/from Ajmer train station costs ₹300 to ₹400, plus a ₹35 toll fee, which bus passengers do not have to pay.

....

Ranthambhore National Park
☎ 07462

This famous national park, open from October 1 to June 30, is the best place to spot wild tigers in Rajasthan. Comprising 1334 sq km of wild jungle scrub hemmed in by rocky ridges, at its centre is the amazing 10th-century Ranthambhore Fort. Scattered around the fort are ancient temples and mosques, hunting pavilions, crocodile-filled lakes and vine-covered *chhatris*.

Seeing a tiger (there were 28 at last count) is partly a matter of luck; leave time for two or three safaris to improve your chances.

It's 10km from Sawai Madhopur (the gateway town for Ranthambhore) to the first gate of the park, and another 3km to the main gate and Ranthambhore Fort. There's a bunch of cheap (and rather grotty) hotels near Sawai Madhopur train station, but the nicest accommodation is stretched out along Ranthambhore Rd, which eventually leads to the park.

It's ₹50 to ₹100 for an auto from the train station to Ranthambhore Rd, depending on where you get off. Many hotels, though, will pick you up from the train station for free if you call ahead.

◎ Sights & Activities

Safaris take place in the early morning and late afternoon, starting between 6am and 7am, and between 2pm and 3pm, depending on the time of year. Each safari lasts for around three hours. The mornings can be exceptionally chilly in the open vehicles, so bring warm clothes.

The best option is to travel by **gypsy** (six-person open-topped jeep; price per safari per person Indian/foreigner ₹528/927). You still have a good chance of seeing a tiger from a **canter** (20-seater open-topped truck; Indian/foreigner ₹400/800), though sometimes other passengers can be rowdy.

Ranthambhore National Park

Be aware that the rules for booking safaris (and prices) are prone to change. At the time of research, hotels and agents could no longer book you onto a safari. You either had to book online through the park's official website (www. rajasthanwildlife.com), which we highly recommend you do, or go in person on the day of your safari to the **Safari Booking Office**, which was inconveniently located 3km from Ranthambhore Rd, in the opposite direction to the park.

🛏 Sleeping

Hotel Tiger Safari Resort
Hotel **$$**

(☏221137; www.tigersafariresort.com; Ranthambhore Rd; r ₹1300-1800; ❄ @ 🛜 ⌕) All-in, this is the best-value option. Rooms are clean, comfortable and spacious and come with cable TV, hot-water showers and free wi-fi. There's a decent restaurant, a well-tended garden, a lovely little swimming pool and it's run by management that is knowledgable, honest and friendly.

Vatika Resort
Hotel **$$$**

(☏222457; www.ranthambhorevatikaresort. com; Ranthambhore Rd; r ₹1800, incl breakfast/ all meals ₹2250/3000; ❄ @ 🛜) Lovely little guesthouse with simple but immaculate rooms, each with terrace seating overlooking a beautifully tended, flower-filled garden. It's about 1km beyond the main strip of accommodation on Ranthambhore Rd (although still 5km before the park's main gate) so it's much quieter than elsewhere.

The Ranthambhore Bagh
Hotel **$$$**

(☏221728; www.ranthambhore.com; Ranthambhore Rd; r/tent ₹3522/4041, incl meals ₹5626/6141; ❄ @ 🛜) This place has more of a safari-camp feel to it than other accommodation on Ranthambhore Rd, with tents dotted around a forested garden as well as well-appointed rooms in the main building. There's no pool, but the gardens have swings and a slide, making this a solid choice for young families.

ℹ Getting There & Away

Trains from Sawai Madhopur run five times daily to **Jaipur** (5.50am, 9.45am, 10.40am, 2.35pm and 6.55pm), although plenty of others run on selected days so you rarely have to wait more than an hour. The journey takes two hours. Unreserved 2nd-class seats cost ₹50; sleepers cost ₹140.

Five trains run daily to **Delhi** (6.28am, 7.05am, 12.30pm, 9.15pm and 11.02pm). Sleeper/3AC tickets cost around ₹190/490. Two daily trains go to **Agra**. The 13238 Kota-PNBE Express to Agra Cantonment leaves at 4.47pm, arrives at 11.05pm and costs ₹144 for a sleeper. The 59811 Haldighati Passenger leaves at 11.25pm, arrives at 6am and costs ₹85 for a sleeper.

Ranthambhore Fort
DAVID GARRY/GETTY IMAGES ©

Only one direct train goes to **Udaipur**; the 2963 Mewar Express. It leaves at 11.50pm, arrives at 7.20am and costs ₹201/529 for a sleeper/3AC ticket.

SOUTHERN RAJASTHAN

Udaipur

☏0294 / POP 451,000

Beside shimmering Lake Pichola, with the ochre and purple ridges of the wooded Aravalli Hills stretching away in every direction, Udaipur has a romantic setting unmatched in Rajasthan and arguably in all India. Fantastical palaces, temples, *havelis* and countless narrow, crooked, colourful streets add the human counterpoint to the city's natural charms. Its tag of 'the most romantic spot on the continent of India' was first applied in 1829 by Colonel James Tod, the East India Company's first Political Agent in the region. Today the romance is wearing ever so slightly thin as Udaipur strains to exploit this reputation for tourist rupees.

Take a step back from the hustle, however, and Udaipur still has its magic, not just in its marvellous palaces and monuments but in its matchless setting, the tranquillity of boat rides on the lake, the bustle of its ancient bazaars, the quaint old-world feel of its better hotels, its tempting shops and lovely surrounding countryside, which can be explored on foot, by bike or on horseback.

◉ Sights

Lake Pichola   Lake
(boat rides adult/child 10am-2pm ₹200/100, 3pm-5pm ₹500/250) Limpid and large, Lake Pichola reflects the cool grey-blue mountains on its rippling mirror-like surface. It was enlarged by Maharana Udai Singh II, following his foundation of the city. It is now 4km long and 3km wide, but remains shallow and dries up completely in severe droughts.

Udaipur

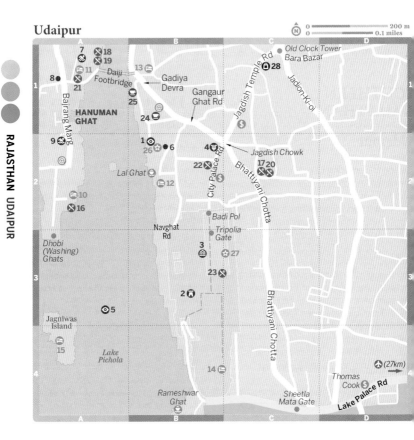

Boat rides leave roughly hourly from Rameshwar Ghat, within the City Palace complex (note, you have to pay ₹25 to enter). The trips make a stop at Jagmandir Island. You can also take 30-minute boat rides from **Lal Ghat**, without the need to enter the City Palace complex.

City Palace
Palace

(www.eternalmewar.in; adult/child ₹25/15, not charged if visiting City Palace Museum; ⏰7am-11pm) Surmounted by balconies, towers and cupolas towering over the lake, the imposing City Palace is Rajasthan's largest palace, with a facade 244m long and 30.4m high. Construction was begun by Maharana Udai Singh II, the city's founder, and it later became a conglom-

eration of structures built and extended by various maharanas, though it still manages to retain a surprising uniformity of design.

City Palace Museum
Museum

(adult/child ₹100/50, camera or video ₹200, audio guide ₹225, human guide ₹250; ⏰9.30am-5.30pm, last entry 4.30pm) The main part of the palace is open as the City Palace Museum, with rooms extravagantly decorated with mirrors, tiles and paintings, and housing a large, varied collection of artefacts.

Jagdish Temple
Hindu Temple

(⏰5.30am-2pm & 4-10pm) Entered by a steep, elephant-flanked flight of steps 150m north of the City Palace's Badi Pol entrance, this busy Indo-Aryan temple

Udaipur

was built by Maharana Jagat Singh in 1651.

Bagore-ki-Haveli Notable Building

(admission ₹30; ◷10am-5pm) This gracious 18th-century *haveli,* set on the water's edge in the Gangaur Ghat area, was built by a Mewar prime minister and has been carefully restored.

◉ Activities & Courses

Several hotels allow nonguests to use their swimming pools, including **Karohi Haveli** (₹200) and **Udai Kothi** (₹300), which has the only rooftop pool in town.

Krishna Ranch Horse Riding

(☎9828059505; www.krishnaranch.com; full day incl lunch ₹1200) A Dutch-Indian company specialising in guided horse safaris (it also does guided walks) through the beautiful countryside around Udaipur. The ranch, where accommodation is also available (single/double including meals and pick-up ₹1500/2500), is near Badi village, around 7km from town.

Millets of Mewar City Walks

(☎8890419048; www.milletsofmewar.com) As well as running cooking courses, management at the excellent restaurant Millets of Mewar also helps organise 2½-hour city walking tours where you can meet local artisans who live and work in Udaipur. Tours, which should be booked a day in advance, start from the restaurant at 10am.

Queen Cafe Cooking

(☎2430875, 9783786028; 14 Bajrang Marg, Hanuman Ghat; 2/4hr class ₹900/1500; ◷8.30am) Learn how to make Indian tea, flat breads, rice and four types of curries with the affable Meenu; owner, chef and busy mum at this homely little eatery. Class sizes: two to five people.

Hotel Krishna Niwas Painting

(☎2420163; www.hotelkrishnaniwas.com; 35 Lal Ghat; 2hr class ₹850; ◷11am-7pm) Jairaj Soni is a renowned artist who teaches miniature and classical painting. You can buy miniature paintings here too.

Detour:
History-Laden Day Trip

If you like fantastic forts or exquisite temples, then consider hiring a taxi for the day from Udaipur to visit the huge, remote fort of Kumbhalgarh and the sublime Jain temples at Ranakpur. It will cost you around ₹1500 per vehicle for the return trip. The drive through the forested Aravalli Hills is a highlight in itself.

An incredible stone fort, **Kumbhalgarh** (Indian/foreigner ₹5/100; ⏱9am-6pm) is situated 84km north of Udaipur. Built by Maharana Kumba in the 15th century, the colossal structure fulfills romantic expectations of Rajput grandeur. The fort's thick walls stretch for around 12km and it's possible to walk along them to complete a circuit of the fort (allow four to five hours). The walls enclose hundreds of temples (some intact, others in ruins), some of which date back to the 2nd century BC, plus palaces, gardens, step-wells and cannon bunkers.

Ninety kilometres north of Udaipur, the Jain Temples at **Ranakpur** (camera/video ₹100/300; ⏱Jains 6am-7pm, non-Jains noon-5pm) are an incredible feat of religious devotion. Carved from milk-white marble, the main temple contains a complicated series of 29 halls, supported by a forest of 1444 pillars (no two alike). It is the finest of its type in Rajasthan, and one the most important in India.

🛏 Sleeping

LAL GHAT AREA

Nukkad Guest House
Guesthouse $

(📞2411403; nukkad_raju@yahoo.com; 56 Ganesh Ghati; r ₹300-500, s/d without bathroom ₹100/200; @ 📶) Always busy with travellers, Nukkad has a relaxed atmosphere and a sociable, breezy upstairs restaurant with good Indian and international dishes (mains ₹60 to ₹85). Your hosts Raju and Kala are helpful, and you can join afternoon cooking classes and morning yoga sessions without stepping out the door. Rooms are simple, fan-cooled, clean and decent value; there's plenty of hot water and many rooms have cushioned window seats. Wi-fi wasn't working when we were here, but should be available.

Jagat Niwas Palace Hotel
Heritage Hotel $$$

(📞2420133; www.jagatniwaspalace.com; 23-25 Lal Ghat; r ₹1850-2950, lake facing ₹3250-4250; ❄ @ 📶) This leading Lal Ghat hotel set in two converted lakeside *havelis* takes the location cake. The lake-view rooms are charming, with carved wooden furniture, cushioned window seats and pretty prints. Non-lake-facing rooms are almost as comfortable and attractive, and considerably cheaper. The building is full of character, with lots of attractive sitting areas, terraces and courtyards, and it makes the most of its position with a picture-perfect rooftop restaurant. Wi-fi in lobby only.

Kankarwa Haveli
Heritage Hotel $$$

(📞2411457; www.kankarwahaveli.com; 26 Lal Ghat; r incl breakfast ₹3000-5000; ❄ @ 📶) This is one of Udaipur's few hotels that is a genuine old *haveli*. It's right by the lake, and the whitewashed rooms, set around a courtyard, have a lovely simplicity with splashes of colour. They are very small for the price, but have bags of character and the pricier ones look right onto Lake Pichola. Wi-fi in ground-floor courtyard only.

HANUMAN GHAT AREA

Dream Heaven
Guesthouse $

(☏2431038; www.dreamheaven.co.in; r ₹200-1000; ❄@☎) The best-value digs in Udaipur, Dream Heaven has a fabulous location (the views from the rooftop restaurant are sublime), simple but well-looked-after rooms and a friendly manager who is very helpful without being too keen to please. Deservedly popular. Wi-fi only on rooftop and upper rooms.

Karohi Haveli
Heritage Hotel $$$

(☏2430026; www.karohihaveli.com; r from ₹3500; ❄@☎≋) A beautifully renovated, three-storey 19th-century haveli with tastefully decorated rooms off a cool central marble courtyard. Quiet but welcoming. Has a rooftop restaurant, bar, garden lawn with lake views, lovely pool (nonguests ₹200) and wi-fi throughout.

Amet Haveli
Heritage Hotel $$$

(☏2431085; www.amethaveliudaipur.com; s/d ₹4800/5700; ❄@☎) This 350-year-old heritage building on the lake shore has delightful rooms with cushioned window seats and coloured glass with little shutters. They're set around a pretty little courtyard and pond. Splurge on one with a balcony or giant bathtub. One of Udaipur's most romantic restaurants, Ambrai, is part of the hotel. A swimming pool was under construction at the time of research.

CITY PALACE AREA

Taj Lake Palace
Heritage Hotel $$$

(☏2428800; www.tajhotels.com; r from ₹40,000; ❄@☎≋) The icon of Udaipur, this romantic white-marble palace seemingly floating on the lake is extraordinary, with open-air courtyards, lotus ponds and a small, mango-tree-shaded pool.

Rooms are hung with breezy silks and filled with carved furniture. Service is superb. Access is by boat from the hotel's own jetty in the City Palace gardens. Rates can vary a lot with season and demand: check the website.

Shiv Niwas Palace Hotel
Heritage Hotel $$$

(☏2528016; www.eternalmewar.in; City Palace Complex; r from ₹15,000; ❄@☎≋) This hotel, in the former palace guest quarters, has opulent common areas like its pool courtyard, bar and lovely lawn garden with a 30m-long royal procession mural. Some of the suites are truly palatial, filled with fountains and silver, but the standard rooms are not great value. Go for a suite, or just come for a drink (beer from ₹475), meal (mains ₹500 to ₹1000), or swim in the gorgeous marble pool (9am to 6pm, nonguests ₹300). Rates drop dramatically from April to September.

Mosaic, City Palace (p164)
DE AGOSTINI/L. ROMANO/GETTY IMAGES ©

Right: Traditional dancers **Below:** Jagdish Temple

(RIGHT) ANIA BLAZEJEWSKA/GETTY IMAGES ©; (BELOW) DIANA MAYFIELD/GETTY IMAGES ©

Eating

FURTHER AFIELD

Krishna Ranch　　　Cottages **$$**

(☏3291478, 9602192902; www.krishnaranch.com; s/d incl meals ₹1500/2500) 🌿 This delightful countryside retreat has five cottages set around the grounds of a small farm. Each comes with attached bathroom (with solar-heated hot-water shower), tasteful decor and farm views. All meals are included in the price and are prepared using organic produce grown on the farm. It's an ideal base for the hikes and horse treks which the management – a Dutch-Indian couple – organises from here, although you don't have to sign up for the treks to stay. The ranch is 7km from town, near the village of Badi, but there's free pick-up from Udaipur.

LAL GHAT AREA

Jagat Niwas Palace Hotel　　　Indian **$$**

(☏2420133; 23-25 Lal Ghat; mains ₹150-375; ⏱7-10am, noon-3pm & 6-10pm) A classy rooftop restaurant with superb lake views, delicious Indian cuisine and good service. Choose from an extensive selection of rich curries (tempered for Western tastes) – mutton, chicken, fish, veg – as well as the tandoori classics. There's a tempting cocktail menu (from ₹255) and the beer (from ₹165) is icy. It's wise to book ahead for dinner.

Lotus Cafe　　　Multicuisine **$**

(15 Bhattiyani Chotta; dishes ₹50-150; ⏱9am-10.30pm) Run by an Australian-Indian couple, this funky little restaurant produces fabulous chicken dishes (predominantly Indian, including some Rajashtani specialities), plus salads, baked potatoes and plenty of vegetarian fare. It's ideal

for meeting and greeting other travellers, with a mezzanine to loll about on and cool background sounds. The management's latest venture, a multicuisine rooftop restaurant called **Hinglish**, was about to open two doors up from here when we last visited.

O'Zen Restaurant Multicuisine $$
(mains ₹100-300; ⏱8.30am-11pm) A trendy new addition to City Palace Rd, this stylish 1st-floor restaurant-cafe does a range of Indian curries plus Italian pizza and pasta. It's bright and modern, does good coffee (₹50 to ₹70) and beer (₹180), has free wi-fi and some interesting views of the street below.

HANUMAN GHAT AREA

Millets of Mewar Indian $
(www.milletsofmewar.com; Hanuman Ghat; mains ₹80-140; ⏱8.30am-10.30pm; 📶) 🌱 Our favourite restaurant in Udaipur, this place not only does the healthiest food in town, but its dishes are also super tasty and fabulous value for money. Local millet is

used where possible instead of less environmentally sound wheat and rice, there are vegan options, gluten-free dishes, fresh salads, and juices and herbal teas. There are multigrain sandwiches and millet pizzas, but also regular curries, Indian street-food snacks, pasta and even pancakes. The coffee is deliciously unhealthy, and there's ice cream and chocolate pudding to go with the millet cookies on the unusual desert menu. The manager is young, friendly and laid back, and organises cookery classes and guided city walks.

Jasmin Multicuisine $
(mains ₹60-90; ⏱8.30am-11pm) Tasty vegetarian dishes are cooked up here in a lovely, quiet, open-air spot looking out on the quaint Daiji footbridge. There are plenty of Indian options, and some original variations on the usual multicuisine theme, including Korean and Israeli dishes. The ambience is super-relaxed and service is friendly. Next door the **Little Prince** (mains ₹80-130) has the same

setting and a very similar menu with slightly higher prices.

Ambrai   North Indian $$$
(☏2431085; Amet Haveli hotel; mains ₹250-400; ☺12.30-3pm & 7.30-10.30pm) The cuisine at this scenic restaurant – at lakeshore level, looking across to Lake Palace Hotel, Lal Ghat and the City Palace – does justice to its fabulous position. Highly atmospheric at night, Ambrai feels like a French park, with its wrought-iron furniture, dusty ground and large shady trees, and there's a terrific bar to complement the dining. Call ahead to reserve a table by the water's edge.

CITY PALACE

Note, you have to pay the ₹25 City Palace entrance fee to access the following.

Paantya Restaurant   Indian $$$
(☏2528016; Shiv Niwas Palace Hotel; mains ₹500-1000; ☺noon-3pm & 7-10.30pm) Most captivating in the evening, this semi-formal restaurant in the ritzy Shiv Niwas Palace has indoor seating, but if the weather's warm enough it's best out in the open-air courtyard by the pool. Indian classical music is performed nightly, and the food is great. For local flavour try the very tasty *laal maas dhungar,* a Rajasthani spiced and smoked mutton dish. A beer will set you back a cool ₹475.

Palki Khana   Italian $$$
(City Palace; mains ₹300-500; ☺9am-6pm) This informal terrace restaurant is the most popular place to refuel during a tour of the City Palace complex. Located centrally in the large open courtyard beside the entrance to the museum, it does mostly Italian dishes as well as good-quality wine, beer (from ₹350) and coffee (₹110 to ₹150). Note, drinks are half price between 4.30pm and 5.30pm.

🍷 Drinking

Most guesthouses have a roof terrace serving up cold Kingfishers with views over the lazy waters of Lake Pichola. Particularly worth considering are Jagat Niwas Palace and Dream Heaven. For a drink beside the water's edge, try Jasmin restaurant or its neighbour The Little Prince. For something more upmarket, head to Ambrai restaurant.

Cafe Edelweiss   Cafe
(73 Gangaur Ghat Rd; coffee from ₹50; ☺8.30am-8pm; 📶) An itsy piece of Europe that appeals to homesick and discerning travellers with its baked snacks (sticky cinnamon rolls, squidgy blueberry chocolate cake, apple strudel) and good strong coffee.

Jheel's Ginger Coffee Bar   Cafe
(Jheel Guest House; coffee ₹50-100; ☺8am-8pm; 📶) Small but slick aircon-cooled cafe by the water's edge on the ground floor of Jheel

Guest House. Large windows afford good lake views, and the coffee is excellent. Also does a range of cakes and snacks. Note, you can take your coffee up to the open-air rooftop restaurant if you like, but there's no alcohol served here.

Panera Bar
Bar
(Shiv Niwas Palace Hotel; beer from ₹475, shots from ₹250; ⊙11.30am-10pm) Sink into plush sofas surrounded by huge mirrors, royal portraits and beautiful paintwork, or sit out by the pool, and be served like a maharaja.

Anand Bar
Bar
(Ambrai Restaurant, Amet Haveli Hotel; beer from ₹150; ⊙11.30am-10.30pm) The fabulous lakeside restaurant Ambrai, at Amet Haveli hotel, doubles as a terrace bar, and is a classy place for a pre-dinner drink. You can grab a small bottle of Kingfisher for ₹150, but there are also cocktails (from ₹375) and a reasonable wine list (from ₹450 per glass).

⭐ Entertainment

Dharohar
Dance, Puppetry
(☑2523858; Bagore-ki-Haveli; admission Indian/foreigner ₹60/100, camera ₹100; ⊙7-8pm) The beautiful Bagore-ki-Haveli hosts the best (and most convenient) opportunity to see Rajasthani folk dancing, with nightly one-hour shows of colourful, energetic Mewari, Bhil and western Rajasthani dances, as well as some traditional Rajasthani puppetry.

Mewar Sound & Light Show
Cultural Program
(Manek Chowk, City Palace; lower/upper seating English show ₹150/400, Hindi show ₹100/200; ⊙7pm Sep-Feb, 7.30pm Mar-Apr, 8pm May-Aug) Fifteen centuries of intriguing Mewar history are squeezed into one atmospheric hour of commentary and light switching – in English from September to April, in Hindi other months.

🔒 Shopping

Tourist-oriented shops – selling miniature paintings, wood carvings, silver, bangles and other jewellery, traditional shoes, spices, leather-bound handmade-paper notebooks, ornate knives, camel-bone boxes and a large variety of textiles – line the streets radiating from Jagdish Chowk. Bargain hard. Udaipur is known for its local crafts, particularly its miniature paintings in the Rajput-Mughal style. To find out more, ask at the art workshop at Hotel Krishna Niwas.

Sadhna
Clothing
(☑2454655; www.sadhna.org; Jagdish Temple Rd; ⊙10am-7pm) ✒ This is the outlet for Seva Mandir, an NGO set up in 1969 to help rural women. The small shop sells attractive fixed-price textiles, including women's clothing, bags and shawls, plus a small range of jewellery. Profits go to the artisans and towards community development work.

ℹ Information

Medical Services

GBH American Hospital (☑24hr enquiries 2426000, emergency 9352304050; www.gbhamericanhospital.com; Meera Girls College Rd, 101 Kothi Bagh, Bhatt Ji Ki Bari) Modern, reader-recommended private hospital with 24-hour emergency service, about 2km northeast of the Lal Ghat area.

Money

There are a couple of ATMs near Jagdish Temple.

Thomas Cook (Lake Palace Rd; ⊙9.30am-6.30pm Mon-Sat) Changes cash and travellers cheques and gives cash advances on credit cards.

ℹ Getting There & Away

Air

Air India (☑2410999, airport office 2655453; www.airindia.com; Saheli Rd, 222/16 Mumal Towers) Flies to Mumbai and Delhi daily.

Jet Airways (☑5134000; www.jetairways.com; at the airport) Flies direct to Delhi and Mumbai daily.

Train

An autorickshaw between the train station and Jagdish Chowk should cost around ₹50. There's a prepaid autorickshaw stand at the station, though, so use that when you arrive.

There are no direct trains to Jodhpur or Jaisalmer.

For **Pushkar**, four daily trains make the five-hour journey to Ajmer (6.15am, 2.15pm, 5.20pm and 10.20pm).

Three trains run daily to **Jaipur** (6.15am, 2.15pm and 10.20pm), taking around seven hours.

Two daily trains (5.20pm and 6.15pm) make the 12-hour trip to **Delhi**.

Only one daily train runs to **Agra** (10.20pm).

Getting Around

To/From the Airport

A prepaid taxi to the Lal Ghat area costs ₹400.

WESTERN RAJASTHAN

Jodhpur

✆ 0291 / POP 1,000,000 MILLION

Mighty Mehrangarh, the muscular fort that towers over the Blue City of Jodhpur, is a magnificent spectacle and

Jodhpur

an architectural masterpiece. Around Mehrangarh's base, the old city, a jumble of Brahmin-blue cubes, stretches out to the 10km-long, 16th-century city wall. The 'Blue City' really is blue! Inside is a tangle of winding, glittering, medieval streets, which never seem to lead where you expect them to, scented by incense, roses and sewers, with shops and bazaars selling everything from trumpets and temple decorations to snuff and saris.

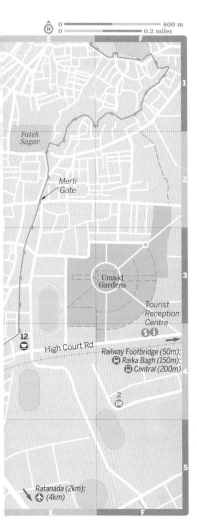

◎ Sights & Activities

Mehrangarh   Fort

(www.mehrangarh.org; museum admission Indian/foreigner ₹60/400, camera/video ₹100/200, guide ₹200; ☺9am-5pm) Rising perpendicular and impregnable from a rocky hill that itself stands 120m above Jodhpur's skyline, Mehrangarh is one of the most magnificent forts in India. The battlements are 6m to 36m high, and as the building materials were chiselled from the rock on which the fort stands, the structure merges with its base. Still run by the Jodhpur royal family, Mehrangarh is packed with history and legend.

🛌 Sleeping

The old city has something like 100 guesthouses, most of which scramble for your custom as soon as you get within breathing distance of Sardar Market.

To avoid the madness, arrange a hotel pick-up from the train or bus station if you can.

OLD CITY

Shivam Paying Guest House
Guesthouse $

(☎2610688; www.shivamguesthouse.com; r ₹200-800; ❄) Decent, hassle-free budget guesthouse run by honest management. Has cosy rooms, (very) steep staircases and a lovely little rooftop restaurant with free wi-fi.

Krishna Prakash Heritage Haveli
Heritage Hotel $$

(☎2633448; www.kpheritage.net; Nayabas; r incl breakfast ₹1000-4000; ❄@✈) This multilevel 1902 *haveli* right under the fort walls is good value and a peaceful choice. It has prettily painted furniture, murals and old family portraits, and rooms are well proportioned; the deluxe ones are a bit more spruced up, generally a bit bigger, and set on the upper floors, so airier. There's a small covered swimming pool and a relaxing terrace restaurant.

Shahi Guest House
Heritage Guesthouse $$

(☎2623802; www.shahiguesthouse.net; Gandhi St, City Police; r ₹1500-2750; ❄🛜) Shahi is an interesting guesthouse developed from a 350-year-old zenana. There's lots of cool stone, and narrow walkways surrounding a petite courtyard. The six rooms are individual and spacious yet cosy, and Anu and her family, who run the place, are charming. There is a delightful rooftop restaurant with fort views.

Pal Haveli
Heritage Hotel $$$

(☎3293328; www.palhaveli.com; Gulab Sagar; r incl breakfast ₹3500-8500; ❄@🛜) This stunning *haveli*, the best and most attractive in the old city, was built by the Thakur of Pal in 1847. There are 21 charming, spacious rooms, mostly large and elaborately decorated in traditional heritage style, surrounding a cool central courtyard. The family still lives here and can show you its small museum. Three restaurants serve excellent food, including rooftop **Indique** with its fine views.

Raas
Boutique Hotel $$$

(☎2636455; www.raasjodhpur.com; Tunvarji-ka-Jhalra; r incl breakfast ₹17,000-21,000; ❄@🛜✈) Developed from a 19th-century city mansion, Jodhpur's first contemporary-style boutique hotel is a splendid retreat of clean, uncluttered style, hidden behind a big castle-like gateway. If you fancy a change from the heritage aesthetic that prevails in Rajasthan's top-end hotels, Raas' clean, uncluttered style and subtle lighting are just the ticket. The red-stone-and-terrazzo rooms are not massive, but they come with plenty of luxury touches and have balconies with great Mehrangarh views or small private gardens. The terrace restaurant

Mehrangarh (p173) outer walls
WALTER BIBIKOW/GETTY IMAGES ©

(mains ₹400 to ₹800) is also a classy affair.

OLD CITY (NAVCHOKIYA)

Singhvi's Haveli
Heritage Guesthouse **$$**

(☏2624293; www.singhvihaveli.com; Ramdevji-ka-Chowk, Navchokiya; r ₹400-2400; ❄@🛜) This red-sandstone, family-run, 500-year-old *haveli* is an understated gem. Run by two friendly brothers, Singhvi's has 13 individual rooms, ranging from the simple to the magnificent Maharani Suite with 10 windows and a fort view. The relaxing and romantic vegetarian restaurant is decorated with sari curtains and floor cushions, and the interior lounge is a delight.

SOUTH OF THE OLD CITY

Durag Niwas Guest House
Guesthouse **$**

(☏2512385; www.durag -niwas.com; 1st Old Public Park Lane; r ₹400-600, with AC ₹1000-1400; ❄) 🍃 A warm, friendly, well-
established family guesthouse set away from the hustle of the old city. Has good home-cooked food, a cute interior court-yard, a cushion-floored, sari-curtained area on the roof for relaxing, and honest, helpful staff. Management also offers cultural tours – including half-day Bishnoi Village tours – and the opportunity to do volunteer work with the women's em-powerment NGO, **Sambhali Trust** (www. sambhali-trust.org). To get here, cross the railway footbridge near Raika Bagh Train Station then take the second right. Note, don't confuse this place with nextdoor Durag Villas Guesthouse, another colour-ful place, but which has nothing to do with the the Sambhali Trust.

✖ Eating

As well as the places reviewed here, remember that most guesthouses have restaurants (usually on the roof, with a fort view).

Countryside Retreat

Rohet Garh (☏02936-268231; www.rohetgarh.com; s/d ₹5000/6000; ❄@🛜♨), in Rohet village, 40km south of Jodhpur on the Pali road, is one of the area's most appealing heritage hotels. This 350-year-old, lovingly tended manor has masses of character and a tranquil atmosphere, which obviously helped Bruce Chatwin when he wrote *The Songlines* here, and William Dalrymple when he began *City of Djinns* in the same room, No 15. Rohet Garh has a gorgeous colonnaded pool, charming green gardens, great food (breakfast/lunch/dinner ₹500/600/700) and lovely, individual rooms. It also possesses a stable of fine Marwari horses and organises rides, from two-hour evening trots (₹2000) to six-day countryside treks, sleeping in luxury tents.

A taxi here is around ₹800 from Jodhpur.

Jhankar Choti Haveli
Multicuisine **$**

(mains ₹90-150; ⏰8am-10pm; 🛜) Stone walls, big cane chairs, prettily painted woodwork and whirring fans set the scene at this front-garden travellers' favourite. It serves up Rajasthani specialities as part of its pure vegetarian Indian menu (the owners are Jain, so no eggs or alcohol either), has fresh coffee for breakfast and there's candlelit seating on the rooftop come evening.

Kalinga Restaurant
Indian **$$**

(off Station Rd; mains ₹130-300; ⏰8am-11pm) This smart restaurant near Jodhpur train station has air-con, a well-stocked bar (beer from ₹130), and tasty veg and non-veg North Indian tandooris and curries, including a selection of kebabs. Try the

Jodhpur shopkeeper

GUYLAIN DOYLE/GETTY IMAGES ©

lal maans, a mouthwatering Rajasthani mutton curry.

Mid Town
Indian $$

(off Station Rd; mains ₹100-150; ⏱7am-10.30pm) This clean, air-conditioned place does great vegetarian food, including some Rajasthani specialities,

and some particular to Jodhpur, such as *chakki-ka-sagh* (wheat dumpling cooked in rich gravy), *bajara-ki-roti pachkuta* (*bajara* wheat roti with local dry vegetables) and *kabuli* (vegetables with rice, milk, bread and fruit). Also does beer (from ₹188).

Indique
Indian $$$

(3293328; Pal Haveli; mains ₹250-350) This candlelit rooftop restaurant at the Pal Haveli hotel is the perfect place for a romantic dinner. Even murky Gulab Sagar glistens at night and the views to the fort, clock tower and Umaid Bhawan are superb. The food covers traditional tandoori, biryanis and North Indian curries, and you won't be disappointed by the old favourites – butter chicken and rogan josh. Has a full drinks menu too (beer from ₹200).

🍷 Drinking

Coffee drinkers will enjoy the precious beans and espresso machines at the deliciously air-conditioned **Cafe Sheesh Mahal** (Pal Haveli; coffee from ₹80; ⏱9am-9pm), which also has free wi-fi. Plenty of rooftop restaurants do real coffee too, with varying results. For a reliable dose of double-shot espresso, there's a branch of **Café Coffee Day** (High Court Rd, Ansal Plaza; coffee from ₹50; ⏱10am-11pm) in the shopping mall on High Court Rd.

Shri Mishrilal Hotel
Cafe

(Sardar Market; lassi ₹30; ⏱8.30am-10pm) Just inside the southern gate of Sardar Market, this place has been going since 1927 and although it looks nothing fancy it whips up the most superb creamy *makhania* lassis; the best you're likely to try anywhere on your travels. Also does tasty *kachori* (₹30) and other Indian snacks.

18 Century Bar
Bar

(Pal Haveli; beer from ₹200; ⏱11am-5pm) Pal Haveli's delightful hotel bar, halfway up the stairs to the rooftop restaurant

Indique, is replete with horse-saddle stools and enough heritage paraphernalia to have you ordering pink gins. It closes at 5pm, after which you can continue ordering drinks on the rooftop until the restaurant closes.

🔒 Shopping

MV Spices   Food, Drink
(www.mvspices.com; ⊙9am-9pm) The most famous and reputable spice shop in Jodhpur (and believe us, there are lots of pretenders!), MV Spices has several small branches around town (including a stall outside the entrance to the fort) that are run by the seven daughters of the founder of the original stall. It will cost around ₹80 to ₹100 for 100g bags of spices, and the owners will email you recipes so you can use your spices correctly when you get home.

Sambhali Boutique   Clothing, Accessories
(⊙10am-8pm Mon-Sat, noon-8pm Sun) 🖉 This small but interesting fixed-price shop sells colourful clothes and handicrafts made by women who have learned craft skills with the Sambhali Trust.

ℹ️ Information

There are foreign-friendly **ATMs** dotted around the city. We've marked some on our map. There are very few in the old city, apart from one near Shahi Guest House. **Internet cafes** charge around ₹30 to ₹40 per hour. Again, they're dotted around town, especially in the old city.

Om Forex (Sardar Market; internet per hr ₹30; ⊙9am-10pm) Internet place which also exchanges currency and travellers cheques.

Police (Sardar Market; ⊙24hr) Small police post inside the market's north gate.

Tourist Reception Centre (📞2545083; High Court Rd; ⊙9am-6pm Mon-Fri) Offers a free city map and willingly answers questions.

ℹ️ Getting There & Away

Air

Jet Airways (📞2515551; www.jetairways.com; airport) and **Air India** (📞2510758, airport office 2512617; www.airindia.com; 2 West Patel Nagar, Circuit House Rd) both fly daily to Delhi and Mumbai. (To find the Air India office, walk along Ratanada Rd then turn left.)

Taxi

You can organise taxis for intercity trips (or longer) through most accommodation places, or deal direct with drivers. There's a taxi stand outside Jodhpur train station.

Train

The computerised **booking office** (Station Rd; ⊙8am-8pm Mon-Sat, to 1.45pm Sun) is 300m northeast of Jodhpur train station.

Two daily trains make the six-hour trip to **Jaisalmer** (5.10am and 11.45pm). Five go to **Jaipur** (6.10am, 9.45am, 8pm, 8.30pm and 11pm) in five to six hours. Two go to **Delhi** (8pm and 11pm), arriving at 6.25am and 11.10am respectively. Two also go to **Mumbai** (3pm and 6.45pm), arriving at 9.40am and 11.35am respectively.

For **Pushkar**, only one train goes to Ajmer (7am). There are no direct trains to Udaipur.

Major Trains from Jodhpur

DESTINATION	TRAIN	DEPARTURE TIME	ARRIVAL TIME	FARE (₹; SLEEPER/3AC)
Ajmer	54801 Jodhpur-Ajmer Fast Passenger	7am	12.40pm	88/362
Delhi	12462 Mandor Exp	8pm	6.25am	272/734
Jaipur	14854 Marudhar Exp	9.45am	3.30pm	158/428
Jaisalmer	14810 Jodhpur-Jaisalmer Exp	11.45pm	5.30am	155/419
Mumbai	14707 Ranakpur Exp	3pm	9.40am	323/912

Jaisalmer

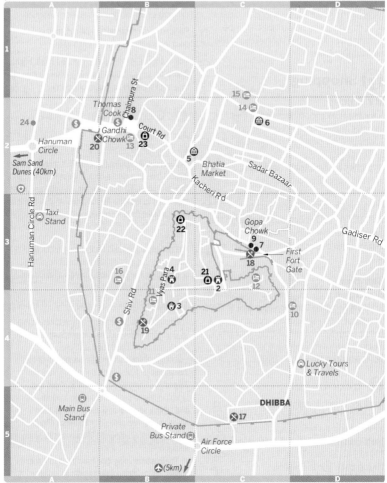

Thomas Cook

Chatrpura St

Court Rd

24

Hanuman Circle

Gandhi Chowk

20

13 23

5

Bhatia Market

Kacheri Rd

Sadar Bazaar

15

14

6

Sam Sand Dunes (40km)

Hanuman Circle Rd

Taxi Stand

22

Gopa Chowk

9 7

18

First Fort Gate

Gadiser Rd

16

Shiv Rd

Vyas Para

4

11

3

19

21

2

12

10

Lucky Tours & Travels

Main Bus Stand

Private Bus Stand

DHIBBA

17

Air Force Circle

✈(5km)

ⓘ Getting Around

To & From the Airport

The airport is 5km south of the city centre; at least ₹100/200 by auto/taxi.

Autorickshaw

Autorickshaws between the clock tower area and the train stations or central bus stand should be about ₹20 to ₹30.

Jaisalmer

📞02992 / POP 78,000

The fort of Jaisalmer is a breathtaking sight: a massive sandcastle rising from the sandy plains like a mirage from a bygone era. No place better evokes exotic camel-train trade routes and desert mystery. Ninety-nine bastions encircle the fort's still-inhabited twisting lanes. Inside are shops swaddled in bright em-

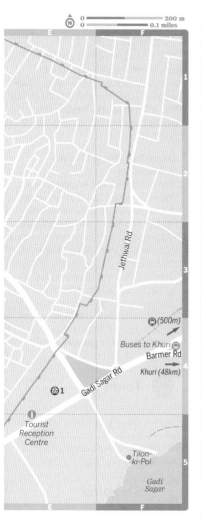

0   200 m
0   0.1 miles

Jaisalmer

◎ Sights

◎ Activities, Courses & Tours

◎ Sleeping

◎ Eating

◎ Shopping

◎ Transport

◎ Sights

Jaisalmer Fort   Fort

Founded in 1156 by the Rajput ruler Jaisal and reinforced by subsequent rulers, Jaisalmer Fort was the focus of a number of battles between the Bhatis, the Mughals of Delhi and the Rathores of Jodhpur. You enter the fort from its east side, near Gopa Chowk, and pass through four massive gates on the zigzagging route to the upper part. The fourth gate opens into a square, Dashera Chowk, where Jaisalmer Fort's uniqueness

broideries, a royal palace and numerous businesses looking for your tourist rupee. Despite the commercialism it's hard not to be enchanted by this desert citadel. Beneath the ramparts, particularly to the north, the narrow streets of the old city conceal magnificent *havelis,* all carved from the same golden-honey sandstone as the fort – hence Jaisalmer's designation as the Golden City.

179

If You Like...
Havelis

Inside the fort but outside it, too (especially in the streets to the north), Jaisalmer is replete with the fairy-tale architecture of *havelis* – gorgeously carved stone doorways, *jali* (carved lattice) screens, balconies and turrets.

1 PATWA-KI-HAVELI
(Indian/foreigner ₹20/50; ◷10am-5pm) The biggest fish in the *haveli* pond is Patwa-ki-Haveli, which towers over a narrow lane, its intricate stonework like honey-coloured lace. It is divided into five sections and was built between 1800 and 1860 by five Jain brothers who made their fortunes in brocade and jewellery. It's most impressive from the outside, though the first of the five sections is open as the privately owned **Kothari's Patwa-ki-Haveli Museum** (Indian/foreigner ₹50/150, camera/video ₹50/70), which richly evokes 19th-century life. Touts in the lane outside can be a pain here.

2 NATHMAL-KI-HAVELI
(◷8am-7pm) This late-19th-century *haveli* also used to be a prime minister's house and is still partly inhabited. It also contains some tourist shops. It has an extraordinary exterior, dripping with carvings, and the 1st floor has some beautiful paintings using 1.5kg of gold. A doorway is surrounded by 19th-century British postcards and there's a picture of Queen Victoria. The left and right wings were the work of two brothers, whose competitive spirits apparently produced this virtuoso work – the two sides are similar, but not identical.

becomes apparent: this is a living fort, with about 3000 people residing within its walls.

Towering over the fort's main square, and partly built on top of the Hawa Pol (the fourth fort gate), is the former rulers' elegant seven-storey **Fort Palace** (Indian/foreigner incl compulsory audio guide ₹50/300, camera/video ₹100/200; ◷8am-6pm Apr-Oct, 9am-6pm Nov-Mar). The 1½-hour audio-guide tour, available in six languages, is included in your ticket price (whether you

want it or not). It's worthwhile, but you must deposit ₹2000 or an official form of photo ID to get it.

Within the fort walls is a mazelike, interconnecting treasure trove of seven beautiful yellow-sandstone **Jain temples** (Indian/foreigner ₹30/150, camera ₹50; ◷Chandraprabhu 7am-1pm, other temples 11am-1pm) dating from the 15th and 16th centuries.

Desert Cultural Centre & Museum   Museum
(Indian/foreigner ₹20/50, puppet shows Indian/foreigner ₹30/50, camera/video ₹20/50, combined museum-show ticket ₹70; ◷9am-8pm, puppet shows 6.30pm, 7.30pm) Next to the Tourist Reception Centre, this interesting little museum has material on the history of Rajasthan's different princely states, and exhibits on traditional Rajasthani culture. Features include Rajasthani music (with video), textiles and a *phad* scroll painting. It also hosts nightly half-hour **puppet shows** with English commentary.

Tours

The Tourist Reception Centre runs a handful of tours, including sunset tours to the Sam sand dunes (₹200 per person, minimum four people). Add ₹100 if you'd like a short camel ride too.

Sleeping

Staying in the fort is the most atmospheric and romantic choice, but be aware of the pressure tourism is exerting on the fort's infrastructure.

OUTSIDE THE FORT

Residency Centre Point   Guesthouse $
(☏252883, 9414760421; residency_guesthouse@yahoo.com; Kumbhara Para; r ₹450; @) Near Patwa-ki-Haveli, this friendly, family-run guesthouse has five clean, spacious doubles in a lovely 250-year-old

building. Rooms vary in size – budget by price but midrange in quality. The rooftop restaurant has superb fort views and offers home-cooked food.

Roop Mahal
Hotel **$**

(📞 251700; www.hotelroopmahal.com; r ₹300-1500) Clean spacious rooms in a new building, trustworthy management, fort views from the rooftop restaurant (mains ₹80 to ₹180) and free wi-fi throughout. A solid budget choice, but with some fancier rooms too.

Desert Moon
Guesthouse **$$**

(📞 250116, 9414149350; www.desert-moonguesthouse.com; Achalvansi Colony; s ₹500-800, d ₹800-1200; ❄ @ 🛜) Run by Lois (a New Zealander who's been living in Jaisalmer for more than 12 years) and her Rajasthani husband, Chanesar, this smart guesthouse, a 10-minute walk from Gandhi Chowk, enjoys a wonderfully peaceful location beneath the royal *chhatri* (burial tombs). Rooms are cool, clean and comfortable,and the rooftop vegetarian restaurant has fort and *chhatri* views. It's ₹50 to ₹60 in an auto from the train station, but there's free pick-up if you call ahead. If you're walking here, head north from Hanuman Circle until you reach Marina Mahal Jain Restaurant (500m) on your left. Desert Moon is down a track about 100m behind this restaurant.

KB Lodge
Hotel **$$$**

(📞 253833; www.killabhawan.com; Patwa Haveli; r ₹1800, with AC ₹2500; ❄ 🛜) Under the same management as the luxury Hotel Killa Bhawan, KB Lodge has more of a guesthouse feel to it, with just five stylish rooms in a small building overlooking the plaza behind Patwa Haveli. There's wi-fi throughout and the pleasant rooftop restaurant, KB Cafe, is has delightful views of the old town and the fort.

Hotel Nachana Haveli
Heritage Hotel **$$$**

(📞 252110; www.nachanahaveli.com; Gandhi Chowk; s/d ₹3150/3500; ❄ @) This 280-year-old royal *haveli,* set around three courtyards – one with a tinkling

Jaisalmer Don't Miss List

RADHIKA DHUMAL IS A DELHI-BASED CONSERVATION ARCHITECT, OVERSEEING JAISALMER IN JEOPARDY'S STREETSCAPE PROJECT

1 THE FORT
Jaisalmer Fort owes its magnificence to its location on the main trade route linking India to Egypt, Arabia, Persia, Africa and the West. Its prosperity was reflected in its *havelis,* intricately carved wood and sandstone mansions, in the magnificent Royal Palace complex, among the oldest recorded buildings in Rajasthan, and in the incomparable Jain Temple complex, dating from the 12th and 13th centuries. Carved in the Dilwara style from the local yellow sandstone, the complex is dedicated to Rakhab and Shambhaydev, the famous Jain hermits known as *tirthankars*.

2 CAMEL TREKKING
No visit to Jaisalmer is complete without a visit to the Thar desert. I recommend a moonlight camel trek over the dunes followed by dinner under the stars.

3 SUNSET VIEWS
The most sublime view of Jaisalmer Fort is from the roof of **Jawahar Niwas Hotel** (www.jawaharniwaspalace.co.in; 1 Bada Bagh Rd); sip a gin and tonic as the setting sun reflects on the golden sandstone. Originally a royal guesthouse, Jawahar Niwas is 800m from the bustle of the fort.

4 HIKING
I would recommend the 5km hike around Jaisalmer Fort's 99 bastions, preferably at dawn, as the city sleeps and your only companions are the slumbering cows.

5 DINING
At Jaisal Italy, you can dine indoors if the desert nights turn cold, or out on the terrace while watching a performance of Rajasthani musicians and dancers.

Jaisalmer Camel Safaris

Trekking by camel is the most evocative and fun way to sample Thar Desert life. Don't expect dune seas – it's mostly arid scrubland sprinkled with villages and wind turbines, with occasional dune areas popping out here and there.

Most trips now include jeep rides to get you to less frequented areas. The camel riding is then done in two-hour batches, one before lunch, one after. It's hardly camel *trekking*, but it's a lot of fun nevertheless.

BEFORE YOU GO

Competition between safari organisers is cut-throat and standards vary. Most hotels and guesthouses are very happy to organise a camel safari for you. While many provide a good service, some may cut corners and take you for the kind of ride you didn't have in mind. A few low-budget hotels in particular exert considerable pressure on guests to take 'their' safari. Others specifically claim 'no safari hassle'.

You can also organise a safari directly with one of the several reputable specialist agencies in Jaisalmer. Since these agencies depend exclusively on safari business it's particularly in their interest to satisfy their clients. It's a good idea to talk to other travellers and ask two or three operators what they're offering.

The best-known dunes, at Sam (40km west of Jaisalmer), are always crowded in the evening and are more of a carnival than a back-to-nature experience. The dunes near Khuri are also quite busy at sunset, but quiet the rest of the time. Operators all sell trips now to 'nontouristy' and 'off the beaten track' areas. Ironically, this has made Khuri quieter again, although Sam still hums with day-dripper activity.

With jeep transfers included, typical rates are between ₹1100 and ₹1700 per person for a one-day-one-night trip (leaving one morning, and returning the next). This should include meals, mineral water and blankets, and sometimes a thin mattress. Check that there will be one camel for each rider. You can pay for greater levels of comfort (eg tents, better food), but always get it all down in writing.

You should get a cheaper rate (₹900 to ₹1500 per person) if you leave Jaisalmer in the afternoon and return the following morning. A quick sunset ride in the dunes at Sam costs around ₹550 per person, including jeep transfer.

WHICH SAFARI?

○ **Sahara Travels** (☎252609; www.saharatravelsjaisalmer.com; Gopa Chowk) Now run by the son of the late LN Bissa (aka Mr Desert), a real Jaisalmer character, this place is still very professional and transparent. Trips are to 'nontouristy' areas only. Prices for an overnight trip (9am to 11am): ₹1400 per person, all inclusive.

○ **Trotters** (☎9828929974; www.trotterscamelsafarijaisalmer.com; ◷5.30am-7.30pm) Run by 'Del Boy' – who else? – this company is also run transparently, with a clear price list in the office showing everything on offer. Does trips to 'nontouristy' areas as well as cheaper jaunts to Sam or Khuri. Prices for an overnight trip (8am to 10am): ₹1100 to ₹1200 per person, all inclusive.

○ **Thar Desert Tours** (☎255656; www.tharcamelsafarijaisalmer.com; Gandhi Chowk; ◷8.30am-7.30pm) Located at Gandhi Chowk, this well-run operator charges ₹950 per person per day, adjusting prices depending on trip times. They are slightly pricier than Sahara or Trotters, but we also receive good feedback about them. Their system is for customers to pay 80% up front.

○ There are several other options, including hotel-organised safaris. Note that recommendations here should not be a substitute for doing your own research.

fountain – is a fascinating hotel. The raw sandstone rooms have arched stone ceilings and the ambience of a medieval castle. They are sumptuously and romantically decorated, though some lack much natural light.

1st Gate
Hotel $$$

(☏8696008365; www.1stgate.in; r incl breakfast ₹6500; ✳@🛜) Italian-designed and super slick, this newcomer is Jaisalmer's most sophisticated modern hotel and it is beautiful throughout. The location lends it one of the most dramatic fort views in town, especially from its split-level open-air restaurant-cafe. Rooms are immaculate and the food (Italian and Indian) and coffee are both top notch. Wi-fi throughout. No pool.

IN THE FORT

Desert Boy's Guest House
Heritage Hotel $$

(☏253091; www.desertboysguesthouse.com; r ₹500-3000) Has 15 beautifully decorated rooms. The cheaper ones have interior windows, but others have sweeping desert views. Rooms are bright and colourful, bathrooms are modern and the place is littered with antique-looking furniture. Wi-fi in some areas only. Restaurant has great views.

Hotel Killa Bhawan
Heritage Hotel $$$

(☏251204; www.killabhawan.com; 445 Kotri Para; r incl breakfast ₹6500-11,000; ✳@🛜) A mini-labyrinth of a place combining three old houses set right on the fort walls. French-owned and designed, it has vividly coloured rooms, attractive little sitting areas and all sorts of intriguing arts and crafts. Rooms are small for the prices, but are decorated exquisitely. No restaurant, but tea, coffee and breakfast are all included.

Eating

Sun Set Palace
Multicuisine $

(Fort; mains ₹90-200) This restaurant has floor cushions and low tables on an airy terrace on the fort's west side. Pretty good vegetarian Indian dishes are

Courtyard inside Jaisalmer Fort (p179)

MARTIN CHILD/GETTY IMAGES ©

prepared, as well as Chinese and Italian options. Beer available.

Desert Boy's Dhani
Indian $$

(mains ₹100-135; ⏰11am-4pm & 7-11pm) An unusual walled-garden restaurant where tables are spread around a large stone-paved courtyard with a big tree. Rajasthani music and dance is performed from 8pm to 10pm most nights, and it's a very pleasant place to eat excellent, good-value Rajasthani and other Indian veg dishes. Does beer too (from ₹200).

Jaisal Italy
Italian $$

(First Fort Gate; mains ₹120-200; ⏰8.30am-10.30pm; 📶) Though it's run by the same family as Lassi Shop, you won't have to worry about *bhang*-laced pizzas. Instead you'll find superb all-veg bruschetta, antipasti, pasta, pizza, salad and desserts, plus Spanish omelettes, served in an exotically decorated indoor restaurant (cosy in winter, deliciously air-conditioned in summer) or on a delightful terrace with cinematic views atop the lower fort walls . Fresh coffee, free wi-fi.

Trio
Indian $$

(📞252733; Gandhi Chowk; mains ₹100-190) Under a tented roof atop the wall of the Mandir Palace, this long-running restaurant does Indian (including some Rajasthani specialities), Chinese and Continental. The thalis, biryanis and tandoori items are all excellent, and the restaurant has a lot more atmosphere than most places in town. Musicians play in the evening and there's a partial fort view.

Saffron
Multicuisine $$$

(Gandhi Chowk; mains ₹100-300) This romantic open-air restaurant, on the spacious roof terrace of Hotel Nachana Haveli, has candle-lit tables overlooking a fountain courtyard below. The Indian food – including tandoori kebabs – is hard to beat, though the Italian comes a close second. Has a range of beers (small bottle ₹160) and a wine list.

1st Gate
Italian $$$

(mains ₹150-300; ⏰7am-11pm; 📶) A small but excellent menu of authentic Italian dishes as well as some delicious Indian food served on a split-level, open-air terrace with dramatic fort views. Also does good strong Italian coffee (₹100 to ₹150) as well as some fine wines.

🔒 Shopping

Hari Om Jewellers
Handicrafts

(Chougan Para, Fort; ⏰10am-8.30pm) This family of silversmiths makes beautiful, delicate silver rings and bracelets featuring world landmarks and Hindu gods. Asking prices for rings start at ₹1800 (at a rate of ₹300 per day's work).

Rajasthani embroidered bedspreads

Jaisalmer Handloom Handicrafts
(www.jaisalmerhandloom.com; Court Rd; ☺9am-10pm) Has a big array of bedspreads, tapestries, clothing (readymade and custom-made, including silk) and other textiles, made by its own workers and others, and doesn't belabour you with too much of a hard sell.

Bellissima Handicrafts
(Fort; ☺8am-9pm) Small shop selling beautiful patchworks, embroidery, paintings, bags, rugs, cushion covers and all types of Rajasthani art. Proceeds assist underprivileged women from surrounding villages, including those who have divorced or been widowed.

❶ Information

Internet Access

There are several internet cafes scattered around town. Typical cost is ₹40 per hour.

Money

Foreign-friendly ATMs are dotted round town, although none inside the fort.

Thomas Cook (Gandhi Chowk; ☺9.30am-7pm Mon-Sat, 10am-5pm Sun) A reliable moneychanger, changing travellers cheques and cash, and providing credit- and debit-card advances.

Tourist Information

Tourist Reception Centre (☏252406; Gadi Sagar Rd; ☺9.30am-6pm) Friendly office with a free map of town, and basic sand-dune tours.

Travel Agencies

Hanuman Travels (☏9413362367)

Swagat Travels (☏252557)

❶ Getting There & Away

Taxi

One-way taxis should cost from around ₹3000 to Jodhpur, ₹4000 to Bikaner, or ₹6000 to Udaipur. There's a **taxi rank** south of Hanuman Circle. Otherwise, try **Lucky Tours & Travels** (☏251818), behind Hotel Maru Palace. They sometimes have cheaper 'returning taxis' available.

Train

Three daily trains go to **Jodhpur** (8am, 5.15pm and 11.30pm). They take eight, five and six hours respectively. Unreserved 'general tickets' cost ₹50 to ₹75.

Two daily trains go to **Bikaner** (10.30am and 10.40pm) in around six hours. Unreserved 'general' seats cost around ₹75; reserved sleepers are around ₹160.

One daily train goes to **Delhi** (5.15pm, 18 hours) via **Jaipur** (12 hours).

❶ Getting Around

Autorickshaw

Around ₹30 from the train station to Gandhi Chowk.

Car

It's possible to hire taxis or jeeps from the stand near Hanuman Circle Rd. To Khuri or the Sam sand dunes; expect to pay ₹800 to ₹1000 one way.

Major Trains from Jaisalmer

DESTINATION	TRAIN	DEPARTURE TIME	ARRIVAL TIME	FARE (₹)
Bikaner	14701 Jaisalmer-Bikaner Exp	10.40pm	4.35am	158 (A)
Delhi (Old Delhi)	14660 Jaisalmer-Delhi Exp	5.15pm	11.10am	317/862 (B)
Jaipur	14660 Jaisalmer-Delhi Exp	5.15pm	5.08am	252/703 (B)
Jodhpur	14809 Jaislamer-Jodhpur Exp	11.30pm	5.15am	155/419 (B)

Fares: (A) sleeper; (B) sleeper/3AC

Goa & Around

It's green, it's glistening and it's gorgeous: just three of the reasons Goa has lured travellers for decades. They come for the silken sand, crystalline shores, coconut culture and *susegad* – a Portuguese-derived term that translates loosely to 'laid-backness'.

But Goa is far more than its old-school reputation as a hippie haven or its relatively new status as a package-holiday beach getaway. Goa is as beautiful and culturally rich as it is tiny and hassle-free, so you can go birdwatching in a butterfly-filled forest, marvel at centuries-old cathedrals, venture out to waterfalls or meander the capital's charming alleyways. Add a dash of Portuguese-influenced food and architecture, infuse with a colourful blend of religious traditions, pepper with parties and you've got a heady mix that makes Goa easy to enjoy and extremely hard to leave – although the pull of nearby Hampi, a stunning World Heritage site just across the state border in Karnataka, might well be strong enough to finally lure you away.

Palolem beach (p214)
KIMBERLEY COOLE/GETTY IMAGES ©

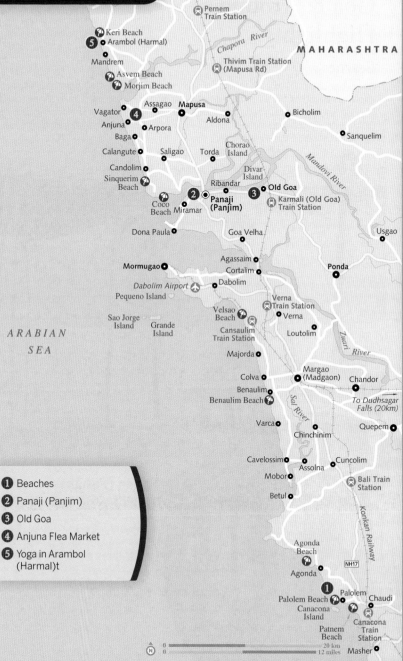

Goa & Around

MAHARASHTRA

Pernem Train Station

Chapora River

Keri Beach
Arambol (Harmal)
Mandrem
Asvem Beach
Morjim Beach

Thivim Train Station
(Mapusa Rd)

Bicholim

Vagator
Assagao
Mapusa
Aldona
Sanquelim

Anjuna
Arpora
Baga
Calangute
Saligao
Torda
Chorao
Island

Mandovi River

Candolim
Sinquerim
Beach
Divar
Island
Ribandar
Old Goa
Usgao

Coco
Beach
Miramar
Panaji
(Panjim)
Karmali (Old Goa)
Train Station

Dona Paula
Goa Velha

Agassaim
Mormugao
Cortalim
Ponda

Dabolim Airport
Dabolim

*ARABIAN
SEA*

Pequeno Island
Verna
Train Station

Sao Jorge
Island
Grande
Island
Velsao
Beach
Verna

Cansaulim
Train Station
Loutolim

Majorda

Colva
Margao
(Madgaon)
Chandor

Benaulim
Benaulim Beach
*To Dudhsagar
Falls (20km)*

Sal River

Varca
Chinchinim
Quepem

Cavelossim
Assolna
Cuncolim

Mobor
Bali Train
Station

Betul

Konkan Railway

Agonda
Beach
NH17
Agonda

Palolem Beach
Palolem
Chaudi
Canacona
Island
Canacona
Train
Station
Patnem
Beach
Masher

Legend

1. Beaches
2. Panaji (Panjim)
3. Old Goa
4. Anjuna Flea Market
5. Yoga in Arambol (Harmal)t

20 km
12 miles

Goa & Around's Highlights

Beaches

Goa is one of India's best places to kick back on powder-white beaches. In some places the coast has become built up, but there's still plenty of paradise-style, palm-shaded coastline where it's easy to escape, relax and tuck into fresh-from-the-boat seafood. Arguably, Palolem (p214) is the best beach of the lot, but there are dozens to choose from along the length of the Goan coastline. Mandrem beach

1

Panaji (Panjim)

2

Is Panaji (p196) India's cutest capital? It's a friendly, manageable, walkable city and its Portuguese-era colonial charms make it a perfect place to lull away a day or two. Stroll the peaceful streets, take a kitschy river cruise, eat delicious vindaloos and end the evening in a cosy local bar. Viva Panjim (p199)

Old Goa

3

Gaze at the cathedral-filled remains of Old Goa (p201), which from the 16th to the 18th century was the 'Rome of the East'. Only shadows of this history remain, but it's a picturesque place that's full of faded vestiges of Catholic splendour, adapted to the local environment. It's home to the largest church in Asia, as well as some beautiful 16th- and 17th-century chapels. Basilica of Bom Jesus (p203)

GREG ELMS/GETTY IMAGES ©

Anjuna Flea Market

Once an infamous hangout for hippies smoking jumbo joints, the weekly Wednesday flea market in Anjuna (p206) is more mainstream these days. Peruse the multitude of open-air stalls for clothes, souvenirs and knick-knacks before retreating to a beach bar for sunset.

Yoga in Arambol (Harmal)

5

Goa is a great place to practise some alternative therapies and yoga. From ashtanga through to zen, every kind of spiritually oriented health regime is to be found here. There are plenty of places all over the state to take courses or have treatments such as ayurvedic massage. Try the lovely beach of Arambol (p206) to track down some local practitioners.

191

Goa's Best…

Wining & Dining

○ **Upper House** Fabulous home-style regional dishes in Goa's charming capital. (p200)

○ **Viva Panjim** Streetside eatery in an old Portuguese house. (p199)

○ **Longhuino's** Old wooden chairs, whirring fans and very good Goan food. (p209)

○ **Café Inn** Great nighttime barbecue in Palolem. (p216)

○ **Home** Hip Mediterranean-style restaurant right by the beach. (p216)

○ **Seasonal beach shacks** Fresh fish on the menu, toes in the sand; found all over.

Rooms with Character

○ **Hotel Bougainvillea** Ridiculously pretty hotel in a 200-year-old mansion. (p205)

○ **Palacete Rodrigues** Cool and quirky mansion with themed rooms. (p204)

○ **Panjim Inn** 19th-century hotel with four-poster beds, colonial furniture and local artworks. (p199)

○ **Bhakti Kutir** A unique jungle retreat. (p215)

○ **Ciaran's** Rustic yet sophisticated Palolem beach huts. (p215)

Local Culture

○ **Panaji** Chilled-out Goan capital. (p196)

○ **Old Goa** Centre of Indian Catholicism, full of colonial-era churches. (p201)

○ **Braganza House** Glorious, faded 17th-century mansion. (p210)

○ **Goa Chitra** Ethnographic museum preserving Goa's domestic past. (p211)

Adventures & Activities

- **Paragliding** Popular on the cliffs above Arambol beach, but also possible in Anjuna on flea-market day.

- **Yoga** Arambol is your best bet, but you can find yoga classes all over Goa.

- **Kayaking** Rent kayaks at Palolem beach. (p214)

- **Trekking** French-run Goa Jungle Adventure, based in Palolem, gets great reviews (p215)

- **Dudhsagar Falls** India's second-highest waterfall makes a fun day trip from Panaji or Margao. (p208).

Need to Know

ADVANCE PLANNING

- **One month before** Book any particularly special accommodation.

- **Two weeks before** Reserve long train trips.

- **One or two days before** Arrange any local tours that take your fancy.

RESOURCES

- **Goa Tourism** (www.goa-tourism.com) Good background and tour info.

- **Goacom** (www.goacom.com) One of Goa's original news and views sites.

- **Goa's English dailies** (www.navhindtimes.in, www.oheraldo.in) For the news.

GETTING AROUND

- **Taxi** Cars and drivers are available for hire in most towns; try your hotel or the local taxi stand. Full-day tours cost ₹1000 to ₹1500.

- **Pilots** Motorcycles, known as 'pilots', are also a licensed form of taxi in Goa. They're cheap, easy to find and can be identified by a yellow front mudguard.

- **Motorcycles & mopeds** Many tourists rent these (₹200 to ₹500 per day), but take care on the potholed, haphazard Goan roads and insist on using a helmet.

- **Bus** There's an extensive network of buses serving even the smallest towns.

- **Arriving at the airport** There are two prepaid taxi counters at Dabolim Airport. Use them.

BE FOREWARNED

- **Illegal substances** Being caught, even with small quantities of illegal drugs, can mean a hefty sentence in jail.

- **Strong currents** Check where it's safe to swim before launching into the Arabian Sea.

- **Christmas & New Year** If you're looking for peace and quiet, be aware that this is the most crowded and expensive period.

Left: Panaji (p196)
Above: Braganza House (p210)
(LEFT & ABOVE) LONELY PLANET/GETTY IMAGES ©;

Goa Itineraries

Central Goa is the state's most cultural region – with its gracious capital Panaji – while the north is the liveliest, harbouring the last remnants of the region's fabled party scene. For utter peace and relaxation, head to the quieter beaches in the south.

5 DAYS

PANAJI TO ARAMBOL
NORTH GOA EXPLORER

Start your trip in the charming Goan capital, ❶ **Panaji (Panjim)**, where you can wander the old town, see its historic buildings, take cruises along the Mandovi River and dine at delicious, laid-back restaurants. Factor in a side-trip to ❷ **Old Goa**, the former state capital that was abandoned in the 17th century but which still houses some architectural gems, including the largest cathedral in Asia.

Return to Panaji before hitting the northern beaches. First up: ❸ **Anjuna**, the much-loved former hippie hangout. Try to time your visit to coincide with the weekly Wednesday flea market, or else drop in on a yoga class and then just chill with a drink at a beach bar. From here you could head still further north to the appealing beach town of ❹ **Arambol (Harmal)**, a corner of Goa that's a well-known traveller magnet with something of a mainstream festival vibe – the main drag leading to the beach is known as 'Glastonbury St'. This is also the best place in Goa for yoga, there are beach huts aplenty and you can even try your hand at paragliding.

ARABIAN SEA

④ ARAMBOL (HARMAL)

③ ANJUNA

OLD GOA
① ② ②
PANAJI (PANJIM)

MARGAO (MADGAON)
BENAULIM ③

CHANDOR ④

PALOLEM ⑤

Top Left: Sé Cathedral (p202)
Top Right: Palolem beach (p214)
(TOP LEFT) STEVEN MIRIC/GETTY IMAGES ©; (TOP RIGHT) NICHOLAS PITT/GETTY IMAGES ©

1
WEEK

PANAJI TO PALOLEM
SOUTH GOA RELAXER

his itinerary explores the tranquil coastal stretches in the south of Goa, with its white-
and beaches and unspoiled coves, but you can kick off in the relaxed regional capital
f **① Panaji (Panjim)**, as with the first itinerary.

Next travel south, either taking the train from **② Old Goa** to the transport hub of Margao
(Madgaon) and then taking a taxi, or by hiring a taxi all the way to the coastal resort of
③ Benaulim, to relax on its long white-sand beach, and explore the surrounding empty
.nd gorgeous coastline, dotted with Portuguese-era mansions and whitewashed churches.
rom here you can also take a trip to explore inland, heading to the town of **④ Chandor**,
vhich is home to several fantastical mansions, including the sumptuous, 17th-century
3raganza House. Next, travel still further south (again, most easily by taxi) to the stunning
rescent-shaped beach of **⑤ Palolem**, one of Goa's most beautiful spots, with calm seas
.nd plenty of opportunities for yoga and to indulge in alternative therapies while resting up
h picturesque beach huts or lusher, low-key resorts set back from the beach.

Discover
Goa & Around

CENTRAL GOA

Panaji (Panjim)

POP 115,000

One of India's most relaxed state capitals, Panaji (more commonly known as Panjim) sits at the mouth of the broad Mandovi River and boasts a fascinating old quarter containing a tangle of narrow streets. Nowhere is the Portuguese influence felt more strongly than here, where the late-afternoon sun lights up yellow houses with purple doors, and around each corner you'll find crumbling ochre-coloured mansions with wrought-iron balconies and cats lying in front of bicycles parked beneath oyster-shell windows. Panjim is a place for walking, enjoying the peace of the afternoon siesta, eating well and meeting real Goans. It's not to be missed.

◎ Sights & Activities

One of the pleasures of Panaji is long, leisurely strolls through the sleepy Portuguese-era Sao Tomé, Fontainhas and Altinho districts.

Church of Our Lady of the Immaculate Conception   Church

(cnr Emilio Gracia & Jose Falcao Rds; ⏱10am-12.30pm & 3-5.30pm Mon-Sat, 11am-12.30pm & 3.30-5pm Sun) Panaji's spiritual and geographical centre is its gleamingly white and oh-so-photogenic main church, consecrated in 1541. When Panaji was little more than a sleepy fishing village this place was the first port of call for sailors from Lisbon, who would clamber up here to thank their lucky stars for a safe

Church of Our Lady of the Immaculate Conception
BEN PIPE/GETTY IMAGES ©

crossing before continuing to Old Goa, the state's capital until the 19th century, further east up the river. It's usually closed in the evening, but the exterior is wonderfully illuminated at night. Mass in English is held at 8am weekdays and 8.15am Sunday.

Tours

The Goa Tourism Development Corporation (GTDC, Goa Tourism; p200) operates a range of popular boat trips along the Mandovi River, including hour-long sunset and evening **cruises** (₹150; ☉6pm & 7.15pm) and two-hour **dinner cruises** (₹500; ☉8.45pm Wed & Sat) aboard the *Santa Monica*. All include a live band and dancers – sometimes lively, sometimes lacklustre – performing Goan folk songs and dances. Cruises depart from the Santa Monica jetty beside the New Patto Bridge, where the **GTDC boat counter** (☎2438754; Santa Monica Jetty) also sells tickets.

Three private companies offer similar one-hour **night cruises** (adult/child ₹150/free; ☉6.15pm, 7.30pm & 8.45pm) also departing from Santa Monica jetty. With bars and DJs playing loud music, these tend to be a lot livelier than the GTDC cruises but can get rowdy with groups of local male tourists – avoid on weekends.

GTDC also runs a full-day **backwater cruise** (₹750; ☉9.30am-4pm) to Old Goa, then a bus to a spice farm where lunch is included.

Heritage walking tours (☎9823025748; ajit_sukhija@yahoo.com; per person ₹500, per person for five or more ₹250), covering the old Portuguese quarter from Tobacco Sq through Sao Tomé, Fountainhas and the Hindu Mala district, are conducted by experienced local guides on demand.

Sleeping

Pousada Guest House
Guesthouse **$**
(☎2422618; sabrinateles@yahoo.com; Luis de Menezes Rd; s/d ₹525/630, d with AC ₹750; ❄)
The four rooms in this bright-yellow place in the old quarter are simple but clean

Local Knowledge

Don't-Miss Goa Beaches

ANTHONY DAS WAS BORN AND BRED IN GOA AND HAS WORKED IN THE TOURIST INDUSTRY FOR MANY YEARS

1 ARAMBOL BEACH
To the extreme north of Goa, this beach used to be a hippie hang-out in the 1970s and it's still popular with backpackers rather than mainstream tourists. A short walk away from the beach there's a sweet-water lake. It's scenic, hasn't been over-exploited and is extremely laid back.

2 KERI BEACH
Even further north than Arambol, there is Keri Beach, shaded by pine trees – a hassle-free place. Here there are hardly any buildings, just a few shacks. There's a little ferry that runs across the Keri River to arrive at Terekhol Fort, an old Portuguese fortress on the Goa–Maharashtra border.

3 PALOLEM BEACH
Again this is a quiet south Goa beach. The accommodation here is all in tents and cottages, without any big hotels. It's long been on the traveller radar, but it's quite far from the main towns so retains a secluded feel, assisted by strict building regulations. The beach is a little cove so there are no big waves – it's an ideal place to swim.

4 AGONDA BEACH
Previously a lot of long-stayers in caravans from Europe used to come to Agonda, in south Goa. Visitors also used to stay in local houses as paying guests. But nowadays people tend to stay in cottages; the beach is well-equipped and also very clean, more so than many beaches in the north.

5 BENAULIM BEACH
This is beautiful. It's big: a 15km to 20km stretch of white sand. It's very popular with foreign tourists – local tourists tend to prefer the busier beaches close to the main towns. There are lots of five-star hotels close by and watersports are popular here; they tend to be safer and better organised than in other more remote places.

GOA & AROUND PANAJI (PANJIM)

Panaji (Panjim)

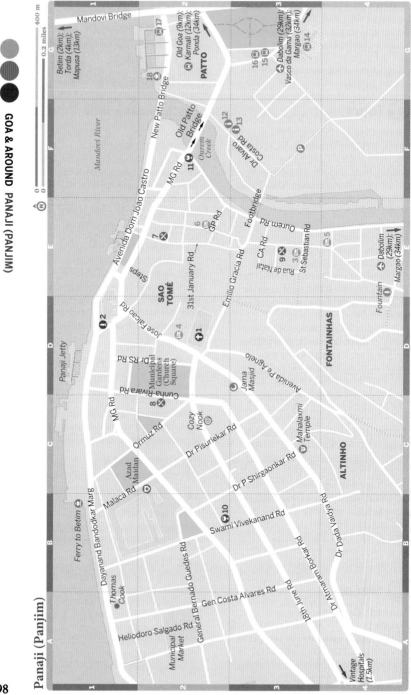

and come with comfy spring-mattress beds and TV. Owner Sabrina is friendly and no-nonsense, and at this price it's one of the better budget deals.

Afonso Guest House
Guesthouse **$$**

(☏2222359, 9764300165; www.afonsoguest house.com; St Sebastian Rd; r ₹1500-2000; ❋)
Run by the friendly Jeanette, this place in a pretty Portuguese-era townhouse offers spacious, well-kept rooms with timber ceilings. The little rooftop terrace makes for sunny breakfasting. It's a simple, serene stay in the heart of the most atmospheric part of town; checkout is 9am and bookings are accepted online but not by phone.

Casa Paradiso
Hotel **$$**

(☏3290180; www.casaparadisogoa.com; Jose Falcao Rd; r ₹1575-2100; ❋) The location alone makes this place worth a look. It's a little cramped but just steps away from the Church of Our Lady of the Immaculate Conception, with bright, air-con rooms, cable TV and friendly staff.

Panjim Inn
Heritage Hotel **$$**

(☏2226523, 9823025748; www.panjiminn. com; 31st January Rd; s/d incl breakfast from ₹2900/3450, ste ₹5950; ❋@🛜) A long-standing Panaji favourite for its heritage character, this beautiful 19th-century hotel has a variety of charismatic original rooms, along with some newer rooms with more modern touches, but all with four-poster beds, colonial furniture and local artworks. Across the road and run by the same family is the **Panjim Peoples**, with four enormous rooms upstairs and the Gitanjali Gallery downstairs; also across the road is the tranquil nine-room **Panjim Pousada**, in an old Hindu home.

❎ Eating

A stroll down 18th June or 31st January Rds will turn up a number of great, cheap canteen-style options, as will a quick circuit of the Municipal Gardens.

Viva Panjim
Goan **$**

(31st January Rd; mains ₹90-120; ⊙11.30am-3.30pm & 7-11pm Mon-Sat, 7-11pm Sun) Though well known to tourists, this little sidestreet eatery, in an old Portuguese house, still delivers tasty Goan classics at reasonable prices – there's a whole page of the menu devoted to pork dishes, as well as tasty *xacuti* (spicy meat or chicken in coconut) and *cafreal* (spicy chicken) dishes and desserts like *bebinca* (16-layer cake) and *serra durra* (pudding). Fair drink prices too.

Upper House
Goan $$

(☏ 2426475; www.theupperhousegoa.com; Cunha Rivara Rd; mains ₹125-385; ⏱11am-10pm) Climbing the stairs to the Upper House is like stepping into a cool European restaurant, with a modern but elegant dining space overlooking the Municipal Gardens at the front, a chic neon-lit cocktail bar next door and more formal restaurant space at the back. But the food is very much Goan – a high standard of regional specialities such as crab *xec xec* (crab cooked in a roasted-coconut gravy), pork vindaloo, and fish-curry-rice done the old-fashioned way. Even the veg adaptations (eg mixed veg and mushroom *xacuti*) are show-stoppers.

Hotel Venite
Goan $$

(31st January Rd; mains ₹210-280; ⏱9am-10.30pm) Atmospheric Venite is a long-time tourist favourite: its tiny, rickety balcony tables make the perfect lunchtime spot. Success may have gone to Venite's head – the Goan food is OK but the prices are exorbitant. We still love the place though – call in for a cold beer or snack and chill out on the balcony before deciding.

🍷 Drinking & Nightlife

Panaji's got pick-me-up pit stops aplenty, especially in Sao Tomé and Fontainhas. Mostly simple little bars with a few plastic tables and chairs, they're a great way to get chatting with locals over a glass of *feni* (coconut liquor).

Cafe Mojo
Bar

(www.cafemojo.in; Menezes Braganza Rd; ⏱10am-4am Mon-Thu, to 6am Fri-Sun) Cafe Mojo is cool. The decor is cosy English pub, the clientele is young and up for a party, and the hook is the e-beer system. Each table has its own beer tap and LCD screen: you buy a card (₹1000), swipe it at your table and start pouring – it automatically deducts what you drink (you can also use the card for spirits, cocktails or food). Wednesday night is

ladies' night and the weekends go till late.

Riverfront & Down the Road
Bar

(cnr MG & Ourem Rd; ⏱11am-3am) The balcony of this bar-restaurant overlooking the creek and Old Patto Bridge makes for a great sundowner spot; the ground-floor bar has occasional live music.

ℹ️ Information

A new tourism complex has been established at Patto on the east side of the Ourem Creek, housing the GTDC (Goa Tourism), Indiatourism and various travel agents. ATMs are plentiful, especially on 18th June Rd and around the Thomas Cook office.

Cozy Nook (18th June Rd; per hr ₹45; ⏱9am-8.30pm) Welcoming internet joint and travel agent.

Goa Tourism Development Corporation (GTDC; ☏ 2424001; www.goa-tourism.com; Dr Alvaro Costa Rd, Paryatan Bhavan; ⏱9.30am-5.45pm Mon-Sat) Pick up maps of Goa and Panaji here and book one of GTDC's host of tours.

Indiatourism (Government of India tourist office; ☏ 2223412; www.incredibleindia.org; Dr Alvaro Costa Rd, Paryatan Bhavan; ⏱9.30am-6pm Mon-Fri, to 2pm Sat) Helpful staff can provide a list of qualified guides for tours and trips in Goa. A half-/full-day tour for up to five people costs ₹700/875.

Thomas Cook (☏ 2221312; 8 Alcon Chambers, Dayanand Bandodkar Marg; ⏱9.30am-6pm Mon-Sat) Changes travellers cheques commission-free and handles currency exchange, wire transfers, cash advances on credit cards and air bookings.

Vintage Hospitals (☏ 6644401, ambulance 9764442220; www.vintagehospitals.com; Caculo Enclave, St Inez; ⏱24hr) A couple of kilometres southwest of Panaji, Vintage is a reputable hospital with all the fixings.

ℹ️ Getting There & Away

A taxi from Panaji to Dabolim Airport takes about an hour and costs ₹600.

Bus

All government buses depart from the huge and busy **Kadamba bus stand** (🔗interstate enquiries 2438035, local enquiries 2438034; www.goakadamba.com; ⏰reservations 8am-8pm), with local services heading out every few minutes. To get to south Goan beaches, take an express bus to Margao and change there. Destination include Margao (express shuttle; ₹30, 35 minutes) and Old Goa (₹9, 15 minutes).

State-run long-distance services also depart from the Kadamba bus stand. Private operators have booths outside Kadamba, but the buses depart from the interstate bus stand next to New Patto Bridge. One reliable company is **Paulo Travels** (🔗2438531; www.paulotravels.com; Kardozo Bldg). Destinations include Hampi (private sleeper; ₹700 to ₹800, 10 to 11 hours) and Mumbai (₹650, 12 to 14 hours).

Train

Panaji's closest train station is Karmali (Old Goa), 12km to the east, where many long-distance services stop (check timetables). A taxi there costs ₹300. Panaji's **Konkan Railway reservation office** (🔗2712940; www.konkanrailway.com; ⏰8am-8pm Mon-Sat) is on the 1st floor of the Kadamba bus stand.

ⓘ Getting Around

Panaji is generally a pleasure to explore on foot. An autorickshaw from Kadamba to the city centre will cost ₹60.

To Old Goa, a taxi or autorickshaw costs around ₹300.

Scooters and motorbikes can easily be hired from around the post office from around ₹200/300 per day.

....

Old Goa

From the 16th to the 18th centuries, when Old Goa's population exceeded that of Lisbon or London, this former capital of Goa was considered the 'Rome of the East'. You can still sense that grandeur as you wander the grounds, with its towering churches and cathedral and majestic convents. Its rise under the Portuguese, from 1510, was meteoric, but cholera and malaria outbreaks forced the abandonment of the city in the 1600s. In 1843 the capital was officially shifted to Panaji.

Some of the most imposing churches, the cathedral and a convent or two are still in use and are remarkably well preserved, while other historical buildings have become museums or ruined sites.

Old Goa

◉ Don't Miss Sights

◉ Sights

Old Goa

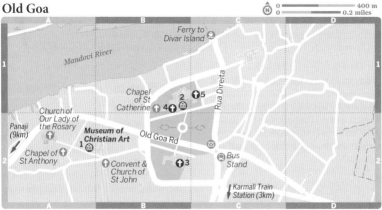

/GETTY IMAGES ©

★ Don't Miss
Museum of Christian Art

This excellent museum, in a stunning space in the restored 1627 **Convent of St Monica**, has a fine collection of 16th- and 17th-century Christian art from Old Goa and around the state. There are some exquisite pieces here – wooden sculptures glittering with gilt and polychrome, processional lamps, tabernacle doors, polychrome paintings and other religious objects from Old Goa's prime – that are almost, but not quite, outdone by the atmospheric interior. The four-storey-high ceilings, exposed wood-beams and terracotta work, and all-around beauty of the place, are worth a visit in their own right.

NEED TO KNOW

http://christianartmuseum.goa-india.org; adult/child ₹30/free; ⊙9.30am-5pm

It's a fascinating day trip, but it can get crowded: consider visiting on a weekday morning, when you can take in Mass (in Konkani) at Sé Cathedral or the Basilica of Bom Jesus (remember to cover your shoulders and legs in the churches and cathedral).

◎ Sights

Sé Cathedral   Church
(⊙7.30am-6.30pm) The largest church in Old Goa, the Sé de Santa Catarina, is also the largest in Asia, at over 76m long and 55m wide. Construction began in 1562, under orders from Portugal's King Dom Sebastião, and the finishing touches were

made 90 years later. Fairly plain all-round, the cathedral has three especially notable features: the first, up in the belfry, is the **Golden Bell**, the largest bell in Asia; the second is in the screened chapel inside to the right, known as the **Chapel of the Cross of Miracles**, wherein sits a cross said to have miraculously, and vastly, expanded in size after its creation by local shepherds in 1619. The third is the massive gilded reredos (ornamental screen behind the altar), which depicts the life of St Catherine, to whom the cathedral is dedicated and who came to a sticky end in Alexandria, Egypt, where she was beheaded.

❶ Getting There & Away

Frequent buses from Old Goa head to Panaji's Kadamba bus stand (₹10, 25 minutes) from Old Goa Rd, just beside the Tourist Inn and at the main roundabout to the east.

NORTH GOA

Anjuna

Dear old Anjuna. The stalwart of India's hippie scene still drags out the sarongs and sandalwood each Wednesday for its famous – and once infamous – flea market, and still has that floating in-between-town feel that we love. With its long beach, rice paddies and cheap guesthouses huddled in relatively peaceful pockets, it continues to pull in droves of backpackers and long-term hippies, while midrange tourists are also increasingly making their way here. The village itself might be a bit ragged around the edges, but that's all part of its haphazard charm, and Anjuna remains a favourite of long-stayers and first-timers alike.

◉ Sights & Activities

Anjuna's charismatic **beach** runs for almost 2km from the northern village area to the flea market. The northern end is mostly cliffs lined with cheap cafes and

♥ If You Like...
Churches

If you enjoy Old Goa churches and architecture, seek out these two gems.

1 BASILICA OF BOM JESUS
(⏱7.30am-6.30pm; English-language mass 10.15am Sun) Famous throughout the Roman Catholic world for its rather grizzled and grizzly long-term resident, the basilica's vast, gilded interior forms the last resting place of Goa's patron saint, St Francis Xavier. Construction of the imposing red-stone basilica was completed in 1605; St Francis himself is housed in a **mausoleum** to the right, in a glass-sided coffin amid a shower of gilt stars.

2 CHURCH OF ST FRANCIS OF ASSISI
(⏱8.30am-5.30pm) The gorgeous interior of this 1661 church, built over a 16th-century chapel, is filled with gilded and carved woodwork, murals depicting the life of St Francis, frescoes of decorative flowers and various angels, 16th-century Portuguese tombstones and a stunning reredos.

basic guesthouses, but the beach proper (starting just south of San Francisco Restaurant) is a lovely stretch of sand with a bunch of beach bars at the southern end. For more action, **paragliding (tandem rides ₹1800)** sometimes takes place on market days off the headland at the southern end of the beach.

YOGA

There's lots of yoga, reiki and ayurvedic massage offered around Anjuna; look for notices at Café Diogo and the German Bakery. Drop-in classes are organised by **Brahmani Yoga** (☎9370568639; www.brahmaniyoga.com), next to Hotel Bougainvillea, and **Oceanic Yoga** (☎9545112278; www.oceanicyoga.com; ⏱1½hr classes ₹400), which also offers intensive courses and teacher training.

🛏 Sleeping

Elephant Art Cafe   Tented Camp **$**
(📞9970668845; elephantartcafe@gmail.com;
tents ₹800-1000) The spacious tents here
are lined with embroidered fabric, have
tile floors and attached bathrooms, and
are set in pretty grounds – like a little tent
village – with winding, lamp-lit paths. The
location, behind the beach shack of the
same name, isn't bad either.

Paradise   Guesthouse **$**
(📞9922541714; janet_965@hotmail.com;
Anjuna-Mapusa Rd; d ₹1000, with AC ₹2000;
❄@📶) The friendly Paradise is fronted
by an old Portuguese house, and its clean
rooms are set in rustic grounds full of
crowing roosters and sleeping cats. Pro-
prietor Janet and her enterprising family
also run a general store, restaurant, internet cafe and more.

**Palacete
Rodrigues**   Heritage Hotel **$$**
(📞2273358; www.palacetegoa.com; Mazal
Vaddo; s/d from ₹1575/2100, d/ste with AC
₹2620/3150; ❄) This old-fashioned man-
sion, crammed with antiques, elaborately
carved furniture, odd corners and bags of
fun, tacky charm, is as cool and quirky as
they come. Choose your theme: rooms
come in Chinese, Vietnamese, Portuguese
and, of course, Goan flavours.

Banyan Soul   Boutique Hotel **$$**
(📞9820707283; www.thebanyansoul.com; d
₹2200; ❄) A slinky 12-room option, tucked
just behind Anjuna's German bakery,
lovingly conceived and run by a young
escapee from the Mumbai technology rat
race. Rooms are chic and well equipped
with cable TV and air-con. It's certainly
among the better midrange choices in
town.

Left: Altarpiece, Sé Cathedral (p202)
Below: Paraglider over Anjuna beach (p203)

(LEFT) DANITA DELIMONT/GETTY IMAGES ©; (BELOW) KIMBERLEY COOLE/GETTY IMAGES ©

Hotel Bougainvillea

Heritage Hotel **$$$**

(Granpa's Inn; ☏2273270, 2273271; www.granpasinn.com; Anjuna Beach Rd; d/ste incl breakfast from ₹3950/4450; ❄☎☒) This old-fashioned hotel in a 200-year-old yellow mansion is ridiculously pretty. Elegant rooms have that rare combination of charm and luxury, and the pool area is gorgeous. The grounds are so lush and shady that it seems a good few degrees cooler than the rest of Anjuna. The downside is that it's a long way back from the beach.

🍴 Eating & Drinking

The southern end of Anjuna beach boasts a string of super-sized semipermanent beach shacks serving all day food and drinks. Good ones include Cafe Lilliput and the Shore Bar. At the far end, **Curlie's** (mains ₹90-280; ⏲9am-3am) is a notorious spot for an evening sunset drink, with an alternative crowd and the odd impromptu party.

Café Diogo Cafe **$**

(Market Rd; snacks ₹60-140; ⏲8.30am-7pm) Probably the best fruit salads in Goa are sliced and diced at Café Diogo, a small locally run cafe on the way to the market. Also worth a munch are the generous toasted avocado, cheese and mushroom sandwiches.

Whole Bean Tofu Cafe **$**

(Market Rd; mains ₹60-150; ⏲8am-5pm) One of the few places in Goa where vegans can eat well, this tofu-filled health-food cafe focuses on all things created from the versatile soya bean.

Martha's Breakfast Home Cafe **$$**

(meals ₹80-300; ⏲7am-2pm) Martha's specialises in all-day breakfasts, served up in a quiet garden on the way down to the flea-market site. The porridge and juice may be mighty tasty, but the star of the breakfast parade is undoubtedly the

205

piping-hot plates of pancakes and waffles, just crying out to be smothered in real maple syrup. There are a few tidy rooms (₹1000) at the side.

German Bakery Multicuisine $$
(www.german-bakery.in; bread & pastries ₹40-80, mains ₹80-270; ⊙8am-11pm; 🛜) Leafy and filled with prayer flags, jolly lights and atmospheric curtained nooks, this is a local favourite for breakfast, crepes or a relaxed vegetarian lunch or dinner. Innovative tofu dishes are a speciality.

Shore Bar Multicuisine $$
(mains ₹120-400) The Shore Bar has been crowded out by the beachfront competition over the years but it's still an Anjuna institution and with the addition of a soundproof upstairs lounge-bar-nightclub, it's back in the good books. The food here is excellent but pricey, and it's always a cool spot for a sunset drink on market day.

Anjuna Flea Market

Wednesday's weekly **flea market** (⊙8am-late Wed, usually late Oct-late Mar) at Anjuna is as much part of the Goan experience as a day on the beach. More than three decades ago it was the sole preserve of hippies smoking jumbo joints and convening to compare experiences on the heady Indian circuit. Nowadays things are far more mainstream. A couple of hours here and you'll never want to see a mirrored bedspread, brass figurine or floaty Indian cotton dress again in your life. But it's still a good time, a place to meet and mingle, and you can find some interesting one-off souvenirs and clothing in among the tourist tat.

ℹ️ Information

Anjuna has three ATMs, clustered together on the main road to the beach.

Speedy Travels (☎2273266; ⊙9am-6.30pm Mon-Sat, 10am-1pm Sun) Reliable agency for air and train ticket booking, a range of tours, and credit-card advances or currency exchange.

ℹ️ Getting There & Away

Buses to Mapusa (₹15), where you can get onward connections, depart every half-hour or so from the main bus stand near the beach; some from Mapusa continue on to Vagator and Chapora. Taxis and pilots (motorcycle taxis) gather at the bus stop, and you can hire scooters and motorcycles easily from the crossroads.

Arambol (Harmal)

Beautiful Arambol, with its craggy cliffs and sweeping beach, first emerged in the 1960s as a mellow paradise for long-haired long-stayers, and ever since, travellers attracted to the hippie atmosphere have been drifting up to this blissed-out corner of Goa. As a result, in the high season the beach and the road leading down to it (known as Glastonbury St) can get pretty crowded – with huts, people and nonstop stalls selling the usual tourist stuff. If you're looking for a committed traveller vibe, this is the place to come; if you're seeking laid-back languidness, you might be better off heading down the coast to Mandrem or Morjim.

🤸 Activities

The cliffs north of Arambol beach are a popular spot for **paragliding**. **Arambol Paragliding School** (☎9822867570) and **Arambol Hammocks** (☎9822389005; www.arambol.com; per 20min ₹1800; ⊙9am-6pm) both offer tandem flights in season from around ₹1800. Several places also offer **yoga** classes and courses.

Follow the cliff path north of Arambol Beach to pretty **Kalacha Beach**, which meets the small 'sweetwater' lake, a great spot for swimming.

Himalayan Iyengar Yoga Centre
Yoga

(www.hiyogacentre.com; Madhlo Vaddo; 5-day yoga course ₹3000; ⊙Nov-Mar) This is the winter retreat for the popular Dharamsala-based Iyengar yoga centre. Five-day courses (beginning on Fridays, orientation every Tuesday), intensive workshops, children's classes and teacher training are all available. The centre is a five-minute walk from the beach, off the main road; look out for the big banner. HI also has **huts** (s/d without bathroom ₹250/300) for students.

🛌 Sleeping

Arambol is well known for its sea-facing, cliff-hugging budget huts – trawl the cliffside to the north of Arambol's main beach stretch for the best hut options. It's almost impossible to book in advance: simply turn up early in the day to check who's checking out.

Chilli's
Hotel $

(☎9921882424; d ₹300-450, with AC ₹600; ⊙year-round; ❄) The bright yellow house on the main road to the beach, run by the helpful Derick Fernandes, is one of Arambol's best non-cliff bargains. Chilli's offers 10 bright, no-frills rooms, all with attached bathroom, fan and hot-water shower, some with fridge and balcony.

Shree Sai Cottages
Beach Huts $

(☎9420767358, 3262823; shreesai_cottages@yahoo.com; huts without bathroom ₹500-600) The last set of huts on the cliffs before Kalacha (Sweet Water) Beach, Shree Sai has a calm, easygoing vibe and basic but cute hut-cottages with little balconies and lovely views out over the water.

Detour:
Baga

Nilaya Hermitage (☎2269793, 2269794; www.nilaya.com; Arpora; d incl breakfast, dinner & spa €350; ❄@🛜⊠) Prepare to be pampered. This spa hotel is the ultimate in Goan luxury. A stay at this hilltop hideaway, set 5km inland from Baga beach at Arpora, will see you signing the guestbook with the likes of Giorgio Armani, Sean Connery and Kate Moss. Ten beautiful red-stone rooms undulate around a swimming pool, alongside four luxury tents. The food is as dreamy as the surroundings, and the ayurvedic spa (all inclusive) will spoil you rotten.

GOA & AROUND   ARAMBOL (HARMAL)

Market stalls on the road to Arambol

Detour:
Dudhsagar Falls

On the eastern border with Karnataka, Dudhsagar Falls (603m) are Goa's most impressive waterfalls and the second highest in India, best seen as soon as possible after the rains. To get here, take the 8.13am train to Colem from Margao (there are only three trains daily in each direction) and from there catch a jeep for the bumpy 40-minute trip to the falls (₹4000 for the six-passenger jeep). It's then a short but rocky clamber to the edge of the falls themselves. A much easier option is to take a full-day GTDC tour from Panaji (₹750, Wednesday and Sunday) or arrange an excursion with travel agencies at any of the beach resorts.

Om Ganesh Beach Huts **$**
(☎ 9404436447; r & huts ₹400-800) Popular huts and some more solid rooms on the cliffs overlooking the water, managed by the friendly Sudir. The seaside Om Ganesh Restaurant is also a great place for lunch or dinner. Note that almost everyone in the area will tell you that their place is Om Ganesh.

Famafa Beach Resort Hotel **$$**
(☎ 2242516; www.famafaarambolgoa.com; Glastonbury St; r from ₹1200; ❄ @) For a little bit of comfort (including some air-con rooms) close to the beach, Famafa is a staid but clean and reliable midranger.

✖ Eating & Drinking

Beach shacks with chairs and tables on the sand and parachute-silk canopies line the beach at Arambol. Many change annually, but **21 Coconuts** (for seafood) and **Relax Inn** (for Italian) are mainstays.

Shimon Middle Eastern **$**
(meals ₹70-140; ⏰ 9am-11pm) Just back from the beach and understandably popular with Israeli backpackers, Shimon is the place to fill up on an exceptional falafel (₹110) or other specialities like *sabikh*, aubergine slices stuffed into pita bread with boiled egg, potato, salad and spicy relishes in pita. Follow either up with Turkish coffee or fruit shake.

Fellini Italian **$$**
(mains ₹140-300; ⏰ 11am-11pm) Pizza's the big deal here – the menu has more than 40 different kinds – and they're good. The pastas, calzones and paninis, especially with seafood, are also tasty. The tiramisu will keep you up at night, thinking back on it fondly.

Double Dutch Multicuisine **$$**
(mains ₹100-290) Longtime popular place for steaks, salads, Thai and Indonesian dishes, and famous for its apple pies, all in a pretty garden setting.

❶ Information

Internet outfits, travel agents and money changers are as common as monsoon frogs on the road leading down to Arambol's beach. The nearest ATM is in Arambol village near the bus stop.

❶ Getting There & Around

Buses to Mapusa (₹27, 1½ hours) depart from Arambol village every half-hour. It's only about 1.5km from the main beach area, but you're lucky if you get a cab, or even an autorickshaw, for ₹60. A prepaid taxi to Arambol from Dabolim Airport costs ₹1000; from Mapusa it's ₹400.

Lots of places in Arambol rent scooters and motorbikes, for ₹200 and ₹300, respectively, per day.

SOUTH GOA

Margao (Madgaon)
POP 94,400

Margao (also known by its train station name of Madgaon) is the main population centre of south Goa and for travellers is chiefly a transport hub, with the state's major train and bus stations.

Sights

It's worth a walk around the lovely, small **Largo de Igreja** district, home to lots of atmospherically crumbling and gorgeously restored old Portuguese homes, and the quaint and richly decorated 17th-century **Church of the Holy Spirit**.

Sleeping

Om Shiv Hotel Hotel **$$**

(☎2710294; www.omshivhotel.com; Cine Lata Rd; d ₹2700-3800, ste ₹4850; ❄) In a bright-yellow building tucked away behind the Bank of India, Om Shiv does a fine line in 'executive' rooms, which all have air-con, balcony and an ordered air. The suites have exceptional views, and it's home to Margao's 'only night hotspot', the Rockon Pub.

Eating

Swad Indian **$**

(New Market; ₹25-110; ☺7.30am-8pm) Many regard this family-friendly favourite as having Margao's best pure veg food. The North Indian thalis are reliably good, as are the snacks, South Indian tiffins and dosas.

Longhuino's Goan, Multicuisine **$$**

(Luis Miranda Rd; mains ₹80-160; ☺8.30am-11pm) Since 1950, quaint old Longhuino's bar and restaurant, with its old wooden chairs, whirring fans and slow service, has been serving up tasty Goan, Indian and Chinese dishes popular with locals and tourists alike. They also do a decent job of desserts like bebinca and tiramasu. Great place to watch the world go by.

Information

Banks offering currency exchange and 24-hour ATMs are all around town.

Apollo Victor (☎2728888; Station Rd, Malbhat) Reliable medical services.

Goa Tourism Desk (☎2715096; www.goa-tourism.com; Margao Residency, Luis Miranda Rd) Book GTDC trips here.

Fishing boats, Arambol (p206)

MICHAEL TAYLOR/GETTY IMAGES ©

Detour:
Chandor

The lush village of Chandor, 15km east of Margao, makes a perfect day away from the beaches and it's here more than anywhere else in the state that the opulent lifestyles of Goa's former landowners, who found favour with the Portuguese aristocracy, are still visible in its quietly decaying colonial-era mansions.

Braganza House, built in the 17th century, is possibly the best example of what Goa's scores of once grand and glorious mansions have today become. Built on land granted by the king of Portugal, the house was divided from the outset into two wings, to house two sides of the same family. The **West Wing** (☎2784201; admission ₹150; ⊙9am-5pm, last admission 4pm) belongs to one set of the family's descendants, the Menezes-Bragança, and is filled with gorgeous chandeliers, Italian marble floors, rosewood furniture and antique treasures from Macau, Portugal, China and Europe. Despite the passing of the elderly Mrs Aida Menezes-Bragança in 2012, the grand old home, which requires considerable upkeep, remains open to the public. Next door the **East Wing** (☎2857630; admission ₹100; ⊙9am-5.30pm) is owned by the Braganza-Pereiras, descendants of the other half of the family. It's nowhere near as grand, but it's beautiful in its own lived-in way and has a small but striking family chapel that contains a carefully hidden fingernail of St Francis Xavier – a relic that's understandably a source of great pride. Both homes are open daily and there's almost always someone around to let you in.

The best way to get here is by taxi from Margao: it's a ₹350 round trip, including waiting time.

ℹ Getting There & Around

Bus

Government and private long-distance buses both depart from Kadamba bus stand, about 2km north of the Municipal Gardens. Shuttle buses (₹30, 35 minutes) run to Panaji every few minutes. For North Goa destinations it's best to head to Panaji and change there. Local buses to Benaulim (₹10, 20 minutes), Colva (₹10, 20 minutes) and Palolem (₹30, one hour) stop at the bus stop on the east side of the Municipal Gardens every 15 minutes or so.

Private buses ply interstate routes several times daily, most departing between 5.30pm and 7.30pm, and can be booked at offices around town; try Paulo Travel Masters. (☎2702922; Luis Miranda Rd, 1st fl, Bella Vista Apt; ⊙8am-7pm). Destinations include Hampi (sleeper; ₹750, nine hours) and Mumbai (private; without/with AC ₹700/1000, 14 hours); these are high-season fares.

Taxi

Taxis are plentiful around the Municipal Gardens, train station and Kadamba bus stand, and they'll go anywhere in Goa, including Palolem (₹800), Panaji (₹800), Dabolim Airport (₹600), Anjuna (₹1200) and Arambol (₹1700). Except for the train station, where there's a prepaid booth, you'll have to negotiate the fare with the driver.

Train

Margao's well-organised train station, about 2km south of town, serves the Konkan Railway and other routes. Its reservation hall (☎PNR enquiry 2700730, information 2712790; ⊙8am-2pm & 2.15-8pm Mon-Sat, 8am-2pm Sun) is on the 1st floor. Services to Mumbai, Mangalore, Ernakulum and Thiruvananthapuram are the most frequent. A 7.50am train runs to Hospet (for Hampi) on Tuesday, Thursday, Friday and Sunday. It takes seven hours. Sleeper/3AC/2AC tickets cost ₹195/520/740.

A taxi or autorickshaw between the train station and the town centre is around ₹100.

Colva & Benaulim

POP 12,000

Colva and Benaulim boast broad, open beaches, but are no longer the first place backpackers head in south Goa. There's no party scene as in north Goa and they lack the beauty and traveller vibe of Palolem. Still, these are the closest beaches to the major transport hubs of Margao and Dabolim Airport. And from here you can explore this part of the southern coast (the beach stretches unbroken as far as Velsao in the north and the mouth of the Sal River at Mobor in the south), which in many parts is empty and gorgeous. The inland road that runs this length is perfect for gentle cycling and scootering, with lots of picturesque Portuguese-era mansions and white-washed churches along the way.

◎ Sights & Activities

The beach entrances at Colva, and to a lesser extent Benaulim, throng with operators keen to sell you **parasailing** (per ride ₹700), **jet-skiing** (per 15min ₹800), and one-hour **dolphin-watching trips** (per person from ₹400).

Goa Chitra   Museum
(☏6570877; www.goachitra.com; St John the Baptist Rd, Mondo Vaddo, Benaulim; admission ₹200; ◔9am-6pm Tue-Sun) Artist and restorer Victor Hugo Gomes has created this ethnographic museum from the more than 4000 cast-off objects that he has collected from across the state over 20 years. Admission to the museum is via a one-hour guided tour (held on the hour). In addition to the organic traditional farm out back, you'll see tons of tools and household objects,

Christian artefacts and some fascinating farming implements. Goa Chitra is 3km east of Maria Hall.

🛏 Sleeping

COLVA

Sam's Guesthouse   Hotel **$**
(☏2788753; r ₹500) Up away from the fray, about 1km north of Colva's main drag, Sam's is a cheerful place with good-value rooms arranged around a garden. It's a short hop across the road to the beach.

Skylark Resort   Hotel **$$**
(☏2788052; www.skylarkresortgoa.com; 4th Ward; r without/with AC from ₹2380/2970; ❄☲) Easily the pick of Colva's hotels for value, Skylark has colourful, immaculate rooms – the more expensive ones face the large pool. Locally made teak furniture, block-print bedspreads and giant shower heads add to the charm, and Colva's best bar is next door.

Braganza House
AMAR GROVER/GETTY IMAGES ©

GOA & AROUND COLVA & BENAULIM

BENAULIM

Rosario's Inn
Guesthouse $

(☎2770636; r without/with AC ₹400/700; ❄) Across a football field flitting with young players and dragonflies, Rosario's is a big family-run place that's been around for a while and is still a steal at this price.

Palm Grove Cottages
Hotel $$

(☎2770059, 2771170; www.palmgrovegoa.com; d ₹1450, with AC ₹1730-3100; ❄) Ensconsed in the leafiest garden you'll find, Palm Grove Cottages is close to the Benaulim shops but feels a world away. Guest rooms are atmospheric (some have balconies), and the ever-popular Palm Garden Restaurant graces the garden. The deluxe rooms in the new Portuguese-style building are top notch.

Anthy's Guesthouse
Guesthouse $$

(☎0832 2771680; anthysguesthouse@rediffmail. com; Sernabatim Beach; r ₹1400-1950) One of just a handful of places actually on the beach, Anthy's is a firm favourite with travellers (book ahead). Well-kept chalet-style rooms, which stretch back from the beach, are surrounded by a pretty garden and restaurant.

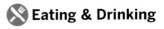

Eating & Drinking

COLVA

Colva's beach has a string of shacks offering the standard fare and fresh seafood.

Sagar Kinara
Indian $

(Colva Beach Rd; mains ₹40-160; ⏰7am-10.30pm) A pure-veg restaurant with tastes to please even committed carnivores, this top-floor place is super-efficient and serves up cheap and delicious North and South Indian cuisine.

Leda Lounge & Restaurant
Continental, Bar

(mains ₹200-600; ⏰7.30am-midnight) The food at stylish Leda – everything from seafood, steaks and Indian standards to pasta – is pricey but the attraction here is the comfy, cosmopolitan bar with live music most nights.

BENAULIM

Malibu Restaurant
Indian, Italian $$

(mains ₹100-180; ⏰8.30am-11pm) With a secluded garden setting full of flowers, cool breezes and butterflies, Malibu is off the beach but still one of Benaulim's tastier and more sophisticated dining experiences, with great renditions of Italian favourites. In season the same owners operate the Malibu beach shack.

Paragliders at Colva beach (p211)

Fish curry, rice and beer in Belaulim

GREG ELMS/GETTY IMAGES ©

Pedro's Bar & Restaurant
Goan, Multicuisine **$$**

(Vasvaddo Beach Rd; mains ₹110-300; ⊘7am-midnight) In a large, shady garden just back from the beachfront and popular with local and international tourists alike, Pedro's offers standard Indian, Chinese and Italian dishes, as well as a good line in Goan choices and some super 'sizzlers'.

Johncy Restaurant
Goan, Multicuisine **$$**

(Vasvaddo Beach Rd; mains ₹110-195; ⊘7am-midnight) At the main entrance to the beach, Johncy has been around forever, dispensing standard beach-shack favourites from its semipermanent location just off the sands.

ℹ Information

Colva has plenty of banks and ATMs strung along the east–west Colva Beach Rd. Benaulim has a Bank of Baroda ATM at Maria Hall and an HDFC ATM on the back road to Colva. Most useful services (pharmacies, supermarkets, internet, travel agents) are clustered around Benaulim village, which runs along the east–west Vasvaddo Beach Rd.

ℹ Getting There & Around

As with other beaches, scooters can be rented at Colva and Benaulim for around ₹200.

Colva

Buses run from Colva to Margao every few minutes (₹10, 20 minutes) until around 7pm. An autorickshaw/taxi to Margao costs ₹200/250.

Benaulim

Buses from Benaulim to Margao are also frequent (₹10, 20 minutes); they stop at the Maria Hall crossroads, 1.2km east of the beach. Some from Margao continue south to Varca and Cavelossim. Autorickshaws and pilots charge around ₹200 for Margao, and ₹60 for the five-minute ride to the beach.

Benaulim to Agonda

Immediately south of Benaulim are the beach resorts of **Varca** and **Cavelossim**, with wide, pristine sands and a line of flashy five-star hotels set amid landscaped private grounds fronting the beach. About 3km south of Cavelossim, at the end of the peninsula, **Mobor** and its

Detour: Cotigao Wildlife Sanctuary

Cotigao Wildlife Sanctuary
(☎ 2965601; admission/camera ₹5/25; ⊙ 7am-5.30pm) About 9km south of Palolem is this beautiful, remote-feeling sanctuary. Don't expect to bump into its more exotic residents (including gaurs, sambars, leopards and spotted deer), but frogs, snakes, monkeys and blazingly plumed birds are plentiful. Trails are marked; set off early for the best sighting prospects from one of the sanctuary's two forest watchtowers, 6km and 9km from the entrance. A rickshaw/taxi from Palolem to the sanctuary will charge ₹600/700 including a couple of hours' waiting time.

beach is one of the prettiest spots along this stretch of coast, with simple beach shacks serving good food. From here you can catch a ferry (or use the bridge once it's finished) over the river estuary to Betul.

From Betul heading south to Agonda, the road winds over gorgeous, undulating hills thick with palm groves. About 2.5km before Agonda is a 2km dirt track leading to **Cola Beach**, one of south Goa's most gorgeous hidden beach gems complete with emerald-green lagoon.

Agonda is a small village with a wide, relatively empty stretch of white-sand beach. Although there's a string of beach huts and restaurants here in season, Agonda is low-key compared with Palolem. Note, strong currents here make swimming dangerous.

Palolem & Around

Palolem has long been 'discovered' but it's still the tropical star of Goa's beaches – a stunning crescent of sand, calm waters and leaning coconut palms lend it a castaway vibe, but it does get crowded in season! It's a backpacker- and family-friendly, laid-back sort of place with lots of bamboo-hut budget accommodation along the sands, good places to eat, safe swimming and kayaking in calm seas, and all the yoga, massage and alternative therapies you could wish for.

If even Palolem's version of action is too much for you, head south, along the small rocky cove named **Colomb Bay**, which hosts several basic places to stay, to **Patnem Beach**, where a fine selection of beach huts, and a less pretty – but infinitely quieter – stretch of sand awaits.

Note that Palolem, even more so than other beach towns, operates seasonally; many places aren't up and running until November.

🏃 Activities

YOGA

Palolem and Patnem are the places to be if you're keen to yoga, belly dance, reiki, t'ai chi or tarot the days away. There are courses and classes on offer all over town, with locations and teachers changing seasonally. Bhakti Kutir (p215) offers daily drop-in yoga classes, as well as longer residential courses, but it's just a single yogic drop in the area's ever-changing alternative-therapy ocean. You'll find info on daily yoga classes (₹200) and cooking classes (₹1000) at **Butterfly Book Shop** (☎ 9341738801; www.yogavilla palolem.com; ⊙ 9am-10.30pm).

BEACH ACTIVITIES

Kayaks are available for rent on both Patnem and Palolem beaches; an hour's paddling will cost ₹100 to ₹150, including life jacket. Fishermen and other boat operators hanging around the beach offer dolphin-spotting trips or rides to beautiful **Butterfly Beach**, north of Palolem, for ₹1000 for two people, including one hour's waiting time. There are so many outrigger boats around that you should be able to bargain them down.

TREKKING

Goa Jungle Adventure
Outdoor Adventure

(☏9850485641; www.goajungle.com; trekking/canyoning trips from ₹1700/1900) Run by a couple of very professional French guys, this adventure outfit gets rave reviews from travellers for its jungle trekking and canyoning trips. Tours run from a half-day to several days, and rafting trips are also occasionally offered. Shoes can be rented for ₹190 per day. Book or enquire at Casa Fiesta restaurant.

🛏 Sleeping

Most of Palolem's accommodation is of the simple seasonal beach-hut variety. Since the huts are dismantled and rebuilt each year, standards and ownership can vary – for this reason the places listed here are either permanent guesthouses or well-established hut operations.

Bhakti Kutir
Cottage **$**

(☏2643472; www.bhaktikutir.com; Colomb Bay; cottages ₹1000-1600; @) Ensconced in a thick wooded grove between Palolem and Patnem, Bhakti's rustic cottages are looking a little worn, and you might find yourself sharing with the local wildlife, but they still make for a unique jungle ecoretreat. There are daily drop-in yoga classes and ayurvedic treatments, a relaxing vibe, and the outdoor restaurant serves up imaginative, healthful food.

Palolem Beach Resort
Resort **$$**

(☏2645775, 9764442778; www.cubagoa.com/palolem; r without/with AC ₹1750/2500, cottages ₹2000; ❄🛜) You can't beat the location, right at the main beach entrance, and although it's not flash, the seasonal cottages are clean and comfortable, and the staff are efficient and friendly. It also has some of the only beachfront air-con rooms (which are open year-round). The plywood non-AC rooms at the back are disappointing for the price.

Ciaran's
Beach Hut **$$$**

(☏2643477; www.ciarans.com; huts incl breakfast ₹3500-4000, r with AC ₹3500; ❄🛜) Ciaran's has some of the sturdiest and best-designed huts on the beach, with real windows, stone floors, full-length mirrors, wood detailing and nicer bathrooms than you'll find in most hotels, all arranged around peaceful palm-filled gardens and a genuine lawn. It's the perfect balance of rustic and sophisticated. There's also a free library, free breakfast and afternoon

Kayaks on Palolem beach
KIMBERLEY COOLE/GETTY IMAGES ©

Beach shacks, Palolem

GREG ELMS/GETTY IMAGES

tea and two quality restaurants, one of which is Palolem's only tapas bar.

Eating

Shiv Sai
Indian $

(thalis ₹50-60, mains ₹40-100; ⊙9am-11pm) A local lunch joint knocking out cheap and tasty thalis, including Goan fish and veggie versions.

Café Inn
Cafe $$

(www.cafeinn.in; meals ₹110-330; ⊙10am-11pm; 🛜) This fun semi-outdoor place has loud music, servers in saris and a cool cafe vibe. The Italian coffee, snacks, shakes, burgers and salads are great, but it's the evening barbecue that stands out: pick your base, toppings, sauces and bread to create a grilled mix-and-match masterpiece.

Fern's By Kate's
Goan $$

(☑9822165261; meals ₹120-350; ⊙8.30am-10.30pm; 🛜) Back from the beach, this solid timber place with a nautical feel serves up excellent authentic Goan food such as local sausages and shark amok-tik. Upstairs are two beautifully finished

air-con rooms (₹4000) with large bathrooms, four-poster beds and sea views.

Magic Italy
Italian $$

(mains ₹230-380; ⊙3pm-midnight) On the main beach road, Magic Italy has been around for a while but the quality of its pizza and pasta is getting even better, with imported Italian ingredients like ham, salami and olive oil, imaginative wood-fired pizzas and homemade pasta. The atmosphere is busy but chilled.

Casa Fiesta
Mexican $$

(mains ₹90-280; ⊙8.30am-midnight) Fiesta serves up a bit of a 'world menu' but its speciality (or point of difference) is Mexican, and it makes a pretty good fist of fajitas, burritos and tacos with most dishes under ₹200. The mellow hut ambienceworks, as do the margaritas.

Home
Continental $$

(☑2643916; www.homeispatnem.com; Patnem Beach; mains ₹160-260; ⊙8.30am-9.30pm) A hip, relaxed veg restaurant serving up pasta, salads, Mediterranean-style goodies and desserts, this is a Patnem favourite. Home also rents out nicely decorated, bright **rooms (s/d ₹1000/3000)**; call to book or ask at the restaurant.

Information

Palolem's main road is lined with travel agencies, internet places and money changers. The nearest ATM is about 1.5km away, where the main highway meets Palolem Beach Rd, or head to nearby Chaudi.

Sun-n-Moon Travels (Palolem Beach Rd; per hr ₹40; ⏰9am-10.30pm; 📶) One of several travel agencies with fast internet. Also sells SIM cards and mobile-phone top-ups.

Getting There & Around

Scooters and motorbikes can easily be hired along the main road leading to the beach from ₹200. Bicycles (₹100 per day) can be hired from the shop next to Palolem Dental Clinic.

Bus

Services to Margao (₹30, one hour, every 30 minutes) and Chaudi (₹5, every 15 minutes), the nearest town, depart from the bus stand down by the beach and stop at the Patnem turn-off. Chaudi has good bus connections, but for Panaji and north Goa, it's much better to go to Margao and catch an express from there.

Taxi & Autorickshaw

An autorickshaw from Palolem to Patnem costs ₹60, as it does to Chaudi. To Agonda it's ₹200. A prepaid taxi from Dabolim Airport to Palolem costs ₹1100.

Train

Many trains that run north or south out of Margao stop at the **Cancona Train Station** (📞2712790, 2643644).

KARNATAKA

Hampi

📞08394

Unreal and bewitching, the forlorn ruins of Hampi dot an unearthly landscape that will leave you spellbound the moment you cast your eyes on it. Heaps of giant boulders perch precariously over miles of undulating terrain, their rusty hues offset by jade-green palm groves, banana plantations and paddy fields. A World Heritage Site, Hampi is a place where you can lose

Hampi Bazaar

While in 1865 it was the Deccan sultanates who leveled Vijayanagar, today a different battle rages in Hampi between conservationists bent on protecting Hampi's architectural heritage and the locals who have settled there. In mid-2012 the master plan that had been in the works since the mid-2000s, and which aims to classify all of Hampi's ruins as protected monuments, was finally put into action. Overnight many shops, hotels and homes in the bazaar were bulldozed, reducing the main strip to rubble overnight, as villagers who'd made the site a living monument were evicted.

While villagers were compensated with a small plot of land in Kaddirampur, 4km from the bazaar (where there is talk of new guesthouses eventually opening up), many locals remained displaced months later as they awaited their payout.

So what does this mean for tourism, and are any guesthouses remaining in Hampi Bazaar? For now, little has changed in terms of tourist infrastructure. While at the time of research rubble from demolished buildings remained, and the main temple road resembled a bombed-out town, all hotels just back from the bazaar remained intact and the owners were confident of continuing to do so. There was talk, however, that height restrictions may be enforced, which would see three-storey buildings having to be cut back to two floors. This would mean a lot Hampi's appealing rooftop restaurants would disappear.

ANDERS BLOMQVIST/GETTY IMAGES ©

Don't Miss
Vittala Temple

The undisputed highlight of the Hampi ruins, the 16th-century Vittala Temple stands amid the boulders 2km from Hampi Bazaar. Though a few cement scaffolds have been erected to keep the main structure from collapsing, the site is in relatively good condition.

Work possibly started on the temple during the reign of Krishnadevaraya (r 1509–29). It was never finished or consecrated, yet the temple's incredible sculptural work remains the pinnacle of Vijayanagar art.

The ornate **stone chariot** that stands in the courtyard is the temple's showpiece and represents Vishnu's vehicle with an image of Garuda within. Its wheels were once capable of turning.

NEED TO KNOW
Indian/foreigner ₹10/250; ☉8.30am-5.30pm

yourself among wistful ruins, or simply be mesmerised by the vagaries of nature.

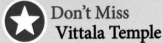 Sights

Set over 36 sq km, there are some 3700 monuments to explore here, and it would take months if you were to do it justice. The ruins are divided into two main areas: the Sacred Centre, around Hampi Bazaar; and the Royal Centre, towards Kamalapuram.

Be aware that the ₹250 ticket for Vittala Temple entitles you to same-day admission into most of the paid sites across the ruins, so don't lose your ticket.

Virupaksha Temple   Hindu Temple
(admission ₹2, camera ₹50; ☉dawn-dusk)
The focal point of Hampi Bazaar is the

Virupaksha Temple, one of the city's oldest structures, and Hampi's only remaining working temple. The main *gopuram* (gateway tower), almost 50m high, was built in 1442, with a smaller one added in 1510. The main shrine is dedicated to Virupaksha, an incarnation of Shiva.

If Lakshmi (the temple elephant) and her attendant are around, she'll smooch (bless) you for a coin. The adorable Lakshmi gets her morning bath at 8am, just down the way by the river ghats.

Royal Centre
Historic Site

While it can be accessed by a 2km foot trail from the Achyutaraya Temple, the Royal Centre is best reached via the Hampi–Kamalapuram road. A number of Hampi's major sites stand here, inlcuding **Mahanavami-diiba**, a 12m-high three-tierd platform, and **Hazarama Temple**, with exquistive carvings and polished black granite pillars.

Sleeping & Eating

Due to Hampi's religious significance, meat is strictly off the menu in all restaurants, and alcohol is banned (though some restaurants can order it for you).

Padma Guest House
Guesthouse $

241331; padmaguesthouse@gmail.com; ₹500-800, with AC from ₹1600; ❄ ?) In a quiet corner of Hampi Bazaar, the astute and amiable Padma has basic but squeaky-clean rooms and is a pleasant deviation from Hampi's usual offerings. Those on the 1st floor have good views of the Virupaksha Temple, while new rooms

have creature comforts of TV and air-con. There's free wi-fi downstairs.

Garden Paradise
Indian, Multicuisine $

(mains from ₹120) Not only does it have a sublime riverside location, but easily the best food. Dine at outdoor tables under shady mango trees or indoors on cushions and psychedelic murals. Also has accommodation.

ⓘ Information

There's no ATM in Hampi; the closest is 3km away in Kamalapuram – a ₹100 autorickshaw return trip.

Internet (per hour ₹40) is ubiquitous; some guesthouses have paid wi-fi. A good tourist resource for Hampi is www.hampi.in.

ⓘ Getting There & Away

Local buses (₹15, 30 minutes, half-hourly from 6.30am to 8.30pm) connect Hampi Bazaar with Hospet, Hampi's nearest train station. An autorickshaw costs ₹150 to ₹200.

A 6.30am train leaves Hospet for Madgaon (seven hours) in Goa every Monday, Wednesday, Thursday and Saturday. For the south, take the daily 8.40pm Hampi Express to Bengaluru (sleeper/2AC ₹191/785, nine hours).

Numerous travel agents in Hampi Bazaar book onward tickets or arrange taxis.

ⓘ Getting Around

Bicycles cost about ₹30 per day in Hampi Bazaar, while mopeds cost ₹100 to ₹150.

Walking the ruins is recommended too, but expect to cover at least 7km just to see the major sites. Hiring an autorickshaw for the day costs ₹750.

Kerala & South India

A sliver of a state in India's deep south, Kerala is shaped by its landscape – almost 600km of glorious Arabian Sea coast and beaches, a languid network of backwaters and the spice- and tea-covered hills of the Western Ghats. As relaxing as an ayurvedic massage, just setting foot on this swathe of soul-quenching green will slow your stride to a blissed-out amble. Besides its famous backwaters, elegant houseboats and delicately spiced, tastebud-tingling cuisine, Kerala is home to wild elephants, exotic birds and the odd tiger, as well as vibrant traditions such as Kathakali plays and snake-boat races.

Not far from here, in Karnataka, the magical city of Mysore is another South India highlight. Kerala is also just a simple step away from the riches of Tamil Nadu, homeland of one of humanity's living classical civilisations, as well as the French-tinged town of Puducherry and the inspirational temples of Mamallapuram and Madurai.

Backwaters near Alappuzha (p238)

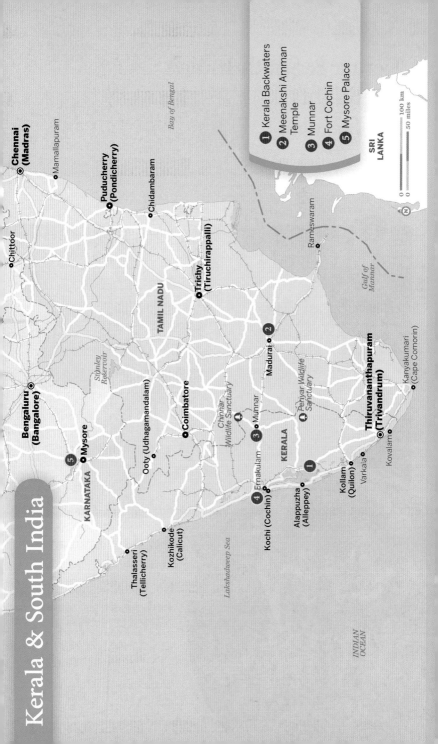

Kerala & South India

Kerala & South India's Highlights

Kerala Backwaters

Exploring Kerala's 900km network of waterways that fringe the coast and trickle inland is an experience not to be missed. The main jumping-off point to explore Kerala's southern backwaters is Alappuzha (Alleppey; p238) – from here you can hire an overnight houseboa or travel around through the narrower canals by canoe.

Meenakshi Amman Temple

The labyrinthine Meenakshi Amman Temple (p282) is one of India's most breathtaking religious sites, a 6-hecta complex enclosed by 12 *gopurams* (entrance towers). It's the pinnacle c South Indian temple architecture and an amazing place to observe the bus rituals and constant activity that cent on the shrine.

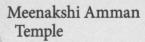

MAHESH/GETTY IMAGES ©

Munnar

The countryside around Munnar (p246) consists of rolling tea plantations, hued in a thousand shades of green. The hills are covered by a sculptural carpet of tea trees and the mountain scenery is magnificent. Stay in a remote guesthouse and take a trek – you'll often find yourself up above the clouds, watching veils of mist cling below the mountaintops.

Fort Cochin

The historic port of Kochi (Cochin; p248) is full of old colonial-era mansions, many turned into some of South India's loveliest heritage hotels. It's the ideal place to splash out on some atmospheric, stately accommodation to use as a base for your explorations of Kochi's islands, its synagogue, museums and excellent restaurants.

Mysore Palace

For many travellers, this most royal of ancient cities (p258) is a highlight of South India. Most are enticed by the magnificent Maharaja's Palace, but it's the bustling markets, cosmopolitan culture and famously friendly locals that persuade visitors to linger longer than first planned.

Kerala & South India's Best...

Wining & Dining

○ **Indian Coffee House** Trivandrum's extraordinary spiralling cafe tower. (p233)

○ **Dal Roti** Fort Cochin's finest, with the freshest, tastiest Indian cuisine. (p254)

○ **Malabar Junction** Another Fort Cochin culinary gem; come here for European cuisine, seafood and healthy indulgence. (p254)

○ **Sapphire** Food fit for a king, served in the grand ballroom of Mysore's Lalitha Mahal Palace hotel. (p264)

○ **Satsanga** Tuck into a proper cut of steak at one of Puducherry's finest continental restaurants. (p280)

Heritage Accommodation

○ **Raheem Residency** Lovely 1860s beachside home in the backwater hub of Alappuzha. (p239)

○ **Tea Sanctuary** Charming bungalows scattered around the tea plantations of the Munnar hills. (p248)

○ **Brunton Boatyard** Faithful 16th- and 17th-century Dutch and Portuguese architecture in Fort Cochin. (p252)

○ **Les Hibiscus** Arguably the pick of Puducherry's impressive collection of heritage hotels. (p279)

○ **Royal Orchid Metropole** Once housed the maharaja's guests, now one of Mysore's finest hotels. (p263)

Architecture

○ **Meenakshi Amman Temple, Madurai** A labyrinthine structure that ranks among the greatest temples of India. (p282)

○ **Mysore Palace, Mysore** Fantastic 20th-century palace – among the grandest of India's royal buildings. (p259)

○ **French Quarter, Puducherry** Romantic white and mustard colonial-era buildings on the cobbled streets of old Pondi. (p277)

○ **Pardesi Synagogue, Kochi** Exquisite synagogue in the spice port of Mattancherry. (p249)

○ **Shore Temple, Mamallapuram** Rock-cut elegance by the sea. (p272)

Chill-Out Spots

o **Backwaters** Kick back on a houseboat and watch the coconut groves float by. (p241)

o **Varkala** Stunning red-streaked coastal cliffs and white-sand beaches at Kerala's beachside traveller hot spot. (p236)

o **Munnar** Trek, chill and sip chai in the tea plantations around Munnar. (p246)

o **Periyar** Explore wildlife and trek the jungle in this popular national park. (p242)

o **Kovalam** Laze on the beach at Kerala's biggest resort or hide yourself away at a nearby ayurvedic retreat. (p234)

Left: Fish seller near Kovalam (p234)
e: Paths connect Kerala's waterside villages

Need to Know

ADVANCE PLANNING

o **One month before** Book ahead at heritage hotels.

o **Two weeks before** Reserve train tickets, or arrange a car and driver through an agency.

o **One day before** Call to reconfirm hotel bookings and reserve a place on your favoured tours.

RESOURCES

o **Kerala Tourism** (www.keralatourism.org) Kerala's official tourism site.

o **Manorama Online** (www.manoramaonline.com) Keralan newspaper with an online English edition.

o **Kerala.com** (www.kerala.com) News, tourism and loads of links.

o **Tamilnadu** (www.tamilnadu.com) News and directory.

o **Tamil Nadu Tourism** (www.tamilnadutourism.org)

GETTING AROUND

o **Train** Often the quickest way between towns along the coast.

o **Car & driver** A taxi – for one or several days – is the most convenient way to travel, but can be slower than the train on some routes, especially after the monsoon.

o **Boat** Ferries serve towns around Kerala's backwaters.

o **Bus** Good for getting to smaller towns.

BE FOREWARNED

o **High season** Kerala's backwaters and beach resorts have a high season around November to March; around mid-December to mid-January, prices creep up further.

o **Great deals** To be had during the monsoon (June to September).

Kerala & South India Itineraries

The first of these itineraries concentrates on the temple-rich state of Tamil Nadu, while the second allows time to explore the gloriously laid-back region of Kerala.

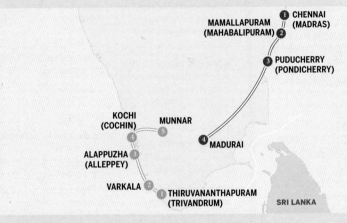

CHENNAI TO MADURAI
TAMIL NADU TEMPLE HOP

This tour starts in ❶**Chennai (Madras)**, the underrated state capital that's thin on top-draw sights but great for top-notch food. Build up an appetite by poking around the Government Museum complex and taking an early-evening stroll along Marina Beach before tucking into the city's culinary delights.

The following day, head south to nearby ❷**Mamallapuram (Mahabalipuram)**, where you can pick your way through the dramatic ruined temples and impressive ancient rock carvings, before gorging on fresh seafood as the sun goes down. If time allows, sign up for a bicycle tour around the neighbouring villages, before making your way to French-tinged ❸**Puducherry (Pondicherry)**. With its colonial-era buildings and bohemian vibe, you'll want to base yourself here for a couple of days – eat steak, browse boutiques and practise some yoga – before heading further south to ❹**Madurai**. The highlight here is the extraordinary Meenakshi Amman Temple, a riot of Dravidian sculpture that's regarded as South India's finest temple complex and ensures a dramatic to end your tour.

THIRUVANANTHAPURAM TO MUNNAR
A TASTE OF KERALA

Launch off from Kerala's gentle state capital, ❶ **Thiruvananthapuram (Trivandrum)**, popping in to its appealing museums and zoological park before heading straight for the beach. The laid-back, traveller-oriented resort of ❷ **Varkala** straggles along the top of stunning coastal cliffs and is formed of a cluster of small hotels and guesthouses. It's a Hindu place of pilgrimage as well as a holiday destination and you'll see priests doing *puja* (worship) on the beach. From here, head to ❸ **Alappuzha (Alleppey)** for a boat trip along Kerala's magical backwaters. Then continue north (either by boat, bus or a combination of the two) to the fascinating historic spice port of ❹ **Kochi (Cochin)**. Stay in lovely Fort Cochin, with its colonial-era mansions, excellent restaurants and age-old cantilevered Chinese fishing nets. The marvelous synagogue is within walking distance, in nearby Mattancherry. If you still have some time, it's an easy trip from Kochi into the foothills of the Western Ghats to the scrappy-looking town of ❺ **Munnar**, which is sublimely set, surrounded by rolling tea plantations. It's the perfect place to stay in a remote mansion, relax and go trekking into the hills.

Five Rathas temple (p273), Mamallapuram
IMAGES OF INDIA/GETTY IMAGES ©

Discover Kerala & South India

Varkala beach (p236)
CRAIG PERSHOUSE/GETTY IMAGES ©

KERALA

Thiruvananthapuram (Trivandrum)

☏0471 / POP 752,490

Kerala's capital – for obvious reasons still often referred to by its colonial name, Trivandrum – is an energetic place and an easygoing introduction to city life down south. Most travellers merely springboard from here to the nearby beachside resorts of Kovalam and Varkala, but Trivandrum has enough sights – including its zoo and cluster of Victorian museums in glorious neo-Keralan buildings – to justify a stay.

◎ Sights

Zoological Gardens & Museums   Zoo, Museum

Yann Martel famously based the animals in his *Life of Pi* on those he observed in Trivandrum's **zoological gardens** (☏2115122; adult/child ₹10/5, camera/video ₹25/75; ☺9am-5.15pm Tue-Sun). Shaded paths meander through woodland and lakes, where animals, such as tigers, macaques and birds, frolic in large open enclosures. There's a **reptile house** where cobras frequently flare their hoods – just don't ask what the cute guinea pigs are for.

The surrounding park contains a gallery and two museums. Housed in an 1880 wooden building, the **Napier Museum** (adult/child ₹5/2; ☺10am-5pm Tue & Thu-Sun, 1-5pm Wed) has an eclectic display of bronzes, Buddhist sculptures, temple carts and ivory carvings. The carnivalesque interior is stunning and worth a look in its own right. The dusty **Natural History Museum** (adult/child ₹5/2; ☺9am-4.30pm Tue

& Thu-Sun, 1-4.30pm Wed) has hundreds of stuffed animals and birds, and a fine skeleton collection. Just inside the eastern gate, the **Shri Chitra Art Gallery** (admission ₹5; ⏱9am-5pm Tue & Thu-Sun, 1-5pm Wed) has paintings by the Rajput, Mughal and Tanjore schools, and works by Ravi Varma.

Museum of History & Heritage
Museum

(☎9567019037; www.museumkeralam.org; Park View; Indian adult/child ₹20/10, foreigner adult/child ₹200/50, camera ₹25; ⏱10am-5.30pm Tue-Sun) In a lovely heritage building within the Kerala Tourism complex, this spacious new museum traces Keralan history and culture through superb static displays and interactive audiovisual presentations.

Shri Padmanabhaswamy Temple
Hindu Temple

(⏱Hindus only 4am-7.30pm) This 260-year-old temple is Trivandrum's spiritual heart.

🎯 Tours

KTDC (Kerala Tourist Development Corporation) runs several tours, all leaving from the Tourist Reception Centre at the KTDC Hotel Chaithram on Central Station Rd.

🛏 Sleeping

YMCA International Guesthouse
Hostel $

(☎2330059; www.ymcatvm.org; YMCA Rd; s/d ₹376/732, with AC ₹788/1125; ❄) Centrally located but down a relatively quiet street, this is one of the best budget deals in town; rooms are spacious and spotless and come with tiled bathrooms and TV. Both men and women accepted.

Graceful Homestay
Homestay $$

(☎2444358; www.gracefulhomestay.com; Pothujanam Rd, Philip's Hill; incl breakfast downstairs s/d ₹1300/1500, upstairs & ste s/d ₹2000/2500; @ 📶) In Trivandrum's leafy western suburbs, this lovely, serene house set in a couple of hectares of garden is owned by Sylvia and run by her brother Giles. The four rooms are all neatly furnished with access to kitchen, living areas and balconies. The pick of the rooms has an amazing covered terrace with views overlooking a sea of palms.

Varikatt Heritage
Homestay $$$

(☎2336057; www.varikattheritage.com; Punnen Rd; r incl breakfast ₹3950-5050; 📶) Trivandrum's most charismatic place to stay is the 250-year-old home of Colonel Roy

Transport from Trivandrum

BUSES LEAVING FROM TRIVANDRUM (KSRTC BUS STAND)

DESTINATION	FARE (₹)	DURATION (HR)	FREQUENCY
Alleppey	100, AC 191	3½	every 15min
Ernakulam (Kochi)	135, AC 250	5	every 20min
Kollam	43	1½	every 15min
Kumily (for Periyar)	200	8	2 daily
Munnar	250	7	2 daily
Varkala	40	1¼	hourly

MAJOR TRAINS FROM TRIVANDRUM

DESTINATION	TRAIN NO & NAME	FARE (₹, SLEEPER/3AC/2AC)	DURATION (HR)	DEPARTURES (DAILY)
Chennai	12696 Chennai Express	341/936/1425	16½	5.10pm
Delhi	12625 Kerala Express	595/1676/2780	50½	11.15am

Thiruvananthapuram (Trivandrum)

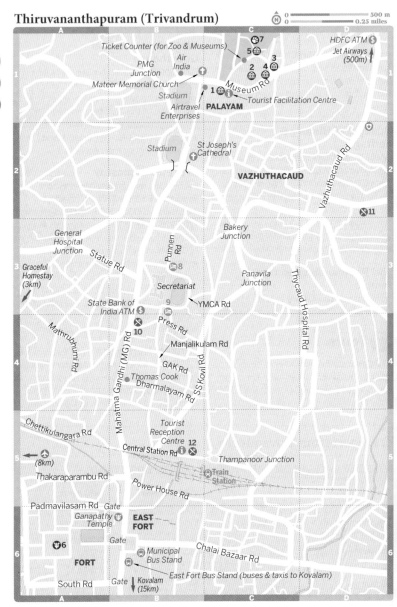

Kuncheria. It's a wonderful Indo-Saracenic bungalow with four rooms flanked by verandas facing a pretty garden. Every antique – and the home itself – has a family story attached. Lunch and dinner available (₹300).

✗ Eating

For some unusual refreshments with your meal, look out for *karikku* (coconut water) and *sambharam* (buttermilk with ginger and chilli).

Thiruvananthapuram (Trivandrum)

Indian Coffee House
Indian $

(Maveli Cafe; Central Station Rd; snacks ₹10-45; ◎7am-11pm) The Central Station Rd branch of Indian Coffee House serves its strong coffee and snacks in a crazy red-brick tower that looks like a cross between a lighthouse and a pigeon coop, and has a spiralling interior lined with concrete benches and tables. You have to admire the hard-working waiters. There's another, more run-of-the-mill branch near the zoo.

Cherries & Berries
Cafe $$

(www.cherriesandberries.in; Carmel Towers, Cotton Hill; ₹45-130; ◎9.45am-10pm; 🛜) For serious comfort food, icy air-con and free wi-fi, take a trip east of the centre to Cherries & Berries. Waffles, mini-pizzas, toasties, good coffee and indulgent chocolate-bar milkshakes.

Azad Restaurant
Indian $$

(Press Rd; dishes ₹75-145; ◎noon-11.30pm) A busy family favourite serving up authentic Keralan fish dishes, like fish *molee*, and excellent biryanis and tandoori.

ℹ Information

KIMS (Kerala Institute of Medical Sciences; ☎3041000, emergency 3041144; www.kimskerala.com; Kumarapuram; ◎24hr) About 3km northwest of Trivandrum.

Thomas Cook (☎2338140, 2338141; MG Rd; ◎10.30am-6pm Mon-Sat) Changes cash and travellers cheques.

Tourist Facilitation Centre (☎2321132; Museum Rd; ◎24hr) Near the zoo; supplies maps and brochures.

Tourist Reception Centre (KTDC Hotel Chaithram; ☎2330031; Central Station Rd; ◎7am-9pm) Arranges KTDC-run tours.

ℹ Getting There & Away

Air

Between them, **Air India** (☎2317341; Mascot Sq), **Jet Airways** (☎2728864; Sasthamangalam Junction) and **SpiceJet** (☎09871803333; www.spicejet.com; Trivandrum airport) fly from Trivandrum airport to Mumbai, Kochi, Bengaluru (Bangalore), Chennai (Madras) and Delhi.

There are also direct flights from Trivandrum to Colombo in Sri Lanka, Male in the Maldives and major Gulf regions such as Dubai, Kuwait and Bahrain.

All airline bookings can be made at the efficient **Airtravel Enterprises** (☎3011300; www.ate.travel; New Corporation Bldg, MG Rd).

Bus

For Tamil Nadu destinations, the State Express Transport Corporation (SETC) buses leave from the eastern end of the KSRTC bus stand.

Buses leave for Kovalam beach (₹15, 30 minutes, every 20 minutes) between 6am and 9pm from the southern end of the East Fort bus stand on MG Rd

Train

Trains are often heavily booked, so it's worth visiting the **reservation office** (☎139; ◎8am-8pm Mon-Sat, to 2pm Sun) at the main train station.

Within Kerala there are frequent express trains to Varkala (sleeper/3AC ₹57/175, one hour), Kollam (₹64/175, 1¼ hour) and Ernakulam (₹128/342, 4½ hours), with trains passing through either Alleppey (₹120/267, three hours) or Kottayam (₹120/313, 3½ hours).

ℹ Getting Around

The **airport** (☎2501424) is 8km from the city and 15km from Kovalam; take local bus 14 from the East Fort and City Bus stand (₹7). Prepaid taxi vouchers from the airport cost ₹350 to the city and ₹500 to Kovalam.

Autorickshaws are the easiest way to get around, with short hops costing ₹20 to ₹30.

Kovalam

☎0471

Once a calm fishing village clustered around its crescent beaches, these days Kovalam is Kerala's most developed resort. The main stretch, **Lighthouse Beach**, is touristy with hotels and restaurants built up along the shore, while **Hawa Beach** to the north is usually crowded with day-trippers.

There are strong rips at both ends of Lighthouse Beach that carry away several swimmers every year. Swim only between the flags in the area patrolled by lifeguards and avoid swimming during the monsoon.

◎ Sights & Activities

Vizhinjam Lighthouse   Lighthouse
(Indian/foreigner ₹10/25, camera/video ₹20/25; ⊙10am-5pm) Kovalam's most distinguishing feature is the candy-striped lighthouse at the southern end of the beach. Climb the spiral staircase for endless views along the coast.

Santhigiri   Ayurveda
(☎2482800; www.santhigiriashram.org; Lighthouse Beach Rd; ⊙9am-8pm) Excellent massages and ayurvedic treatments from ₹1000.

🛏 Sleeping

Paradesh Inn   Guesthouse **$$**
(☎9995362952; inn.paradesh@yahoo.com; Avaduthura; d incl breakfast ₹1600, ste ₹2500; @) Well back from the beach above the palms, tranquil Italian-run Paradesh Inn resembles a Greek island hideaway – a whitewashed house highlighted in blue. Each of the six fan-cooled rooms has a hanging chair outside, and there are sweeping views from the rooftop, fab breakfasts and *satya* cooking ('yoga food') for guests.

Treetops   Guesthouse **$$**
(☎9847912398, 2481363; treetopsofkovalam@ yahoo.in; r ₹1000; @) Indeed in the treetops

high above the beach next to Paradesh Inn, this friendly expat-owned place is a breath of fresh air. The three bright, sparkling-clean rooms have hanging chairs on the terraces, TVs, hot water and rooftop views; yoga classes available.

Beach Hotel II   Hotel **$$$**
(☎9400031243, 2481937; www.thebeachhotel -kovalam.com; d ₹4500, with AC ₹5600; ❄) Tucked into the southern end of Lighthouse Beach, this stylish pad has 10 seafacing rooms all with balcony and large sliding French windows. Decor is simple chic. It's also home to the excellent Fusion terrace restaurant.

Leela   Hotel **$$$**
(☎2480101; www.theleela.com; d from ₹14,000, ste from ₹33,750; ❄@🛜🏊) The sumptuous Leela is set in extensive grounds on the headland north of Hawa beach. Expect to find three swimming pools, an ayurvedic centre, a gym, two private beaches, several restaurants and more. Spacious rooms have period touches, colourful textiles and Keralan artwork.

🍴 Eating & Drinking

Each evening dozens of the restaurants lining the beach promenade display the catch of the day – just pick a fish, settle on a price (per fillet serve around ₹350, tiger prawns ₹550 per half kilo) and decide how you want it prepared. Unlicensed places will serve alcohol in mugs, or with the bottles hidden discreetly out of sight.

Suprabhatham   Keralan **$**
(meals ₹60-125; ⊙9am-10pm) This little veg place hidden back from the beach doesn't look like much, but it dishes up excellent, dirt-cheap Keralan cooking in a rustic setting of dirt floor and plastic chairs.

Waves Restaurant & German Bakery   Multicuisine **$$**
(Beach Hotel; breakfast ₹70-300, mains ₹150-550; ⊙7am-11pm) With its broad, burntorange balcony, ambient soundtrack and wide-roaming menu, Waves is always busy with foreigners. It morphs with the

German Bakery, a great spot for breakfast with fresh bread, croissants, pastries and decent coffee, while dinner turns up Thai curries, German sausages and seafood.

Fusion Multicuisine **$$**
(mains ₹120-340; ⊙8.30am-10.30pm) The terrace restaurant at Beach Hotel II is one of the best dining experiences on Lighthouse Beach with an inventive East-meets-West menu, a range of Continental dishes, Asian fusion and interesting seafood numbers like lobster steamed in vodka. Also serves French press coffee and herbal teas.

🅘 Information

Almost every shop and hotel will change money. Near the hospital is a CBS ATM taking Visa cards. About 500m uphill from the beach are HDFC and Axis ATMs. There are several small internet cafes charging around ₹30 per hour.
Tourist Facilitation Centre (☑2480085; Kovalam Beach Rd; ⊙9.30am-5pm) Helpful; in the entrance to Government Guesthouse near the bus stand and Leela Resort.

Upasana Hospital (☑2480632) Has English-speaking doctors who can take care of minor injuries.

🅘 Getting There & Around

Bus

Buses start and finish at an unofficial stand on the main road outside the entrance to Leela resort and all buses pass through Kovalam Junction, about 1.5km north of Lighthouse Beach. Buses connect Kovalam and Trivandrum every 20 minutes between 5.30am and 10.10pm (₹9, 30 minutes). There are two buses daily to Ernakulam (₹200, 5½ hours), stopping at Kallambalam (for Varkala, ₹70, 1½ hours), Kollam (₹80, 2½ hours) and Alleppey (₹120, four hours). There's another 6.30am bus to Ernakulam via Kottayam that bypasses Varkala.

Taxi

A taxi between Trivandrum and Kovalam beach is around ₹400; an autorickshaw should cost ₹250. From the bus stand to Lighthouse Beach costs around ₹50.

♥ If You Like…
Ayurvedic Retreats

Around 8km south of Kovalam, amid seemingly endless swaying palms, colourful village life and some empty golden-sand beaches, are some ayurvedic resorts that make tantalising high-end alternatives to Kovalam's crowded centre.

1 DR FRANKLIN'S PANCHAKARMA INSTITUTE
(☑2480870; www.dr-franklin.com; Chowara; s/d hut €15/20, r from €25/32, with AC €38/55; @ 🛜) A reputable and less expensive alternative to the flashier resorts. Daily treatment with full board costs €56. Accommodation is tidy and comfortable but not resort style.

2 SURYA SAMUDRA PRIVATE RETREATS
(☑2480413; www.suryasamudra.com; Pulinkudi; r incl breakfast ₹14,100-22,600; ❄🏊) A-list seclusion, featuring 22 transplanted traditional Keralan homes, with four-poster beds and open-air bathrooms, set in a palm grove above sparkling seas. There's an infinity pool carved out of a single block of granite, ayurvedic treatments, gym and spectacular outdoor yoga platforms.

3 BETHSAIDA HERMITAGE
(☑2267554; www.bethsaidahermitage.com; Pulinkudi; s €80-140, d €140-155; ❄) A resort with a difference: this is a charitable organisation that helps support two nearby orphanages and an old people's home. It's also an inviting, somehow old-fashioned beachside escape with sculpted gardens, a friendly welcome and putting-green-perfect lawns.

4 THAPOVAN HERITAGE HOME
(☑2480453; www.thapovan.com; s/d hillside from ₹2700/3480, cottages ₹4500/5700, beachfront cottage ₹4800/6000) Has two properties about 100m apart – one has beachfront cottages in Keralan style and the other is on a gorgeous hilltop location, with teak cottages filled with handcrafted furniture and set amid perfectly manicured grounds with wonderful views to the ocean and swaying palm groves.

Varkala

0470 / POP 42,270

Perched almost perilously along the edge of dizzying cliffs, the resort of Varkala has a naturally beautiful setting and the cliff-top stretch has steadily grown into Kerala's most popular backpacker hang-out. A strand of golden beach nuzzles Varkala's cliff edge, where restaurants play innocuous trance music and stalls sell T-shirts, baggy trousers and silver jewellery.

Activities

Laksmi's Massage

(**9895948080; Clafouti Beach Resort; manicure/pedicure from ₹400/600, henna ₹300, massage ₹800; 9am-7pm**) This tiny place offers treatments such as threading and waxing as well as massages (women only).

Haridas Yoga Yoga

(**www.pranayogavidya.com; Hotel Green Palace; classes ₹250; 8am & 4.30pm Aug-May**) Recommended 1½-hour hatha yoga classes with experienced teachers.

Eden Garden Massage

(**2603910; www.eden-garden.net; massage from ₹1000**) Offers a more upmarket ayurvedic experience, including single treatments and packages.

Sleeping

Jicky's Guesthouse $

(**2606994; www.jickys.com; s ₹400, d ₹600-1000, cottage ₹1250-1750, r with AC ₹2500;**) In the palm groves just back from the cliffs and taxi stand, family-run Jicky's remains as friendly as they come and has spread into several buildings offering plenty of choice for travellers. The rooms in the main whitewashed building are lovely and fresh, and nearby are two charming octagonal double cottages, and some larger air-con rooms.

Kaiya House Guesthouse $$

(**9746126909, 9995187913; www.kaiyahouse.com; s/d incl breakfast ₹1500/2000, d with AC ₹2500;**) Well back from the cliffs, what Kaiya House lacks in sea views it makes up for with charm, welcoming owners and sheer relaxation. There's a lovely rooftop terrace and rear courtyard with calming vibe. The cliff-top is 10 minutes' walk away.

Blue Water Beach Resort Cottages $$$

(**94468 48534; www.bluewaterstay.com; Odayam Beach; cottages ₹3000-5000**) At quiet Odayam Beach, north of Varkala, Blue Water is the pick of the beachfront places with sturdy individual timber cottages with tiled roofs arranged in a pleasant lawn area sloping down to the beach.

Taj Gateway Hotel Hotel $$$

(**6673300; www.thegatewayhotels.com; d incl breakfast from ₹7700;**

Fish stall, Varkala

MAX PADDLER/GETTY IMAGES ©

✱ @ 🛜 🏊) Varkala's flashiest hotel is looking hot – refurbished rooms with gleaming linen and mocha cushions overlook the garden, while the more expensive rooms have sea views and private balconies. There's a fantastic pool with bar (nonguests ₹500), tennis court and the well-regarded GAD restaurant.

🍴 Eating & Drinking

Most restaurants in Varkala offer the same mishmash of Indian, Asian and Western fare to a soundtrack of easy-listening trance and Bob Marley, but the quality of the cliffside 'shacks' has improved out of sight over the years and most offer free wi-fi. Join in the nightly Varkala saunter till you find a place that suits. Unlicensed places will usually serve alcohol discreetly.

Sreepadman South Indian **$**
(thali ₹40) For dirt-cheap and authentic Keralan fare – think dosas and thalis – where you can rub shoulders with rickshaw drivers rather than tourists, check out hole-in-the-wall Sreepadman opposite the Janardhana temple.

Trattorias Multicuisine **$$**
(meals ₹100-400; ⏰8.30am-11pm) Trattorias aims to specialise in Italian with a decent range of pasta and pizza but also offers Japanese – including sushi – and Thai dishes. This was one of the original places with an Italian coffee machine, and the wicker chairs and sea-facing terrace are cosy.

Coffee Temple Cafe
(⏰from 6am; 🛜) For your early-morning coffee fix it's hard to beat this English-run place, where the coffee beans are freshly ground. Also good cakes and fresh bread.

ℹ Information

A 24-hour ATM at Temple Junction takes Visa cards, and there are more ATMs in Varkala town. Many of the travel agents lining the cliff do cash advances on credit cards and change travellers

Detour:
Kappil Beach

About 9km north of Varkala, Kappil Beach is a beautiful and, as yet, undeveloped stretch of sand. It's also the start of a mini network of backwaters. The **Kappil Lake Boat Club**, near the bridge, hires out boats for short trips on the lake.

Just steps from the golden sand of Kappil and with very little around to disturb the peace, **Kappil Paradise Resort** (📞938775509; mohdrafi20@rediffmail.com; r ₹1200) has a handful of solid cottage-style rooms among the palms. Meals are available and the owner can help with transport to/from Varkala (around ₹150) and motorbike rental.

cheques. Internet cafes (per hr around ₹40) dot the cliff top.

Dangers & Annoyances

The beaches at Varkala have strong currents; even experienced swimmers have been swept away. This is one of the most dangerous beaches in Kerala. Take care walking on the cliff path, especially at night – much of it is unfenced and can be slippery in parts.

If women wear bikinis or even swimsuits on the beach at Varkala, they are likely to feel uncomfortably exposed to stares.

ℹ Getting There & Away

There are frequent local and express trains to Trivandrum (sleeper/3AC ₹140/249, one hour) and Kollam (₹140/249, 40 minutes), as well as four daily services to Alleppey (2nd class/chair class ₹50/185, two hours). From Temple Junction, three daily buses pass by on their way to Trivandrum (₹40, 1½ to two hours), with one heading to Kollam (₹30, one hour).

A taxi to Trivandrum costs ₹1100 and to Kollam ₹800.

Environmental Issues

Pollution from houseboat motors is becoming a major problem as boat numbers swell every season. The Keralan authorities have introduced an ecofriendly accreditation system for houseboat operators. Among the criteria an operator must meet before being issued with the 'Green Palm Certificate' are the installation of solar panels and sanitary tanks for the disposal of waste – ask operators whether they have the requisite certification. Consider choosing one of the few remaining punting, rather than motorised, boats if possible, though these can only operate in shallow water.

ⓘ Getting Around

It's about 2.5km from the train station to Varkala beach, with rickshaws going to Temple Junction for ₹60 and north cliff for ₹80. Local buses also travel regularly between the train station and Temple Junction (₹4).

Alappuzha (Alleppey)

☑ 0477 / POP 174,200

Alappuzha – still more romantically known as Alleppey – is the hub of Kerala's backwaters, home to a vast network of waterways and more than 1000 houseboats. Wandering around the small but chaotic city centre, with its modest grid of canals, you'd be hard-pressed to agree with the 'Venice of the East' tag. But step out of this mini-mayhem and head west to the beach – or in practically any other direction towards the backwaters – and Alleppey is graceful and greenery-fringed, disappearing into a watery world of villages, canoes, toddy shops and, of course, houseboats.

🏃 Activities

Kerala Kayaking Kayaking

(☑ 2245001, 9846585674; www.kerala kayaking.com; 4/7/10hr per person ₹1000/3000/4000) The first (and only) kayaking outfit in Alleppey, the young crew here offer excellent guided kayaking trips through narrow backwater canals. Paddles in single or double kayaks include a support boat and motorboat transport to your starting point.

🚩 Tours

Any of the dozens of travel agencies in town, guesthouses, hotels, or the KTDC can arrange canoe or houseboat tours of the backwaters. See p241.

🛌 Sleeping

Even if you're not planning on boarding a houseboat, Alleppey has some of the most charming and best-value accommodation in Kerala.

Mandala Beach House Guesthouse

(www.mandalabeachhouse.com; Alleppey Beach; d ₹600-900, cottage ₹750, ste ₹2000) Beachfront accommodation on a budget doesn't get much better than this in Alleppey. Super laid-back Mandala sits on the edge of the sand and has a range of simple rooms – the best being the glass-fronted 'penthouse' with unbeatable sunset views. Impromptu parties are known to crank up here in season.

Johnson's Guesthouse $

(☑ 2245825; www.johnsonskerala.com; d ₹400-750; @ 🛜) This backpacker favourite in a tumbledown mansion is as quirky as its owner, the gregarious Johnson Gilbert. It's a rambling residence with themed rooms filled with funky furniture, loads of plants outside and a canoe-shaped fish tank for a table. Johnson hires out his 'eco-houseboat' (₹6500 to ₹9000) and has a secluded riverside guesthouse in the backwaters.

Cherukara Nest   Homestay $$
(☎2251509; www.cherukaranest.com; d/tr incl breakfast ₹750/900, with AC ₹1200, AC cottage ₹1500; ❄@🛜) Set in well-tended gardens, with a pigeon coop at the back, this lovely heritage home has the sort of welcoming family atmosphere that makes you want to stay. In the main house there are four large character-filled rooms, with high ceilings, lots of polished wood touches and antediluvian doors with ornate locks – check out the spacious split-level air-con room. Owner Tony also has a good-value houseboat (₹5500 for two people) – one of the few that still uses punting power.

Tharavad   Homestay $$
(☎242044; www.tharavadheritageresort.com; west of North Police Station; d ₹1200-1500, with AC ₹2000; ❄) In a quiet canalside location between the town centre and beach, this charming ancestral home has lots of glossy teak and antiques, shuttered windows, five interesting rooms and well-maintained gardens.

Raheem Residency   Hotel $$$
(☎2239767; www.raheemresidency.com; Beach Rd; d €112-146; ❄🛜🏊) This thoughtfully renovated 1860s heritage home is a joy to visit, let alone stay in. The 10 rooms have been restored to their former glory and have bathtubs, antique furniture and period fixtures. The common areas are airy and comfortable, and there are pretty courtyards, a well-stocked library, a great little pool and an excellent restaurant.

✕ Eating & Drinking

Mushroom   Arabian, Indian $
(near South Police Station; mains ₹40-90; ⊙noon-midnight) Breezy open-air restaurant with wrought-iron chairs specialising in cheap, tasty and spicy halal meals like chicken *kali mirch*, fish tandoori and chilli mushrooms. Lots of locals and travellers give it a good vibe.

Kream Korner Art Cafe   Multicuisine $
(☎2252781; www.kreamkornerartcafe.com; Mullackal Rd; dishes ₹25-150; ⊙9am-10pm) The most colourful dining space in town, this food-meets-art restaurant greets you

Houseboats, Alappuzha

Don't Miss
Kerala's Backwaters

The undisputed highlight of a trip to Kerala is travelling through the 900km network of waterways that fringe the coast and trickle inland – preferably onboard a traditional houseboat designed like a *kettuvallam* (rice barge). Drifting through quiet canals lined with coconut palms, eating delicious Keralan food, meeting local villagers and sleeping on the water – it's a world away from the clamour of India.

tourist cruise ₹400

departs Kollam or Alleppey at 10.30am, arrives at 6.30pm

⊘ daily Aug-Mar, every second day Apr-Jul

Tourist Cruises

The popular tourist cruise between Kollam and Alleppey departs from either end at 10.30am, arriving at 6.30pm, daily from August to March and every second day at other times. It's a scenic and leisurely way to get between the two towns, but the boat travels along only the major canals.

Houseboats

Houseboats cater for couples (one or two double bedrooms) and groups (up to seven bedrooms!). Food (and an onboard chef to cook it) is generally included in the quoted cost, as is a driver/captain. Houseboats can be chartered through a multitude of private operators in Alleppey, Kollam and Kottayam. This is the biggest business in Kerala: some operators are unscrupulous. The quality of boats varies widely, from rust buckets to floating palaces – try to check out the boat before agreeing on a price. Most guesthouses and homestays can also book you on a houseboat.

It's possible to travel by houseboat between Alleppey and Kollam, and north all the way to the Kochi backwaters – the DTPC in Kollam can organise these trips. Expect a boat for two people for 24 hours to cost about ₹5000 to ₹8000 at the budget level; for four people, ₹8000 to ₹12,000; for larger boats or for air-conditioning expect to pay from ₹12,000 to ₹30,000. Shop around. Prices triple from around 20 December to 5 January.

Village Tours

More and more travellers are opting for village tours. They usually involve small groups of five to six people, a knowledgeable guide and an open canoe or covered *kettuvallam*. The tours (from Kochi, Kollam or Alleppey) last from 2½ to six hours and cost from around ₹400 to ₹800 per person. They include visits to villages to watch coir-making, boat building, toddy (palm beer) tapping and fish farming.

Kerala Backwaters Don't Miss List

BROUGHT UP ALONGSIDE THE BACKWATERS, DINESH KUMAR RUNS LOCAL TOURS AND HOUSEBOAT TRIPS

1 **CANOE & CHAVARA**
A motorised canoe ride through Alleppey's inland waters allows a glimpse of the local social life, the nature and its landscape. I recommend seeing a church, the 250-year-old birth house and Chavara Bhavan (Kuttamangalam) of the Reverend Kuriakose Elias. The journey will take you through the zigzagging canals, past rice fields – really, you are in the lap of nature.

2 **COIR MAKING**
In 1902, Londoner William Goodacre started a coir handloom in Muhamma, a village 16km north of Alleppey. When the British left India, Goodacre gave his handloom workers ownership – Kerala's first co-operative society. There are 150 workers here, the oldest aged 82. Take a bus from Alleppey and alight at Muhamma junction (40 minutes). Entry is free and it's open Monday to Saturday.

3 **RICE PADDIES & A CHURCH**
There are three famous rice fields below the water level, called Q, S and T Kayals. Kayal, in Malayalam, refers to the rice fields artificially created from Vembanad Lake. The project was led by local man Paul Murikkan, and it was his dream that he and his wife should be buried near the rice fields, so he built a church and burial grounds here. Sadly, his dream was never fulfilled, and he died alone in Trivandrum, but the church still exists on the deserted lakeshore.

4 **HOUSEBOAT ROUTE**
There are so many routes, but I suggest leaving from Alleppey at noon, docking overnight in a small lake called Vattakayal, south of C-block rice fields. This location is surrounded by paddy fields and the landscape is lush and green.

5 **PUBLIC FERRY**
I recommend the public ferries: Alleppey to Nedumudy (via Venattukadu) and Alleppey to Kavalam (via Venattukadu). Being from the backwaters, I know the beauty of the landscape, and these are some of the loveliest routes.

Detour:
Green Palm Homes

Just 12km from Alleppey on a backwater island, **Green Palm Homes** (9495557675, 0477-2724497; www.greenpalmhomes.com; Chennamkary; r incl full board ₹3250-4000, without bathroom ₹2250) is a series of homestays that seem a universe away, set in a picturesque village, where you sleep in simple rooms in villagers' homes among rice paddies (though 'premium' rooms with attached bathroom and air-con are available). It's splendidly quiet, there are no roads in sight and you can take a guided walk or hire bicycles (₹50 per hour) or canoes (₹100 per hour).

To get here, call ahead and catch one of the hourly ferries from Alleppey to Chennamkary (₹5, 1¼ hours). This is a traditional village; dress appropriately.

with brightly painted tables and contemporary local art on the walls. It's a relaxed, airy place popular with Indian and foreign families for its inexpensive and tasty menu of Indian and Chinese dishes.

Harbour Restaurant   Multicuisine $$
(2230767; Beach Rd; meals ₹100-290; 10am-10pm) This enjoyable beachside place is run by the nearby Raheem Residency. It's more casual and budget-conscious than the hotel's restaurant, but promises a range of well-prepared Indian, Chinese and Continental dishes, and some of the coldest beer in town.

Chakara Restaurant   Multicuisine $$$
(2230767; Beach Rd; mini Kerala meal ₹420, mains from ₹450; 12.30-3pm & 7-10pm) The restaurant at Raheem Residency is Alleppey's finest, with seating on a bijou open rooftop, reached via a spiral staircase, with views over to the beach. The menu creatively combines traditional Keralan and European cuisine, specialising in locally caught fish.

🛈 Information

DTPC Tourist Reception Centre (2251796; www.dtpcalappuzha.com; Boat Jetty Rd; 9am-5pm) Close to the bus stand and boat jetty. Staff can advise on homestays and houseboats.

UAE Exchange (2264407; cnr Cullan & Mullackal Rds; 9.30am-6pm Mon-Fri, to 4pm Sat, to 1pm Sun) For changing cash and travellers cheques.

🛈 Getting There & Away

Boat
Ferries run to Kottayam from the boat jetty on Boat Jetty (VCSB) Rd.

Bus
From the KSRTC bus stand, frequent buses head to Trivandrum (₹120, 3½ hours, every 20 minutes), Kollam (₹55, 2½ hours) and Ernakulam (Kochi; ₹50, 1½ hours). Buses to Kottayam (₹40, 1¼ hours, every 30 minutes) are much faster than the ferry. The Varkala bus (₹100, 3½ hours) leaves at 9am and 10.40am daily.

Train
There are several trains to Ernakulam (2nd-class/sleeper/3AC ₹39/120/218, 1½ hours) and Trivandrum (₹59/120/267, three hours) via Kollam (₹66/140/250, 1½ hours). Four trains a day stop at Varkala (2nd-class/AC chair ₹71/218, two hours). The train station is 4km west of town.

🛈 Getting Around

An autorickshaw from the train station to the boat jetty and KSRTC bus stand is around ₹60.

Periyar Wildlife Sanctuary
 04869

South India's most popular wildlife sanctuary, **Periyar** (224571; www.periyar tigerreserve.org; Indian/foreigner ₹25/300; 6am-6pm, last entry 5pm) encompasses 777 sq km and a 26-sq-km artificial lake created by the British in 1895. The vast region is home to bison, sambar, wild boar, angur, 900 to 1000 elephants and 35 to 40 hard-to-spot tigers. Firmly established on both the Indian and foreigner tourist trails, the place can sometimes feel a bit like Disneyland-in-the-Ghats, but its mountain scenery and jungle walks make for an enjoyable visit. Bring warm and waterproof clothing.

Kumily, 4km from the sanctuary, is the closest town and home to a growing strip of hotels, spice shops, chocolate shops and Kashmiri emporiums. **Thekkady** is the sanctuary centre, with the KTDC hotels and boat jetty. Confusingly, when people refer to the sanctuary they tend to use Kumily, Thekkady and Periyar interchangeably.

⊙ Sights & Activities

Various tours and trips access Periyar Wildlife Sanctuary. Most hotels and agencies around town can arrange all-day 4WD **jungle safaris (per person ₹1600-2000; ☺5am-6.30pm)**, which cover over 40km of trails in jungle bordering the park, though many travellers complain that at least 30km of the trip is on sealed roads.

You can arrange **elephant rides (per 30min/1hr/2hr ₹350/750/1000)** at most hotels and agencies in town. If you want the extended elephant experience, you can pay ₹2500 for a 2½-hour ride that includes elephant feeding and washing. **Cooking classes** (around ₹200-400) are offered by many local homestays.

Spice Gardens & Tea Plantation
Gardens, Tea Estate
Several spice planta-tions are open to visitors and most hotels can arrange tours (₹450/750 by autorickshaw/taxi for two to three hours). If you want to see a tea factory in operation, do it

from here – working tea-factory visits are not permitted in Munnar.

If you'd rather do a spice tour independently, you can visit a few excellent gardens outside Kumily. The one-hectare **Abraham's Spice Garden** (☏222919; www.abrahamspice.com; Spring Valley; tours ₹100; ☺7am-6.30pm) has been going for 56 years. **Highrange Spices** (☏222117; tours ₹100; ☺7am-6pm), 3km from Kumily, has 4 hectares where you can see ayurvedic herbs and vegetables growing. A rickshaw/taxi to either spice garden and back will be around ₹200/300.

Periyar Lake Cruise   Boating
(adult/child ₹150/50; ☺departures 7.30am, 9.30am, 11.15am, 1.45pm & 3.30pm) These 1½-hour boat trips around the lake are the main way to tour the sanctuary without taking a guided walk. You might see deer, boar and birdlife but it's generally more of a cruise – often a rowdy one – than a wildlife-spotting experience. Boats are operated by the forest department and by KTDC – the **ticket counters** are together in the main building above the boat jetty,

Elephants with a calf, Periyar Wildlife Sanctuary
CHRISTER FREDRIKSSON/GETTY IMAGES ©

and you must buy a ticket before boarding the boat.

Ecotourism Centre
Outdoor Adventure

(☎224571; www.periyartigerreserve.org; Thekkady Rd; ☻9am-1pm & 2-5pm) A number of more adventurous explorations of the park can be arranged by the Ecotourism Centre, run by the Forest Department. These include border hikes, 2½-hour nature walks (₹200), full-day bamboo rafting (₹1500) and 'jungle patrols' (₹750), which cover 4km to 5km and are the best way to experience the park close up, accompanied by a trained tribal guide. Trips usually require a minimum of four or five people. There are also overnight 'tiger trail' treks (per person ₹4000, solo ₹6000), which are run by former poachers retrained as guides, and cover 20km to 30km.

Santhigiri Ayurveda
Ayurveda

(☎223979; www.santhigiri.co.in; Munnar Rd, Vandanmedu Junction; ☻8am-8pm) An excellent and authentic place for the ayurvedic experience, offering top-notch massage (₹650 to ₹1500) and long-term treatments.

🛏 Sleeping

INSIDE THE SANCTUARY

The KTDC runs three steeply priced hotels in the park, including Periyar House, Aranya Nivas and the grand **Lake Palace** (☎223887; www.lakepalacethekkady.com; r incl all meals ₹20,000-25,000). Make reservations (at any KTDC office), particularly for weekends. Note that there's effectively a curfew at these places – guests are not permitted to roam the sanctuary after 6pm.

The Ecotourism Centre can arrange tented accommodation inside the park at the **Jungle Camp** (d tent ₹5000). Rates include trekking and meals but not the park entry fee. Also ask about **Bamboo Grove** (d ₹1500), a group of basic cottages and treehouses not far from Kumily town.

Left: Bonnet Macaques grooming each other
Below: Hikers in Periyar Wildlife Sanctuary
(LEFT) WILL GRAY/GETTY IMAGES ©; (BELOW) CHRISTER FREDRIKSSON/GETTY IMAGES ©

KUMILY

Green View
Homestay   Homestay $$
(📞224617; www.sureshgreenview.com; Bypass
Rd; r incl breakfast ₹500-1750; 📶) It has
grown from its humble homestay origins
but Greenview is a lovely place that manages to retain its personal and friendly
family welcome from owners Suresh and
Sulekha. The two buildings house several
classes of beautifully maintained rooms
with private balconies, some overlooking a lovely rear spice garden. Excellent
vegetarian **meals** and **cooking lessons**
(veg/nonveg ₹200/350) are available.

El-Paradiso   Homestay $$
(📞222350; www.goelparadiso.com; Bypass Rd; d
₹750-1250, q ₹1850; @ 📶) This immaculate
family homestay has fresh rooms with
balconies and hanging chairs, or opening
onto a terrace overlooking greenery at the
back. Cooking classes (₹400 incl meal)
are a speciality here.

Spice Village   Hotel $$$
(📞04843011711; www.cghearth.com; Thekkady
Rd; villas ₹14,000-20,000; 📶 🏊) 🌿 This CGH
Earth place takes its green credentials
very seriously and has captivating, spacious cottages that are smart yet cosily
rustic, in pristinely kept grounds. Its
restaurant does lavish lunch and dinner
buffets (₹1000 each), there's a colonial-
style bar and the **Wildlife Interpretation
Centre** (📞222028; ⏰6am-6pm), which
has a resident naturalist showing slides
and answering questions about the park.
Good value out of high season when rates
halve.

Eating

There are plenty of good cheap veg restaurants in the bazaar area.

Ebony's Cafe   Multicuisine $
(Bypass Rd; meals ₹40-240; ⏰8.30am-9.30pm)
This friendly rooftop joint with lots of pot

245

plants, check tablecloths and traveller-friendly tunes serves up a tasty assortment of Indian and Western food from mashed potato to pasta and cold beer (₹150).

French Restaurant & Bakery
Cafe, Bakery **$**

(meals ₹40-175; ⊙7.30am-10pm) This family-run shack set back from the main road is a good spot for breakfast or lunch, serving up croissants, pancakes and baguettes, along with decent pasta and noodle dishes.

Chrissie's Cafe
Multicuisine **$$**

(Bypass Rd; meals ₹80-200; ⊙8am-9.30pm) A perennially popular haunt, this airy 1st-floor cafe satisfies travellers with cakes and snacks, excellent coffee, and well-prepared Western faves like pizza and pasta.

ⓘ Information

There's a Federal Bank ATM accepting international cards at the junction with the road to Kottayam, and several internet cafes in the bazaar area.

DTPC Office (☏222620; ⊙10am-5pm Mon-Sat) Behind the bus stand; not as useful as the Ecotourism Centre.

Ecotourism Centre (☏224571; www.periyartigerreserve.org; ⊙9am-1pm & 2-5pm) For park tours, information and walks.

State Bank of Travancore (⊙10am-3.30pm Mon-Fri, to 12.30pm Sat) Changes travellers cheques and currency; has an ATM accepting foreign cards.

ⓘ Getting There & Away

Eleven buses daily operate between Ernakulam (Kochi) and Kumily (₹120, five hours). Buses leave every 30 minutes for Kottayam (₹71, four hours), with two direct buses to Trivandrum at 8.45am and 11am (₹210, eight hours) and one daily bus to Alleppey at 1.10pm (₹120, 5½ hours). Private buses to Munnar (₹75, four to five hours) also leave from the bus stand at 6am, 6.30am and 9.45am.

Tamil Nadu buses leave every 30 minutes to Madurai (₹80, four hours) from the Tamil Nadu bus stand just over the border.

ⓘ Getting Around

It's only about 1.5km from Kumily bus stand to the main park entrance, but another 3km from there to Periyar Lake (autorickshaw ₹50). Autorickshaws will take you on short hops around town for ₹30. **Bicycle hire** is available from many guesthouses.

Munnar

☏04865 / POP 68,200 / ELEV 1524M

South India's largest tea-growing region, the rolling hills around Munnar are carpeted in emerald-green tea plantations, contoured, clipped and sculpted like ornamental hedges. The low mountain scenery is magnificent – you're often up above the clouds watching veils of mist clinging to the mountain-tops. Munnar itself is a scruffy administration centre, not unlike a North Indian

Tea plantation, Munnar
BRUNO MORANDI/GETTY IMAGES ©

hill station, but wander just a few kilometres out of town and you'll be engulfed in a sea of a thousand shades of green.

Sights & Activities

The best way to experience the hills is on a **guided trek**, which can range from a few hours' 'soft trekking' around tea plantations to more arduous full-day mountain treks, which open up some stupendous views. Trekking guides can easily be organised through hotels and guesthouses or the DTPC for around ₹100 per person per hour (usually a minimum of four hours).

Tours

The DTPC (p248) runs three fairly rushed full-day tours to points around Munnar. The **Sandal Valley Tour** (per person ₹350; ⊙9am-6pm) visits Chinnar Wildlife Sanctuary, several viewpoints, waterfalls, plantations, a sandalwood forest and villages. The **Tea Valley tour** (per person ₹300; ⊙10am-6pm) visits Echo Point, Top Station and Rajamalai (for Eravikulam National Park), among other places. The **Village Sightseeing Tour** (₹400; ⊙9.30am-6pm) covers Devikulam, Anayirankal Dam, Ponmudy and a farm tour among others. You can hire a taxi to visit the main local sights for around ₹1200 for the day.

Sleeping

AROUND TOWN

JJ Cottage   Homestay $
(☏230104; jjcottagemunnar@sancharnet.in; d ₹350-800; @) The sweet family at this superb purple place a couple of kilometres south of town (but easy walking distance from the main bus stand) will go out of its way to make sure your stay is comfortable. The varied and uncomplicated rooms are ruthlessly clean, bright, great value and have TV and hot water. The one deluxe room on the top floor has a separate sitting room and sweeping views. Free internet but no wi-fi.

Green View   Guesthouse $
(☏230940; www.greenviewmunnar.com; d ₹450-700; @ ☏) This tidy guesthouse has 10

Detour:
Chinnar Wildlife Sanctuary

About 10km past Marayoor and 60km northeast of Munnar, this **wildlife sanctuary** (www.chinnar. org; Indian/foreigner ₹100/150, camera/ video ₹25/150; ⊙7am-6pm) hosts deer, leopards, elephants and the endangered grizzled giant squirrel. Trekking and **tree house** (s/d ₹1000/1250) or **hut** (s/d ₹1500/1800) accommodation within the sanctuary are available, as well as ecotour programs like river trekking, cultural visits and waterfall treks (around ₹150). For details contact the Forest Information Centre in Munnar. Buses from Munnar can drop you off at Chinnar (₹35, 1½ hours), or taxi hire for the day will cost ₹1300.

fresh budget rooms, a friendly welcome and reliable tour advice. The best rooms are on the upper floor and there's a super rooftop garden where you can sample 15 kinds of tea. The young owner organises trekking trips and also runs **Green Woods Anachal** (d incl breakfast ₹750) outside Munnar – a four-room budget option out in the tea and spice plantations.

MUNNAR HILLS

Dew Drops   Guesthouse $$
(☏04842216455; wilsonhomes2003@yahoo. co.in; Kallar; r incl breakfast ₹1500) Set in thick forest around 20km south of Munnar, this fantastic, remote place lies on 97 hectares of spice plantation and farmland. The resplendent building has eight bright, simple rooms each with a veranda on which you can sit and enjoy the chirping of birdlife and expansive views. The peace here is zen; call for a pick-up (₹50 per person).

Tea Sanctuary
Bungalows $$$

(☎230141; www.theteasanctuary.com; KDHP House; s/d incl breakfast ₹4500/5000) The Kannan Devan Hills Plantation Company operates four charming old heritage bungalows scattered around the Munnar hills under the banner of Tea Sanctuary. The secluded locations are amazing, surrounded by tea plantations. You can book through KDHP House in Munnar town.

Rose Gardens
Homestay $$$

(☎04864278243; www.munnarhomestays.com; NH49 Rd, Karadipara; r incl breakfast ₹4000; @ 🛜) Despite its handy location on the main road to Kochi, around 10km south of Munnar and with good bus connections, this is a peaceful spot overlooking the owner Tomy's idyllic plant nursery, with over 240 types of plants, and his mini spice and fruit plantation. The five rooms are large and comfortable with balconies overlooking the valley, and the family is charming. Cooking lessons are free, including fresh coconut pancakes for breakfast and delicately spiced Keralan dishes for dinner.

✴ Eating

Rapsy Restaurant
Indian $

(Bazaar; dishes ₹30-140; ⊙8am-9pm) This spotless glass-fronted sanctuary from the bazaar is packed at lunchtime, with locals lining up for Rapsy's famous *paratha* or biryani (from ₹50). It also makes a decent stab at fancy international dishes like Spanish omelette, Israeli *shakshuka* (eggs with tomatoes and spices) and Mexican salsa.

Aromas
Indian $

(www.royalretreat.co.in; Kannan Devan Hills; dishes ₹35-120; ⊙7.30-10am, noon-3pm, 7-9pm) In the Royal Retreat Hotel, just south of town, this longstanding favourite has reliably tasty and fresh Indian cooking served in nicely twee rooms with checked tablecloths.

Eastend
Indian $$

(Temple Rd; dishes ₹110-250; ⊙7.30-10.30am, noon-3.30pm & 6.30-10.30pm) In the slightly fancy hotel of the same name, this brightly lit, smartish place is one of the best in town for nonveg Indian dishes, with Chinese, North and South Indian and Kerala specialities on the menu.

ℹ Information

There are ATMs near the bridge, south of the bazaar.

DTPC Tourist Information Office (☎231516; keralatourismmunnardtpc@gmail.com; Alway-Munnar Rd; ⊙8.30am-7pm) Marginally helpful; operates a number of tours and can arrange trekking guides.

Forest Information Centre (☎231587; enpmunnar@gmail.com; ⊙10am-5pm) Wildlife Warden's Office, for accommodation bookings in Chinnar Wildlife Sanctuary.

ℹ Getting There & Away

Roads around Munnar are in poor condition and can be affected by monsoon rains. The main **KSRTC bus station** (AM Rd) is south of town, but it's best to catch buses from stands in Munnar town (where more frequent private buses also depart). The main stand is in the bazaar.

There are around 13 daily buses to Ernakulam (Kochi, ₹81, 5½ hours), two direct buses to Alleppey (₹110, five hours) at 6.20am and 1.10pm, and five to Trivandrum (₹226, nine hours). Private buses go to Kumily (₹75, four hours) at 11.25am, 12.20pm and 2.25pm.

A taxi to Ernakulam costs around ₹2000, and to Kumily ₹1800.

ℹ Getting Around

Autorickshaws ply the hills around Munnar with bone-shuddering efficiency; they charge up to ₹700 for a full day's sightseeing.

Kochi (Cochin)
☎0484 / POP 601,600

Serene Kochi has been drawing traders and explorers to its shores for over 600 years. The result is an unlikely blend of medieval Portugal, Holland and an English village grafted onto the tropical Malabar Coast. It's a delightful place to spend some time and nap in some of India's finest homestays and heritage accommodation.

NOBLEIMAGES/ALAMY ©

Don't Miss
Pardesi Synagogue

Originally built in 1568, this synagogue was partially destroyed by the Portuguese in 1662, and rebuilt two years later when the Dutch took Kochi. It features an ornate gold pulpit and elaborate hand-painted, willow-pattern floor tiles from Canton, China, which were added in 1762. It's magnificently illuminated by chandeliers (from Belgium) and coloured-glass lamps. The graceful clock tower was built in 1760. There is an upstairs balcony for women who worshipped separately according to Orthodox rites. Note that shorts, sleeveless tops, bags and cameras are not allowed inside.

NEED TO KNOW

admission ₹5; ⊙10am-1pm & 3-5pm Sun-Thu, closed Jewish hols

Mainland Ernakulam is the hectic transport and cosmopolitan hub of Kochi, while the historical towns of Fort Cochin and Mattancherry, though well-touristed, remain wonderfully serene.

 Sights

FORT COCHIN

A popular promenade winds around to the unofficial emblems of Kerala's backwaters: cantilevered **Chinese fishing nets**. A legacy of traders from the AD 1400 court of Kublai Khan, these enormous, spiderlike contraptions require at least four people to operate their counterweights at high tide. Modern fishing techniques are making these labour-intensive methods less and less profitable.

MATTANCHERRY & JEW TOWN

About 3km southeast of Fort Cochin, Mattancherry is the old bazaar district and centre of the spice trade. These days it's packed with spice shops and overpriced

Detour:
Cherai Beach

On Vypeen Island, 25km from Fort Cochin, Cherai Beach makes a fantastic day trip or getaway from Kochi. It's a lovely stretch of as-yet-undeveloped white sand, with miles of lazy backwaters just a few hundred metres from the seafront. Cherai is easily visited on a day trip from Kochi – it's an excellent ride if you hire a scooter or motorbike in Fort Cochin – but a growing number of low-key resorts along the single road running parallel to the beach make it worth hanging out a few days.

Brighton Beach House (☏9946565555; www.brightonbeachhouse.org; d ₹1100) has five basic rooms in a small building by the shore. The beach is rocky here, but the place is wonderfully secluded, filled with hammocks to loll in, and has a neat, elevated stilt-restaurant overlooking the seawall.

A collection of distinctive cottages lying around a meandering lagoon, **Cherai Beach Resort** (☏04842416949; www.cheraibeachresorts.com; villas from ₹3750, with AC from ₹4500; ❄@) has the beach on one side and backwaters on the other. Bungalows are individually designed using natural materials, and there's a bar and restaurant.

Hidden back from the beach but with the backwaters on your doorstep, **Les 3 Elephants** (☏04842480005, 9349174341; www.3elephants.in; Convent St; cottages ₹4000-8000; ❄☎) is a superb French-run ecoresort.

To get here from Fort Cochin, catch the vehicle-ferry to Vypeen Island (per person ₹2) and either hire an autorickshaw from the jetty (around ₹350) or catch one of the frequent buses (₹15, one hour) and get off at Cherai village, 1km from the beach.

Kashmiri-run emporiums. In the midst of this, Jew Town is a bustling port area with the fine Pardesi Synagogue.

Mattancherry Palace   Museum
(Dutch Palace; ☏2226085; Palace Rd; adult/child ₹5/free; ☉9am-5pm Sat-Thu) The Mattancherry Palace was a generous gift presented to the Raja of Kochi, Veera Kerala Varma (1537–61), as a gesture of goodwill by the Portuguese in 1555. More probably, it was used as a sweetener to securing trading privileges. The Dutch renovated the palace in 1663, hence its alternative name, the Dutch Palace.

The star attractions here are the astonishingly preserved Hindu **murals**, depicting scenes from the Ramayana, Mahabharata and Puranic legends in intricate detail. The central hall on the 1st floor is now a portrait gallery of maharajas from 1864. There's an impressive collection of palanquins (hand-carried carriages), bejewelled

outfits and splendidly carved ceilings in every room. Information panels detail the history of the Kochi royal dynasty. Photography is prohibited.

Tours

Most hotels and tourist offices can arrange the popular day trip out to the **elephant training camp** (☉7am-6pm) at Kudanadu, 50km from Kochi. Here you can go for a ride (₹200) and even help out with washing the gentle beasts if you arrive at 8am. Entry is free, though the elephant trainers will expect a small tip. A return trip out here in a taxi should cost around ₹1000 to ₹1200.

Tourist Desk
Information Counter   Boat Tour
(☏2371761; www.touristdesk.in) This private tour agency runs the popular full-day **Water Valley Tour** (₹650) through local backwater canals and lagoons. A canoe

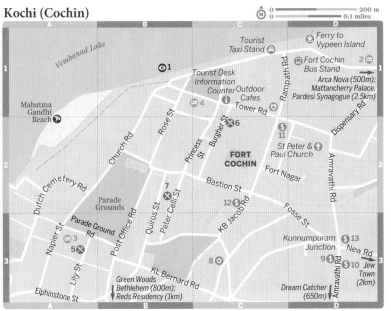

Kochi (Cochin)

trip through smaller canals and villages is included, as is lunch and hotel pick-ups. It also offers a two-night **Wayanad Wildlife tour** (₹6000), and an overnight **Munnar Hillstation tour** (₹3000). Prices include accommodation, transport and meals.

KTDC   Boat Tour

(☎2353234; backwater tours ½-day ₹450, motor-boat tours 2½hr ₹250, houseboat backwater trips day tour ₹650) The KTDC has **backwater tours** at 8.30am and 2pm, and tourist **motor-boat tours** around Fort Cochin at 9am and 2pm. Its full-day **houseboat backwater trips** visit local weaving factories, spice gardens and toddy tappers.

🛌 Sleeping

Book ahead during December and January. At other times you can bargain for a discount.

FORT COCHIN

**Green Woods
Bethlehem**   Homestay $

(☎3247791; greenwoodsbethlehem1@vsnl.net; opposite ESI Hospital; s/d incl breakfast ₹800/900) With a smile that brightens

Kochi (Cochin)

weary travellers, welcoming owner Sheeba looks ready to sign your adoption papers the minute you walk through her front door. Down a quiet laneway and

MARTIN HARVEY/GETTY IMAGES

with a walled garden thick with plants and palms, this is one of Kochi's most serene homestays. The rooms are humble but cosy; breakfast is served in the fantastic leafy rooftop cafe, where cooking classes/demonstrations are often held.

Dream Catcher Homestay $
(2217550; www.dreamcatcherhomestays.com; Vasavan Lane; r ₹800-1000, with AC from ₹2000; ❄) Tucked away on a narrow laneway, this rambling old colonial house has spotless mid-priced rooms, an almost gothic sitting room and balconies lined with pot plants: it offers a warm backpacker-friendly welcome from the Portuguese-descended family.

Reds Residency Homestay $$
(3204060; www.redsresidency.in; 11/372 A, KJ Herschel Rd; d incl breakfast ₹800-1000, with AC ₹1000-1200, AC cottage ₹1500; ❄ @ 🛜) Reds is a relatively new homestay with hotel-quality rooms but a true family welcome from knowledgeable hosts Philip and Maryann. The five double rooms are modern and immaculate, and there's a self-contained 'penthouse' cottage with

kitchen on the rooftop. It's in a peaceful location near the Maritime Museum.

Malabar House Hotel $$$
(2216666; www.malabarhouse.com; Parade Ground Rd; r €230, ste incl breakfast €330-380; ❄ @ 🛜) What may just be one of the fanciest boutique hotels in Kerala, Malabar flaunts its uber-hip blend of modern colours and period fittings like it's not even trying. While the suites are huge and lavishly appointed, the standard rooms are more snug. The award-winning restaurant and wine bar are top notch.

Brunton Boatyard Hotel $$$
(2215461; bruntonboatyard@cghearth.com; River Rd; r ₹21,000, ste ₹28,000; ❄ @ 🛜) This imposing hotel faithfully reproduces 16th- and 17th-century Dutch and Portuguese architecture in its grand complex. All of the rooms look out over the harbour, and have bathtub and balconies with a refreshing sea breeze that beats air-con any day. It has the excellent History Restaurant and Armoury Bar, along with a couple of open-air cafes.

Old Harbour Hotel
Hotel $$$

(☎ 2218006; www.oldharbourhotel.com; Tower Rd; r ₹9250-13,050; ❄ @ ☒) Set around an idyllic garden with lily ponds and a small pool, the dignified Old Harbour is housed in a 300-year-old Dutch/ Portuguese heritage building. The elegant mix of period and modern styles lend it a more intimate feel than some of the more grandiose competition. There are 13 rooms, some facing directly onto the garden, and some with plant-filled, open-air bathrooms.

MATTANCHERRY & JEW TOWN

Caza Maria
Homestay $$$

(☎ 9846050901; cazamaria@rediffmail.com; Jew Town Rd, Mattancherry; r incl breakfast ₹4500; ❄) Right in the heart of Jew Town, this unique place has just two enormous, gorgeous heritage rooms overlooking the bazaar. Fit for a maharaja, the rooms feature an idiosyncratic style – with each high-ceilinged room painted in bright colours, filled to the brim with antiques.

AROUND KOCHI

Olavipe
Homestay $$

(☎ 04782522255; www.olavipe.com; Olavipe; s/d incl meals ₹5100/8500) This gorgeous 1890s traditional Syrian-Christian home is on a 16-hectare farm surrounded by backwaters, 28km south of Kochi. A restored mansion of rosewood and glistening teak, it has several large and breezy rooms beautifully decorated in original period decor. There are lots of shady awnings and sitting areas, a fascinating archive with six generations of family history, and the gracious own-ers will make you feel like a welcome friend rather than a guest.

🍴 Eating & Drinking

FORT COCHIN

Behind the Chinese fishing nets are several **fishmongers**, from whom you can buy fish (or prawns, scampi or lobster), then take your selection to one of the row of simple but popular restaurants on nearby Tower Rd where the folks there will cook it and serve it to you for an additional charge. Market price varies.

Kashi Art Cafe
Cafe $

(Burgher St; breakfast & snacks ₹80-110; ⏰ 8.30am-7.30pm) An institution in Fort Cochin, this natural light–filled place has a zen-but-casual vibe and solid wood tables that spread out into a semi-courtyard space. The coffee is as strong as it should be and the daily Western breakfast and lunch specials are excellent. A small gallery shows off local artists.

KERALA & SOUTH INDIA KOCHI (COCHIN)

Fisher mending Chinese fishing nets (p249)
ANTHONY PLUMMER/GETTY IMAGES ©

Right: Mattancherry street **Below:** Mattancherry Palace (p250)

(RIGHT) ANDERS BLOMQVIST /GETTY IMAGES ©; (BELOW) DE AGOSTINI PICTURE LIBRARY/GETTY IMAGES ©

Teapot
Cafe $

(Peter Celli St; mains ₹60-250) This atmospheric cafe is the perfect venue for 'high tea', with 16 types of tea, sandwiches, cake and full meals served in chic, airy rooms. Witty tea-themed accents include loads of antique teapots, tea chests for tables and a gnarled glass table with a tea-tree base.

Dal Roti
Indian $$

(✆9746459244; 1/293 Lily St; meals ₹100-230; ⊗noon-3.30pm & 6.30-10.30pm Wed-Mon) There's a lot to like about busy Dal Roti. Friendly and knowledgeable owner Ramesh will hold your hand through his expansive North Indian menu, which even sports its own glossary, and help you dive into his delicious range of vegetarian, eggetarian and nonvegetarian options. From kati rolls to seven types of thali, you won't go hungry. No alcohol.

Arca Nova
Seafood $$

(2/6A Calvathy Rd; mains ₹220-380; ⊗7.30am-10.30pm) The waterside restaurant at the Fort House Hotel is a prime choice for a leisurely lunch. It specialises in fish dishes and you can sit out at tables overlooking the water or in the serenely spacious covered garden area.

Malabar Junction
International $$$

(✆2216666; Parade Ground Rd; mains ₹350-650) Set in an open-sided pavilion, the restaurant at Malabar House is movie-star cool, with white-tableclothed tables in a courtyard close to the small pool. There's a seafood-based, European-style menu – the signature dish is the impressive seafood platter with grilled vegetables.

MATTANCHERRY & JEW TOWN

Ramathula Hotel
Indian $

(Kayees Junction, Mattancherry; biryani ₹40-60; ⊗lunch & dinner) This place is legendary among locals for its chicken and mutton

biryanis – get here early or miss out. It's better known by the chef's name, Kayikka's.

Caza Maria   Multicuisine **$$**
Bazaar Rd; mains ₹150-290; ⊙10am-8pm) This enchanting 1st-floor place across from the hotel of the same name is a bright-blue, antique-filled space with funky music and a changing daily menu of North Indian, South Indian and French dishes.

Café Jew Town   Cafe **$$**
Bazaar Rd; snacks ₹120-150; ⊙9.30am-6pm) Walk through chic antique shops and galleries to reach this sweet Swiss-owned cafe; the few tables proffer good cakes, snacks and Italian coffee.

✪ Entertainment

There are several places in Kochi where you can view Kathakali. The performances are certainly made for tourists, but they're a good introduction to this intriguing art form. The standard program starts with the intricate make-up application and costume-fitting, followed by a demonstration and commentary on the dance and then the performance – usually two hours in all. The fast-paced traditional martial art of *kalarippayat* can also be easily seen in Fort Cochin.

FORT COCHIN
Kerala Kathakali Centre   Cultural Program
(🕿2217552; www.kathakalicentre.com; KB Jacob Rd; admission ₹250; ⊙make-up from 5pm, show 6-7.30pm) In an intimate, wood-lined theatre, this place provides a useful introduction to Kathakali, complete with amazing demonstrations of eye movements, plus handy translations of the night's story. The centre also hosts performances of the martial art of *kalarippayat* at 4pm to 5pm daily, traditional music at 8pm to 9pm Sunday to Friday and classical dance at 8pm to 9pm on Saturday.

ERNAKULAM

See India Foundation
Cultural Program
(2376471; devankathakali@yahoo.com; Kalathiparambil Lane; admission ₹200; make-up 6pm, show 7-8pm) One of the oldest Kathakali theatres in Kerala, it has small-scale shows with an emphasis on the religious and philosophical roots of Kathakali.

Information

Internet Access
There are several internet cafes around Princess St in Fort Cochin charging ₹40 per hour, and a number of homestays offer free wi-fi.

Medical Services
Lakeshore Hospital (2701032; www.lakeshorehospital.com; NH Bypass, Marudu) Modern hospital 8km southeast of central Ernakulam.

Money
UAE Exchange (9.30am-6pm Mon-Fri, to 4pm Sat) Ernakulam (2383317; MG Rd, Perumpillil Bldg); Ernakulam (3067008; Chettupuzha Towers, PT Usha Rd Junction); Fort Cochin (2216231; Amravathi Rd) Foreign exchange and travellers cheques.

Tourist Information
There's a tourist information counter at the airport. Many places distribute a free brochure that includes a map and walking tour entitled *Historical Places in Fort Cochin*.

KTDC Tourist Reception Centre (2353234; Shanmugham Rd, Ernakulam; 8am-7pm) Organises tours. There's another office at the jetty at Fort Cochin.

Tourist Desk Information Counter Ernakulam (2371761; www.touristdesk.in; Boat Jetty; 8am-6pm); Fort Cochin (2216129; 8am-7pm) A private tour agency that's extremely knowledgeable and helpful about Kochi and beyond.

Tourist Police Ernakulam (2353234; Shanmugham Rd; 8am-6pm); Fort Cochin (2215055; 24hr)

Getting There & Away

Air
Kochi International Airport has flights to the Gulf states, Sri Lanka and Singapore. Between them **Jet Airways** (2359334; MG Rd), **Air India** (2351295; MG Rd) and Spicejet fly direct daily to Chennai, Mumbai and Bengalaru. Air India also flies to Delhi daily, while IndiGo flies to Trivandrum.

Bus
At the time of writing there were plans afoot for buses to operate directly between Fort Cochin and tourist centres like Munnar, Alleppey and Periyar. Until then, all long-distance services operate from Ernakulam. The **KSRTC bus stand** (2372033; reservations 6am-10pm) is next to the railway, halfway between the two train stations. Government and private buses pull into the

Kathakali dancer

massive new Vyttila Mobility Hub (☎2306611; www.vyttilamobilityhub.com; ⏱24hr), a state-of-the-art transport terminal about 2km east of Ernakulam Junction train station. Numerous private bus companies have super-deluxe, air-con, video and Volvo buses to long-distance destinations such as Chennai and Trivandrum; prices vary depending on the standard but the best buses are about 50% higher than government buses. Agents in Ernakulam and Fort Cochin sell tickets. Private buses also use the **Kaloor bus stand**, 1km north of the city.

A prepaid autorickshaw from Vyttila costs ₹67 to the boat jetty, ₹62 to the train station and ₹171 to Fort Cochin.

Train

Ernakulam has two train stations, **Ernakulam Town** and **Ernakulam Junction**. Reservations for both are made at the Ernakulam Junction reservations office (☎132; ⏱8am-8pm Mon-Sat, to 2pm Sun).

There are local and express trains to Trivandrum (2nd-class/AC chair ₹73/264, 4½ hours), via either Alleppey (₹39/171, 1½ hours) or Kottayam (₹39/171, 1½ hours).

ⓘ Getting Around

To/From the Airport

Kochi International Airport (☎2610125; http://cochinairport.com) is at Nedumbassery, 30km northeast of Ernakulam. A new bus services runs between the airport and Fort Cochin (₹70, one hour, eight daily), some going via Ernakulam. Taxis to/from Ernakulam cost around ₹650, and to/from Fort Cochin around ₹900.

Boat

Ferries are the fastest and most enjoyable form of transport between Fort Cochin and the mainland. The jetty on the eastern side of Willingdon Island is called **Embarkation**; the west one, opposite Mattancherry, is **Terminus**; and the main stop at

Ernakulam Bus & Train Services

MAJOR BUSES FROM ERNAKULAM

The following bus services operate from the KSRTC bus stand and Vyttila Mobility Hub.

DESTINATION	FARE (₹)	DURATION (HR)	FREQUENCY
Alleppey	41	1½	every 10min
Chennai	555	16	1 daily, 2pm
Kollam	94	3½	every 30min
Kottayam	51	2	every 30min
Kumily (for Periyar)	120	5	8 daily
Munnar	90	4½	every 30min
Trivandrum	138	5	every 30min

MAJOR TRAINS FROM ERNAKULAM

The following are major long-distance trains departing from Ernakulam Town.

DESTINATION	TRAIN NO & NAME	FARE (₹, SLEEPER/ 3AC/2AC)	DURATION (HR)	DEPARTURES (DAILY)
Bengaluru	16525 Bangalore Express	257/719/1085	13	5.55pm
Chennai	12624 Chennai Mail	292/793/1185	12	6.40pm
Delhi	12625 Kerala Express (A)	579/1630/2685	46	3.50pm
Goa	16346 Netravathi Express	305/858/1315	15	2.05pm
Mumbai	16382 Mumbai Express	469/1337/2130	40	1.30pm

(A) Departs from Ernakulam Junction

Fort Cochin is **Customs**, with another stop at the **Mattancherry Jetty** near the synagogue. One-way fares are ₹2.50 (₹3.50 between Ernakulam and Mattancherry).

Ernakulam

There are services to both Fort Cochin jetties (Customs and Mattancherry) every 25 to 50 minutes from Ernakulam's main jetty.

Ferries also run every 20 minutes or so to Willingdon and Vypeen Islands.

Fort Cochin

Ferries run from Customs Jetty to Ernakulam. Ferries also hop between Customs Jetty and Willingdon Island 18 times a day.

Car and passenger ferries cross to Vypeen Island from Fort Cochin virtually nonstop.

Local Transport

There are no real bus services between Fort Cochin and Mattancherry Palace, but it's an enjoyable 30-minute walk through the busy warehouse area along Bazaar Rd. Autorickshaws should cost around ₹40, much less if you promise to look in a shop. Most autorickshaw trips around Ernakulam shouldn't cost more than ₹35.

To get to Fort Cochin after ferries stop running you'll need to catch a taxi or autorickshaw – Ernakulam Town train station to Fort Cochin should cost around ₹300; prepaid autorickshaws during the day cost ₹150.

SOUTHERN KARNATAKA

Mysore

☏ 0821 / POP 887,500 / ELEV 707M

If you haven't been to Mysore, you just haven't seen South India. Conceited though it may sound, this is not an overstatement. An ancient city with more than 600 glorious years of legacy,

Mysore

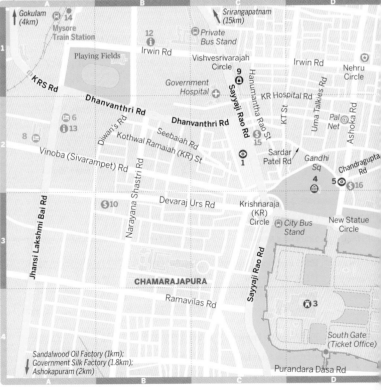

Mysore is one of the most flamboyant places in India. Known for its glittering royal heritage, bustling markets, magnificent monuments, cosmopolitan culture and a friendly populace, it is also a thriving centre for the production of premium silk, sandalwood and incense. It also flaunts considerable expertise in yoga and ayurveda, two trades it markets worldwide.

◉ Sights

Mysore Palace   Palace
(Maharaja's Palace; www.mysorepalace.tv; Indian/foreigner ₹40/200, children under 10 free, Sound & Light show adult/child ₹40/25; ⊙10am-5.30pm) Among the grandest of India's royal buildings, this fantastic palace was the former seat of the Wodeyar maharajas. The old palace was gutted by fire in 1897; the one you see now was completed in 1912 by English architect Henry Irwin at a cost of ₹4.5 million.

The interior of this Indo-Saracenic marvel – a kaleidoscope of stained glass, mirrors and gaudy colours – is undoubtedly over the top. The decor is further embellished by carved wooden doors, mosaic floors and a series of paintings depicting life in Mysore during the Edwardian Raj. The way into the palace takes you past a fine collection of sculptures and artefacts. Don't forget to check out the armoury, with an intriguing collection of 700-plus weapons.

Entrance to the palace grounds is at the South Gate on Purandara Dasa Rd. While you are allowed to snap the palace's exterior, photography within is strictly prohibited. Cameras must be deposited in lockers at the palace entrance.

Also available within the compound is a multilingual guided audiotour of the palace, the price of which is included in the foreigners' ticket.

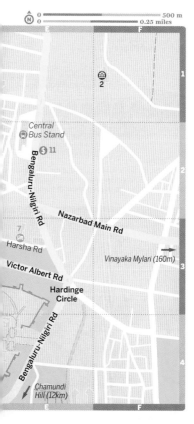

Mysore Palace

The interior of Mysore Palace houses opulent halls, royal paintings, intricate decorative details, as well as sculptures and ceremonial objects. There is a lot of hidden detail and much to take in, so be sure to allow yourself at least a few hours for the experience. A guide can also be invaluable.

After entering the palace the first exhibit is the **Doll's Pavilion** **1**, which showcases the maharaja's fine collection of traditional dolls and sculptures acquired from around the world. Opposite the **Elephant Gate** **2** you'll see the seven cannons that were used for special occasions, such as the birthdays of the maharajas. Today the cannons are still fired as part of Dasara festivities.

At the end of the Doll's Pavilion you'll find the **Golden Howdah** **3**. Note the fly whisks on either side; the bristles are made from fine ivory.

Make sure you check out the paintings depicting the Dasara procession in the halls on your way to the **Marriage Pavilion** **4** and look into the courtyard to see what was once the wrestling arena. It's now used during Dasara only. In the Marriage Pavilion, take a few minutes to scan the entire space. You can see the influence of three religions in the design of the hall: the glass ceiling represents Christianity, stone carvings along the hallway ceilings are Hindu design and the top-floor balcony roof (the traditional ladies' gallery) has Islamic-style arches.

When you move through to the **Private Durbar Hall** **5**, take note of the intricate ivory inlay motifs depicting Krishna in the rosewood doors. The **Public Durbar Hall** **6** is usually the last stop where you can admire the panoramic views of the gardens through the Islamic arches.

Private Durbar Hall
Rosewood doors lead into this hall, which is richly decorated with stained-glass ceilings, steel grill work and chandeliers. It houses the Golden Throne, only on display to the public during Dasara.

Entry to
the Palace

Doll's Pavilion
The first exhibit, the Doll's Pavilion, displays the gift collection of 19th- and early-20th-century dolls, statues and Hindu idols that were given to the maharaja by dignitaries from around the world.

Public Durbar Hall
The open-air hall contains a priceless collection of paintings by Raja Ravi Varma and opens into an expansive balcony supported by massive pillars with an ornate painted ceiling of 10 incarnations of Vishnu.

Marriage Pavilion
This lavish hall used for royal weddings features themes of Christianity, Hindu and Islam in its design. The highlight is the octagonal painted glass ceiling featuring peacock motifs, the bronze chandelier and the colonnaded turquoise pillars.

Elephant Gate
Next to the Doll's Pavilion, this brass gate has four bronze elephants inlaid at the bottom, an intricate double-headed eagle up the top and a hybrid lion-elephant creature (the state emblem of Karnataka) in the centre.

Golden Howdah
At the far end of the Doll's Pavilion, a wooden elephant howdah decorated with 80kg of gold was used to carry the maharaja in the Dasara festival. It now carries the idol of goddess Chamundeswari.

STUCK PIXEL/GETTY IMAGES ©

Devaraja Market Market

(Sayyaji Rao Rd; ⊙6am-8.30pm) Dating from Tipu Sultan's reign, this lively bazaar has local traders selling traditional items such as flower garlands, spices and conical piles of *kumkum* (coloured powder used for bindi dots), all of which makes for some great photo-ops. Refresh your bargaining skills before shopping.

Chamundi Hill Viewpoint

At a height of 1062m, on the summit of Chamundi Hill, stands the **Sri Chamundeswari Temple** (⊙7am-2pm, 3.30-6pm & 7.30-9pm), dominated by a towering 40m-high *gopuram* (entrance gateway). It's a fine half-day excursion, offering spectacular views of the city below. Queues are long at weekends, so visit during the week. You can take bus 201 (₹23, 30 minutes) that rumbles up the narrow road to the summit. A return autorickshaw trip will cost about ₹400.

Alternatively, you can take the foot trail comprising 1000-plus steps that Hindu pilgrims use to visit the temple. One-third of the way down is a 5m-high statue of **Nandi** (Shiva's bull) that was carved out of solid rock in 1659.

Colonial Architecture Architecture

For architecture buffs, Mysore has quite a handful of charming buildings. Dating from 1805, **Government House** (Irwin Rd), formerly the British Residency, is a Tuscan Doric building set in 20 hectares of gardens. Facing the north gate of the Maharaja's Palace is the 1927 **Silver Jubilee Clock Tower** (Ashoka Rd); nearby stands the imposing **Rangacharlu Memorial Hall**, built in 1884. The beauty of towering **St Philomena's Cathedral** (St Philomena St; ⊙8am-5pm), built between 1933 and 1941 in neo-Gothic style, is emphasised by beautiful stained-glass windows.

🕵 Tours

KSTDC runs a daily Mysore city tour (from ₹725), taking in the entire city, Chamundi Hill, Srirangapatnam and Brindavan Gardens. It starts daily at 6.30am, ends at 11.30pm and is likely to leave you breathless! The tour leaves from the tours office at Hotel Mayura Hoysala (p263). Bookings can be made at the KSTDC Transport Office (located at the hotel) or at travel agencies around town.

Royal Mysore Walks   Walking

(☎ 9632044188; www.royalmysorewalks.com; 2hr walks from ₹600) A walking tour is an excellent way to familiarise yourself with Mysore's epic history and heritage. Techie-turned-historian Vinay and his team organise weekend walks with a specific focus on either the city's royal history, its markets, its old quarters or its handicrafts. They also conduct cycling and jeep tours.

🛏 Sleeping

Hotel Mayura Hoysala   Hotel $

(☎ 2426160; 2 Jhansi Lakshmi Bai Rd; s/d incl breakfast from ₹953/1050; ❄) Government-owned hotel that continues to offer its blend of mothballed heritage (lace-lined curtains, heavy wooden doors, assorted cane furniture and old photographs lining its corridors) at affordable prices. The bar here is popular with Mysore's tipplers.

Green Hotel   Heritage Hotel $$

(☎ 4255000; www.greenhotelindia.com; 2270 Vinoba Rd, Jayalakshmipuram; s/d incl breakfast from ₹3550/4050; 🛜) 🍃 Undergoing several fascinating reincarnations over the years, the character-filled Green Hotel was originally built as the Chittaranjan Palace in the 1920s by the marajah for his three daughters, before becoming a major film studio from the 1950s to 1987. Today its 31 rooms, set among charming gardens, are all run on solar power and those in the palace building include themes such as a Writers Room or kitschy Bollywood decor. Best of all, the profits are distributed to charity and environmental projects across India. It's 3km west of town.

Parklane Hotel   Hotel $$

(☎ 4003500; www.parklanemysore.com; 2720 Harsha Rd; r from ₹2000; ❄@🛜🏊) Travellers' central on Mysore's tourist circuit, the Parklane is over-the-top kitsch but it's hard to dislike with its massive rooms which are immaculate, ultra comfortable and thoughtfully outfitted with mobile-chargers and very useful toiletry kits. The restaurant on the 1st floor is always busy and has a lively atmosphere.

Lalitha Mahal Palace   Heritage Hotel $$$

(☎ 8212526100; incl breakfast turret room ₹4834, heritage classic room ₹12,080; ❄@🛜) A former maharaja's guesthouse built in 1921, this grand majestic heritage building has been operating as a hotel since 1974. Old-world charm comes in bucketloads, from the 1920s birdcage elevator to mosaic tiled floors. The 'standard' turret room offers good value with wooden floors and bright bathrooms, but the heritage classic rooms are where you'll feel the history. Spacious four-poster beds sit next to antique furniture, claw-foot baths sit on marble bathroom floors and shuttered windows look out to stately landscaped gardens. There's also a gym and tennis courts. Watch out for the cheeky monkeys here.

Royal Orchid Metropole   Heritage Hotel $$$

(☎ 4255566; www.royalorchidhotels.com; 5 Jhansi Lakshmi Bai Rd; s/d incl breakfast from ₹6568/7160; ❄🛜🏊) Originally built by the Wodeyars to serve as the residence of the Maharaja's British guests, this is undoubtedly one of Mysore's leading heritage hotels. The charming colonial-era structure has 30 rooms oozing historical character, and there are performances of magic shows, music, dance and snake charming when tour groups pass through.

🍴 Eating & Drinking

Malgudi Café   Cafe $

(Green Hotel; mains ₹60-80; ⏱10am-7pm; 🛜) 🍃 Set around an inner courtyard within the Green Hotel, this ambient cafe brews excellent coffees and Himalayan teas to be enjoyed with tasty snacks, cakes or fresh bread baked on the premises daily. Staff here come from underprivileged backgrounds and are mostly women, and profits assist with downtrodden communities, so you can do your bit by ordering a second cuppa. Service can be slow.

Vinayaka Mylari   South Indian $

(769 Nazarbad Main Rd; mains ₹30-50; ⏱7.30-11.30am & 4-8pm) Local foodies say this is

one of the best eateries in town to try South Indian classics of masala dosa and *idlis*. There's a similar branch up the road run by the owner's brother.

Pelican Pub   Pub $
(Hunsur Rd; mains ₹75-150; ⊙11am-11pm) A popular watering hole located en route to Green Hotel, this laid-back joint serves beer for ₹65 a mug in the indoor classic pub or al fresco garden setting out back. Tasty food pairs nicely with a cold beer; try some sinful pork chilli for ₹135 a platter, or spinach balls in a sticky sauce. There's live music Wednesdays.

Sapphire   Indian $$
(mains ₹180-450; ⊙lunch 12.30-2.45pm, snacks 2.45-7.45pm, dinner 8-11pm) Dine in absolute royal Indian style in the grand ballroom of the Lalitha Mahal Palace hotel. And grand it is, with high stained-glass ceilings, lace tablecloths and polished teak floors. Order the royal Mysore silver thali, which gets you an assortment of vegetables, breads and sweets served on lavish brassware (₹390), while enjoying live Indian sitar performances over lunch and dinner.

Parklane Hotel   Multicuisine $$
(Parklane Hotel, 2720 Harsha Rd; mains ₹100-140) Mysore's most social restaurant with buzzing picnic-style garden tables, lit up moodily by countless lanterns. The food here is stock standard, with the usual Indian dishes, but live traditional music, and a fully stocked bar, make for a great night out.

🔒 Shopping

Mysore is a great place to shop for its famed sandalwood products, silk saris and wooden toys. It is also one of India's major incense-manufacturing centres.

Look for the butterfly-esque 'Silk Mark' on your purchase; it's an endorsement for quality silk.

Government Silk
Factory   Clothing
(Mananthody Rd, Ashokapuram; ⊙10am-6.30pm Mon-Sat, outlet 10.30am-7.30pm Mon-Sat) Given that Mysore's prized silk is made under its very sheds, this is the best and cheapest place to shop for the exclusive textile. Behind the showroom is the factory, where you can drop by to see how the fabric is made.

Sandalwood Oil
Factory   Souvenirs
(Mananthody Rd, Ashokapuram; ⊙9.30am-1pm & 2-5pm Mon-Sat) A quality-assured place for sandalwood products such as incense, soap, cosmetics and the prohibitively expensive pure sandalwood oil. Guided tours are available to show you around the factory and explain how the products are made.

Mysore silk saris

Cauvery Arts & Crafts Emporium
Clothing

(Sayyaji Rao Rd; ⏰10am-7.30pm) Not the cheapest place, but the selection is extensive, and there's no pressure to buy.

ℹ Information

Internet Access

Pal Net (per hr ₹40; ⏰9am-9pm Mon-Sat, to 2pm Sun)

Medical Services

Government Hospital (☎4269806; Dhanvanthri Rd) Has a 24-hour pharmacy.

Money

State Bank of Mysore (cnr Irwin & Ashoka Rds; ⏰10.30am-2.30pm & 3-4pm Mon-Fri, 10.30am-12.30pm Sat) Changes cash and has an ATM.

Thomas Cook (☎2420090; 9/2 Ashoka Rd, Silver Tower; ⏰9.30am-6pm Mon-Sat) Foreign currency.

Tourist Information

Karnataka Tourism (☎2422096; adtourismmysore@gmail.com; Old Exhibition Bldg, Irwin Rd; ⏰10am-5.30pm Mon-Sat) Extremely helpful, and plenty of brochures.

KSTDC Transport Office (☎2423652; 2 Jhansi Lakshmi Bai Rd; ⏰8.30am-8.30pm) Offers general tourist information and provides a useful map. Has counters at the train station and central bus stand, as well as this office next to Hotel Mayura Hoysala.

ℹ Getting There & Away

Air

Mysore's airport was not operating any flights at the time of research.

Bus

The central bus stand (BN Rd) handles all KSRTC long-distance buses. The city bus stand (Sayyaji Rao Rd) is for city, Srirangapatnam and Chamundi Hill buses.

The private bus stand (Sayyaji Rao Rd) also has services to Ernakulam. You'll find several ticketing agents around the stand.

Train

From Mysore's railway booking office (☎131; ⏰8am-8pm Mon-Sat, to 2pm Sun), buy a ticket on the 6.45am Chamundi Express (2nd class/AC chair ₹57/202) or the 11am Tippu Express to Bengaluru (₹66/233, three hours), from where train connections are much better. The 2.15pm Shatabdi Express also connects Bengaluru (AC chair/AC executive chair ₹285/620, two hours) and Chennai (₹741/1535, seven hours) daily except Wednesday. The 10.30pm Mysore Dharwad Express goes to Hubli (sleeper/2AC ₹212/880, 9½ hours), from where there are connections to Hospet (for Hampi; three hours) and Goa (four hours).

ℹ Getting Around

Agencies at hotels and around town rent taxis for about ₹7 per kilometre, with a minimum of 250km per day, plus a daily allowance of ₹200 for the driver.

The flagfall on autorickshaws is ₹20, and ₹10 per kilometre is charged thereafter. Count on around ₹800 for a day's sightseeing.

KSRTC Buses from Mysore

DESTINATION	FARE (₹)	DURATION (HR)	FREQUENCY
Bengaluru	110 (O), 162 (R), 270 (V)	3	every 20min
Chennai	930 (V), 531 (R)	12	4 daily
Ernakulam	593 (V)	11	4 daily
Hospet	372 (O), 491 (R)	10	4 daily

O – Ordinary; R – Rajahamsa Semideluxe; V – Airavath AC Volvo

TAMIL NADU

Chennai (Madras)

♪044 / POP 7.7 MILLION

The 'capital of the south' has always been the rather dowdy sibling among India's four biggest cities, with its withering southern heat, roaring traffic, and scarcity of outstanding sights. For many travellers, it is as much a gateway as a destination in itself. If you're just caught here between connections, it's certainly worth poking around one of the museums or taking a sunset stroll along Marina Beach. If you have more time to explore Chennai's varied neighbourhoods and appreciate its role as keeper of South Indian artistic and religious traditions, the odds are this 70-sq-km conglomerate of urban villages will grow on you. Recent years have added a new layer of cosmopolitan glamour in the shape of luxury hotels, shiny boutiques, classy contemporary restaurants and even a smattering of clubs and bars open into the wee hours.

◉ Sights

Government Museum　　　　Museum
(www.chennaimuseum.org; Pantheon Rd, Egmore; Indian/foreigner ₹15/250, camera/video ₹200/500; ⏱9.30am-5pm Sat-Thu) Housed across several British-built buildings known as the Pantheon Complex, this excellent museum is Chennai's best. You may find some sections temporarily closed as renovation meanders on.

The main building (No 1) has a respectable archaeological section representing all the major South Indian periods.

The big highlight is building 3, the **Bronze Gallery**, with a superb, beautifully presented collection of South Indian bronzes from the 7th-century Pallava era through to modern times, with English-language explanatory material.

The same ticket gets you into the **National Art Gallery**, **Contemporary Art Gallery** and **Children's Museum**, in the same complex.

Marina Beach　　　　Beach
Take an early-morning or evening stroll (you really don't want to fry here at any other time) along the 3km-long main stretch of Marina Beach and you'll pass cricket matches, flying kites, fortune-tellers, fish markets and families enjoying the sea breeze. Try a cob of roast corn with lime and chilli powder from one of the vendors – delicious. Don't swim: strong rips make it dangerous.

Tours

The Tamil Nadu Tourism Development Corporation (p271) conducts half-day city tours (non-AC/AC ₹215/235) and day trips to Mamallapuram (₹275/350). Book ahead for weekends and holidays; be ready for cancellations on quiet weekdays.

Storytrails　　　　Walking Tours
(♪42124214, 9940040215; http://storytrails. in; 1, 2nd Cross St, CIT Colony, Mylapore; 3hr tour ₹695-795.) Runs entertaining and informative neighbourhood walking tours based around themes such as dance, temples, jewellery and bazaars, as well as tours specially aimed at children.

🛌 Sleeping

EGMORE & AROUND

YWCA International Guest House　　　　Guesthouse $$
(♪25324234; ywcaigh@indiainfo.com; 1086 Poonamallee High Rd; s/d incl breakfast ₹785/1045, with AC ₹1300/1500; ❄@🛜) The YWCA guesthouse, set in green and shady grounds, offers a calm atmosphere and exceptionally good value. Very efficiently run by an amiable staff, it provides good-sized, impeccably clean rooms, spacious common areas and good-value meals (₹150/225 for veg/nonveg lunch or dinner). Wi-fi (in the lobby) costs ₹100 per day.

Hotel Chandra Park　　　　Hotel $$
(♪28191177; www.hotelchandrapark.com; 9 Gandhi Irwin Rd; incl breakfast s ₹1319-2279, d ₹1499-2578; ❄) Chandra Park's prices remain mysteriously lower than most comparable establishments. Standard rooms are small but have air-con, clean towels and

tight, white sheets. Throw in a decent bar and a hearty buffet breakfast and this is good value by Chennai standards.

SOUTHERN CHENNAI

Footprint B&B
B&B $$

(☎ 9840037483; http://chennaibedandbreakfast.com; Gayatri Apartments, 16 South St, Alwarpet (behind Sheraton Park Hotel); r incl breakfast ₹4045; ❄ @ ☎) This is a wonderfully comfortable and relaxed base for your Chennai explorations, in a quiet street in a leafy neighbourhood. Bowls of pretty flowers and old-Madras drawings set the scene. The nine cosy, spotless rooms have king-size or wide twin beds. Breakfasts (Western or Indian) are generous, wi-fi is free and the hospitable owners can tell you all you need to make the most of your time. Phone or email in advance; walk-ins are discouraged.

Lotus
Hotel $$

(☎ 28157272; www.thelotus.in; 15 Venkatraman St, T Nagar; incl breakfast s ₹2980-4170, d ₹3930-4470; ❄ ☎) An absolute gem, the Lotus offers a quiet setting away from the main roads, a good veg restaurant, and fresh, stylish rooms with wood floors and cheerful decor. Wi-fi is free (but doesn't reach all rooms).

Residency Towers
Hotel $$$

(☎ 28156363; www.theresidency.com; Sir Thyagaraya Rd, T Nagar; incl breakfast s ₹7135-8994, d ₹7675-8994; ❄ @ ☎ ✈) Residency Towers combines five-star elegance with personality at very good prices for this level of accommodation. Rooms have sliding doors in front of windows to block out noise, walnut-veneer furniture, weighing scales and other thoughtful touches. Also here are three restaurants, a nice outdoor pool and a 'pub' that

becomes a heaving weekend night spot. Wi-fi is free.

Park Hotel
Boutique Hotel $$$

(☎ 42676000; www.theparkhotels.com; 601 Anna Salai; s ₹12,592-17,988, d ₹13,791-17,988, ste from ₹19,187; ❄ @ ☎ ✈) We love this superstylish large boutique hotel, which flaunts design everywhere you look, from the bamboo, steel and gold cushions of the towering lobby to the posters from classic South Indian movies shot in Gemini Studios, the previous incarnation of the hotel site. Rooms have lovely lush bedding, all mod cons and stylish touches including glass-walled bathrooms. It's all pretty swish, and that goes for the three restaurants, large open-air pool, luxurious spa and two night spots too!

Eating

EGMORE

Hotel Saravana Bhavan
Indian $

(www.saravanabhavan.com; 21 Kennet Lane; mains ₹60-150; ⏱ 6am-10pm) Dependably delish, lunchtime and evening South Indian thali

Hindu temple priest, Chennai
LONELY PLANET/GETTY IMAGES ©

Chennai (Madras)

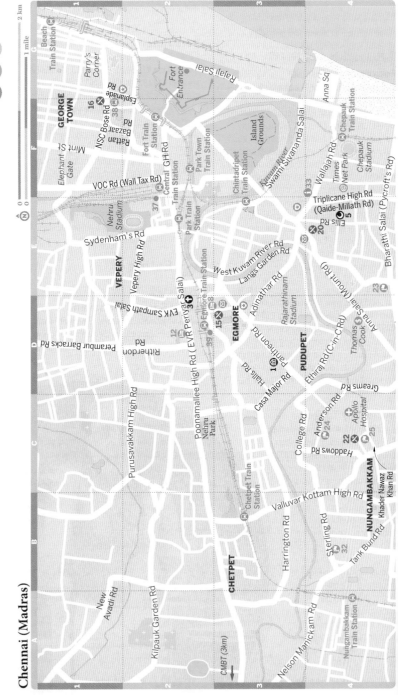

0 1 mile
0 2 km

GEORGE TOWN

Beach Train Station

Parry's Corner

Fort Entrance

Rajaji Salai

Esplanade Rd

NSC Bose Rd

Rattan Bazaar Rd

Mint St

Elephant Gate

16

38

Fort Train Station

Park Town Train Station

Chintadripet Train Station

Island Grounds

Kuvam River

Swami Sivananda Salai

Anna Sq

Chepauk Train Station

Chepauk Stadium

Wallajah Rd

Times @ Net Park

133

Triplicane High Rd (Qaide-Millath Rd)

Ellis Rd

20

5

Bharathi Salai (Pycroft's Rd)

VOC Rd (Wall Tax Rd)

Central GH Rd

Central Train Station

37

Park Train Station

Nehru Stadium

Sydenham's Rd

VEPERY

Vepery High Rd

EVK Sampath Salai

Egmore Train Station

West Kuvam River Rd

Langs Garden Rd

Adinathar Rd

Rajarathinam Stadium

Anna Salai (Mount Rd)

23

Perambur Barracks Rd

Ritherdon Rd

Poonamallee High Rd (EVR Periyar Salai)

12

3

18

39

15

22

EGMORE

Panthreon Rd

Halls Rd

PUDUPET

Ethiral Rd (C-in-C Rd)

Thomas Cook

1

Casa Major Rd

Greams Rd

Purusavakkam High Rd

Nehru Park

Chetpet Train Station

College Rd

Anderson Rd

Apollo Hospital

24

22

25

Haddows Rd

NUNGAMBAKKAM

Khader Nawaz Khan Rd

Valluvar Kottam High Rd

Harrington Rd

CHETPET

Sterling Rd

Tank Bund Rd

32

New Avadi Rd

Kilpauk Garden Rd

CMBT (3km)

Nelson Manickam Rd

Nungambakkam Train Station

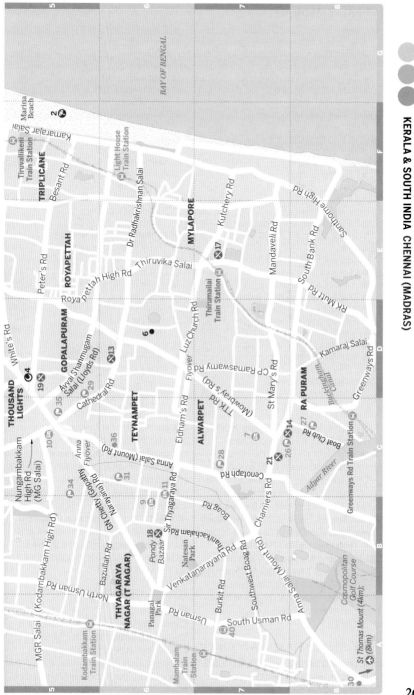

KERALA & SOUTH INDIA CHENNAI (MADRAS)

BAY OF BENGAL

Marina Beach

Kamarajar Salai

TRIPLICANE

Tiruvalliken Train Station

Besant Rd

Light House Train Station

Dr Radhakrishnan Salai

Kutchery Rd

Santhome High Rd

MYLAPORE

Peter's Rd

ROYAPETTAH

Thiruvika Salai

Pettah High Rd

Roya Pettah High Rd

Mandaveli Rd

South Bank Rd

RK Mutt Rd

GOPALAPURAM

Ayyai Shanmugam Salai (Lloyds Rd)

Cathedral Rd

Thirumailai Train Station

Luz Church Rd

Flyover

CP Ramaswamy Rd

TTK Rd (Mowbray's Rd)

St Mary's Rd

Kamaraj Salai

Greenways Rd

RA PURAM

THOUSAND LIGHTS

White's Rd

Nungambakkam High Rd (MG Salai)

Anna Flyover

TEYNAMPET

Eldham's Rd

ALWARPET

Buckingham Canal

Boat Club Rd

Greenways Rd Train Station

Adyar River

Anna Salai (Mount Rd)

GN Chetty (Gandhi) Rd

Sir Thyagaraya Rd

Boag Rd

Cenotaph Rd

Chamiers Rd

Anna Salai (Mount Rd)

THYAGARAYA NAGAR (T NAGAR)

Pondy Bazaar

Natesan Park

Thanikachalam Rds

Venkatanarayana Rd

Southwest Boag Rd

Bazullah Rd

North Usman Rd (Kodambakkam High Rd)

MGR Salai (Kodambakkam High Rd)

Panagal Park

Usman Rd

Burkit Rd

South Usman Rd

Cosmopolitan Golf Course

St Thomas Mount (4km); (8km)

Kodambakkam Train Station

Mambalam Train Station

Chennai (Madras)

'meals' at the Saravana Bhavans usually run ₹80 to ₹100. This famous Chennai vegetarian chain is also excellent for South Indian breakfasts (*idlis* and *vadas* for ₹49), ice cream, filter coffee and other Indian vegetarian fare including biryanis and pilaus. Branches include **George Town** (209 NSC Bose Rd; ⊙6am-10.30pm), **Triplicane** (Shanthi Theatre Complex, 44 Anna Salai; ⊙7am-11pm), **Thousand Lights** (293 Peter's Rd; ⊙11.30am-11pm), **Mylapore** (70 North Mada St; ⊙6am-11pm) and **T Nagar** (102 Sir Thyagaraya Rd; ⊙6am-11pm), not to mention London, Paris and New York! The Thousand Lights branch is more upscale than most, with silver cutlery.

NUNGAMBAKKAM & AROUND

Tuscana Pizzeria   Italian $$$
(☎45038008; www.tuscana.in; 19, 3rd St, Wallace Garden; pizzas & pasta ₹315-690; ⊙noon-11.30pm) This, my pizza-loving friends, is the real deal, and Chennai has embraced it enthusiastically. Tuscana serves authentic thin-crust pizzas with toppings such as prosciutto, as well as interesting takes such as hoisoin chicken pizza. Pasta and desserts are also top-notch. There's another branch, **Tuscana on Chamiers** (☎45000008; www.tuscanaonchamiers.in; 89 Chamiers Rd, Alwarpet; ⊙12.30-3.15pm & 6.30-11.15pm), in Alwarpet. Reservations are a good idea at both.

SOUTH CHENNAI

Eco Cafe   Multicuisine $$
(Chamiers, 106 Chamiers Rd, RA Puram; mains ₹250-375, breakfasts ₹175-305; ⊙8.30am-9.30pm) This 1st-floor cafe feels a continent away from Chennai, except that Chennai-ites love it too. Leafy wallpaper, leaves through the windows, discreetly

spaced tables, wonderful banana nut bread and cappuccino, English breakfasts, American pancakes, pasta, quesadillas, waffles, salads...

Copper Chimney   North Indian **$$$**
(☏28115770; 74 Cathedral Rd, Gopalapuram; mains ₹200-575; ☉noon-3pm & 7-11.30pm)
The vegetarian dishes aren't the priority here, but meat eaters will drool over the yummy North Indian tandoori dishes served in stylishly minimalist surroundings. The *machchi* tikka – skewers of tandoori-baked fish – is superb.

ℹ Information

Dangers & Annoyances`

Never get into an autorickshaw before agreeing the fare, and never pay the driver upfront. Tempting offers of ₹50 'city tours' by autorickshaw drivers precede a day being dragged from one shop or emporium to another.

Internet Access

'Browsing centres' are dotted all over town.

Medical Services

Apollo Hospital (☏28293333, emergency 1066; www.apollohospitals.com; 21 Greams Lane) State-of-the-art, expensive hospital popular with 'medical tourists'.

Money

ATMs are everywhere, including at Central train station, the airport and the main bus station.

Thomas Cook (Phase I, Spencer Plaza, Anna Salai; ☉10am-6pm Mon-Sat, to 4pm Sun) Charges only ₹50 commission on all foreign cash exchanges. Also changes American Express travellers cheques.

Tourist Information

Tamil Nadu Tourism Development Corporation (TTDC; ☏25383333; www.tamilnadutourism. org; Tamil Nadu Tourism Complex, 2 Wallajah Rd, Triplicane; ☉24hr) The state tourism body's main office takes bookings for its own bus tours and mediocre hotels, and also answers questions and hands out a few leaflets.

Major Trains from Chennai

DESTINATION	TRAIN NO & NAME	FARE (₹)	DURATION (HR)	DEPARTURE
Bengaluru	12007 Shatabdi Express*	529/1155	5	6am CC
	12609 Chennai-Bangalore Intercity Express	110/386	6½	1.35pm CC
Delhi	12621 Tamil Nadu Express	528/1482/2375	33	10pm CC
Goa	17311 Vasco Express (Friday only)	343/971/1500	22	2.10pm CC
Kochi	16041 Alleppey Express	275/770/955	12¼	8.45pm CC
Kolkata	12842 Coromandel Express	461/1242/1955	27	8.45am CC
Madurai	12635 Vaigai Express	132/488	8	1.20pm CE
	12637 Pandyan Express	232/594/880	9	9.20pm CE
Mumbai	11042 Mumbai Express	383/1085/1700	26	11.55am CC
Mysore	12007 Shatabdi Express*	679/1470	7	6am CC
	16222 Kaveri Express	212/564/850	10¼	9.30pm CC
Trivandrum	12623 Trivandrum Mail	337/925/1405	15¾	7.45pm CC

Departure codes: CC – Chennai Central; CE – Chennai Egmore
*Daily except Wednesday
Shatabdi fares are chair/executive; Express and Mail fares are 2nd/chair car for day trains, sleeper/3AC/2AC for overnight trains

ℹ️ Getting There & Away

Air

Chennai Airport (☏22560551) is at Tirusulam in the far southwest of the city. A brand-new domestic terminal was due to open soon, with the international terminal expanding to occupy the whole of the old building.

There are direct flights to over 20 Indian cities plus Colombo, Singapore, Kuala Lumpur and Bangkok, as well as the Gulf states.

Bus

Most government buses operate from the large but surprisingly orderly CMBT (Chennai Mofussil Bus Terminus; Jawaharlal Nehru Rd, Koyambedu), 6km west of the centre. Routes include to Madurai (₹420, 10 hours, frequent), Mamallapuram (₹80, two hours, twice hourly) and Puducherry (₹100, four hours, twice hourly).

The T Nagar Bus Terminus (South Usman Rd) has a few daily departures to Bengaluru, Madurai, Mysore, Thanjavur and Trichy, plus bus 599 to Mamallapuram (₹27, two hours, about hourly).

Car

Renting a car with a driver is the easiest way of going almost anywhere and is easily arranged through most travel agents, midrange or top-end hotels, or the airport's prepaid taxi desks. Sample rates for non-AC/AC cars are ₹1300/1550 to Mamallapuram and ₹2700/3200 to Puducherry.

Train

Interstate trains and those heading west generally depart from Central station, while trains heading south mostly leave from Egmore. The advance reservations office (1st fl, Chennai Central local station; ⊙8am-8pm Mon-Sat, 8am-2pm Sun), with its extremely helpful Foreign Tourist Cell, is in a separate 11-storey building just west of the main Central station building. The Passenger Reservation Office (☏28194579) at Egmore station keeps the same hours.

ℹ️ Getting Around

To/From the Airport

The Chennai Metro Rail system, expected to open in 2014, will provide a cheap and easy link between the airport and city. Meanwhile, the cheapest option is a suburban train to or from Tirusulam station, connected by a pedestrian underpass to the parking areas outside the international terminal. Trains run several times hourly from 4am to midnight to/from Chennai Beach station (₹7, 42 minutes) with stops including Kodambakkam, Egmore, Chennai Park and Chennai Fort.

Prepaid taxi kiosks at the airport charge ₹380/515 for a non-AC/AC cab to Egmore, and slightly less to T Nagar.

Autorickshaw

Drivers don't use meters. Expect to pay at least ₹40 for a short trip down the road, around ₹80 for a 3km trip and ₹100 to ₹120 for 5km. Prices are at least 25% higher after 10pm. There are prepaid booths outside the CMBT (₹160 to Egmore) and Central station.

Mamallapuram (Mahabalipuram)

☏044 / POP 17,666

Mamallapuram was the major seaport of the ancient Pallava kingdom based at Kanchipuram, and a wander round the town's great World Heritage–listed temples and carvings inflames the imagination, especially at sunset.

◎ Sights

You can easily spend a full day exploring Mamallapuram's marvellous temples and rock carvings. Most of them were carved from the rock in the 7th century during the reign of Pallava king Narasimhavarman I, whose nickname Mamalla (Great Wrestler) gave the town its name. Apart from the Shore Temple and Five Rathas, admission is free. Official Archaeological Survey of India guides can be hired at the sites for around ₹50; they're worth the money.

Shore Temple   Hindu Temple

(combined 1-day ticket with Five Rathas Indian/foreigner ₹10/250, video ₹25; ⊙6am-6pm) Standing like a magnificent fist of rock-cut elegance overlooking the sea, the two-towered Shore Temple symbolises the heights of Pallava architecture and the maritime ambitions of the Pallava kings. Its small size belies its excellent proportion and the supreme quality of the carvings, many of which have been eroded into vaguely Impressionist embel

PAUL HARDING/GETTY IMAGES ©

Arjuna's Penance

The crowning masterpiece of Mamallapuram's stonework, this giant relief carving is one of the greatest works of ancient art in India. Inscribed on a huge boulder, the Penance bursts with scenes of Hindu myth and everyday vignettes of South Indian life.

In the centre *nagas*, or snake-beings, descend a cleft once filled with water, meant to represent the Ganges. To the left Arjuna performs self-mortification (fasting and standing on one leg), so that the four-armed Shiva will grant him his most powerful weapon, the god-slaying Pasupata. Shiva is attended by dwarves, and celestial beings fly across the upper parts of the carving, including the moon god (above Shiva) and sun god (right of the cleft) with orbs behind their heads. Below Arjuna/Bagiratha appears a temple to Vishnu, mythical ancestor of the Pallava kings. The many wonderfully carved animals include a small herd of elephants and – humour amid the holy – a cat performing penance to a crowd of appreciative mice.

NEED TO KNOW
West Raja St

lishments. Built under Narasimhavarman II in the 8th century, it's the earliest significant freestanding stone temple in Tamil Nadu. The two towers rise above shrines to Shiva and their original linga (phallic symbols of Shiva) captured the sunrise and sunset. Between the Shiva shrines is one to Vishnu, shown sleeping.

Five Rathas Hindu Temple
(Pancha Ratha; Five Rathas Rd; combined 1-day ticket with Shore Temple Indian/foreigner ₹10/250, video ₹25; ⊙6am-6pm) Huddled together at the south end of Mamallapuram, the Five Rathas look like buildings, but they were, astonishingly, all carved from single large rocks. Each of these

273

Mamallapuram (Mahabalipuram)

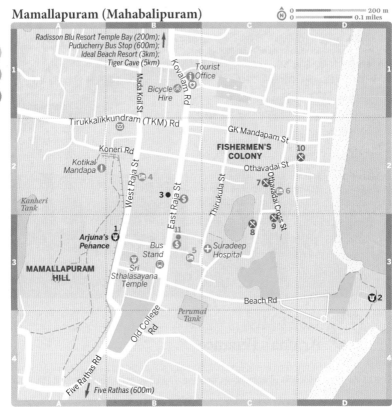

Mamallapuram (Mahabalipuram)

7th-century temples was dedicated to a Hindu god and is now named after one or more of the Pandavas, the five hero-brothers of the epic Mahabharata, or their common wife, Draupadi. Outside each one is a carving of its god's animal mount.

The *rathas* were hidden in the sand until excavated by the British 200 years ago. It's thought they didn't originally serve as actual places of worship, but were created as models for structures to be built elsewhere.

Tours

Hi! Tours Cycling, Birdwatching
(☎27443360; www.hi-tours.com; 123 East Raja
St; bicycle tours ₹350-400; ⏱9.30am-6pm Mon-
Fri, to 2pm Sat) Runs half-day bicycle tours
to nearby villages, observing activities
like rice- and masala-grinding and *kolam*
drawing (the 'welcome' patterns outside
doorways, also called *rangoli*).

Sleeping

Lakshmi Cottage Hotel $
(☎27442463; lakshmilodge2002@yahoo.co.in; 5
Othavadai Cross St; r ₹400-800, with AC ₹1200;
❄) One of the better of several backpacker-oriented places along Othavadai
Cross St, the Lakshmi has lots of rooms
in primary colours, and assorted travel
services on the ground floor. Beds range
from concrete to carved wood.

**Butterball Bed 'n
Breakfast** B&B $$
(☎9094792525; suhale2009@gmail.com; 9/26
West Raja St; s/d incl breakfast ₹1600/1800;
❄🛜) There's a great view of the epony-
mous giant rock from the roof terrace,
and a nice lawn. The smallish but clean,
pleasant rooms have old English prints,
writing desks and blue-tiled bathrooms.
Breakfast is a good Western-style affair;
also welcome is the civilised 24-hour
checkout, rare in Mamallapuram.
Free wi-fi throughout.

**Hotel
Mahabs** Hotel $$
(☎27442645; www.hotel
mahabs.com; 68 East Raja St;
r ₹1319, with AC ₹2159-2518;
❄@🛜☀) Friendly
Mahabs is centred
on an attractive pool
(₹300 for nonguests)
surrounded by trees,
plants and murals.
Rooms are in shades
of brown but very clean
and comfy. There's a de-
cent in-house restaurant;

internet use is ₹50/200 per hour/24
hours.

**Radisson Blu Resort
Temple Bay** Resort $$$
(☎27443636; http://radissonblu.com/hotel-
mamallapuram; 57 Kovalam Rd; s/d incl breakfast
from ₹8934/9893; ❄@🛜☀) The Radis-
son's 144 luxurious chalets, villas and
bungalows are spread around manicured
gardens stretching 500m to the beach.
Somewhere in the midst is India's longest
swimming pool, all 220m of it.

Eating

Eateries on Othavadai and Othavadai
Cross Sts provide semi-open-air settings,
decent Western mains and bland Indian
curries. Most of them can serve you a
beer. For real Indian food, there are a few
decent cheap veg and biryani places near
the bus stand.

Le Yogi Multicuisine $$
(19 Othavadai St; mains ₹120-350; ⏱7.30am-
11pm) This is some of the best Western
food in town; the steaks, pasta, pizzas and

Rickshaw driver, Chennai (p266)
TOM COCKREM/GETTY IMAGES ©

crepes are genuine and tasty (if small), service is good, and the airy setting, with bamboo posts and pretty hanging lamps, has a touch of the romantic.

Gecko Café
Multicuisine $$

(www.gecko-web.com; 14 Othavadai Cross St; mains ₹150-290; ⊗8am-10.30pm) Two friendly brothers run this cute little spot on a thatch-covered rooftop overlooking a large pond. The offerings and prices aren't that different from other tourist-oriented spots, but there's more love put into the cooking here and it comes out tastier. At research time they were building a **second location** around the corner.

Freshly 'n Hot
Cafe $$

(Othavadai Cross St; mains ₹60-225; ⊗7.30am-9pm) Yes, the name makes no sense, but the ambience is relaxed and the decor clean and fresh. A comparatively small menu of perfectly OK pizza, pasta, sandwiches, egg items and crepes accompanies a long list of coffees. The iced coffees are excellent.

ℹ Information

Head to East Raja St for ATMs.

Suradeep Hospital (☏27442448; 15 Thirukula St; ⊗24hr) Recommended by travellers.

Tourist Office (☏27442232; Kovalam Rd; ⊗10am-5.45pm Mon-Fri) Quite helpful and friendly.

ℹ Getting There & Away

From the **bus stand** (East Raja St), bus 599 heads to Chennai's T Nagar Bus Terminus (₹27, two hours) 24 times daily, and AC bus 568C (588C on Saturday and Sunday) runs to Chennai's CMBT (₹85, two hours) about hourly, 8am to 9pm. For Chennai Airport take bus 515 to Tambaram (every 30 minutes, 6.20am to 9.30pm), then a taxi, autorickshaw or suburban train from there. Buses to Puducherry (₹50, two hours) stop about every half-hour at the junction of Kovalam Rd and the Mamallapuram bypass, 1km north of the town centre.

Taxis are available from the bus stand, travel agents and hotels. It's about ₹1000 to ₹1200 to Chennai, or ₹1500 to Puducherry.

South Indian thali meal

GREG ELMS/GETTY IMAGES ©

You can make train reservations at the Southern Railway Reservation Centre (32 East Raja St, 1st fl; ⏰10am-1pm & 2.30-5pm Mon-Sat, 8am-2pm Sun)

ℹ️ Getting Around

The easiest way to get around is on foot, though on a hot day it's quite a hike to see all the monuments. Bicycles can be hired at some guesthouses and hotels, and at a few rental stalls, usually for ₹50 per day.

Puducherry (Pondicherry)

📞0413 / POP 241,773

Puducherry (formerly called Pondicherry and almost always referred to as 'Pondy') is certainly no Provençal village, but the older part of this former French colony (where you'll probably spend most of your time) does have a lot of quiet, clean, shady, cobbled streets, lined with mustard-yellow colonial townhouses. In fact, if you've come from Chennai or some of the inland cities, old Pondy may well seem a sea of tranquillity.

◎ Sights

French Quarter Neighbourhood
Pocketed away just behind the seafront is a series of cobbled streets, with white and mustard buildings in various states of romantic *déshabillé*, and a slight sense of Gallic glory gone by, otherwise known as the French Quarter. A do-it-yourself **heritage walk** through this area could start at the French Consulate near the north end of Goubert Ave, the seafront promenade. Head south then turn inland to shady **Bharathi Park**, with the neoclassical governor's residence, **Raj Nivas**, facing its north side. Return to the seafront at the **Gandhi Memorial**, pass the **Hôtel de Ville** (City Hall) and then it's a matter of pottering south through what's known as the 'white town' – Dumas, Romain Rolland, Suffren and Labourdonnais Sts.

❤️ If You Like...
Colonial-Era Architecture

Puducherry has one of the best collections of over-the-top churches and cathedrals in India. If you enjoyed strolling around the French Quarter, go in search of these too.

1 **OUR LADY OF THE IMMACULATE CONCEPTION CATHEDRAL**
(Mission St) Completed in 1791, this is a robin's-egg-blue and cloud-white typically Jesuit edifice in a Goa-like Portuguese style.

2 **SACRED HEART BASILICA**
(Subbayah Salai) The brown-and-white grandiosity of this church is set off by stained glass and a Gothic sense of proportion.

3 **NOTRE DAME DES ANGES**
(Dumas St) This mellow pink-and-cream church, built in 1858, looks sublime in the late-afternoon light. The smooth limestone interior was made using eggshells in the plaster.

Sri Aurobindo Ashram Ashram
(www.sriaurobindoashram.org; Marine St; ⏰general visits 8am-noon & 2-6pm) Founded in 1926 by Sri Aurobindo and a French-born woman known as 'the Mother', this spiritual community has about 1200 members who work in the ashram's many departments.

General visits to the main ashram building on Marine St are cursory – you just see the flower-festooned samadhi (shrine) of Aurobindo and the Mother, then the bookshop, then you leave. People staying in ashram guesthouses have access to other areas and activities. Collective meditation around the samadhi from 7.25pm to 7.50pm Monday, Tuesday, Wednesday and Friday is open to all.

Sri Manakula Vinayagar Temple Hindu Temple
(Manakula Vinayagar Koil St; ⏰5.45am-12.30pm & 4-9.30pm) Pondy may have more churches than most towns, but this is still India,

277

Puducherry (Pondicherry)

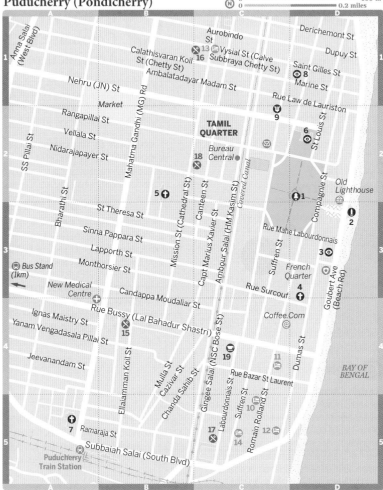

and the Hindu faith still reigns supreme. Don't miss the chance to watch tourists, pilgrims and the curious get a head pat from the temple elephant at this temple dedicated to Ganesh. The temple also contains over 40 skilfully painted friezes.

Tours

Shanti Travel (☏4210401; www.shantitravel.com; 13 Romain Rolland St; ☺10am-7pm) offers recommended two-hour **walking tours** (per person ₹400) of Puducherry with English- or French-speaking guides.

Sleeping

Sri Aurobindo Ashram (p277) runs several simple but clean guesthouses. They're primarily intended for ashram visitors, but many accept other guests who are willing to abide by their rules: 10.30pm curfew and no smoking, alcohol or drugs. Only some accept advance bookings. The ashram's **Bureau Central** (☏2233604; bureaucentral@sriaurobindoashram.org; Ambour Salai; ☺6am-8pm) has a list.

Puducherry (Pondicherry)

Kailash Guest House   Hotel **$**
(📞2224485; http://kailashguesthouse.in; 43 Vysial St; s/d ₹600/800, with AC d ₹1000; ❄️) The best value for money in this price range; Kailash has simple, super-clean rooms with well mosquito-proofed windows, and friendly management. It's geared to traveller needs, with communal areas, clothes-drying facilities and laundry service.

Les Hibiscus   Heritage Guesthouse **$$**
(📞2227480; www.leshibiscus.in; 49 Suffren St; s/d incl breakfast ₹2200/2500; ❄️@🛜) Hibiscus has just four pristine, high-ceilinged rooms with gorgeous antique beds, coffee-makers and a mix of quaint Indian art and old-Pondy photos. The whole place is immaculately tasteful, the breakfast is fabulous, internet is free and management is genuinely friendly and helpful. Well worth booking ahead for.

Coloniale Heritage Guest House   Heritage Guesthouse **$$**
(📞2224720; http://colonialeheritage.com; 54 Romain Rolland St; r incl breakfast ₹2000-4000; ❄️🛜) This colonial home with six comfy rooms is chock-full of character thanks to the owner's amazing collection of gem-studded Tanjore paintings, Ravi Varma lithographs and other 19th- and 20th-century South Indian art. Breakfast is served in a sunken patio next to the leafy garden. Free wi-fi.

Hotel de Pondichéry   Heritage Hotel **$$**
(📞2227409; www.hoteldepondicherry.com; 38 Dumas St; incl breakfast s ₹2000, d ₹2800-3800; ❄️🛜) A heritage spot with comfy, quiet, high-ceilinged, colonial-style rooms and a dash of original modern art. The large front courtyard area houses the good restaurant, Le Club (p280). Staff are lovely and there's free wi-fi in the lobby.

Hotel De L'Orient   Heritage Hotel **$$$**
(📞2343067; www.neemranahotels.com; 17 Romain Rolland St; r incl breakfast ₹3760-8056; ❄️🛜) A grand restored colonial mansion with breezy verandas, charming rooms kitted out with antique furniture and *objets*, and a large, pretty courtyard at its heart. A place to get that old Pondy feel while enjoying polished service and French, Italian or creole (French-Indian) food in the courtyard **Carte Blanche Restaurant** (mains ₹250-400; ⏱7.15-10.30am, noon-6pm & 7-9.30pm).

🍴 Eating & Drinking

Puducherry is a culinary highlight of Tamil Nadu; you get good South Indian cooking plus several restaurants specialising in well-prepped French and Italian cuisine.

Baker Street   Cafe $

(123 Rue Bussy; items ₹40-130; ⏰7am-10pm) A very popular upmarket, French-style bakery with delectable cakes, croissants and eclairs. Baguettes, brownies and quiches aren't bad either. Eat in or take away.

Surguru   South Indian $

(235 (old 99) Mission St; mains ₹65-110; ⏰7.30am-10.30pm) Simple South Indian served in a relatively posh setting. Surguru is the fix for thali and dosa addicts who like their veg accompanied by good strong AC. Thali is available at lunchtime.

Satsanga   Multicuisine $$

(☎2225867; www.satsanga.co.in; 54 Labourdonnais St; mains ₹150-340; ⏰8am-11pm) Deservedly popular for its excellent Continental cuisine, Satsanga, like most places in this genre, offers a full Indian menu as well. It's especially strong on steaks, fish, prawns and pâtés. There are good vegetarian options too, and the homemade bread and butter goes down a treat. For a table on the breezy terrace, it's a good idea to book.

La Pasta   Italian $$

(http://lapastapondy.blogspot.com; 55 Vysial St; mains ₹125-350; ⏰noon-2pm & 6-9.30pm Tue-Sun) Pasta aficionados, make a little pilgrimage to this spot with just three check-cloth tables, where a real Italian whips up her own yummy sauces and concocts her own perfect pasta in an open kitchen as big as the dining area. No alcohol: it's all about the food, and she even has wholemeal options.

Le Club   Continental, Indian $$$

(38 Dumas St; mains ₹330-440; ⏰8.30am-10.30pm) Steaks (with sauces such as Béarnaise or blue cheese), pizzas and crepes are all top-class at this romantically lit garden restaurant. Tempting local options include creole prawn curry and Malabarstyle fish, and there are plenty of cocktails and even wine to go with your meal.

L'e-Space   Cafe, Bar

(2 Labourdonnais St; cocktails ₹200, pancakes ₹100; ⏰5-11pm) A quirky little semi-open-air upstairs cafe that serves decent cocktails and where some people may be away on something other than alcohol. Locals and tourists congregate here, and during the season it can be a social traveller spot.

ℹ Information

ATMs are plentiful and there are numerous currency-exchange offices on Mission St near the corner of Nehru St.

Rue Bussy between Bharathi St and MG Rd is packed with clinics and pharmacies.

Coffee.Com (11A Romain Rolland St; per hr ₹80; ⏰9am-10pm) A genuine internet cafe, with good coffee and light food (₹60 to ₹100) to help your browsing.

New Medical Centre (☎2225289; www.nmcpondy.com; 470 MG Rd; ⏰24hr) Recommended private clinic and hospital.

ℹ Getting There & Away

Bus

The **bus stand** (Maraimalai Adigal Salai) is in the west of town, 2km from the French Quarter.

Train

Puducherry station has only a few services. Two daily trains run to Chennai Egmore, with unreserved seating only (₹28 to ₹53, four to five hours). You can connect at Villupuram, 38km west of Puducherry, for many more services north and south. Puducherry station has a computerised booking office for trains throughout India.

Buses from Puducherry (Pondicherry) Bus Stand

DESTINATION	FARE (₹)	DURATION (HR)	FREQUENCY (DAILY)
Bengaluru	188-200 (Volvo AC 500-600)	8	6 (Volvo AC 8.30am, 10.30pm)
Chennai	97 (Volvo AC 190)	4	124 (25 Volvo AC)
Mamallapuram	50	2	70

Getting Around

One of the best ways to get around Pondy's flat streets is by walking. Autorickshaws are plentiful. From the bus stand to the French Quarter it costs ₹25 if the driver uses the meter, otherwise the price will be at least double.

Madurai

☎ 0452 / POP 1.02 MILLION

Chennai may be the capital of Tamil Nadu, but Madurai claims its soul. Madurai is Tamil-born and Tamil-rooted, one of the oldest cities in India, a metropolis that traded with ancient Rome and was a great capital long before Chennai was even dreamt of.

Tourists, Indian and foreign, usually come here to see the Meenakshi Amman Temple, a labyrinthine structure ranking among the greatest temples of India. Otherwise, Madurai, perhaps appropriately given her age, captures many of India's glaring dichotomies with a centre dominated by a medieval temple and an economy increasingly driven by IT, all overlaid with the energy and excitement of a large Indian city and slotted into a much more manageable package than Chennai's sprawl.

Sights

Gandhi Memorial Museum
Museum

(Gandhi Museum Rd; camera ₹50; ⊙10am-1pm & 2-5.45pm Tue-Sun) FREE Housed in a 17th-century Nayak queen's palace, this excellent museum contains an impressively moving and detailed account of India's struggle for independence from 1757 to 1947, and the English-language text pulls no punches about British rule. Included in the exhibition is the blood-stained dhoti (long loincloth) that Gandhi was wearing when he was assassinated in Delhi in 1948; it's here because it was in Madurai, in 1921, that he first took up wearing the dhoti as a sign of native pride. Bus 75 from Periyar Bus Stand goes to the Tamukkam bus stop on Alagarkoil Rd, 600m from the museum.

Sleeping

Hotel West Tower
Hotel $

(☎2346908; 42/60 West Tower St; s/d ₹473/825, r with AC ₹1238 ; ❄) The West Tower's best asset is that it's very near the temple, but it's also acceptably clean and friendly.

Madurai Residency
Hotel $$

(☎438000; www.madurairesidency.com; 15 West Marret St; incl breakfast s ₹2039-2518, d ₹2398-2878; ❄ ⏸) The service is stellar and the rooms are comfy and fresh at this winner, which has one of the the highest rooftop restaurants in town. It's very popular, so book at least two days ahead. There's wi-fi in the lobby.

Pilgrim with offerings, Meenakshi Amman Temple (p282)
PAUL BEINSSEN/GETTY IMAGES ©

Don't Miss
Meenakshi
Amman Temple

camera/video ₹50/250

🕙 4am-12.30pm & 4-9.30pm

The abode of the triple-breasted goddess Meenakshi ('fish-eyed' – an epithet for perfect eyes in classical Tamil poetry) is considered by many to be the height of South Indian temple architecture, as vital to the aesthetic heritage of this region as the Taj Mahal is to North India.

The Temple Complex

Not so much a temple as a 6-hectare complex with 12 tall *gopurams*, all encrusted with a staggering array of gods, goddesses, demons and heroes (1511 of them on the south *gopuram* alone). The four streets surrounding the temple are pedestrian-only. The main entrance is by the eastern *gopuram*. First, have a look round the **Pudhu Mandapa** (East Chitrai St), the 100m-long, 16th-century pillared hall facing the *gopuram*. It's filled with colourful textile and craft stalls and tailors at sewing machines, partly hiding some of the lovely pillar sculptures, but it's easy to find the triple-breasted Meenakshi near the southeast corner, and her marriage to Shiva, accompanied by Vishnu, just inside the western entrance. A particularly handsome light-blue Nandi bull (Shiva's vehicle) sits outside the eastern entrance of the *mandapa*.

Inside

Once inside the eastern *gopuram*, you'll find the Nayak-period Thousand Pillar Hall on your right. This is now an **Art Museum** (Indian/foreigner ₹5/50, camera/video ₹50/250; ⏱7am-7.30pm) where you can admire at your leisure a Shiva shrine with a large bronze Nataraja at the end of a corridor of superbly carved pillars, plus many other fine bronzes and colourful painted panels. Moving on into the temple, you'll reach a Nandi shrine surrounded by more beautifully carved columns. Ahead is the main Shiva shrine, and further ahead to the left is the main Meenakshi shrine, both of which only Hindus can enter. Anyone can, however, wander round the temple tank and leave the temple from there via a hall of flower sellers and the arch-ceilinged Ashta Shakti Mandapa.

Note, dress codes are fairly strict for the temple itself: no women's shoulders, or legs of either gender, may be exposed.

Meenakshi Amman Temple Don't Miss List

BOBY JOSE IS A TOUR GUIDE SPECIALISING IN MADURAI AND TAMIL NADU

1 THE SOUTH GOPURAM

This is the only *gopuram* (entrance tower) with parabolic design, and is one of the most beautiful *gopurams* structurally. The *gopuram* was constructed during the late 16th century, and has both Vijayanagar and Nayak architectural characteristics.

2 SCULPTURE ON THE SHIVA SHRINE

There is some marvellous marriage-ceremony sculpture on one of the pillars in front of the *sundareswar* or Shiva shrine. In this scene, Lord Vishnu offers his sister Meenakshi or Parvati to Sundareswarar or Shiva. Vishnu is in a gentle mood, Parvati looks shy, and Shiva courageous – it's a visual feast. This sculpture, along with the Nandi *mandapa* (pillared pavilion), is housed under a high ceiling supported by ornamental pillars typical of the Nayak period.

3 THOUSAND PILLAR HALL

This is a wonder because of the remarkable angularity between all the pillars. The *mandapa* is a huge edifice located in the northeast corner of the temple that actually houses 985 pillars. The group of figures on two rows of pillars at the entrance is a masterpiece in itself.

4 THE GOLDEN VIMANAS

You may view the two golden *vimanas* (towers) from the eastern side of the golden lotus tank. The two *vimanas* and the golden lotus tank are as old as the legends connected with the origin of the shrine.

5 PATH AROUND THE SHIVA SHRINE

I advise visitors to walk around the outside of the Shiva shrine: this circular route is particularly stunning. The monolithic pillars and granite roof are dazzling structures – you can see how the engineering of the era embraced artistry.

Madurai

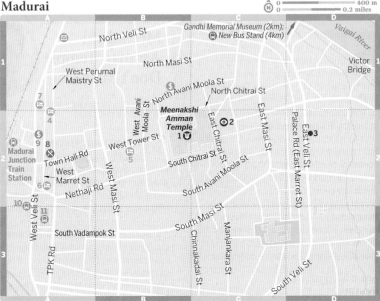

Madurai

Hotel Supreme   Hotel $$
(☎ 2343151; www.hotelsupreme.in; 110 West Perumal Maistry St; incl breakfast s ₹2278-3118, d ₹2578-3298; ❄ 🛜) The Supreme is a well-presented hotel with friendly service that is very popular with domestic tourists. Don't miss the chance to walk into Apollo 96, a bar built to look like a spaceship, and wonder if someone laced your lassi last night. There's good food at the Surya Restaurant (p285), and free in-room wi-fi.

Royal Court   Hotel $$$
(☎ 4356666; www.royalcourtindia.com; 4 West Veli St; incl breakfast s ₹3957-4917, d ₹4797-5636; ❄ @ 🛜) The Royal Court manages to blend a bit of white-sheeted, hardwood-floored colonial elegance with comfort, good eating options, professional service and free in-room wi-fi. It's an excellent, central choice for someone who needs a bit of spoiling.

Government Buses from Madurai

DESTINATION	FARE (₹)	DURATION (HR)	FREQUENCY
Chennai	325	9-10	40 daily
Ernakulam (Kochi)	340	8	9am & 9pm
Mysore	280-360	16	7 buses 4.30-9.45pm
Puducherry	265	8	8.45pm & 9.30pm

🍴 Eating

For a great evening tasting Madurai specialities with a local food enthusiast, call or email **Foodies Day Out** (☏9840992340; www.foodiesdayout.com; 2nd fl, 56 East Veli St; tour per person ₹1500). They'll pick you up around 5.30pm and take you to seven or eight restaurants and stalls to sample the signature dish at each. Vegetarian tours are available; at least two people are needed.

Anna Meenakshi Restaurant
Indian **$**

(West Perumal Maistry St; mains ₹60-100; ⊙6am-11pm) With marginally more attention to decor and ambience than other cheapies along the street, Anna Meenakshi is a busy spot where you can get a decent South Indian thali for ₹60.

Surya Restaurant
Multicuisine **$$**

(110 West Perumal Maistry St; mains ₹70-160; ⊙4pm-midnight) The rooftop restaurant of Hotel Supreme offers a superb view over the city, stand-out service and good pure-veg food, but the winner here has got to be the iced coffee, which might have been brewed by God when you sip it on a dusty, hot day.

ℹ️ Information

State Bank of India (West Veli St) Has foreign-exchange desks and an ATM.

Supreme Web (110 West Perumal Maistry St; per hr ₹30; ⊙7am-11pm) An efficient place with browsing, printing, scanning and photocopying. Take your passport.

ℹ️ Getting There & Away

Air

SpiceJet (www.spicejet.com) flies at least once daily to Bengaluru, Chennai, Colombo, Delhi, Hyderabad and Mumbai. Further Chennai flights are operated by **JetKonnect** (☏2690771; www.jetkonnect.com; Airport) three or four time daily, and **Air India** (☏2341795; www.airindia.com; 7A West Veli St) once daily.

Bus

Most government buses arrive and depart from the **New Bus Stand** (Melur Rd), 4km northeast of the old city. Tickets for more expensive (and mostly more comfortable) private buses are sold by agencies on the south side of the **Shopping Complex Bus Stand** (btwn West Veli St & TPK Rd). Most travel overnight.

Train

From Madurai Junction station, nine trains go daily to Chennai, the fastest being the 6.45am Vaigai Express (2nd/chair class ₹132/488, eight hours) via Trichy (₹71/253, two hours). A good overnight train for Chennai is the 8.35pm Pandyan Express (sleeper/3AC/2AC/1AC ₹232/730/880/1500, nine hours). Trivandrum (three trains daily), Coimbatore (two daily) and Bengaluru (one daily) are among other destinations.

ℹ️ Getting Around

The airport is 12km south of town and taxis cost ₹300 to the centre. Alternatively, buses 15 and 16 run to/from the **Periyar Bus Stand** (West Veli St). From the **New Bus Stand**, bus 5 (₹4) shuttles into the city; an autorickshaw is ₹100.

Darjeeling, Varanasi & the Northeast

Up in the cool northern hills the 'toy train' of the Darjeeling Himalayan Railway chugs its way to the British-era hill station of Darjeeling. It's a quintessential remnant of the Raj, where views of massive Khangchendzonga towering over the surrounding tea estates rank as one of the region's most inspiring sights. The West Bengal capital Kolkata (Calcutta) is a cultural and gastronomic, somewhat mind-blowing feast, peppered with remnants of grandiose colonial-era architecture. It's a fascinating metropolis full of head-spinning contrasts, and forms a perfect springboard to exploring the region, including the tiger-filled swamps of the Sunderbans. Not far away, on the central plains, life and death rituals are played out on the banks of the Ganges in the extraordinary holy city of Varanasi, while tourists flock to Khajuraho to marvel at the breathtaking, virtuoso erotic carvings of its Unesco-protected temples.

Tea estate, Darjeeling hills
RICHARD I'ANSON/GETTY IMAGES ©

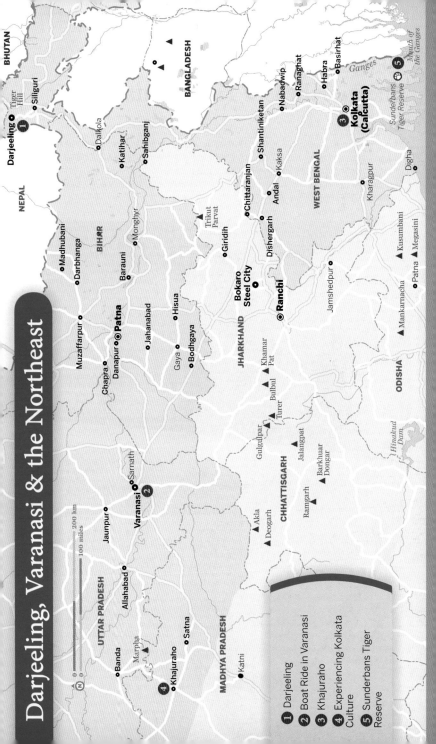

Darjeeling, Varanasi & the Northeast

1 Darjeeling
2 Boat Ride in Varanasi
3 Khajuraho
4 Experiencing Kolkata Culture
5 Sunderbans Tiger Reserve

Darjeeling, Varanasi & the Northeast's Highlights

Darjeeling

A quintessential Indian hill station, Darjeeling (p309) is a place to escape the heat of the plains, relax and drink tea. It resonates with Raj-era history, its views of massive Khangchen-zonga towering over the surrounding tea estates rank as one of the region's most inspiring sights, and the approach via 'toy train' through the mountains is one of India's iconic journeys. Darjeeling Himalayan Railway

1

2

Boat Ride in Varanasi

The best way to see the tumultuous-ness of the holy city of Varanasi (p316) is to take a dawn boat trip along the Ganges. It's inspiring to see the colour and clamour of pilgrims bathing and performing *puja* (worship) in the mellow morning light. Early evening is another great time to be by the ghats, lighting a lotus candle and letting it float away on the water.

BRIAN D CRUICKSHANK/GETTY IMAGES ©

Experiencing Kolkata Culture **3**

India's intellectual and cultural capital, Kolkata (Calcutta; p296) is full of faded colonial-era buildings such as the grandiose Victoria Memorial and St Paul's Cathedral (right), with its pre-Raphaelite stained glass. On first glance, this might seem a frenetic, bamboozling city, but it's a fantastic place to wander, dine and experience local culture.

TIM BARKER/GETTY IMAGES ©

4

Khajuraho

The temples at Khajuraho (p328) are exquisite examples of Indo-Aryan architecture, but it's their liberally embellished carvings that have made them famous. Around the outsides of the temples are bands of virtuoso stonework showing a storyboard of life a millennium ago – gods, goddesses, warriors, musicians, real and mythological animals, and lots and lots of sex.

5

Sunderbans Tiger Reserve

Home to the world's largest population of tigers, the Sunderbans (p306) is a 10,000-sq-km area (split roughly 40-60 between India and Bangladesh), which encompasses a huge network of broad channels and semi-submerged mangroves. Around 400 Royal Bengal tigers roam the swamps here, as well as other wildlife such as spotted deer, 2m-long water monitors and darting kingfishers, and a number of companies based in Kolkata run recommended guided tours.

Darjeeling, Varanasi & the Northeast's Best...

Wining & Dining

○ **Oh! Calcutta** Don't let the shopping-mall location fool you; this is Bengali-fusion with a touch of class. One of Kolkata's best. (p303)

○ **Bhojohari Manna** Top-notch Bengali food at bargain prices in this great-value Kolkata chain. (p305)

○ **Glenary's** Elegant dining above a famous Darjeeling teahouse. (p314)

○ **Brown Bread Bakery** Well worth hunting for in Varanasi's back alleys, Brown Bread is organic, international and terrifically tasty.. and all for a good cause. (p324)

○ **Raja's Café** Khajuraho's finest; lovely setting and superb Indian menu. (p333)

Heritage Hotels

○ **Oberoi Grand** Transporting you from the chaos of Kolkata's streets to an oasis of genteel calm. (p301)

○ **Windamere Hotel** Rambling relic of the Raj and one-time boarding house for Darjeeling's British tea planters. (p313)

○ **Hotel Ganges View** Beautifully renovated, colonial-style house overlooking the Ganges in the holy city of Varanasi. (p322)

○ **Gateway Hotel Ganges** The maharaja's former guesthouse is Varanasi's finest hotel. No river views, but luxury abounds. (p323)

Viewpoints

○ **Bhutia Busty Gompa** Darjeeling monastery with Khangchendzonga providing a spectacular backdrop. Picture perfect. (p314)

○ **Tiger Hill** Darjeeling's most famous sweeping view takes in half a dozen giant peaks (including Everest) and is best seen at dawn. (p309)

○ **Victoria Memorial** The magnificently photogenic view across reflecting ponds from the northeast. (p296)

○ **Sunderbans** Nature at every turn as you float your way through the mangrove forests. (p306)

Sacred Sites

○ **River Ganges, Varanasi**
The river ghats here are where some of the most intimate rituals of life and death are played out in public. (p318)

○ **Observatory Hill**
Sacred to both Buddhists and Hindus, the site of the original Dorje Ling monastery that gave Darjeeling its name. (p311)

○ **Sarnath** Where the Buddha came to preach his message after he achieved enlightenment at Bodhgaya. (p323)

○ **Kalighat Temple** Pilgrims queues into the main hall at the most holy of Kolkata's Hindu temples. (p298)

Need to Know

ADVANCE PLANNING

○ **One month before**
Book accommodation, especially in high season (usually November to March).

○ **One week before** Book any long-distance rail journeys, internal flights, and your tour of the Sunderbans.

○ **One or two days before** Book your seat on the Darjeeling Himayalan Railway (toy train), and any tours that take your fancy.

RESOURCES

○ **West Bengal Tourist Department** (www.westbengaltourism.gov.in) Includes Kolkata and Darjeeling.

○ **Bengali Recipes** (www.sutapa.com)

○ **Calcutta Web** (www.calcuttaweb.com) Kolkata news and listings.

○ **Uttar Pradesh Tourism** (www.up-tourism.com) Includes Varanasi.

○ **Madhya Pradesh Tourism** (www.mptourism.com) Includes Khajuraho.

GETTING AROUND

○ **Air** The most convenient airport is Kolkata. There are also small airports at Varanasi and Khajuraho.

○ **Train** Trains serve Kolkata, Varanasi and Khajuraho; Darjeeling can be reached via picturesque 'toy train'.

○ **Car & driver** Possible to arrange at taxi stands or through hotels in most towns; the most convenient way to reach smaller towns, especially in the mountains.

BE FOREWARNED

○ **Avoid the crowds**
During the month-long 'puja season', starting from Durga Puja and stretching to Diwali, hotels, jeeps and trekking huts are often booked out by travelling Bengali tourists. Pack a jumper and visit in November to avoid the crowds.

○ **Touts** Touts are an annoyance in tourist hotspots such as Khajuraho, but take real care in Varanasi; many tourists get scammed here.

Left: Victoria Memorial (p296)
Above: Pilgrim, Varanasi (p316)
(LEFT) AMITABHA GUPTA/GETTY IMAGES ©;
(ABOVE) CHRIS BEALL/GETTY IMAGES ©

Darjeeling, Varanasi & the Northeast Itineraries

The first trip takes you from Kolkata to Varanasi before ending at Khajuraho. The second lets you sample the best of Bengal: its capital, Kolkata; its tiger domain, the Sunderbans; and its picturesque hill station, Darjeeling.

NEPAL

BHUTAN

❸ DARJEELING

❸ SARNATH

❷

VARANASI

❹

KHAJURAHO

BANGLADESH

KOLKATA (CALCUTTA) ❶

SUNDERBANS TIGER RESERVE ❷

5 DAYS

KOLKATA TO KHAJURAHO
THE SPIRITUAL & THE SACRED

Start your trip in the frenetic yet fascinating city of ❶**Kolkata**. Book yourself into a Raj-era heritage hotel, then take in the city's charming colonial architecture by signing up for one of Kolkata's excellent walking tours. Tuck into top-notch Bengal cuisine at one of the city's many fine restaurants, but don't miss snacking on *kati* rolls or taking a tea break at a roadside chai stall.

From Kolkata, board a train westwards to the mesmerising holy city of ❷**Varanasi**, a place that encompasses life and death in an extraordinary swirl of colour, ritual and mayhem. Take an early-morning boat ride along the Ganges to experience a sense of otherworldly spirituality. And don't miss a half-day trip to nearby ❸**Sarnath**, one Buddhism's four most sacred places.

From Varanasi, board another train, this time towards the steamy centre of India to visit the incredible temples of ❹**Khajuraho**. This World Heritage Site is a dazzling symphony of temple art, famous for its fecund images of rampant sexuality, but also a remarkable feat of virtuoso carving. You can catch a train from here to Delhi, or even fly, which is a neat way of ending this whistlestop trip.

KOLKATA TO DARJEELING

THE BEAUTY OF BENGAL

Again, start your trip in ❶ **Kolkata**, the capital of West Bengal and the home of Bengali cuisine. After a couple of days sightseeing, leave the city chaos behind and make your way to the wilds of the ❷ **Sunderbans Tiger Reserve**. This network of channels and mangrove swamps is part of the world's largest river delta and is home to the magnificent Royal Bengal tiger. Book yourself onto an all-inclusive tour and sleep on board a riverboat or in an 'eco-village' on the riverbank, before exploring the thickly forested reserve with a good pair of binoculars and an expert guide.

Returning to Kolkata, next head further north; if possible, take the 'toy train' for the last section of the scenic trip to ❸ **Darjeeling**, in the lush northeastern corner of India. This graceful hill station is spread over a steep mountain ridge, surrounded by tea plantations, with a backdrop of jagged Himalayan peaks. Climb Tiger Hill, visit a tea estate and explore the local gompas and pagodas set in breathtaking scenery.

Buddhist devotees at Sarnath (p323)
TIM GRAHAM/GETTY IMAGES ©

Darjeeling, Varanasi & the Northeast

KOLKATA (CALCUTTA)

India's second-biggest city is a daily festival of human existence, simultaneously noble and squalid, cultured and desperate. By its old spelling, Calcutta conjures up images of human suffering to most Westerners. But locally, Kolkata is regarded as India's intellectual and cultural capital. While poverty is certainly in your face, the dapper Bengali gentry continues to frequent grand old gentlemen's clubs, back horses at the Calcutta Racetrack and tee off at some of India's finest golf courses.

As the former capital of British India, Kolkata retains a feast of colonial-era architecture, albeit much in a photogenic state of disrepair. Kolkata is also the ideal place to experience the mild, fruity tang of Bengali cuisine.

⊙ Sights

Central Kolkata

Victoria Memorial Historic Building
(VM; Map p304; ☏22235142; www.victoriamemorial-cal.org; Indian/foreigner ₹10/150; ⊙10am-5pm Tue-Sun, last tickets 4.30pm) The incredible Victoria Memorial is a vast, beautifully proportioned festival of white marble: think US Capitol meets Taj Mahal. Had it been built for a beautiful Indian princess rather than a dead colonial queen, this would surely be considered one of India's greatest buildings. It was designed to commemorate Queen Victoria's 1901 diamond jubilee, but construction wasn't completed until nearly 20 years after her death.

The soaring central chamber remains very impressive and leads through to the **Calcutta Gallery**, an excellent, even-handed

Sikh women cooking chapatis
RICHARD I'ANSON/GETTY IMAGES ©

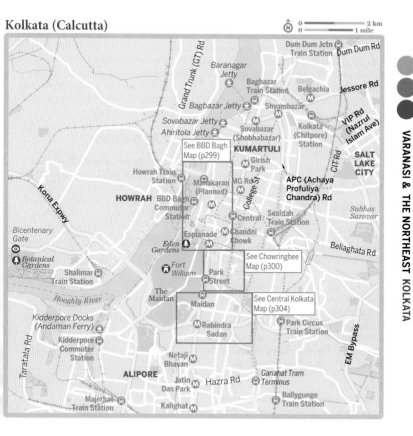

exhibition tracing the city's colonial-era history.

In the evenings the VM makes a spectacular canvas for a 45-minute English-language **sound & light show** (Indian/foreigner ₹10/20; 🕑7.15pm Tue-Sun mid-Oct–Feb, 7.45pm Tue-Sun Mar-Jun). Ticket booth (from 5pm) and entry are at the east gate. Seating is outside and uncovered. No shows in summer.

St Paul's Cathedral   Church
(Map p304; 🕿22230127; Cathedral Rd; 🕑9am-noon & 3-6pm) With its central crenellated tower, St Paul's would look quite at home in Cambridgeshire. Built 1839–47, it has a remarkably wide nave and features a stained-glass west window by pre-Raphaelite maestro Sir Edward Burne-Jones.

Aurobindo Bhawan   Historic Building
(Map p304; 8 Shakespeare Sarani; 🕑8am-8pm) Revolutionary turned guru Sri Aurobindo was born in Calcutta in 1872 and his grand childhood mansion-home has been preserved as an oasis of peace in the city centre.

The Maidan   Park
(Map p304) After the 'Black Hole' fiasco, a moated 'second' Fort William was constructed in 1758 in octagonal, Vauban-esque form. The whole village of Gobind-apur was flattened to give the new fort's cannons a clear line of fire. Though sad for then-residents, this created the Maidan (moi-dan), a 3km-long park that is today as fundamental to Kolkata as Central Park is to New York City. Fort William itself remains hidden within a walled military zone.

Indian Museum
Museum

(Map p300; ☎22499979; www.indianmuseum-kolkata.org; Chowringhee Rd; Indian/foreigner ₹10/150, camera ₹50; ☺10am-4.30pm Tue-Sun, last entry 4pm) Kolkata's old-fashioned main museum fills a colonnaded palace ranged around a central lawn. Extensive exhibits include fabulous 1000-year-old Hindu sculptures, lumpy minerals, a dangling whale skeleton and an ancient Egyptian mummy.

BBD Bagh Area

Esplanade
Area

(Map p299) Rising above chaotic Esplanade bus station, the 1828 **Sahid Minar** is a 48m-tall round-topped obelisk originally celebrating an 1814 British military victory over Nepal. Across one of Kolkata's busiest junctions, the striking **Metropolitan Building** was originally a colonial-era department store. Left derelict for years, a long overdue 2009 restoration saw its corner domes regilded. A block north, the fanciful **Tippu Sultan's Mosque** hides almost invisibly behind street stalls.

BBD Bagh
Area

(Map p299; Dalhousie Sq) Once of Raj-era Calcutta's foremost squares, BBD Bagh is centred on a palm-lined central reservoir-lake ('tank') that once supplied the young city's water. Although concrete intrusions detract from the overall spectacle, many a splendid colonial-era edifice remains.

High Court
Historic Building

(Map p299; http://calcuttahighcourt.nic.in; Esplanade Row West; ☺10.30am-1.15pm & 2-4.30pm Mon-Fri) Another of Kolkata's greatest architectural triumphs, the High Court building was built between 1864 and 1872, loosely modelled on the medieval Cloth Hall in Ypres (Flanders).

South Kolkata

Kalighat Temple
Hindu Temple

(☎22231516; ☺5am-10pm, central shrine closed 2-4pm) This ancient Kali temple is Kolkata's holiest spot for Hindus and possibly the source of the city's name. Today's version, a 1809 rebuild, has floral and peacock-motif tiles that look more Victorian than Indian. More interesting than the architecture are the jostling pilgrim queues that snake into the main hall to fling hibiscus flowers at a crowned, three-eyed Kali image.

🏃 Activities

The 1829 **Royal Calcutta Golf Club** (☎24731288, 24731352; www.rcgc.in; 18 Golf Club Rd), the world's oldest outside Britain, allows foreign nonmembers to play a round for US$50.

👉 Tours

See p306 for excursions to the Sunderbans.

WALKING TOURS

Most start after dawn and last till mid-morning but tailor-made options are possible.

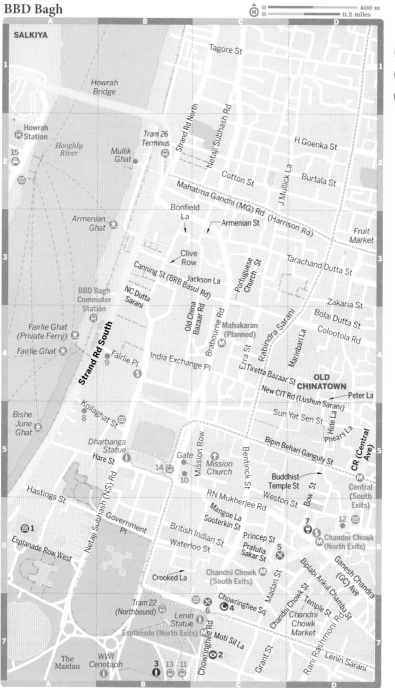

BBD Bagh

SALKIYA

0 — 400 m
0 — 0.2 miles

Tagore St

Howrah Bridge

Howrah Station

Hooghly River

Strand Rd North

Netaji Subhash Rd

Tram 26 Terminus

Mullik Ghat

H Goenka St

Burtala St

J Mullick La

Cotton St

Mahatma Gandhi (MG) Rd (Harrison Rd)

Bonfield La

Armenian St

Armenian Ghat

Clive Row

Canning St (BRB Basul Rd)

Jackson La

Portuguese Church St

Tarachand Dutta St

Fruit Market

BBD Bagh Commuter Station

NC Dutta Sarani

Old China Bazaar Rd

Brabourne Rd

Mahakaran (Planned)

Rabindra Sarani

Zakaria St

Bolai Dutta St

Coolootola Rd

Fairlie Ghat (Private Ferry)

Fairlie Ghat

Fairlie Pl

9

India Exchange Pl

Ezra St

Tiretta Bazaar St

Marimbari La

OLD CHINATOWN

Peter La

New CIT Rd (Lushun Sarani)

Sun Yat Sen St

Hide La

Phears La

Bishe June Ghat

Koilaghat St

8

Dharbanga Statue

Hare St

Gate

Mission Row

Mission Church

Bentinck St

Bipin Behari Ganguly St

Buddhist Temple St

Bow St

CR (Central Ave)

Central (South Exits)

14

10

Hastings St

Netaji Subhash (NS) Rd

Government Pl

RN Mukherjee Rd

Weston St

Mangoe La

Sooterkin St

British Indian St

Waterloo St

Princep St

Prafulla Sakar St

7

12

Chandni Chowk (North Exits)

Madan St

5

Ganesh Chandra (GC) Ave

1

Esplanade Row West

Crooked La

Chandni Chowk (South Exits)

Chandni Chowk

Chowringhee Sq

4

Biplabi Ankul Chamba St

Chandni Chowk Temple St

Chandni Chowk Market

Tram 22 (Northbound)

6

Lenin Statue

Esplanade (North Exits)

Chowringhee Rd

Moti Sil La

2

Madan St

Grant St

Rani Rashmoni Rd

Lenin Sarani

The Maidan

WWI Cenotaph

3

13 11

15

299

0	200 m
0	0.1 miles

Kali Travel Home
Walking
(📞25550581, 9007778504; www.traveleastindia.com; ₹400-700)

CalWalks
Walking
(📞9830184030; www.calcuttawalks.com; from ₹1500)

Footsteps
Walking
(📞9830008033, 9830052688; www.braindropsindia.com/footsteps; from ₹800) Relatively few fixed dates.

Calcutta Photo Tours
Walking, Photography
(📞9831163482; calcuttaphototours.com; from ₹1500)

MOTORBIKE/CAR TOURS

Best known for their mangrove boat trips, Backpackers (p306) also offers innova-

tive two-part city tours on the back of a motorbike (₹1500).

🛌 Sleeping

Sudder Street Area

The nearest Kolkata gets to a traveller ghetto is the area around helpfully located Sudder St. There's a range of backpacker-oriented services, and if you haven't got any advanced booking a big advantage of arriving here is that virtually every second building is a guesthouse or hotel.

Hotel Kempton
Hotel $$
(Map p300; 📞40177888; www.hotelkempton.in; 3 Marquis St; s/d from ₹3757/4110; ❄🛜)
The Kempton's feast of white marble and artificial orchids hint at standards far

above the prices actually charged in this new, relatively suave tower that brings a new level of class to the Sudder St zone. Prices include buffet breakfast.

Fairlawn Hotel　　　　　Hotel $$
(Map p300; ☏ 22521510; www.fairlawnhotel.com; 13A Sudder St; s/d incl breakfast ₹3167/3871; ✳@🛜) Taking guests since 1936, the Fairlawn is a character-filled 1783 Raj-era home fronted by tropical greenery. The stairs and sitting room are smothered with photos, family mementos and articles celebrating the hotel's nonagenarian owner. While not luxurious, most rooms are spacious and well equipped though some bathrooms retain very old tubs. At least one of the downstairs rooms has limited natural light. Wi-fi (₹250) is turned off at midnight.

Oberoi Grand　　Heritage Hotel $$$
(Map p300; ☏ 22492323; www.oberoikolkata.com; 15 Chowringhee Rd; s/d/ste from ₹22,310/24,071/52,840; ✳@🛜🏊) Passing through the almost hidden courtyard gateway, you're transported from the chaos of Chowringhee Rd into a regal oasis of genteel calm that deserves every point on its five stars. Immaculate accommodation oozes atmosphere, the swimming pool is ringed with palms, and proactive staff anticipate your every need.

....

City Centre

Chrome　　　　　　Art Hotel $$
(Map p304; ☏ 30963096; www.chromehotel.in; 226 AJC Bose Rd; s/d from ₹9400/9980; ✳@🛜🏊) Sleep in a brilliantly executed artistic statement that looks like a seven-storey Swiss cheese by day and a colour-pulsing alien communicator by night. Rooms have optical-illusion decor, and the 5th-floor landing hides a mini-library. Droning air-conditioner motors undermine relaxation at the rooftop swimming pool (open 7am to 7pm).

Astor　　　　　　　　Hotel $$
(Map p304; ☏ 22829950; www.astorkolkata.com; 15 Shakespeare Sarani) Artful evening floodlighting brings out the best of the Astor's solid 1905 architecture, and rooms should offer standards to match once the wholesale interior reconstruction is complete, which should be any day now.

Kenilworth　　　　　　Hotel $$$
(Map p304; ☏ 22823939; www.kenilworth-hotels.com/kolkata; 1 Little Russell St; s/d ₹11,750/13,000; ✳🛜) The deep lobby of marble, dark wood and chandeliers contrasts successfully with a more contemporary cafe that spills out onto an attractive lawn. Pleasingly bright, fully equipped rooms have some of Kolkata's most comfortable beds. Discount rates from around ₹7000 are often available. Wi-fi costs ₹335/670 per hour/day.

✳ Eating

Cheaper Bengali places often serve tapas-sized portions so order two or three dishes per person along with either rice or *luchi* plus some sweet *khejur* (chutney).

Most restaurants add 13% tax to bills. Posher places add 18.3%. Tips are welcome at cheaper places and expected at most expensive restaurants. **Times Food Guide** (www.timescity.com/kolkata; book

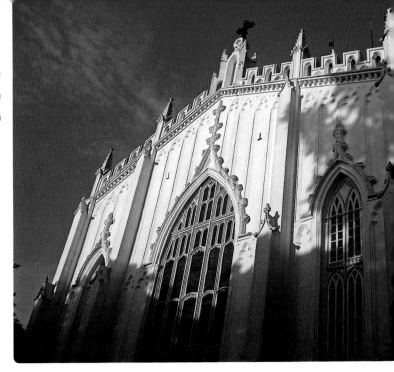

₹100) and **Zomato** (www.zomato.com/kolkata) offer hundreds of restaurant reviews.

For a colourful and very affectionate portrait of Kolkata's ever-vibrant street food scene see www.streetfoodkolkata.com which includes recipes and films and a sells a brilliantly evocative book.

Kati Rolls

Bengal's trademark fast food is the *kati* roll: take a *paratha* roti, fry it with a coating of egg then fill with sliced onions, chilli and your choice of stuffing (curried chicken, grilled meat or paneer). Roll it up in a twist of paper and it's ready to eat, generally on the street from hole-in-the-wall serveries. Standards vary considerably but a classic is **Hot Kati Rolls** (Map p300; 1/1 Park St; rolls ₹15-65; ⏰11am-10.30pm).

Sudder Street & New Market

Raj's Spanish Cafe
Cafe $

(Map p300; off Sudder St; mains ₹80-150; ⏰8am-10pm; 📶) Excellent coffee, juices, pancakes and relatively reliable wi-fi (₹25 per hour, from around 11am) makes this a popular hang-out for medium-term charity volunteers. The menu includes a well-made selection of Spanish dishes (tortilla *pisto manchego*) and various traveller favourites. Decor is simple but welcoming and the small outdoor area has some cursory foliage. It's hidden behind Roop Shrinagar fabric shop.

Aminia
Tandoori, Mughlai $

(Map p300; Hogg St; mains ₹70-135; ⏰10.30am-10.30pm) Aminia's age-old interior has been mildly spruced up to give a vaguely retro-1940s cool feel, the ceiling fans whirring high above a single big white cacophonous hall. Henna-bearded wait-staff in monogrammed magenta tunics

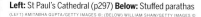

slap down dishes including good chicken tikka and overly oily biryanis.

Blue & Beyond   Multicuisine $$
(Map p300; ☎22521039; 9th fl, Lindsay Hotel, Lindsay St; mains ₹200-300, beer/cocktails from ₹165/200; ⏱12.30-10.30pm) The drawcard here is an open-air rooftop terrace with wide views over New Market and prices that that are relatively reasonable for a restaurant that's licensed to serve alcohol. Menu wild-cards include Greek chicken, vegetable platters and Tom Yam soup.

City Centre

Kookie Jar   Bakery $
(Map p304; www.kookiejar.in; Rawdon St; pastries ₹30-80; ⏱8am-10pm) Takeaway cakes, multi-grain bread, wraps, fluffy pastries and Kolkata's most heavenly fudge brownies.

Vanilla Creperie   Cafe $$
(Map p304; 32 Elgin Rd; pancakes ₹180-250, coffee from ₹50; ⏱9am-11pm) Handy as an Elgin St meeting place, this all-white cafe sports faux shutters and serves baguette sandwiches along with its range of savoury-filled pancakes.

Oh! Calcutta   Bengali $$$
(Map p304; ☎22837161; 4th fl, Forum Mall, Elgin Rd; mains ₹240-650, rice ₹180; ⏱12.30-3.15pm & 7.30-10.45pm) Shutter-edged mirror 'windows', bookshelves and B&W photography create a casually up-market atmosphere in this Bengali-fusion restaurant that is far more suave than you might expect from its shopping-mall location, and portions are unusually large. *Luchi* (₹140 for six) are feather-light, and fresh lime brings out the subtleties of *koraishatir dhokar dalna* (pea-cakes in ginger, ₹430).

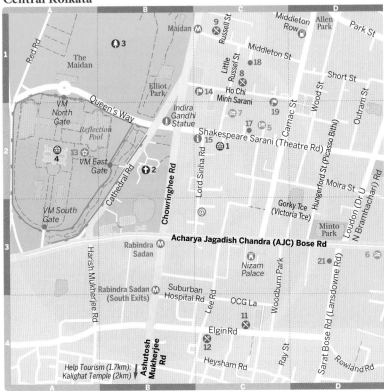

Amigos
Mexican **$$$**

(Map p304; ☎40602507; www.facebook.com/
Amigos.calcutta; 11/1A Ho Chi Minh Sarani;
mains ₹300-450; ⏱noon-3pm & 7.30-10.30pm)
Excellent Tex-Mex food supplemented
with pizzas, served to a relaxed crowd of
upwardly mobile 30-somethings whose
reverberant chatter combines with two
different salsa music tracks to create
quite a din in the tidy stone-effect dining
rooms. Delicious guacamole (extra)
comes in spoon-sized portions; the bill
arrives in a sombrero.

Fire and Ice
Italian **$$$**

(Map p304; ☎22884073; www.fireandicepiz-
zeria.com; Kanak Bldg, Middleton St; mains ₹350-
670; beer/wine/cocktails from ₹210/280/350;
⏱noon-11.15pm) Self-consciously handsome waiters sporting black shirts, red

aprons and bandanas bring forth real Italian pastas, and pizzas with fresh-baked
thin crusts that are Kolkata's best.

BBD Bagh Area

Anand
South Indian **$**

(Map p299; ☎22128344; 19 CR Ave; dosas ₹40-
120; ⏱9am-9.30pm Thu-Tue) Prize-winning
pure-veg dosas served in a well-kept
if old-fashioned family restaurant with
bamboo and mirror-tiled ceilings.

KC Das
Sweets **$**

(Map p299; Lenin Sarani; mishti doi ₹28;
⏱7.30am-9.30pm) Bustling Bengali sweet
shop that claims to have invented *rasgulla*
(rosewater-scented cheese balls) in 1868.
Seating available.

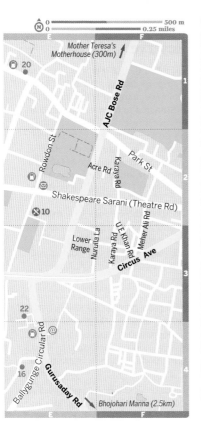

Gariahat Area

Bhojohari Manna   Bengali $$

(☏24663941; www.bhojohorimanna.com; 18/1 Hindustan Rd; dishes ₹50-270, rice ₹45; ☺12.30-10.30pm) Although it's a small chain, each Bhojohari Manna branch feels very different and has a somewhat different menu, though all feature top-quality Bengali food at sensible prices. This branch (number 6) is our favourite; it's comparatively spacious, decorated with tribal implements and has live traditional music some Saturdays. The menu allows diners to pair a wide selection of fish types with the sauce of your choice. Some dishes are rather small so order a spread not missing the *echorer dalna* (green jackfruit curry).

🍷 Drinking & Nightife

Most better bars are in hotels or restaurants. Cheaper places are usually dingy and overwhelmingly male-dominated.

A Kolkata delight is making streetside tea stops for mini-cuppas served in disposable *bhaar* (environmentally friendly earthenware thimbles, around ₹5).

Fairlawn Hotel   Bar

(Map p300; 13A Sudder St; beers ₹110; ☺10am-10pm) The small tropical garden of the historic Fairlawn Hotel is great for a cold brew.

Broadway Bar   Bar

(Map p299; Broadway Hotel, 27A Ganesh Chandra Ave; small/standard beer ₹60/120, shots ₹30-105; ☺11am-10.30pm) Backstreet Paris? Chicago 1930s? Prague 1980s? This cavernous, unpretentious old-men's pub

305

Detour:
Sunderbans Tiger Reserve

Home to one of the largest concentrations of Royal Bengal tigers on the planet, this 2585 sq km **reserve** (☏03218255280; per person per day/video ₹40/200; ☉dawn-dusk) is a network of channels and semi-submerged mangroves that forms the world's largest river delta. Tigers (officially estimated to number close to 300) lurk in the impenetrable depths of the mangrove forests, and also swim the delta's innumerable channels. Although they do sometimes kill villagers and their livestock, tigers are typically shy and sightings are rare. Nevertheless, cruising the broad waterways through the world's biggest mangrove sanctuary (now a Unesco World Heritage Site) and watching wildlife, whether it be a spotted deer, 2m-long water monitor or luminescent kingfisher, is a world away from Kolkata's chaos.

The best time to visit the reserve, which is about three hours drive from Kolkata, is between November and March – entry is restricted in the monsoon months. Organised tours are the best way to navigate this harsh and tricky landscape, not least because all your permits, paperwork, guiding duties and logistical problems are taken care of. Travelling alone is not recommended.

TOURS

Backpackers (☏9836177140; www.tourdesundarbans.com; 11 Tottee Lane, Kolkata; 1/2 nights per person all-inclusive ₹4000/4500; ☉10am-7pm) An extremely professional and knowledgeable outfit that conducts highly recommended tours of the jungles, including birdwatching and local music sessions. Accommodation is in a cruise boat converted from a fishing trawler, or a traditional village-style guesthouse, with folk music in the evenings.

Sunderban Tiger Camp (☏033-32935749; www.waxpolhotels.com; 71 Ganesh Chandra Ave, Kolkata; 1/2 nights per person all-inclusive from ₹3700/6200) Provides expert guides and quality accommodation (on dry land) in lovely red-brick cottages with forest-themed wall murals.

Help Tourism (☏033-24550917; www.helptourism.com; 67A Kali Temple Rd, Kalighat, Kolkata; 2 nights per person all-inclusive ₹15950) Actively associated with local communities, this tour gets you in close proximity to rural life in the delta, in addition to providing wonderful access into the forest. Accommodation is in a luxury eco-themed camp.

defies easy parallels but has a compulsive left-bank fascination with cheap booze, 20 ceiling fans, bare walls, marble floors and, thankfully, no music.

🔒 Shopping

CLOTHING

Kolkata is great value for clothing, with pre-cut shirts costing under ₹100 from the Chowringhee Rd **Hawkers' Market**

(Map p300). Local tailors on Elliot Rd are less tourist-oriented than those around New Market. Fashion-conscious locals head to Hazra Rd and Gariahat.

CRAFTS & SOUVENIRS
Dakshinapan Shopping Centre
Shopping Centre

(Gariahat Rd; ☉10.30am-7.30pm Mon-Sat) It's worth facing the soul-crushing 1970s architecture for Dakshinapan's wide range of government emporia. There's plenty of tack but many shops offer excellent-value souvenirs, crafts and fabrics.

ⓘ Information

Internet Access

Gorukh (Map p300; 7 Sudder St; per hr ₹20; ⊙9am-9.30pm) Traveller-friendly place at the back of a fabric shop beside Raj's Spanish Cafe. Cheap international phone calls.

Medical Services

Handy for Sudder St, Eastern Diagnostics (Map p300; ☎22178080; www.easterndiagnostics.com; Mirza Ghalib St; ⊙10am-2pm or by appointment) offers doctors' consultations from ₹200.

Medical services are listed on www.calcuttaweb.com/doctor.php.

Money

ATMs are widespread. Many private moneychangers around Sudder St offer commission-free exchange rates several per cent better than banks, and some will exchange travellers cheques. Shop around and double-check the maths.

Tourist Information

India Tourism (Map p304; ☎22825813; www.incredibleindia.org; 4 Shakespeare Sarani; ⊙9am-6pm Mon-Fri, to 1pm Sat) Free maps of greater Kolkata.

West Bengal Tourism (Map p299; ☎22437260; westbengaltourism.gov.in; 3/2 BBD Bagh; ⊙10.30am-1.30pm & 2-5.30pm Mon-Fri, 10.30am-1pm Sat) Useful website. Office primarily sells their own tours.

ⓘ Getting There & Away

Air

The total reconstruction of Netaji Subhash Bose International Airport (NSBIA; ☎25118787; http://www.aai.aero/kolkata/index.jsp) is likely to vastly increase international traffic to Kolkata from 2013. Already there are direct connections to around 30 Indian cities plus the following international destinations:

Bangkok Air Asia, Thai, IndiGo, Jet

Dhaka Biman, Jet, United Airways Bangladesh

Doha Qatar Airways

Dubai Emirates

Hong Kong Dragonair

Kathmandu Air India

Kuala Lumpur Air Asia

Kunming China Eastern

Paro, Bhutan Druk

Singapore SilkAir/Singapore Air, Druk

Yangon Air India

Useful local airline contacts:

Air India (Map p299; ☎22114433; 39 Chittaranjan Ave; ⊙10am-6pm Mon-Fri, to 5pm Sat)

Major Trains from Kolkata

Departures daily unless otherwise stated.

USEFUL FOR	TRAIN	DURATION (HR)	DEPARTURES	FARES (₹; SLEEPER/3AC/2AC UNLESS OTHERWISE STATED)
Chennai	12841 Coromandal	26½	2.50pm (HWH)	461/1288/2025
	12839 Chennai Mail	28	11.45pm (HWH)	461/1288/2025
Delhi	12303/12381 Poorva	23	8.10am/8.15am (HWH)	442/1187/1860
	12313 SDAH Rajdhani	17½	4.50pm (SDAH)	3AC/1AC 1592/3395
Mumbai CST	12810 Mumbai Mail	33¼	8.15pm (HWH)	508/1425/2265
Varanasi	13005 Amritsar Mail	14	7.10pm (HWH)	286/805/1225

Departure codes: HWH – Howrah; SDAH – Sealdah

Biman (Map p304; 22266672; www.biman-airlines.com; 6th fl, 99A Park St)

China Eastern Airlines (Map p304; 40448887; InterGlobe, 1st fl, Landmark Bldg, 228A AJC Bose Rd) Flies to Kunming (Yunnan).

Druk Air (Map p304; 22902429; 3rd fl, 51 Tivoli Court, 1A Ballygunge Circular Rd) Most foreigners need to make tour arrangements before flying into Bhutan.

United Airways Bangladesh (Map p300; 9007095363; www.uabdl.com; Saberwal House, 55b Mirza Galib St) Single/return to Dhaka from ₹3052/5400.

Bus

For Darjeeling or Sikkim, start by taking a bus to Siliguri (around 12 hours). Numerous private Siliguri buses drive overnight departing between 6pm and 8pm (from ₹355). SBSTC (₹300) and NBSTC (₹360), with ticket desks in the walled area in the bus station's northeastern corner, also have a few morning services to Siliguri.

Train

Stations

Long-distance trains depart from three major stations. Gigantic Howrah (Haora; HWH) is across the river, often best reached by ferry, Sealdah (SDAH) is at the eastern end of MG Road, and 'Kolkata' (Chitpore; KOAA) Station is around 5km further north (nearest metro Belgachia).

Tickets

To buy long-distance train tickets, foreigners should use the **Eastern Railways' Foreign Tourist Bureau** (Map p299; 22224206; 6 Fairlie Pl;

Car & Motorbike Hire

Car rental companies including **Wenz** (9330018001; http://wenzcars.com) can organise long-distance chauffeured rides. Sudder St agencies might be able to find you better deals: Backpackers (p306) can find cars at ₹2200 for up to eight hours (add ₹22 per km if driving more than 80km).

10am-5pm Mon-Sat, to 2pm Sun). Bring a book to read as waits can be very long but there are sofa-seats. Some folks arrive before opening time and sign a waiting list

For a certain commission, Sudder St travel agencies can save you the trek to the ticket office and can sometimes manage to find tickets on 'full' trains.

🏛 Getting Around

To/From the Airport

NSBIA Airport is around 16km northeast of central Kolkata. By the time you read this, the brand new integrated terminal should have opened 300m/600m south of the ageing former domestic/international terminals.

AC Bus

Air-conditioned airport buses (₹40, around one hour) run every half-hour (9am to 9pm) to Esplanade and/or Howrah.

Taxi

Prepaid, fixed-price taxis cost ₹290 to Sudder St and take around 50 minutes. Long waits are possible after 10pm.

Ferry

Generally faster and more agreeable than road travel, especially between central Kolkata and Howrah train station, **river ferries** (ticket ₹4; 8am-8pm) depart every 15 minutes from various jetties including Bagbazar, Armenian (not Sundays), Fairlie, Bishe June and Babu Ghat. Reduced service on Sundays.

Metro

Kolkata's busy **metro** (www.mtp.indianrailways.gov.in; ticket ₹4-12; 7am-9.45pm Mon-Sat, 2-9.45pm Sun) has trains every five to 15 minutes. For Sudder St use Esplanade or Park St.

There's one operational line but several extensions are planned. Due for completion by 2015, Line 2 (http://kmrc.in) between Howrah, Sealdah and Salt Lake, will massively improve the city's navigability.

Rickshaw

Human-powered 'tana rickshaws' work within limited areas, notably around New Market. Although rickshaw pullers sometimes charge foreigners disproportionate fares, many are virtually destitute, sleeping on the pavements beneath their rented chariots at night, so tips are heartily appreciated.

The Khangchendzonga range from Tiger Hill

JANE SWEENEY/GETTY IMAGES ©

Autorickshaws operate as share-taxis along fixed routes. Usefully for Sudder St travellers, one such route shuttles the length of Mirza Ghalib and Royd streets (₹5, northbound mornings, southbound afternoons).

Taxi

Kolkata's yellow Ambassador cabs are ubiquitous by day but can become hard to find after 10pm.

Be aware that taxi meters do NOT show what you'll pay: the real fare is around 250% of the meter reading. Drivers have a conversion chart. Some cabs, typically stationary ones, won't use the meter especially after 9pm when drivers might ask double if they can't expect to find a return fare.

Beware: around 1pm much of the city's one-way road system reverses direction! Taxis can prove reluctant to make journeys around this time.

There are prepaid taxi booths at Howrah Station, Sealdah Station and at the airport.

DARJEELING

☏ 0354 / POP 120,400 / ELEV 2135M

Spread in ribbons over a steep mountain ridge, surrounded by emerald-green tea plantations and with a backdrop of jagged white Himalayan peaks floating over distant clouds, the archetypal hill station of Darjeeling is rightly West Bengal's premier attraction. When you aren't gazing open-mouthed at Khangchendzonga (8598m), you can explore colonial-era architecture, visit Buddhist monasteries and spot snow leopards and red pandas at the nearby zoo. The steep, narrow streets bustle with an array of Himalayan faces from Sikkim, Bhutan, Nepal and Tibet and when energies start to flag a good, steaming Darjeeling brew is never far away.

⊙ Sights

Tiger Hill   Viewpoint

To watch the dawn light break over a spectacular 250km stretch of Himalayan horizon, including Everest (8848m), Lhotse (8501m) and Makalu (8475m) to the far west, rise early and jeep out to Tiger Hill (2590m), 11km south of Darjeeling, above Ghum. The skyline is dominated by Khangchendzonga ('great five-peaked snow fortress'), India's highest peak and the world's third-highest mountain.

TIM MAKINS/GETTY IMAGES ©

⭐ Don't Miss
The Toy Train

The **Darjeeling Himalayan Railway**, known affectionately as the toy train, is one of the few hill railways still operating in India. The train made its first journey along its precipice-topping, 2ft-wide tracks in September 1881 and these days it passes within feet of local storefronts as it weaves in and out of the main road, bringing traffic to a standstill and tooting its whistle incessantly for almost the entire trip. The train has been a Unesco World Heritage Site since 1999.

Services on the line have been in flux since 2009, when landslides destroyed a section of track. Services to and from NJP station are not expected to resume for the next couple of years, which leaves only the two daily diesel services to Kurseong via Ghum:

TRAIN NO	DARJEELING	GHUM	KURSEONG
52544	10.15am	10.45am	1.10pm
52588	4pm	4.30pm	6.40pm
TRAIN NO	KURSEONG	GHUM	DARJEELING
52587	7am	9.15am	9.45am
52545	3pm	5.20pm	5.50pm

During the high season there are also joy rides (₹270) that leave Darjeeling at 8am, 10.40am, 1.20pm and 4pm for a two-hour steam-powered return trip. The service pauses for 10 minutes at the scenic Batastia Loop and then stops for 20 minutes in Ghum, India's highest railway station, to visit the small **railway museum** (admission ₹20; ⊙10am-1pm & 2-4pm). Enthusiasts can see the locomotives up close in the shed across the road from Darjeeling station. For a budget ride take the 10.15am diesel passenger service to Ghum (₹21).

Book at least a day or two ahead at the **train station** (☎2252555; ⊙8am-5pm Mon-Sat,to 2pm Sun) or online at www.irctc.co.in. For more on the service and efforts to maintain it, see www.dhrs.org.

The sunrise over the Himalaya from here has become a major tourist attraction, with hundreds of jeeps leaving Darjeeling for Tiger Hill every morning at 4am. At the summit you can either pay ₹10 to stand in the pavilion grounds or warm up in one of the heated lounges in the pavilion (₹20 to ₹40).

Organised sunrise trips (usually with a detour to Batastia Loop on the way back) can be booked through a travel agency or directly with jeep drivers at the Clubside taxi stand. Return trips cost ₹800 to ₹1000 per vehicle.

Observatory Hill   Sacred Site

Sacred to both Buddhists and Hindus, this hill was the site of the original Dorje Ling monastery that gave the town its name. Today, devotees come to a temple in a small cave to honour Mahakala, a Buddhist deity and wrathful form of the Hindu god Shiva. The summit is marked by several shrines, a flurry of colourful prayer flags and the ringing notes from numerous devotional bells. A path leading up to the hill through giant Japanese cedars starts about 300m along Bhanu Bhakta Sarani from Chowrasta; watch out for marauding monkeys. Disappointingly, there are no mountain views.

Padmaja Naidu Himalayan Zoological Park   Zoo

(🖉2253709; www.pnhzp.gov.in; admission incl Himalayan Mountaineering Institute Indian/for-eigner ₹40/100; ⏰8.30am-5pm Fri-Wed, ticket counter closes 4pm) This zoo, one of India's best, was established in 1958 to study, conserve and preserve Himalayan fauna. Housed within the rocky and forested environment are Himalayan megafauna such as Himalayan bears, clouded leopards, red pandas and Tibetan wolves. The zoo, and its attached snow leopard breeding centre (closed to the public), are home to the world's largest single captive population of snow leopards.

The zoo is a pleasant 20-minute downhill walk down from Chowrasta

Local Knowledge

Darjeeling Don't Miss List

TEA EXPERT RAJAH BANERJEE IS THE FOURTH GENERATION OF THE BANERJEE FAMILY TO OWN AND RUN THE MAKAIBARI TEA ESTATE, NEAR KURSEONG

1 THE TOY TRAIN
The heritage Darjeeling toy train, a unique steam-powered narrow gauge chugging up from Kurseong ('land of the white orchid') to Darjeeling ('land of the thunderbolt'), is a must for visitors. Passengers can almost touch the flora from the windows, and hop off, make a swift purchase from a shop and hop on, such is the romantic speed of the train. It meanders through the three main valleys of the region, Kurseong, Sonada and Darjeeling, with views of spectacular flora interspersed with well-groomed tea gardens.

2 HISTORICAL REMNANTS
The remnants of the British Raj resonate at the Hotel Windamere and in the memorabilia at the Tea Planters Club, and the Himalayan Mountaineering Institute offers a rare insight into the famous mountaineers who have conquered Everest, while also grooming future conquerors.

3 SUNRISE FROM TIGER HILL
The early-morning sunrise from Tiger Hill is an event to be treasured forever. It's the only spot in the world – regally poised at nearly 3000m – to offer the broad sweep of the eternal Himalyan range from Everest and Khangchendzonga to Makalu. The miracle is not only to witness this majestic display, but also to experience the rapid emergence of the sun over the horizon.

4 TEA PLANTATION VISIT
To discover more about what makes Darjeeling tick, visit a tea plantation for a day trip to understand the process. It's also possible to participate as a long-term volunteer, working on a tea estate – some of the plantations offer programs where you can work as a volunteer while staying with a local village family.

Darjeeling

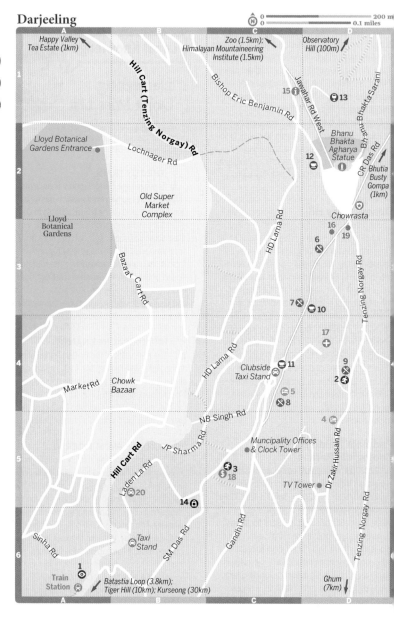

along Jawahar Rd West; alternatively, take a share jeep (₹10, about 10 minutes) from the Chowk Bazaar bus/jeep station, or hire a taxi (₹200).

Himalayan Mountaineering Institute
Museum

(HMI; ☎2254087; www.himalayanmountain eeringinstitute.com; admission incl zoo Indian/foreigner ₹40/100; ⏰8.30am-4.30pm Fri-Wed) Tucked away within the grounds of the

Darjeeling

zoo, this prestigious mountaineering institute was founded in 1954 and has provided training for some of India's leading mountaineers. Within the complex is the **Mountaineering Museum**, with fascinating detail from the 1922 and 1924 Everest expeditions which both set off from Darjeeling.

🎯 Tours

The GTA tourist information centre and travel agencies offer a variety of tours around Darjeeling, usually including the zoo, Himalayan Mountaineering Institute, Tibetan Refugee Self-Help Centre and several viewpoints. Taxis can be hired for custom tours for ₹800 per half-day.

**Adventures
Unlimited**   Outdoor Activities
(☎9933070013; www.adventuresunlimited.in; Dr Zakir Hussain Rd) Offers treks (US$40 to US$45 per day), kayaking, motor paragliding, Enfield motorbike hire and mountain-bike trips. Also rents hiking gear.

🛏 Sleeping

Prices given are for the high season (October to early December and mid-March to June), when it's wise to book ahead. In the low season prices can drop by 50%. A recently introduced rule requires foreigners to present a passport photo when checking in to a hotel, so carry some with you until this rule is withdrawn.

Andy's Guesthouse   Guesthouse **$**
(☎2253125; 102 Dr Zakir Hussain Rd; d ₹500-600) This simple, spotless, stone-walled place has airy, carpeted rooms, a comfy common area and a rooftop terrace with a great view. Mrs Gurung provides a friendly boarding-house atmosphere but runs a tight ship, with dozens of post-it notes admonishing the guests to follow the many house rules, including no smoking and 'complete silence after 9.30pm'. There's a good laundry service.

Dekeling Hotel   Guesthouse **$$**
(☎2254159; www.dekeling.com; 51 Gandhi Rd; d ₹1644-2935, without bathroom ₹935; @ 🛜)
Spotless Dekeling is full of charming touches like coloured diamond-pane windows, a traditional *bukhari* (wood-burning heater) in the cosy and sociable lounge/library, wood panelling and sloping-attic ceilings, plus some of the best views in town. Tibetan owners Sangay and Norbu are the perfect hosts. The whole place is a

If You Like…
Temples with a View

If you liked the views from Tiger Hill, then consider tracking down these scenic sacred sights too.

1 BHUTIA BUSTY GOMPA

This temple originally stood on Observatory Hill, but was rebuilt in its present location by the chogyals of Sikkim in the 19th century. It houses fine murals depicting the life of the Buddha, and Khangchendzonga provides a spectacular backdrop. To get here, follow CR Das Rd steeply downhill for five minutes from Chowrasta Sq, past a trinity of colourful Buddhist rock carvings. Climbing back up is a 10-minute slog.

2 YIGA CHOLING GOMPA
(Ghum; camera per photo ₹10)

The region's most famous monastery has wonderful old murals and is home to 30 monks of the Gelugpa school. Built in 1850, it enshrines a 5m-high statue of Jampa (Maitreya, or 'Future Buddha') and 300 beautifully bound Tibetan texts. It's just west of Ghum, about a 10-minute walk off Hill Cart Rd. The junction of Ghum is 7km from Darjeeling. You can get here by toy train (₹21), shared taxi (₹15) or chartered taxi (₹300 one way).

perfect combination of clean and homey, right down to the adorable dog, Drolma.

Windamere Hotel — Heritage Hotel $$$

(☎ 2254041; www.windamerehotel.com; Jawahar Rd West; incl full board s/d from ₹9133/11,807; @) This quaint, rambling relic of the Raj on Observatory Hill offers Darjeeling's most atmospheric digs. The charming colonial-era Ada Villa was once a boarding house for British tea planters, and the well-tended grounds are spacious with lots of pleasant seating areas. The comfortable rooms, fireplaces and hot-water bottles offer just the right measures of comfort and fustiness; a bit like staying at a rich aunt's house.

Eating & Drinking

Most restaurants close by 8pm or 9pm. Tax will add on 13.5% to most bills. See the boxed text (right) for more on where to drink tea in the area.

Glenary's — Teahouse

(Nehru Rd; small pot ₹45-75, pastries ₹15-35; ⊗8am-8pm; 🛜) Below the restaurant, this teahouse and bakery has massive windows and good views – order your tea, select a cake, grab your book and sink into some wicker. It's a good place to grab breakfast.

Sonam's Kitchen — Continental $

(142 Dr Zakir Hussain Rd; mains ₹80-120; ⊗8am-2.30pm & 5.30-8pm Mon-Sat, 8am-2pm Sun) Providing an island of real brewed coffee in an ocean of tea, Sonam serves up lovely breakfasts, French toast, pancakes, fresh soups (nettle in season) and pasta; the deliciously chunky wholemeal sandwiches can be packed to go for picnics. It's a tiny place so try not to linger during mealtimes.

Kunga — Tibetan $

(51 Gandhi Rd; mains ₹90-120) Kunga is a cosy wood-panelled place run by a friendly Tibetan family, strong on noodles and momos, with excellent juice, fruit muesli curd and shabhaley (Tibetan pies).

Lunar Restaurant — Indian $$

(51 Gandhi Rd; mains ₹90-150) This bright and clean space just below Dekeling Hotel is perhaps the best vegetarian Indian restaurant in town, with good service and great views from the large windows. The masala dosas (lentil-flour pancake filled with vegetables) come with yummy dried fruit and nuts.

Footsteps — Multicuisine $$

(19 Nehru Rd; mains ₹160-240; ⊗7.30am-9.30pm) There's a refreshing focus on healthy options at this new place, with gluten-free baked goods and brown breads on the menu. The best options are the all-day breakfasts, particularly the waffles and pancakes, but there are

Detour:
Tea Tourism

The easiest places to learn about tea production are **Makaibari Estate** (☑ 2330181; www.makaibari.com; Pankhabari Rd; ☺ Tue-Sat) in Kurseong and **Happy Valley** (Pamphawati Gurungni Rd; ☺ 8am-4pm Tue-Sun) outside Darjeeling. March to May is the busiest time, but occasional plucking also occurs from June to November.

You can stay overnight with a tea picker's family at a **homestay** (☑ 9832447774; www.volmakaibari.org; per person incl food ₹600) at Makaibari Estate and you'll get to join your hosts for a morning's work in the tea bushes. Pick your own leaves, watch them being processed and then return home with a batch of your very own hand-plucked Darjeeling tea. If you're in the mood for splurging, accommodation doesn't get any more exclusive than top-end **Glenburn** (www. glenburnteaestate.com; s/d ₹14,500/23,000), between Darjeeling and Kurseong, a working tea estate/resort that boasts five staff for every guest.

Sample different grades of black, white and green teas by the cup at **Sunset Lounge** (20 Chowrasta Sq; cup of tea ₹25-130; ☺ 9am-8pm; 📶) and **House of Tea** (Nehru Rd; tea ₹30-50; ☺ 9.30am-8pm). The pukka afternoon tea at the **Windamere Hotel** (₹450; ☺ 4-6pm) is a joy for aficionados of all things colonial, with shortcake, scones, cheese and pickle sandwiches and brews from the Castleton Tea Estate.

also good grilled sandwiches and dinner thalis. The baked cookies and muffins are served with a Darjeeling brew as a range of afternoon set teas.

Glenary's — Multicuisine **$$**
Nehru Rd; mains ₹100-225; ☺ noon-9pm, later in high season) This elegant restaurant atop the famous bakery and teahouse receives mainly rave reviews: of note are the Continental sizzlers, Chinese dishes, tandoori specials and veg gratin (good if you're off spicy food). The wooden floors, linen table cloths and fabulous tin roof just add to the classy atmosphere.

ℹ️ Information

Internet Access
There are dozens of internet cafes around town; all generally charge ₹30 per hour.

Medical Services
Planter's Hospital (D&DMA Nursing Home; ☑ 2254327; Nehru Rd) The best private hospital.

Money
Poddar's (☑ 2252841; Laden La Rd; ☺ 9.30am-8pm) Better rates, longer hours and shorter queues than the State Bank of India next door (which has an ATM).

Tourist Information
Gorkhland Terriorial Administration (GTA) Tourist Reception Centre (☑ 2255351; Jawahar Rd West, Silver Fir Bldg; ☺ 10am-5pm Mon-Sat, except 9am-1pm every 2nd and 4th Sat, plus 9am-1pm Sun high season) The staff are friendly, well organised and the best source of information in Darjeeling.

ℹ️ Getting There & Away

Air
The nearest airport is 90km away at Bagdogra, about 12km from Siliguri. Budget four hours for the drive, to be safe.
Air India (☑ 2254230; www.airindia.com; Chowrasta; ☺ 9.30am-1pm & 1.45-5.30pm Mon-Fri)

Pineridge Travels (☎2253912; pineridge@ mail.com; Nehru Rd; ☉10am-5pm Mon-Sat) For domestic and international flight tickets.

Bus

Samsara Tours, Travels & Treks (☎2252874; www.samsaratourstravelsandtreks.com; 7 Laden La Rd) Can book 'luxury' air-con buses from Siliguri to Kolkata (₹1000 to ₹1500, 12 hours) and ordinary night buses to Guwahati (₹550, 6pm) and Patna (₹450, 6pm). These tickets don't include transfers to Siliguri.

Jeep & Taxi

Numerous share jeeps leave the crowded Chowk Bazaar bus/jeep stand for Siliguri (₹120, three hours) and Kurseong (₹60, 1½ hours). Jeeps for Mirik (₹80, 2½ hours) leave from the northern end about every 1½ hours. All jeeps depart between 7am and 3.30pm.

Darjeeling Transport Corporation (☎9933071338; 30 Laden La Rd) offers charter jeeps to Gangtok (₹2000), Kalimpong (₹1700), Kurseong (₹1200), Kakarbhitta (₹2000) and Siliguri/Bagdogra Airport (₹1500/1700).

Train

The nearest major train station is at New Jalpaiguri (NJP), near Siliguri. Tickets can be bought for major services out of NJP at the Darjeeling train station (p310). Fares from Darjeeling include Ghum (1st/2nd class ₹115/21, 30 minutes) and Kurseong (₹160/27, three hours).

ⓘ Getting Around

There are several taxi stands around town, but rates are absurdly high for short hops. Darjeeling' streets can be steep and hard to navigate. You car hire a porter to carry your bags up to Chowrasta from Chowk Bazaar for around ₹60.

To Ghum, get a share jeep (₹15) from along Hil Cart Rd.

VARANASI

☎0542 / POP 1.4 MILLION

Brace yourself. You're about to enter one of the most blindingly colourful, unrelentingly chaotic and unapologetically indiscreet places on earth. Varanasi takes no prisoners. But if you're ready for it, this may just turn out to be your favourite stop of all.

Also known at various times in history as Kashi (City of Life) and Benares, this is one of the world's oldest continually inhabited cities and is regarded as one of Hinduism's seven holy cities. Pilgrims come to the ghats lining the River Ganges here to wash away a lifetime of sins in the sacred waters or to cremate their loved ones. Most visitors agree it's a magical place, but it's not for the faint-hearted. Here the most intimate rituals of life and death take place in public and the sights, sounds and smells in and around the ghats – not to mention the almost

---

Varanasi

Varanasi

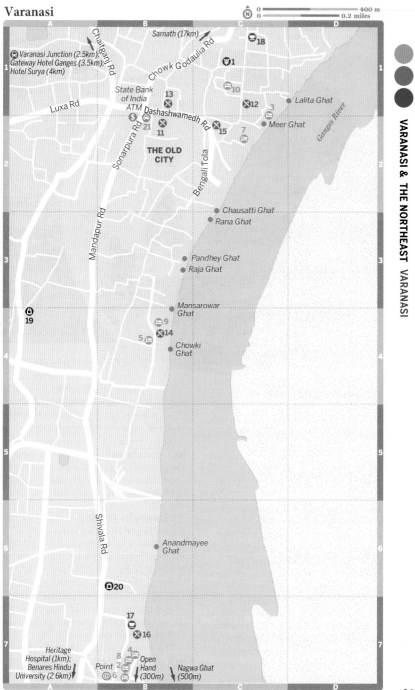

0 — 400 m
0 — 0.2 miles

Sarnath (17km)

Chaitganj Rd

Chowk Godaulia Rd

Varanasi Junction (2.5km);
Gateway Hotel Ganges (3.5km);
Hotel Surya (4km)

Luxa Rd

State Bank
of India
ATM

Dashashwamedh Rd

Sonarpura Rd

THE OLD
CITY

Bengali Tola

Mandapur Py

Lalita Ghat

Meer Ghat

Ganges River

Chausatti Ghat
Rana Ghat

Pandhey Ghat
Raja Ghat

Mansarowar
Ghat

Chowki
Ghat

Shivala Rd

Anandmayee
Ghat

Heritage
Hospital (1km);
Benares Hindu
University (2.6km)

Open
Hand
(300m)

Nagwa Ghat
(500m)

Right: Boats on the Ganges **Below:** Steps leading to the river at Dashashwamedh Ghat

(LEFT) PK GUPTA/GETTY IMAGES ©; (BELOW) GAVIN QUIRKE/GETTY IMAGES ©

constant attention from touts – can be overwhelming. Persevere. Varanasi is unique, and a walk along the ghats or a boat ride on the river will live long in the memory.

◉ Sights

Ghats
Ghats

Spiritually enlightening and fantastically photogenic, Varanasi is at its brilliant best by the ghats, the long stretch of steps leading down to the water on the western bank of the Ganges. Most are used for bathing but there are also several 'burning ghats' where bodies are cremated in public. The main one is Manikarnika: you'll often see funeral processions threading their way through the backstreets to this ghat. The best time to visit the ghats is at dawn when the river is bathed in a mellow light as pilgrims come to perform *puja* to the rising sun, and at sunset when the main *ganga aarti* (river worship ceremony) takes place at Dashashwamedh Ghat.

About 80 ghats border the river, but the main group extends from Assi Ghat, near the university, northwards to Raj Ghat, near the road and rail bridge.

A boat trip along the river provides the perfect introduction, although for most of the year the water level is low enough for you to walk freely along the whole length of the ghats.

Vishwanath Temple
Hindu Temple

(Golden Temple) There are temples at almost every turn in Varanasi, but this is the most famous of the lot. It is dedicated to Vishveswara – Shiva as lord of the universe. The current temple was built in 1776 by Ahalya Bai of Indore; the 800kg of gold plating on the tower and dome was supplied by Maharaja Ranjit Singh of Lahore 50 years later.

The area is full of soldiers because of security issues and communal tensions. Bags, cameras, mobile phones, pens or any other electronic device must be

deposited in lockers (₹20) before you enter the alleyway it's in. Non-Hindus are not allowed inside the temple itself, although this is not always strictly enforced – bring your original passport (not a copy) if you want to enter.

🎯 Activities

It's worth an early rise for at least two of your mornings in Varanasi, one to take in the action on a river boat trip and another to experience the hubbub of activity on the ghats themselves. Nonguests can use the outdoor **swimming pools** at Hotel Surya (₹200) and Hotel Clarks Varanasi (₹500).

River Trips   Boating

A dawn rowing boat ride along the Ganges is a quintessential Varanasi experience. The early-morning light is particularly inspiring, and all the colour and clamour of pilgrims bathing and performing *puja* unfolds before you. An hour-long trip south from Dashashwamedh Ghat to Harishchandra Ghat and back is popular, but be prepared to see a burning corpse at Harishchandra. Early evening is also a good time to be on the river, when you can light a lotus-flower candle (₹10) and set it adrift on the water before watching the nightly *ganga aarti* ceremony (7pm) at Dashashwamedh Ghat directly from the boat.

The official government price of boats is ₹50 per person per hour, but it is not enforced. Count yourself lucky if you manage ₹100 per person per hour and be prepared for some hard bargaining. And be warned: it's best to arrange a boat the day before. If you show up as the sun is about to rise, you'll find yourself in a Varanasi Standoff: a battle of wills between yourself, a boatman and the unforgiving rising sun – to the tune of ₹1000 per person.

Many guesthouses offer boat trips, although they're more expensive than dealing with the boatmen directly. Brown Bread Bakery can arrange a hassle-free boat for less than riverside (₹100 for one

319

The Varanasi Shakedown

If you thought the touts and rickshaw-wallahs were annoying in Agra, wait till you get to Varanasi. The attention here, particularly around the ghats and the Old City, is incredible: you will have to put up with persistent offers from touts and drivers of 'cheapest and best' boat trips, guides, tour operators, travel agents, silk shops and money changers (to name a few). Take it in good humour but politely refuse.

Words to live by in Varanasi:

○ Don't take photos at the 'burning' ghats and resist offers to 'follow me for a better view', where you'll be pressured for money and possibly be placed in an uncomfortable situation.

○ Do not go to any shop with a guide or autorickshaw. Be firm and don't do it. *Ever*. You will pay 40% to 60% more for your item due to insane commissions and you will be passively encouraging this practice. Do yourself a favour and walk there, or have your ride drop you a block away.

○ Imposter stores are rampant in Varanasi, usually spelled one letter off or sometimes exactly the same. The shops we have recomended are the real deal. Ask for a visting card (ie business card) – if the info doesn't match, you have been had.

○ When negotiating with boatmen, confirm the price *and* currency before setting out. They just love to say '100!' and then at the end claim they meant dollars or euros.

○ Do not book unoffical guides; that's who most guesthouses hire. If you want a guide, go through UP Tourism (p327) to avoid most of the hassles above. If not, have fun shopping!

to two people, ₹50 for each additional person) with some à la carte coffee and cakes to boot.

Tours

Varanasi Walks   Walking Tour
(☏8795576225; www.varanasiwalks.com; ₹1500-1800) Travellers have raved about cultural walks on offer from this foreigner-run agency specialising in themed walks that explore beyond the most popular ghats and temples. Walks are usually available between 6am and 9am and 3pm and 7pm and can be reserved online. Three of the five guides were born and raised in Varanasi.

UP Tourism Office   City Tour
(Varanasi Junction Train Station; half-/full-day tour ₹1500/3000; ⊙7am-7pm) If time is short, UP Tourism can arrange guided tours by taxi of the major sites, including a 5.30am boat ride and an afternoon trip to Sarnath.

Sleeping

The majority of Varanasi's budget hotels – and some midrange gems – are concentrated in the tangle of narrow streets back from the ghats along the River Ganges. There's a concentration around Assi Ghat, while others are in the crazy, bustling northern stretch of alleys between Scindhia and Meer Ghat, part of an area we refer to as the Old City.

Varanasi has an active paying-guesthouse scheme with more than 100 family homes available for accommodation from ₹200 to ₹1500 a night (most are under ₹400). UP Tourism has a full list.

Old City Area

Hotel Alka   Guesthouse $

(☏2401681; www.hotelalkavns.com; Meer Ghat; r without bathroom ₹500, r ₹600-800, with AC ₹1124-3597; ❄@🛜) An excellent ghat-side option, Alka has pretty much spotless rooms that open onto, or overlook, a large, plant-filled courtyard. In the far corner, a terrace juts out over Meer Ghat for one of the best views in all of Varanasi, a view shared from the balconies of eight of the pricier rooms.

Teerth Guesthouse   Guesthouse $

(www.teerthguesthouse.com; 8/9 Kalika Gali; r without bathroom ₹350, r ₹600-800; 🛜) This newish guesthouse is a pleasant surprise as you leave the undesirable alleyways that lead to it and enter into a spic-and-span, marble lobby laced with the scent of jasmine. Rooms are on the smaller size,

but are new and spotless and the whole place hogs a load of sunlight through the open atrium. A pleasant rooftop offers Old City views. Best of all, though, it's relatively quiet. Wi-fi is ₹100 per stay.

Kedareswar   Hotel $$

(☏2455568; www.kedareswarguesthouse.com; 14/1 Chowki Ghat; r incl breakfast AC/non-AC ₹1400/2400; ❄🛜) Housed in a brightly painted, aquamarine green building, this friendly six-room place has cramped but immaculate rooms with sparkling bathrooms. There's only two cheaper non-AC rooms, so it might be worth phoning ahead. Chowki Ghat is right beside Kedar Ghat.

Shiva Ganges View Paying
Guest House   Guesthouse $$$

(☏2450063; www.varanasi guesthouse.com; 14/24 Mansarowar Ghat; r ₹3500, with AC ₹4500-5000, ste ₹6000; ❄@🛜) The best Old City top-end place is a delightful, bright-red brick building and part of the city's paying-guesthouse scheme. Huge rooms here ooze character, with central double beds (all with mosquito nets), high ceilings and chunky door and window shutters. All have river

Ritual washing at Dashashwamedh Ghat (p318)

views and spotlessly clean bathrooms. Home-cooked food is also available. The one downside – the manager can be a bit pushy.

Rashmi Guest House   Hotel $$$

(☎2402778; www.rashmiguesthouse.com; 16/28A Man Mandir Ghat; r incl breakfast ₹2780-6670; ❋@☎) Sparkling white-tiled corridors and marble staircases lead to clean and modern rooms, which are tiny but smart. Many have views of Man Mandir Ghat (in fact, the only difference between a deluxe and super deluxe is the view and a courtesy minibar), although the excellent rooftop Dolphin Restaurant offers the best views of all. Ayurvedic massage (₹1200) is also available.

Assi Ghat Area

Sahi River View Guesthouse   Guesthouse $

(☎2366730; sahi_rvgh@sify.com; 1/158 Assi Ghat; incl breakfast s/d from ₹300/350, with AC from ₹950/1250; ❋@) There's a huge variety of rooms at this friendly place.

Most are good quality and clean, and some have interesting private balconies. Each floor has a pleasant communal seating area with river view, creating a great feeling of space throughout.

Chaitanya Guest House   Guesthouse $

(☎2313686; knpsahi@yahoo.com; 1/158A Assi Ghat; r AC/non-AC ₹1000/500; ❋) Chaitanya has just four rooms: a single, two doubles and a double with AC. All are comfortable, with high ceilings and clean bathrooms (though some mattresses are warped), and are well looked after by friendly staff.

Hotel Ganges View   Hotel $$$

(☎2313218; www.hotelgangesview.com; Assi Ghat; r with AC ₹4500-5500; ❋☎) Simply gorgeous, this beautifully restored and maintained colonial-style house overlooking Assi Ghat is crammed with books, artwork and antiques. Rooms are spacious and immaculate and there are some charming communal areas in which to sit and relax, including a lovely 1st-floor garden terrace. Book ahead.

Palace on Ganges   Hotel $$$

(☎2315050; www.palaceonganges.com; 1/158 Assi Ghat; r ₹6184; ❋@☎) Each of the 24 rooms (the four river views are first-come, first-served) in this immaculate heritage accommodation is individually themed in a regional Indian style, using antique furnishings and colourful design themes. The colonial, Rajasthan and Jodhpur rooms are among the best.

Cantonment Area

Hotel Surya   Hotel $$

(☎2508465; www.hotel-suryavns.com; 20/51A The Mall; s/d incl breakfast from ₹2280/2700; ❋@☎🏊) Varanasi's cheapest

Monks at Sarnath
TIM GRAHAM/GETTY IMAGES ©

Detour:
Sarnath

About 10km north of Varanasi, peaceful Sarnath was where the Buddha came to preach his message of the middle way to nirvana after he had achieved enlightenment at Bodhgaya. In the 3rd century BC emperor Ashoka had magnificent stupas and monasteries erected here as well as an engraved pillar. When Chinese traveller Xuan Zang dropped by in AD 640, Sarnath boasted a 100m-high stupa and 1500 monks living in large monasteries. However, soon after Buddhism went into decline and, when Muslim invaders sacked the city in the late 12th century, Sarnath disappeared altogether. It was 'rediscovered' by British archaeologists in 1835.

Set in a peaceful park of monastery ruins, the impressive 34m **Dhamekh Stupa** (Indian/foreigner ₹5/100, video ₹25; ☉dawn-dusk) marks the spot where the Buddha preached his first sermon. The floral and geometric carvings are 5th century AD, but some of the brickwork dates back as far as 200 BC. Nearby is a 3rd-century BC **Ashoka Pillar** with an edict engraved on it. It once stood 15m tall and had the famous four-lion capital (now in the museum) perched on top of it, but all that remains are five fragments of its base.

Beside the entrance to the Dhamekh Stupa is the ticket office for the excellent **Archaeological Museum** (admission ₹5; ☉9am-4.45pm), which is just opposite. Walking distance from here, the large ruined **Chaukhandi Stupa** (☉dawn-dusk) dates back to the 5th century AD, and marks the spot where Buddha met his first disciples.

The best place for lunch is the modest **Vaishali Restaurant** (mains ₹30-160; ☉8am-7.30pm), on the first floor of a building by the main crossroads.

Getting There & Away

An autorickshaw to Sarnath costs about ₹110 from Varanasi's Old City. Trains for Sarnath leave Varanasi Junction at 7am, 11.30am and 1.20pm. Returning to Varanasi, trains leave Sarnath at 9am, 7.30pm and 9.50pm. The journey takes around 20 minutes and a 'general' ticket for an unreserved 2nd-class seat will cost you just a few rupees. Everywhere in Sarnath is reachable on foot.

---

hotel with a swimming pool, Surya has standard 3-star Indian rooms, but a modern makeover in the superior and premium rooms means everything has been tightened up a bit, with new furnishings, upholsteries and the like. Value here is palpable, as all is built around a huge lawn area that includes a laid-back Middle Eastern–style cafe (Mango Verra) flanked by a gorgeous, nearly 200-year-old heritage building (the former stomping ground of a Nepali king), where the excellent-value Canton Royale is housed. There's also the good (but smoky) Sol Bar and the recomended Aarna Spa.

Gateway Hotel Ganges   Hotel $$$
(☏6660001; www.thegatewayhotels.com; Raja Bazaar Rd; r/ste from ₹12,366/15,738; ❄@☎☀) Varanasi's best hotel is on nearly 2 hectares of beautiful gardens with fruit trees, a tennis court, a pool, an outdoor yoga centre and the old maharaja's guesthouse. All the rooms were made over between 2010 and 2012. There's little size difference between standard and deluxe catagories, but the latter are far classier. Service is top class and there are two fine restaurants, two bars and two spa treatment rooms (massages from ₹3000).

🍴 Eating

Look out for locally grown *langda aam* (mangoes) in summer or *sitafal* (custard apples) in autumn. *Singhara* is a blackish root that tastes like water chestnut.

Old City Area

Keshari Restaurant   Indian $

(14/8 Godaulia; mains ₹65-130; ⏱9.30am-11pm) Known as much for excellent cuisine as surly service, this atmospheric spot (carved wood panelling dons the walls and ceilings) has been famously at it for nearly a half-century. Indians pack in here for high-quality veg from all over India – a dizzying array of dishes are on offer (41 paneer curries alone). Those who like to dance with the devil should spring for the paneer Kadahi (spicy tomato-based gravy), sure to make your nose run.

Ayyar's Cafe   South Indian $

(Dashashwamedh Rd; mains ₹30-75; ⏱8am-10pm) Excellent, no-nonsense choice off the tourist beaten path for South Indian masala dosa (₹30), and its spicier cousin, the Mysore dosa (₹70); and one of the few cheapies to serve filtered coffee. It's tucked away at the end of a very short alley signed 'New Keshari Readymade' off Dashashwamedh Rd.

Madhur Milan Cafe   Indian $

(15/81 Dashashwamedh Rd; mains ₹32-85; ⏱6am-11pm) Popular with locals, this simple but friendly restaurant serves up a range of good-value, mostly South Indian dishes. Thalis start from ₹60. The early opening time means it's packed for breakfast, with most folks going for the extremely popular *poori sabji* set breakfast (₹40; fried wheat flour patties used to scoop up spiced potato curry), which comes with *jalebi* (fried batter soaked in sugar syrup).

Brown Bread Bakery   Multicuisine $$

(📞9838888823; www.brownbreadbakery.com; 5/127 Tripura Bhairavi; mains ₹120-350; ⏱7am-10pm; 🛜) 🌿 This restaurant and organic shop's fabulous menu includes more than 40 varieties of European-quality cheese and more than 30 types of bread, cookies and cakes. The partly-AC ambiance – with seating on cushions around low tables on the nonsmoking bottom floor, astounding views from the rooftop patio and live classical-music performances in the evenings – is spot on. Part of the profits go to the charity **Learn for Life** (www.learn-for-life.net). Warning: not to be confused with the location across the street, abandoned by Micha, the 5th-generation German baker, but carried on by his local ex-partners. If there are not four floors and a rooftop, you're at a different place. Call to confirm if you're unsure.

Lotus Lounge   Multicuisine $$

(14/27 Mansarowar Ghat; mains ₹70-240; ⏱8am-10pm; 🛜) The food doesn't move mountains, but Lotus is a supremely great place to chill. The laid-back, half-open-air restaurant, with broken-tile mosaic flooring, wicker chairs and a terrace that juts out over Mansarowar Ghat with lounge cushions and tatami mats, dishes out a world fusion potpourri from its kitchen and there's wi-fi and French press coffee.

Dolphin Restaurant   Indian $$$

(Rashmi Guest House; 16/28A Man Mandir Ghat; mains ₹110-300; ⏱7am-10pm) The atmosphere trumps the food at Dolphin – the rooftop restaurant at Rashmi Guest House – which is perched high above Man Mandir Ghat, but it's still a fine place for an evening meal. The breezy balcony is the most refined table in the Old City and one of the few that serves non-veg as well.

Assi Ghat Area

Open Hand   Cafe $$

(www.openhandonline.com; 1/128-3 Dumraub Bagh; ₹70-210; ⏱8am-8pm ; 🛜) 🌿 This shoes-off cafe/gift shop serves fabulous espresso (from ₹45) and a range of excellent muffins, pancakes, muesli and juices that will delight you to no end. Take breakfast (₹70 to ₹210) on the narrow balcony or lounge around the former home all day on the free wi-fi. There's

HOLGER LEUE/GETTY IMAGES ©

also a large selection of gorgeous handicrafts (jewellery, toys, clothing) made in the local community. Couldn't be more pleasant.

Aum Cafe   Cafe $
(www.touchoflight.us; 1/201 Assi Ghat; mains ₹60-155; ⊙7am-4.30pm Tue-Sun; 🛜) 🥗
Run by a hippie-dippy American woman who has been coming to India for more than 20 years, this colourful cafe has breakfast all day (₹65 to ₹120; good lemon pancakes!), astounding lemon and organic green tea lassis and a handful of light sandwiches and mains. There's also massage therapies and body piercing available.

Pizzeria Vaatika
Cafe   Multicuisine $$
(www.pizzeriavaatika.in; Assi Ghat; pizza ₹150-220; ⊙7.30am-10pm) Italians stop reading now. As for the rest of you, decent (for India) thin-crust pizza is churned out of a wood-fired oven and served on a shady garden terrace overlooking Assi Ghat. An Italian friend of the Indian owner originally showed him the ropes, so his heart is in the right place. Don't forget to leave some

room for the delicious apple pie – it's legitimately tasty.

Cantonment Area

Varuna Restaurant   Indian $$$
(www.thegatewayhotels.com; Gateway Hotel Ganges, Raja Bazaar Rd; mains ₹425-1700; ⊙12.30-2.45pm & 7.30-11pm) Taj Hotels takes its restaurants very seriously and you'll indeed find one of UP's most innovative and interesting menus at the elegant but not stuffy main restaurant at the best hotel in town. New Zealand lamb chops doused with masala, spiritual veg thalis (₹800) and stone-ground mustard-marinated prawns are just a few of the intriguing choices. Service is appropriately on point and there's live sitar and tabla music every evening.

Canton Royale   Indian $$$
(www.hotelsuryavns.com; Hotel Surya, 20/51A The Mall; mains ₹150-280; ⊙11am-11pm) Housed in a nearly 200-year-old heritage building, Hotel Surya's excellent main restaurant has a colonial elegance, and on warm evenings you can eat out on the large lawn. Value for money, it's one of

No 1 Lassi in all Varanasi

Your long, thirsty search for the best lassi in India is over. Look no further than **Blue Lassi** (lassis ₹20-80; ⏱7.30am-10.30pm; 📶), a tiny, hole-in-the-wall yogurt shop that has been churning out the freshest, creamiest, fruit-filled lassis since 1925. The grandson of the original owner still works here, sitting by his lassi-mixing cauldron in front of a small room with wooden benches for customers and walls plastered with messages from happy drinkers.

the best of Varanasi's top-end choices, offering a global hodgepodge that extends from Mexican and Thai to Chinese and Continental. But really, it's the Indian that's excellent, including a wonderful thali (₹280).

🍷 Drinking & Nightlife

Note that it is frowned upon to drink alcohol on or near the holy Ganges, and liquor laws regarding proximity of temples ensure nobody is licensed, but rooftops here can usually discreetly fashion up a beer. For bars, head to midrange and top-end hotels away from the ghats.

There's nightly live **classical music** at Brown Bread Bakery, Puja Hotel and Varuna Restaurant at Gateway Hotel Ganges, to name but a few.

The International Music Centre Ashram has small **performances** (₹100) on Wednesday and Saturday evenings.

Prinsep Bar   Bar
(www.tajhotels.com; Gateway Hotel Ganges, Raja Bazaar Rd; ⏱noon-11pm, to midnight Sat & Sun) For a quiet drink with a dash of history try this tiny bar, named after James Prinsep, who drew wonderful illustrations of Varanasi's ghats and temples, but stick

to beer (from ₹195) as our cocktail (from ₹450) was weak.

Mango Verra   Cafe
(www.hotelsuryavns.com; 20/51A The Mall; ⏱11am-11pm) This laid-back cafe in the garden at Hotel Surya is a relaxing place where you can smoke hookah pipes (₹300) while sipping a beer.

🔒 Shopping

Varanasi is justifiably famous for silk brocades and beautiful Benares saris, but don't believe much of what the silk salesmen tell you about the relative quality of products, even in government emporiums. Instead, shop around and judge for yourself.

Varanasi is also a good place to shop for sitars (starting from ₹3000) and tablas (from ₹2500). The cost depends primarily on the type of wood used. Mango is cheapest (and cracks or warps correspondingly), while black shisham or mahogany are of the highest quality. Serious buyers should be sure to double-check their chosen wood isn't banned for export.

Baba Blacksheep   Silk
(www.babablacksheep.co; B 12/120 A-9, Bhelpura; ⏱9.30am-8pm) If the deluge of traveller enthusiam is anything to go by, this is the most trustworthy, non-pushy shop in India. Indeed it is one of the best places you'll find for silks (scarves/saris from ₹300/2500) and pashminas (shawls from ₹1500). Prices are fixed and the friendly owner refuses to play the commssion game, so autorickshaws and taxis don't like to come here (ignore anyone who says you cannot drive here). It's located at Bhelpura crossing under the mosque.

Benares Art & Culture   Handicrafts
(Shivala Rd; ⏱10am-8pm Mon-Sat) This centuries-old *haveli* (traditional, ornately decorated mansion) stocks fixed-price quality carvings, sculptures, paintings and wooden toys all made by local artists.

ℹ️ Information

Varanasi is pretty wired – even Blue Lassi (above) has wi-fi! Some charge. Many don't. Internet cafes are everywhere, charging between ₹25 and ₹50 per hour. There are several ATMs scattered around town, including State Bank of India in the lobby as you exit the train station.

Heritage Hospital (www.heritagehospitals.com; Lanka) English-speaking staff and doctors; 24-hour pharmacy.

Point (1/156 Assi Ghat Rd; per hr ₹25; ⊘8am-10.30pm) Friendly internet near Assi Ghat.

State Bank of India (The Mall; ⊘10am-2pm & 2.30-4pm Mon-Fri, 10am-1pm Sat) Changes travellers cheques and cash.

State Bank of India ATM (cnr Dashashwamedh Rd & Mandapur Rd)

Tourist Police (UP Tourism office, Varanasi Junction train station; ⊘7am-7pm) Tourist police wear sky-blue uniforms.

UP Tourism (www.up-tourism.com; Varanasi Junction Train Station; ⊘7am-7pm) The patient Mr Umashankar at the office inside the train station has been dishing out reasonably impartial information to arriving travellers for years; he's a mine of knowledge, so this is a requisite first stop if you arrive here by train. Get the heads-up on autorickshaw prices, the best trains for your travels, the lay of the land, details on Varanasi's paying-guesthouse scheme or arrange a guided tour.

ℹ️ Getting There & Away

Air

Lal Bahadur Shashtri Airport, 24km north of town, is served by **Jet Airways** (www.jetairways.com; Lal Bahadur Shastri Airport), with direct flights to Delhi (from ₹7400, daily), Mumbai (from ₹7600, daily) and Kolkata (from ₹2900, daily); and **Air India** (www.airindia.com; Airlines Bhavan 52, Yadunath Marg) to Delhi (₹1799, daily), Mumbai (₹3699, daily), Agra (₹3028, Monday, Wednesday and Saturday), Khajuraho (₹3532, Monday, Wednesday and Saturday) and Kathmandu (₹12,159, Tuesday, Thursday, Saturday and Sunday). Some other airlines are based at the airport.

Train

Luggage theft has been reported on trains to and from Varanasi so you should take extra care. Reports of drugged food and drink aren't uncommon, so it's probably still best to politely decline any offers from strangers.

Varanasi Junction train station, also known as Varanasi Cantonment (Cantt), is the main station. Foreign tourist quota tickets must be purchased at the helpful **Foreign Tourist Centre** (⊘8am-12.50pm & 2-8pm Mon-Sat, 8am-2pm Sun), a ticket office just past the UP Tourism office, on your right as you exit the station.

A few daily trains leave for New Delhi and Kolkata, but only two daily trains go to Agra. The direct train to Khajuraho only runs on Monday, Wednesday and Saturday. On other days, go via Satna from where you can catch buses to Khajuraho.

ℹ️ Getting Around

To/From the Airport

An autorickshaw to the airport in Babatpur, 22km northwest of the city, costs ₹200. A taxi is about ₹400.

Cycle-Rickshaw

A small ride – up to 2km – costs ₹10 to ₹15. Rough prices from Dashashwamedh Rd include:

Handy Trains from Varanasi (BSB)

DESTINATION	TRAIN NO & NAME	FARE (₹)	DURATION (HR)	DEPARTURES
Agra	13237/13239 PNBE-Kota Exp	262/733/1110 (A)	13	4.40pm
Khajuraho	21108 BSB-Kurj Link E	200/551 (B)	12	6.05pm*
Kolkata (Howrah)	12334 Vibhuti Exp	306/836/1255 (A)	14	6.10pm
New Delhi	12559 Shiv Ganga Exp	306/836/1255 (A)	12½	7.15pm

Fares: (A) sleeper/3AC/2AC; (B) sleeper/3AC
*Mon, Wed, Sat only

Assi Ghat ₹40 and Varanasi Junction train station ₹45. Be prepared for hard bargaining.

Taxi & Autorickshaw

Prepaid booths for autorickshaws and taxis are directly outside Varanasi Junction train station and give you a good benchmark for prices around town. First pay a ₹5 administration charge at the booth then take a ticket which you give to your driver, along with the fare, once you've reached your destination. Note that taxis and autorickshaws cannot access the Dashashwamedh Ghat area between the hours of 8am and 8pm due to high pedestrian traffic. You'll be dropped at Godaulia Crossing and will need to walk the remaining 400m or so to the entrance to the Old City; or 700m or so all the way to Dashashwamedh Ghat. Sample fares:

Airport auto/taxi ₹200/400

Assi Ghat auto/taxi ₹70/200

Dashashwamedh Ghat auto/taxi ₹60/150

Sarnath auto/taxi ₹80/250

Half-day tour (four hours) auto/taxi ₹455/₹600

Full-day tour (eight hours) auto/taxi ₹905/₹1200

MADHYA PRADESH

....

Khajuraho

☑ 07686 / POP 23,200

The erotic carvings that swathe Khajuraho's three groups of World Heritage–listed temples are among the finest temple art in the world. The Western Group of temples, in particular, contains some stunning sculptures. See our special colour illustration for details.

Many travellers complain about the tiring persistence of touts here. Their complaints are well founded, but it's not so bad that you should contemplate missing out on these beautiful temples.

⊙ Sights

The temples are superb examples of Indo-Aryan architecture, but it's their liberally embellished carvings that have made Khajuraho famous. Around the outsides of the temples are bands of exceedingly artistic stonework showing a storyboard of life a millennium ago – gods, goddesses, warriors, musicians, real and mythological animals.

Khajuraho temples

CHRIS MELLOR/GETTY IMAGES ©

Two elements appear repeatedly – women and sex. Sensuous, posturing *surasundaris* (heavenly nymphs), *apsaras* (dancing *surasundaris*) and *nayikas* (mortal *surasundaris*) have been carved with a half-twist and slight sideways lean that make the playful figures dance and swirl out from the temple. The *mithuna* (pairs, threesomes etc of men and women depicted in erotic poses) display the great skill of the sculptors and the dexterity of the Chandelas.

Western Group (inside fenced enclosure) Temples

Khajuraho's most striking and best-preserved temples are those within the fenced-off section of the **Western Group** (Indian/foreigner ₹10/250, video ₹25; ☾dawn-dusk) and are the only temples here you have to pay to see. An Archaeological Survey of India (ASI) guidebook to Khajuraho (₹99) and a 90-minute audio guide (₹113) are available at the ticket office. See our special illustration for details on this group.

Western Group (outside fenced enclosure) Temples

Skirting the southern boundary of the fenced enclosure, **Matangesvara** is the only temple in the Western Group still in everyday use. It may be the plainest temple here (suggesting an early construction), but inside it sports a polished 2.5m-high lingam (phallic image of Shiva).

The ruins of **Chausath Yogini**, beyond Shiv Sagar, date to the late 9th century and are probably the oldest at Khajuraho. Constructed entirely of granite, it's the only temple not aligned east to west. The temple's name means 64 – it once had 64 cells for the *yoginis* (female attendants) of Kali, while the 65th sheltered the goddess herself. It is reputedly India's oldest *yogini* temple.

A further 600m west, down a track and across a couple of fields (just ask the locals), is the sandstone-and-granite **Lalguan Mahadev Temple** (AD 900), a small ruined shrine to Shiva.

Eastern Group (old village temples) Temples

The eastern group includes three Hindu temples scattered around the old village and four Jain temples further south, three of which are in a walled enclosure.

The **Hanuman Temple** (Basti Rd) contains a 2.5m-tall statue of the Hindu monkey god. It's little more than a bright orange shrine, but the interest is in the pedestal inscription dating to AD 922, the oldest dateable inscription in Khajuraho.

The granite **Brahma Temple**, with its sandstone *sikhara* overlooking Narora Sagar, is one of the oldest in Khajuraho (about AD 900). The four-faced lingam in the sanctum led to it being incorrectly named, but the image of Vishnu above the sanctum doorway reveals its original dedication to Vishnu.

Resembling Chaturbhuja Temple in the southern group, **Javari Temple** (1075–1100) stands just north of the old village. It's dedicated to Vishnu and is a good example of small-scale Khajuraho architecture for its crocodile-covered entrance and slender *sikhara*.

Vamana Temple (1050–75), 200m further north, is dedicated to the dwarf incarnation of Vishnu. It has quirky touches such as elephants protruding from the walls. Its roofed *mahamandapa* (main hall) is an anomaly in Khajuraho but typical among medieval west Indian temples.

Between the old village and the Jain Enclosure, the small **Ghantai Temple**, also Jain, is named after the *ghanta* (chain and bell) decorations on its pillars. Once similar to nearby Parsvanath, only its pillared shell remains, and it's normally locked.

Eastern Group (Jain enclosure) Temples

While not competing in size and erotica with the western-enclosure temples, **Parsvanath Temple** (AD 950–70), the largest of the Jain temples in the walled enclosure, is notable for the exceptional precision of its construction, and for its sculptural beauty. Some of the best preserved of Khajuraho's most famous images can be seen here, including the woman removing a thorn from her foot

Khajuraho Temples

Western Group

The sheer volume of artwork at Khajuraho's best-preserved temples can be overwhelming. Initiate yourself with this introductory tour, which highlights some of those easy-to-miss details.

First, admire the **sandstone boar** ① in the Varaha shrine before heading towards **Lakshmana Temple** ② to study the south side of the temple's base, which has some of the raunchiest artwork in Khajuraho: first up, a nine-person orgy; further along, a guy getting very friendly with a horse. Up on the temple platform see a superb dancing Ganesh carved into a niche (south side), before walking to the west side for graceful *surasundaris* (nymphs): one removing a thorn from her foot; another draped in a wet sari; a third admiring herself in a mirror.

Next is Khajuraho's largest temple, **Kandariya-Mahadev** ③. Carvings to look for here include the famous handstand position (south side), but the most impressive thing about this temple is the scale of it, particularly its soaring rooftops.

Mahadeva ④ and **Devi Jagadamba** ⑤ share the same stone plinth as Kandariya-Mahadev, as do four beautifully carved *sardula* (part-lion, part-human mythical beasts), each caressing a stone lion – one is at the entrance to Mahadeva; the other three stand alone on the plinth.

Walk north from here to **Chitragupta** ⑥, with beautiful carvings hidden on the west side, as well as elephant friezes around the temple's base (north side). The interior here is particularly impressive.

Continue east to **Vishvanath Temple** ⑦ for more fabulous carvings before admiring the impressive statue of Vishnu's bull in the **Nandi shrine** ⑧ opposite.

Handstand Position
Perhaps Khajuraho's most famous carving, this flexible flirtation is above you as you stand on the south side of the awesome Kandariya-Mahadev.

Sikharas
Despite its many fine statues, perhaps the most impressive thing about Kandariya-Mahadev is its soaring *sikharas* (temple rooftops), said to represent the Himalayan abode of the gods.

Kandariya-Mahadev Temple ③

Devi Jagadamba Temple ⑤

Mahadeva Temple ④

NORTH →

Toilets

Sardula Statue
There are four lion-stroking *sardula* (part-lion, part-human mythical beasts) on this huge stone plinth, but this one, guarding the entrance to Mahadeva, is our favourite.

Kama Sutra Carvings
Although commonly referred to as Kama Sutra carvings, Khajuraho's erotic artwork does not properly illustrate Vatsyayana's famous sutra. Debate continues as to its significance: to appease evil spirits or imply rulers here were virile, thus powerful? Interestingly, the erotic carvings are never located close to the temple deity.

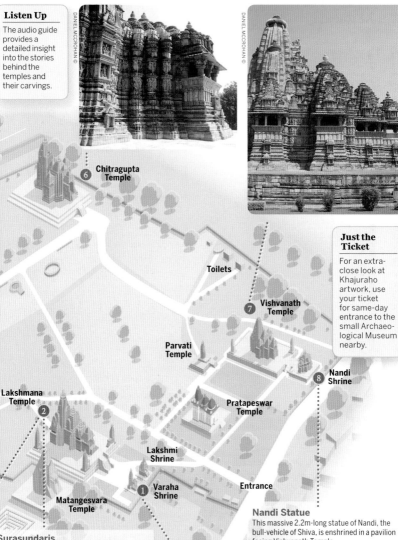

Listen Up
The audio guide provides a detailed insight into the stories behind the temples and their carvings.

6 Chitragupta Temple

Just the Ticket
For an extra-close look at Khajuraho artwork, use your ticket for same-day entrance to the small Archaeological Museum nearby.

Toilets

7 Vishvanath Temple

Parvati Temple

8 Nandi Shrine

Lakshmana Temple **2**

Pratapeswar Temple

Lakshmi Shrine

Matangesvara Temple

Varaha Shrine **1**

Entrance

Nandi Statue
This massive 2.2m-long statue of Nandi, the bull-vehicle of Shiva, is enshrined in a pavilion facing Vishvanath Temple.

Surasundaris
Beautifully graceful depictions of nymphs are found on a number of Khajuraho temples. And despite all the depictions of gymnastic orgies, the wonderfully seductive *surasundari* draped in a wet sari is arguably the most erotic of all.

Vishnu's Boar
This 9th-century statue of Varaha, the boar incarnation of Vishnu, is carved all over with figures of Bramanical gods and goddesses. Under Varaha's foot notice the serpent Seshanaga in a devotional posture, and the feet of a goddess, now missing.

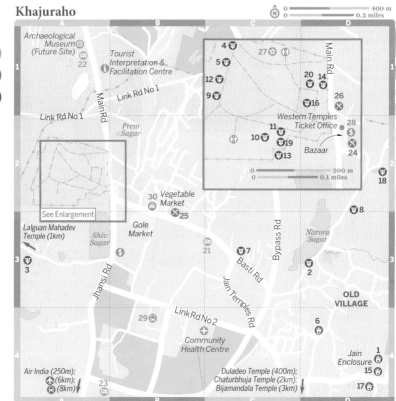

and another applying eye makeup, both on the south side.

The adjacent, smaller **Adinath** has been partially restored over the centuries. With fine carvings on its three bands of sculptures it's similar to Khajuraho's Hindu temples, particularly Vamana. Only the striking black image in the inner sanctum triggers a Jain reminder.

Shanti Nath, built about a century ago, houses components from older temples, including a 4.5m-high Adinath statue with a plastered-over inscription on the pedestal dating to about 1027.

Southern Group   Temples

A dirt track runs to the isolated **Duladeo Temple**, about 1km south of the Jain enclosure. This is the youngest temple, dating to 1100–1150. Its relatively wooden, repetitive sculptures, such as those of

Shiva, suggest that Khajuraho's temple builders had passed their artistic peak by this point, although they had certainly lost none of their zeal for eroticism.

Anticipating Duladeo and its flaws, the ruined **Chaturbhuja Temple** (c 1100) has a fine 2.7m-high, four-armed statue of Vishnu in the sanctum. It is Khajuraho's only developed temple without erotic sculptures.

Just before Chaturbhuja there's a signed track leading to **Bijamandala Temple**. This is the excavated mound of an 11th-century temple, dedicated to Shiva (judging by the white marble lingam at the apex of the mound). Although there are some exquisitely carved figures, unfinished carvings were also excavated, suggesting that what would have been Khajuraho's largest temple was abandoned as resources flagged.

Khajuraho

🛏 Sleeping

Hotel Harmony   Hotel **$**
(☎274135; www.hotelharmonyonline.com; Jain Temples Rd; s/d ₹600/800, with AC s ₹1100, d ₹1200-1600; ❄ @ 🛜) Cosy, well-equipped rooms off marble corridors are tastefully decorated and come with effective mosquito screens and cable TV. Great food is available at the Zorba the Buddha restaurant and you can eat under the stars on the rooftop. Yoga, massage, face- and palm-reading and numerology are all available.

Radisson Jass Hotel   Hotel **$$$**
(☎272777; www.radisson.com; Bypass Rd; r from ₹6600; ❄ @ 🛜 🏊) A marble spiral staircase winds its way up from the fountain in the lobby to stylish 1st-floor rooms that are very smart and fully appointed, albeit with small bathrooms. There's a comfortable bar (with pool table), a restaurant, tennis and badminton courts, and a fine swimming pool and spa. Check the website for latest room deals.

Lalit Temple View   Hotel **$$$**
(☎272111; www.thelalit.com; Main Rd; r from ₹11,700; ❄ @ 🛜 🏊) Sweeps aside all other five-star pretenders with supreme luxury, impeccable service and high prices. Rooms are immaculate with large-screen TVs, carved-wood furniture and tasteful artwork. Guests who don't have temple-view rooms can see the Western Group from the delightful lotus-shaped pool.

🍴 Eating

Madras Coffee House   South Indian **$**
(cnr Main & Jain Temples Rds; mains ₹40-150; ⏰8.30am-9.30pm) Good, honest South Indian fare – dosa, *idli* (spongy round fermented rice cakes), *uttapam* (thick savoury rice pancakes), thali – as well as coffee and chai, served in a narrow cafe. Ideal for breakfast. House speciality is the egg, cheese and veg dosa (₹150).

Raja's Café   Multicuisine **$$**
(Main Rd; mains ₹80-280; ⏰8am-10pm; 🛜) Raja's has been on top of its game for more than 30 years, with espresso coffee, English breakfasts, wood-fired pizzas, and superb Indian, Italian and Chinese dishes. Try the *palak paneer* (unfermented cheese and spinach) and tandoori chicken, in particular. The location, with

333

Frieze at Khajuraho

FRIEDRICH SCHMIDT/GETTY IMAGES ©

a temple-view terrace, is great, as is the restaurant design, with a delightful courtyard shaded by a 170-year-old neem tree. But it's the food that steals the show.

Mediterraneo Italian **$$**
(Jain Temples Rd; mains ₹200-350, pizza ₹290-430; ☉7.30am-10pm) Far removed from its Italian roots, Mediterraneo manages acceptable Italian fare served on a lovely terrace overlooking the street. Dishes include chicken, salads, organic whole-wheat pasta and wood-fired pizzas, and beer and wine are also available.

⭐ Entertainment

Admittedly, the temples do look magical illuminated with technicolour floodlights, but the one-hour **sound and light show** (Indian/foreigner ₹120/350, child ₹60/200; ☉English 6.30pm Nov-Feb, 7.30pm Mar-Oct, Hindi 7.45pm Nov-Feb, 8.45pm Mar-Oct) chronicling the history of Khajuraho is still about 45 minutes too long.

ℹ Information

Community Health Centre (☏272498; Link Rd No 2; ☉9am-1pm & 2-4pm) Limited English, but helpful staff.

State Bank of India (☏272373; Main Rd; ☉10.30am-4.30pm Mon-Fri, to 1.30pm Sat) Changes cash and travellers cheques. There are ATMs beside Raja's Cafe and Paradise Restaurant.

Tourist Interpretation & Facilitation Centre (☏274051; khajuraho@mptourism.com; Main Rd; ☉10am-5pm Mon-Sat, closed 2nd & 3rd Sat of month) Leaflets on statewide tourist destinations. Also has a stand at the airport and train station.

ℹ Getting There & Away

Air

Jet Airways (☏274406; ☉10am-3.30pm), at the airport, has a daily 1.45pm flight to Delhi (from ₹5900, 3½ hours) via Varanasi (from ₹4800, 40 minutes). **Air India** (☏274035; Jhansi Rd; ☉10am-4.50pm Mon-Sat) has 5.20pm flights to the same two cities, but only on Monday, Wednesday and Friday.

Taxi

Yashowaran Taxi Driver Union is opposite Gole Market under a neem tree. Fares including all taxes and tolls: airport (₹200), train station (₹300), Raneh Falls (₹600), Panna National Park (in 4WD, ₹1500), Satna (₹1500), Orchha (₹2300), Chitrakut (₹2800), Bandhavgarh (₹4500), Varanasi (₹6000) and Agra (₹6000).

Train

The daily 22447 Khajuraho–Nizamuddin Express leaves for Delhi (sleeper/3AC/2AC ₹344/935/1365, 6.20pm, 11½ hours) via Agra (₹282/753/1015, 8½ hours).

On Tuesday, Friday and Sunday the 21107 Khajuraho–Varanasi Express leaves for Varanasi (sleeper/3AC ₹275/758, 11.40pm, 11 hours).

Train tickets can be bought from the **train reservation office** (📞274416; 🕐8am-noon & 1-4pm Mon-Sat, 8am-2pm Sun) at the bus stand.

You must book tickets at least four hours before departure.

Coming to Khajuraho, the 21108 Varanasi–Khajuraho Express leaves Varanasi on Monday, Wednesday and Saturday at 6.05pm and arrives in Khajuraho at 5.15am. The 22448 Nizamuddin–Khajuraho Express leaves Delhi's Hazrat Nizamuddin station daily at 8.15pm and passes Agra (11.20pm) before arriving in Khajuraho (6.35am).

🛈 Getting Around

Bicycle is a great way to get around. Several places along Jain Temples Rd rent them (per day ₹50). Cycle-rickshaws cost around ₹20 wherever you go in Khajuraho.

Taxis to and from the airport/train station charge ₹200/250, autorickshaws ₹150/200.

Northern Mountains & Amritsar

Soaring Himalayan peaks and steamy lowland jungles, revered temples and renowned ashrams, peaceful hill stations and busy cities: the Northern Mountains are truly an active traveller's delight, with some of India's best trekking, climbing, rafting, yoga schools, holiday towns and wildlife watching.

In many places to the northwest, you might think you've accidentally stumbled into Tibet. But the ancient Buddhist monasteries clinging to sheer cliffsides, the troves of Buddhist arts and the home-away-from-home of the Dalai Lama are just another part of the essence of Himachal. And from here you're just a hop, skip and a jump away from the realm of the Punjab, with the glorious Golden Temple, Sikhism's holiest shrine, gleaming like a jewel at its heart.

Sikh devotees at the Golden Temple (p372), Amritsar

Northern Mountains & Amritsar

Under Administration of Pakistan

Under Administration of China

External boundaries shown reflect the requirements of the government of India. Some boundaries may not be those recognised by neighbouring countries. Lonely Planet always tries to show on maps where travellers may need to cross a boundary (and present documentation) irrespective of any dispute.

Kargil

Kolahoi Glacier

Leh

Parkachik Glacier

Srinagar

JAMMU & KASHMIR

Darung Drung Glacier

Banggong Co

Padum

Kishtwar

Jammu

Dalhousie

Manali

Bara Shigri Glacier

Pathankot

McLeod Ganj

HIMACHAL PRADESH

PAKISTAN

Beas

CHINA TIBET

Bhakra Dam

Sutlej

ahore

Amritsar

Shimla

Khatling Glacier

Firozpur

Sutlej

Ludhiana

Kalka

UTTARAKHAND

Gangotri Glacier

PUNJAB

Chandigarh

Mussoorie

Dehra Dun

Rishikesh

Abuhar

Bathinda

Yamuna

HARYANA

Corbett Tiger Reserve

Nainital

1 Golden Temple

2 Adrenalin-Seeking in Manali

3 Corbett Tiger Reserve

4 Tibetan Buddhism in McLeod Ganj

5 Rishikesh

Panipat

UTTAR PRADESH

Delhi

Ganges

Bareilly

0 ____ 100 km
0 ____ 50 miles

Northern Mountains & Amritsar's Highlights

Golden Temple

Sikhism's holiest shrine (p373), this gold-plated *gurdwara* (Sikh temple) glitters in the middle of its sacred pool of placid water and draws millions of pilgrims from all over the world. Whatever your faith, Amritsar's gilded temple will undoubtedly be a glowing highlight of your visit to India.

1

2 ## Adrenalin-Seeking in Manali

Manali (p359) might be one of the mountains' most hippie and laid-back traveller magnets, but there's plenty to get the pulse racing here amid breathtaking mountain scenery. This is one of the best places in India for adventure tourism, with activities such as trekking, paragliding and rafting all at your fingertips.

Corbett Tiger Reserve

GRANT DIXON/GETTY IMAGES ©

There are around 200 tigers at the Corbett Tiger Reserve (p352) in Uttarakhand, and that's the reason most visitors come here, but even if you don't spot one, the reserve is an end in itself. It's 1318 sq km of grassland, sal forest and river habitats, populated with wild elephants, sloth bears, languor monkeys, peacocks, deer, crocodiles, wild boars, monitor lizards and over 600 species of birds.

3

4

Tibetan Buddhism in McLeod Ganj

McLeod Ganj (p364), nicknamed 'Little Lhasa', is situated high in the fresh air of the Himalayas. You may feel as if you've stumbled into Tibet – it is the ideal place to clear your head, see Tibet in exile and understand something about Tibetan Buddhism.

CHRISTER FREDRIKSSON/GETTY IMAGES ©

5

Rishikesh

The 'yoga capital of the world' (p348) is a magnet for spiritual seekers, but Rishikesh's laid-back vibe, its outdoor activities and its fabulous mountain setting on the banks of the fast-flowing Ganges, attract all sorts. So if mediation isn't your thing, sign up for a rafting trip, hike your way around the forested hills, or just kick back on a riverside beach and enjoy the view.

Northern Mountains & Amritsar's Best...

Wining & Dining

Imperial Square
Mussoorie's finest, with huge windows overlooking Gandhi Chowk. (p347)

Little Buddha Cafe An ultra-loungey treehouse restaurant in Rishikesh. (p351)

Indian Coffee House Uniformed waiters, ageing booths and a blackboard menu: a Shimla institution. (p358)

La Plage Fabulous French restaurant, housed in an apple orchard. (p364)

Nick's Italian Kitchen Best pizza in McLeod Ganj, damn decent coffee.. and the cheesecake - wow! (p368)

Heritage Accommodation

Kasmanda Palace Hotel Mussoorie's most romantic hotel; a white Romanesque castle (c 1836). (p347)

Hotel Springfields Charming raj-era property in the former summer capital of Shimla. (p358)

Baikunth Magnolia One of Manali's finest; with a garden setting and plenty of balconies. (p361)

Sunshine Guest House Another Manali gem, this one's more ramshackle, but still full of colonial-era charm. (p361)

Walks

Rishikesh Take short walks to nearby waterfalls, or follow pilgrims to Neelkantha Mahadev Temple. (p348)

McLeod Ganj Take a easy walk through the surrounding pine forests, or test your stamina with the uphill hike to Triund. (p364)

Shimla Walk up Prospect Hill for great views, or amble down to the green meadow at Annandale. (p354)

Manali Hike along the Beas River, or sign up for a guided, multi-day trek across the mountains. (p359)

Adventure Activities

○ Tiger Safaris Track tigers in the forests and grasslands of Corbett Tiger Reserve. (p352)

○ Rafting & Kayaking Manali or Rishikesh are your best bets for river-based thrills.

○ Paragliding Popular at Solang Nullah and Gulaba April to October. Sign up with agencies in Manali.

○ Mountain Biking Again, sign up in Manali, although you'll have to take transport out to the best tracks. (p359)

Need to Know

ADVANCE PLANNING

○ One month before Book heritage accommodation or other special hotels, especially in the high season. Book a safari at Corbett Tiger Reserve.

○ One week before Book long-distance train journeys or arrange a long-term driver and car through a local agency.

○ One day before Call to reconfirm your accommodation; ring ahead if you want to take part in adventure activities.

RESOURCES

○ Corbett Tiger Reserve (www.corbettnationalpark. in) Book tiger safaris.

○ Himachal Tourism (www.hptdc.gov.in) Regional tourist-board site, including accommodation and transport information.

○ Haryana Online (www. haryana-online.com) Includes history and cultural information on the Punjab.

○ US Military Maps (www.lib.utexas.edu/ maps/ams/india) Useful for trekking.

GETTING AROUND

○ Air There's an airport at Amritsar, plus seasonal ones near Shimla, Manali and McLeod Ganj.

○ Train The railway will take you as far as Rishikesh and Shimla.

○ Car & driver Hiring a taxi for a day or several days is the easiest way to access more remote places.

○ Bus Serves smaller towns that the train doesn't reach.

BE FOREWARNED

○ Best weather Himachal's best weather seasons are May to mid-July and mid-September to early November.

○ Amritsar accommodation Hotels in Amritsar quickly fill during weekends and festivals, so book ahead.

○ Litter Dispose of litter carefully and consider using refillable water bottles.

: Cyclists near Manali **Above:** Elephants at Corbett Tiger Reserve (p352)

Northern Mountains & Amritsar Itineraries

These itineraries cover tigers, temples, the Himalayan foothills and India's heart of Tibetan Buddhism. Be prepared for some long road journeys... although the scenery should more than make up for the numb bum

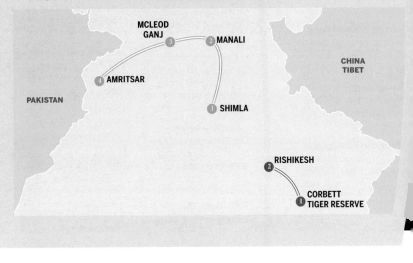

CORBETT TIGER RESERVE TO RISHIKESH

SAFARIS & YOGA

Easily reached from Delhi by train or bus, ❶**Corbett Tiger Reserve** makes a thrilling start to this trip. You'll need to take two or three jeep safaris to give yourself a half-decent change of spotting a tiger, but even if you don't see one, a couple of days spent exploring the grasslands and forests is a wonderfully peaceful way to begin your India adventure.

To experience an even greater level of relaxation, head from here to ❷**Rishikesh**, either with your own car and driver, or by bus via Haridwar. Fabulously laid-back Rishikesh is the self-styled yoga capital of the universe, and the serene mountain setting, with forested hills overlooking the banks of the River Ganges, is highly conducive to meditating, contemplating or just chilling out. If you want to stretch your legs, there are riverside beaches to hike to and nearby waterfalls to explore. End your tour with a splash by signing up for a rafting trip.

THE MOUNTAINS OF HIMACHAL

Assuming you're starting from Delhi, take the train to Kalka, from where you can pick up the Shimla toy train to the lovely hill station of ❶ **Shimla**. With its colonial-era architecture and grand heritage hotels, Shimla is a beautiful place to relax after India's hectic capital, with walks into the thickly forested green on all sides and sweeping views.

From Shimla, hire a car and driver, or hop on a long-distance bus, to ❷ **Manali**, for its beautiful Himalayan setting, laid-back traveller vibe and adrenalin-pumping adventure activities including mountain biking, rafting, walking and trekking.

Retain your car and driver (or brave another mountain bus journey) to get to ❸ **McLeod Ganj**, home of the Dalai Lama in exile. The mountainous setting is just as gorgeous here, but you'll also get a taste of Tibetan culture and the chance to learn more about Tibetan Buddhism.

Again, either retain your car and driver, or take a long-distance bus from nearby Dharamsala, to travel west to ❹ **Amritsar**, the realm of the Punjab and home to the magnificent Golden Temple.

Paragliders, Himachal Pradesh
JITENDRA SINGH/GETTY IMAGES ©

Discover the Northern Mountains & Amritsar

UTTARAKHAND

Mussoorie

0135 / POP 29,500 / ELEV 2000M

Perched on a ridge 2km high, the 'Queen of Hill Stations' vies with Nainital as Uttarakhand's favourite holiday destination. When the mist clears, views of the green Doon Valley and the distant white-capped Himalayan peaks are superb.

Established by the British in 1823, Mussoorie became hugely popular with the Raj set. The ghosts of that era linger on in the architecture of the churches, libraries, hotels and summer palaces. The town is swamped with visitors between May and July.

Sights & Activities

Gun Hill Viewpoint
From midway along the Mall, a **cable car** (return ₹75; 8am-10pm May-Jul & Oct, 10am-7pm Aug, Sep & late Nov-Apr) runs up to Gun Hill (2530m), which, on a clear day, has views of several big peaks.

Walks Walking
When the clouds don't get in the way, the walks around Mussoorie offer great views. **Camel's Back Rd** is a popular 3km promenade from Kulri Bazaar to Gandhi Chowk, but there are plenty of other options. **Trek Himalaya** (2630491; www.trekhimalaya.com; Upper Mall; 11am-9pm) can organise guides for around ₹700 a day.

Sleeping

Peak season is summer (May to July) when hotel prices shoot to ridiculous heights. There's a midseason during the honeymoon period around October and November, and

Manali (p359)
ANAND PUROHIT/GETTY IMAGES ©

over Christmas and New Year. At other times you should be able to get a bargain. The following prices are for midseason, unless otherwise specified.

Hotel Broadway
Hotel $

(2632243; Camel's Back Rd, Kulri Bazaar; d ₹600-1500) The best of the budget places by a country mile, this historic 1880s wooden hotel with colourful flowerboxes in the windows oozes character. It's in a quiet location but close to the Mall. Cheaper downstairs rooms could use a refresh, but upstairs rooms are nice; the best has lovely sunlit bay windows.

Kasmanda Palace Hotel
Heritage Hotel $$$

(2632424; www.kasmandapalace.com; d ₹5000-7200) Located off the Mall, this is Mussoorie's most romantic hotel. The white Romanesque castle was built in 1836 for a British officer and was bought by the Maharaja of Kasmanda in 1915. All of the rooms have charm. An excellent restaurant and pretty garden area complete the picture.

Hotel Padmini Nivas
Heritage Hotel $$$

(2631093; www.hotelpadmininivas.com; The Mall; d ₹2250-2850, ste ₹3450-4050; @) Built in 1840 by a British colonel, this heritage hotel has real old-fashioned charm. Large rooms with quaint sun rooms are beautifully furnished; those in the main house are significantly nicer than those in the side building.

Eating & Drinking

There is a **Café Coffee Day** in Kulri Bazaar and another branch near Gandhi Chowk.

Lovely Omelette Centre
Fast Food $

(The Mall, Kulri Bazaar; mains ₹30-80; 9am-9.30pm Wed-Mon) Mussorie's most famous eatery is also its smallest – a cubbyhole along the Mall that serves what many say are the best omelettes in India. The specialty is the cheese omelette, with chillies, onions and spices, served over toast.

Imperial Square
Continental $$

(2632632; Gandhi Chowk; mains ₹190-350; 7am-11pm; 🛜) With huge windows overlooking Gandhi Chowk, Imperial Square scores high on everything – decor, service and food. The menu is strong on Continental dishes, with long lists of platters and sizzlers, plus big toasted sandwiches.

Kasmanda Palace Restaurant
Multicuisine $$

(2632424; Kasmanda Palace Hotel; mains ₹110-350) The regal restaurant at this Raj-era hotel (found north of the Mall) is the perfect escape from Mussoorie's holiday bustle. The dining room is intimate but not stuffy, and the garden restaurant is fine for a lazy lunch or summer evening.

ℹ️ Information

Connexions (The Mall, Kulri Bazaar; internet per hr ₹60; 10.30am-10.30pm) Above the Tavern.

GMVN Booth (2631281; Library bus stand; 8am-6pm) Can book local tours, treks and far-flung rest houses.

Trek Himalaya (2630491; Upper Mall; 11am-9pm) Exchanges major currencies at a fair rate.

ℹ️ Getting There & Away

Bus

Frequent buses head to Mussoorie (₹47, 1½ hours) from Dehra Dun's Mussoorie bus stand. Some go to the **Picture Palace bus stand** (2632259) while others go to the **Library bus stand** (2632258) at the other end of town – if you know where you're staying, it helps to be on the right bus. There's no direct transport from Mussoorie to Rishikesh or Haridwar – change at Dehra Dun.

Taxi

From taxi stands at both bus stands you can hire taxis to Dehra Dun (₹610) and Rishikesh (₹1610). A shared taxi to Dehra Dun should cost ₹100 per person.

Train

The **Northern Railway booking agency** (2632846; Lower Mall, Kulri Bazaar; 8am-2pm Mon-Sat) books tickets for trains from Dehra Dun and Haridwar.

Rishikesh

📞 0135 / POP 102,130 / ELEV 356M

Ever since the Beatles rocked up at the ashram of the Maharishi Mahesh Yogi in the late '60s, Rishikesh has been a magnet for spiritual seekers. Today it styles itself as the 'Yoga Capital of the World', with masses of ashrams and all kinds of yoga and meditation classes. Most of this action is north of the main town, where the exquisite setting on the fast-flowing Ganges, surrounded by forested hills, is conducive to meditation and mind expansion.

But Rishikesh is not all spirituality and contorted limbs; it's now a popular whitewater rafting centre, backpacker hangout, and gateway to treks in the Himalaya.

◎ Sights

Lakshman Jhula & Around   Area
The defining image of Rishikesh is the view across the Lakshman Jhula hanging bridge to the huge, 13-storey wedding-cake temples of **Swarg Niwas** and **Shri Trayanbakshwar**. Built by the organisation of the guru Kailashanand, they resemble fairyland castles and have dozens of shrines to Hindu deities on each level, interspersed with jewellery and textile shops.

🤸 Activities

YOGA & MEDITATION

Sri Sant Seva Ashram   Mixed Yoga
(📞2430465; santsewa@hotmail.com; Lakshman Jhula; d ₹200-500, with AC ₹1000; 🛜) The yoga classes are mixed styles and open to all. Beginner (₹100) and intermediate and advanced (₹200) sessions run daily. There are also courses in reiki, ayurvedic massage and cooking.

Parmarth Niketan
Ashram   Hatha Yoga
(📞2434301; www.parmarth.com; Swarg Ashram; s/d ₹500/600) Dominating the centre of Swarg Ashram and drawing visitors to its evening *ganga aarti* (lamp lighting) on the riverbank, Parmarth has a wonderfully ornate and serene garden courtyard. The price includes a room with a private bathroom, all meals and hatha yoga lessons.

RAFTING, KAYAKING & TREKKING

Over 100 storefronts offer full- and half-day rafting trips, launching upstream and paddling down to Rishikesh. Some also offer multiday rafting trips, with camping along the river. The official rafting season runs from 15 September to 30 June. A half-day trip starts at about ₹600 per person, while a full day costs from ₹1600. Most companies also offer all-inclusive Himalayan treks to places such as Kuari Pass, Har-ki Dun and Gangotri from around ₹2500 per day.

Red Chilli
Adventure   Trekking, Rafting
(📞2434021; www.redchilliadventure.com; Lakshman Jhula Rd; ⏰9am-9pm) Reliable outfit.

De-N-Ascent
Expeditions   Kayaking, Trekking
(📞2442354; www.kayakhimalaya.com; Lakshman Jhula, Tapovan Sarai) Specialist in kayaking lessons and expeditions.

WALKS & BEACHES

An easy, 15-minute walk to two small **waterfalls** starts 3km north of Lakshman

Rishikesh

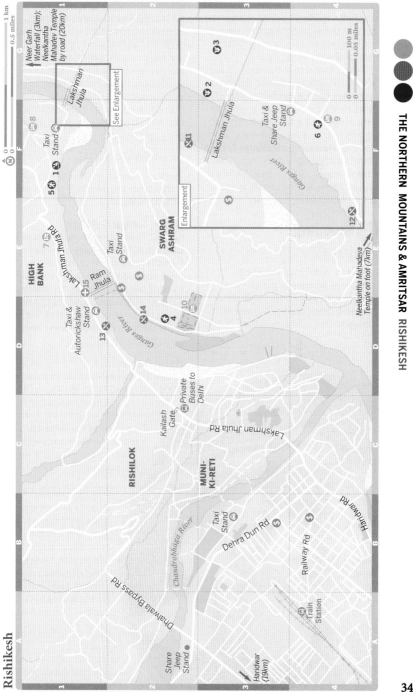

Neer Garh Waterfall (3km); Neelkantha Mahadev Temple by road (20km)

Lakshman Jhula

See Enlargement

HIGH BANK

Lakshman Jhula Rd

Ram Jhula

SWARG ASHRAM

Taxi Stand

Taxi & Autorickshaw Stand

Ganges River

Kailash Gate

Private Buses to Delhi

RISHILOK

Chandrabhaga River

MUNI-KI-RETI

Lakshman Jhula Rd

Dhalwala Bypass Rd

Share Jeep Stand

Haridwar (19km)

Taxi Stand

Dehra Dun Rd

Railway Rd

Haridwar Rd

Train Station

Neelkantha Mahadeva Temple on foot (7km)

Enlargement

Lakshman Jhula

Taxi & Share Jeep Stand

Ganges River

100 m
0.05 miles

1 km
0.5 miles

349

Jhula bridge on the south side of the river. The start is marked by drink stalls and a roadside shrine, and the path is easy to find. Four-wheel-drive taxis cost ₹100 from Lakshman Jhula.

On the other side of the river, it's about 2km north to the signposted walk to lovely **Neer Garh Waterfall** (admission ₹30), from where it's a 20-minute uphill walk.

For a longer hike, follow the dedicated pilgrims who take water from the Ganges to offer at **Neelkantha Mahadev Temple**, a 7km, approximately three-hour walk along a forest path from Swarg Ashram. You can also reach the temple by road (20km) from Lakshman Jhula.

Sleeping

HIGH BANK

This small, leafy travellers' enclave is a 20-minute walk up the hill from Lakshman Jhula and has some of the best backpacker accommodation in Rishikesh.

Bhandari Swiss Cottage   Hotel $
(☎2432939; www.bhandariswisscottage rishikesh.com; r from ₹200, with AC from ₹1000; ❄@☎) The first place you come to, this is a well-run backpacker favourite with rooms in several budgets – the higher up you stay, the higher the price. Rooms with big balconies have expansive views of the river backed by green mountains. Excellent little restaurant, internet cafe and yoga classes.

LAKSHMAN JHULA

There are several good budget options on both sides of the river here, in the liveliest part of Rishikesh.

Divine Ganga Cottage   Hotel $
(☎2442175; www.divinegangacottage.com; r ₹800, with AC ₹2000; ❄@) Tucked away from the hubbub and surrounded by small rice paddies and local homes with gardens, the huge upstairs terrace has supreme river views. Downstairs non-AC rooms are small and overpriced, but the larger stylish upstairs AC rooms are some of the best in town.

Hotel Surya   Hotel $
(☎2440211; www.hotelsuryalaxmanjhula.com; r ₹300-500, with AC ₹1200; ❄) Above Café Coffee Day, the newly renovated Surya is good value in a good location. Even some of the cheapest rooms have balconies with river views, and all are very spacious.

SWARG ASHRAM

If you're serious about yoga and introspection, stay at one of Swarg's numerous ashrams. Otherwise, there's a knot of guesthouses a block back from the river towards the southern end of Swarg.

Samosas at street stall, Rishikesh
RICHARD I'ANSON/GETTY IMAGES ©

Vashishth Guest House
Boutique Hotel $

(☎2440029; www.vashishthgroup.com; r ₹500, with AC ₹850, with AC & kitchen ₹1000) This sweet little boutique hotel has colourfully painted walls, comfortable mattresses, and a small lending library. A couple of the rooms boast good-sized kitchens with cooking utensils and table and chairs. For what you get, this is one of the best deals in Rishikesh.

🍴 Eating

Virtually every restaurant in Rishikesh serves only vegetarian food.

LAKSHMAN JHULA

Devraj Coffee Corner
Cafe $

(snacks & mains ₹30-150; ⊙8am-9pm) Perched above the bridge and looking across the river to Shri Trayanbakshwar temple, this German bakery is a sublime spot for a break at any time of the day. The coffee is the best in town and the menu ranges from specialties like brown bread with yak cheese to soups and sizzlers, along with the usual croissants and apple strudel.

Little Buddha Cafe
Multicuisine $$

(mains ₹60-140; ⊙8am-11pm) This funky treehouse-style restaurant has an ultral-oungey top floor, tables overlooking the Ganga, and really good international food. Pizzas are big and the mixed vegetable platter is a serious feast. It's one of the busiest places in Lakshman Jhula, for good reasons.

SWARG ASHRAM & RAM JHULA

Madras Cafe
Indian $

(Ram Jhula; mains ₹80-120; ⊙8am-10pm) This local institution dishes up tasty South and North Indian vegetarian food, thalis, a mean mushroom curry, whole-wheat pancakes and the intriguing Himalayan health *pilau* ', as well as super-thick lassis.

Tip Top Restaurant
Multicuisine $

(Swarg Ashram; mains ₹60-170; ⊙8am-10pm) The friendly little joint is perched up high, catching river views and breezes. Customize your own sandwich, or dig into the three 'I's – Indian, Italian or Israeli dishes.

HIGH BANK

Backpackers gather at the popular restaurants on High Bank. This is the only area in town where you'll find meat on the menu.

Oasis Restaurant
Multicuisine $$

(mains ₹90-170; ⊙8am-10pm) At New Bhandari Swiss Cottage, this place has some character, with candlelit tables in the garden and hanging lanterns inside. The menu covers oodles of world cuisines, from Mexican and Thai to Israeli and Tibetan, and features a number of chicken dishes including a delicious chilli chicken.

ℹ️ Information

Dangers & Annoyances

Be cautious of befriending sadhus – while some are on genuine spiritual journeys, the orange robes have been used as a disguise by fugitives from the law since medieval times.

The current in some parts of the Ganges is very strong, and as inviting as a dip from one of the beaches may seem, people drown here every year. Don't swim out of your depth.

Internet Access

Internet access is available all over town, usually for ₹20 or ₹30 per hour.

Medical Services

Himalayan Institute Hospital (☎2471133; ⊙24hr) The nearest large hospital, 17km along the road to Dehra Dun and 1km beyond Jolly Grant airport.

Shivananda Ashram (☎2430040; www.sivanandaonline.org; Lakshman Jhula Rd) Provides free medical services and has a pharmacy.

Money

Several travel agents around Lakshman Jhula and Swarg Ashram will exchange travellers cheques and cash.

Getting There & Away

Bus

There are regular buses to Haridwar and Dehra Dun; for Mussoorie change at Dehra Dun.

Private deluxe buses to Delhi (₹475, seven hours) leave from Kailash Gate, just south of Ram Jhula, at 1.30pm and 9.30pm. There's also one direct overnight bus daily from Rishikesh to Dharamsala (₹925) at 4pm.

Private night buses to Jaipur (seat/sleeper/Volvo ₹550/625/1350, 13 hours), Agra (seat/sleeper ₹475/550, 12 hours) and Pushkar (₹550/625, 16 hours) can be booked at travel agencies in Lakshman Jhula, Swarg Ashram and High Bank, but they leave from Haridwar.

Taxi

Private taxis can be hired from Lakshman Jhula, Ram Jhula, and in between the main and *yatra* bus stands. Rates to various destinations include Haridwar (₹660, one hour) and Dehra Dun (₹970, 1½ hours).

Train

Bookings can be made at the reservation office at the train station, or at travel agencies. Only a handful of slow trains run from Rishikesh to Haridwar, so it's usually better to go by bus or taxi.

Getting Around

Shared *vikrams* (outsized autos) run from the downtown Ghat Rd junction up past Ram Jhula (₹1 per person) and the High Bank turn-off to Lakshman Jhula. To hire the entire *vikram* from downtown to Lakshman Jhula should cost ₹80 to 'upside' (the top of the hill on which the Lakshman Jhula area sits) and ₹100 to 'downside' (closer to the bridge). From Ram Jhula to High Bank or Lakshman Jhula is ₹40.

Corbett Tiger Reserve

☎ 05947 / ELEV 400-1210M

This famous **reserve (◷mid-Nov–mid-Jun, Jhirna zone open year-round)** was established in 1936 as India's first national park. It's named for legendary tiger hunter Jim Corbett (1875–1955), who put Kumaon on the map with his book *The Man-Eaters of Kumaon*.

Tiger sightings take some luck, as the 200 or so tigers in the reserve are neither

baited nor tracked. Your best chance of spotting one is late in the season (April to mid-June). The park also has 200 to 300 wild elephants living in the reserve.

Of Corbett's five zones (Bijrani, Dhikala, Domunda, Jhirna and Sonanadi), Dhikala is the highlight of the park. Deep inside the reserve, it's only open from 15 November to 15 June and only to overnight guests, or as part of a one-day tour available only through the park's **reception centre** (☏251489; www.corbettnationalpark.in; Ranikhet Rd; ⊙6am-4pm), opposite Ramnagar's bus stand.

Tours

Jeeps can be hired at the reception centre in Ramnagar, or through your accommodation or a tour agency. Jeep owners have formed a union, so in theory rates are fixed (on a per jeep basis, carrying up to six people). Half-day safaris (leaving in morning and afternoon) should cost ₹1500 to Bijrani, ₹1800 to Jhirna, or ₹2100 to Domunda – not including the entry fees for you and your guide. Full-day safaris cost double. Overnight excursions to Dhikala cost ₹3300. Safaris offered by Karan Singh, who runs Corbett Motel (p354), are highly recommended.

PERMITS

It's highly recommended to make advance reservations. You can book via the park's website or by signing up for a trip with a safari outfit.

Your total costs will be calculated as follows: jeep hire (see left), plus vehicle entrance fee (₹250/500 for Indians/foreigners per day), plus visitor entrance fee (₹100/450 per Indian/foreigner per day), plus, bizarrely, visitors fees for any spare seats in your six-seater jeep (calculated at the Indian-passenger rate).

Arranging everything yourself is marginally cheaper than taking a safari or hotel tour, but they provide expert guides fluent in English, which can be well worth the few extra rupees.

🛏 Sleeping & Eating

For serious wildlife viewing, Dhikala – deep inside the reserve – is the prime place to stay. Book through the reception centre in Ramnagar at least one month in advance. The town of Ramnagar has budget accommodation, while upmarket resorts are strung out along the road skirting the eastern side of the park between Dhikuli and Dhangarhi Gate.

DHIKALA

Easily the cheapest beds in the park are at **Log Huts** (dm Indian/foreigner ₹200/400), resembling 3AC train sleepers, with 24 basic beds (no bedding supplied). **Tourist Hutments** (Indian/foreigner ₹1250/2500) offer the best-value accommodation in Dhikala and sleep up to six people. Dhikala has a couple of restaurants serving vegetarian food. No alcohol is allowed in the park.

RAMNAGAR

A busy, unappealing town, Ramnagar has plenty of facilities, including internet cafes (₹30 per hour), ATMs (State Bank of India ATM at the train station, and a Bank of Baroda ATM on Ranikhet Rd) and transport connections – mostly along Ranikhet Rd.

Corbett Motel   Hotel $
(9837468933; www.corbetmotel.com; tent/d/ tr ₹400/500/600) Set in a beautiful mango orchard only a few hundred metres from the train station, Ramnagar's best budget accommodation is a world away from the traffic-clogged centre and offers exceptional service and hospitality. You can stay in sturdy tents or basic but spotless rooms, and the restaurant serves fine food. The owner, Karan, is a well-known local naturalist and can organise jeep safaris into the park. Call ahead for a pick-up.

NORTH OF RAMNAGAR

Infinity Resorts   Hotel $$$
(251279; www.infinityresorts.com; Dhikuli; s/d incl breakfast from ₹8000/10,000; ❄ ⛱) The most impressive of the resorts in this area, Infinity has luxurious rooms, a roundhouse with restaurant and bar, and a swimming pool in a lovely garden backing onto the Kosi River.

ⓘ Getting There & Away

Buses run almost hourly from Ramnagar to Delhi (₹178, seven hours) and Dehra Dun (₹171, seven hours) from where you can change for Mussoorie.

Ramnagar train station is 1.5km south of the main reception centre. The nightly Ranikhet Express 15013 (sleeper/3AC/2AC ₹133/345/585) leaves Delhi at 10.40pm, arriving in Ramnagar at 4.55am. The return trip on train 25014 leaves Ramnagar at 9.55pm, arriving in Old Delhi at 3.55am. A daytime run from Old Delhi on train 15035 (2nd class/chair ₹77/271) departs at 4pm, reaching Ramnagar at 8.35pm; the return on train 25036 departs Ramnagar at 9.50am, hitting Delhi at 3.20pm.

HIMACHAL PRADESH

Shimla

0177 / POP 170,000 / ELEV 2205M

Strung out along a 12km ridge, Shimla – the one-time official summer home of the Raj – is today an engaging blend of hill town and holiday resort. Indian vacationers stroll the Mall, while the lower bazaars flow with local life and with shops selling hardware, stationery, fabric and spices. With cars banned from the main part of town, walking anywhere is very pleasant – even when huffing and puffing uphill.

Expect a stiff walk to your hotel. Porters will carry your luggage uphill for ₹80 to ₹100 but most double as touts, and hotels will increase your room tariff to cover their commission.

◎ Sights & Activities

Jakhu Temple   Hindu Temple
Shimla's most famous temple is dedicated to the Hindu monkey god Hanuman;

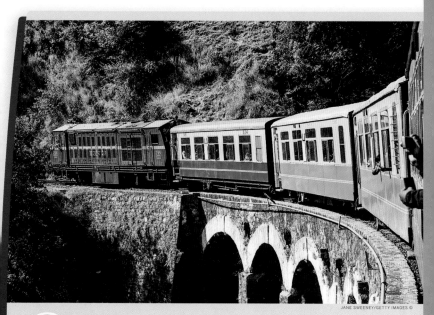

JANE SWEENEY/GETTY IMAGES ©

⭐ Don't Miss
Shimla Toy Train

One of the little joys of Shimla is getting to or from it by the narrow-gauge toy train from Kalka, just north of Chandigarh. Although the steam trains are long gone, it's a scenic four- to six-hour trip, passing through 103 tunnels as it winds up through the hills. Tiny Shimla train station is 1.5km west of Scandal Point on Cart Rd – about a 15-minute uphill walk.

Ordinary trains (1st/2nd class ₹189/16, 5½ hours) run downhill to Kalka at 2.25pm, 4.25pm and 6.15pm, returning at 4am, 5.10am and 6am. Additional high-season services run at 9.25am and 3.50pm, returning at 7am and 12.45pm. To travel in style, catch the posh Shivalik Express at 5.40pm (returning at 5.30am; ₹280 with meals, 4¾ hours).

The easiest way to or from Delhi is on the Himalayan Queen Express; it costs ₹167 (chair car) to Kalka, plus an additional ₹284/75 (chair car/2nd class) on to Delhi. An alternative is to connect with the 5.45pm Kalka Shatabdi to Delhi (4¼ hours). Timings for the Himalayan Queen Express are as follows:

SHIMLA	ARRIVE KALKA	DEPART KALKA	DELHI	TRAIN NOS
10.30am	4.10pm	4.50pm	10.40pm	52456 & 14096
DELHI	**ARRIVE KALKA**	**DEPART KALKA**	**SHIMLA**	**TRAIN NOS**
5.45am	11.10am	12.10pm	5.20pm	14095 & 52455

There's a **rail booking office** (🕑 9am-1pm & 2-4pm Mon-Sat) next to the HPTDC tourist office on the Ridge, or you can book at the train station.

t's therefore appropriate that hundreds of rhesus macaques loiter around, harassing devotees for *prasad* (temple-

blessed food offerings). Getting here involves a steep 30-minute hike from the east end of the Ridge. Primate alert: the

Shimla

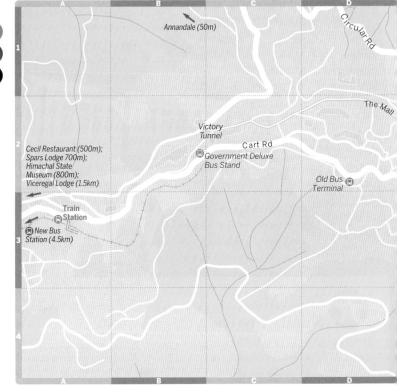

Annandale (50m)

Circular Rd

The Mall

Victory
Tunnel

Cart Rd

Government Deluxe
Bus Stand

Cecil Restaurant (500m);
Spars Lodge (700m);
Himachal State
Museum (800m);
Viceregal Lodge (1.5km)

Old Bus
Terminal

Train
Station

New Bus
Station (4.5km)

monkeys on this route can be a menace, so bring a walking stick to discourage them. Taxis charge around ₹350 return.

Viceregal Lodge Historic Building
(Indian/foreigner ₹30/65, cameras ₹20; ⊙9.15am-1pm & 2-5pm, to 7pm May-Jul, tours every 30min from 10.15am) Built as an official residence in 1888 for the British viceroys, the Viceregal Lodge looks like a cross between Harry Potter's Hogwarts School and the Tower of London. Every brick used in its construction was hauled up here by mule. Today it houses the Indian Institute of Advanced Study, but you can take a guided tour of the buildings. The easily missed photo gallery behind the ticket office is worth a visit.

The lodge is a 4.5km walk west from Scandal Point along the Mall; the path to the left of the Himachal State Museum

entrance leads there in five minutes via Peterhof Hotel (itself a former viceregal residence).

Walking Walking
About 4km northwest of Scandal Point is **The Glen**, a former playground of British colonialists, selected for its similarity to the Scottish highlands. The road here passes through the flat green meadow at **Annandale**, once the site of the gymkhana club and a famous racecourse, and still a popular venue for cricket and polo matches. The army runs the show here now, including a small army museum. The walk down here is pleasant but you should prebook a taxi for the return uphill slog.

There's an interesting temple of Kamna Devi and excellent views at **Prospect Hill**, about 4km west of Shimla and accessible from walking paths at the entrance to

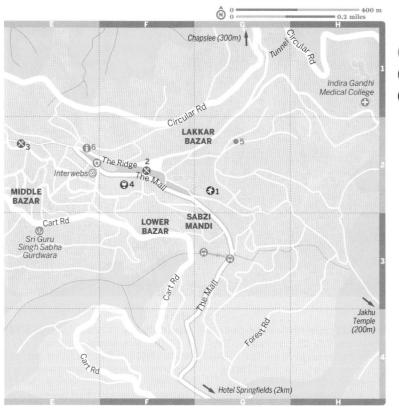

the Viceregal Lodge complex. About 2km further away on the Shimla–Kalka railway line, **Summer Hill** has pleasant, shady walks. Pretty **Chadwick Falls** are 2km further west, best visited just after the monsoon.

YMCA Tours & Treks
Outdoor Adventure

(☎9857102657; www.himalayansites.com; Shimla YMCA, The Ridge) The affable and knowledgeable Anil Kumar runs day trips around Shimla as well as treks throughout Himachal and Uttarakhand.

🛏 Sleeping

Hotels in Shimla charge steep rates during the peak tourist season (April to June, October and Christmas). At all other times, ask about discounts of up to 40%.

RICHARD I'ANSON/GETTY IMAGES ©

YMCA
Hotel $

(☎2650021; ymcashimla@yahoo.co.in; s/d without bathroom ₹550/825, r incl breakfast ₹1761; @) Up the steps beside the Ritz Cineplex, the expansive, bright-red YMCA takes all comers, regardless of age, religion or gender. Rooms are neat and pleasant (the corner rooms in particular have great views), with immaculate shared bathrooms, and there's a nice sunset terrace and sun room, with an internet cafe and lockers for valuables. Rooms with bathroom offer poorer value. Book ahead April to July.

Spars Lodge
Guesthouse $$

(☎2657908; Museum Rd; s/d ₹990/1400, ste from ₹1990; @) On the little road up to the museum, Spars is a budget place with an inviting, homey feel. It's bright, clean and airy with a lovely sunny dining room upstairs. The owners are welcoming and the restaurant serves great food, including local trout. Rates are fixed throughout the year. It's a 25-minute walk from central Shimla but taxis are available.

Hotel Springfields
Heritage Hotel $$$

(☎2621297; www.ushalexushotels.com; Chotta Shimla; r ₹4697; ❄🛜) Built for the wife of the raja of Sheikhapura and featuring charming drawing rooms, a lounge bar and immaculately trimmed lawns, Springfields is a perfect combination of colonial-era charm and mod cons that won't break the bank. It's just below Cart Rd in Chotta Shimla, a pleasant 30-minute walk or ₹200 taxi ride from Shimla centre.

🍴 Eating & Drinking

Indian Coffee House
Cafe $

(The Mall; dishes ₹20-40; ⏰8am-8.30pm) A Shimla institution, the Indian Coffee House is like an old boys' club with its ageing booths, uniformed waiters and blackboard menu. It's the most atmospheric place in town for breakfast, cheap dosas and coffee (don't even ask for tea!), though it's more about the experience than the food.

Ashiana
Indian $$

(The Ridge; dishes ₹75-180; ⏰9am-10pm) In a fanciful circular building on the Ridge, this is an almost elegant restaurant and a good people-watching spot, with a delightful sunny terrace. As well as tasty Indian dishes there are sizzlers, Chinese and a few Thai favourites. In Ashiana's basement, Goofa serves the same food, from the same kitchen, for 25% less. You don't get the views but at night, who cares?

Cecil Restaurant Multicuisine $$$
(☎2804848; The Mall, Chaura Maidan; mains ₹700-1000; ⏰10am-10pm) For a formal night out, look no further than the colonial-era elegance of the Cecil Restaurant at the Oberoi. The à la carte menu is strong on Indian and Thai curries and there are sumptuous buffets when a group is in town. Book ahead.

Himani's Bar
(The Mall; mains ₹100-225, beer ₹150; ⏰9am-10pm) The neon and marble decor is straight out of the 1980s, but Himani's is a decent place for a casual drink or plate of chicken tikka. The lower floors are smoky and male-dominated but the top-floor terrace overlooking the Mall is perfect on a sunny afternoon.

ℹ️ Information

Emergency
Indira Gandhi Medical College (☎2803073; Circular Rd; ⏰24hr)

Tourist police (☎2812344; Scandal Point)

Internet Access
Interwebs (The Mall; per hr ₹30, wi-fi ₹60; ⏰10am-10pm) One of two internet cafes next to each other, and a rare wi-fi hot spot.

Money
Numerous ATMs are dotted around Scandal Point and the Mall.

Punjab National Bank (The Mall; ⏰10am-2pm & 3-4pm Mon-Fri, 10am-2pm Sat) Changes major currencies in cash and travellers cheques.

Tourist Information
HPTDC Tourist Office (Himachal Pradesh Tourist Development Corporation; ☎2652561; www.hptdc.gov.in; Scandal Point; ⏰9am-8pm, to 7pm mid-Jul-Sep & Dec-Mar) Helpful for advice, brochures and booking HPTDC buses, hotels and tours, along with a railway booking window and bus ticket booth next door.

Travel Agencies
Great Escape Routes (☎6533037; www.greatescaperoutes.com; 6 Andi Bhavan, Jakhu; 📶) Specialises in trekking and adventure tours around the state, including some local hikes that overnight in homestays. Can put you in touch with local mountain-bike guides and has an internet cafe with wi-fi. Contact Nitin.

ℹ️ Getting There & Away

Air
At the time of research there were no flights to Jubbarhatti airport, 23km south of Shimla, though seasonal services to Delhi should resume at some point.

Bus
HPTDC and private travel agencies offer overnight deluxe Volvo buses to Delhi (₹880, nine hours), plus morning and evening buses to Manali (₹500, nine hours) in season (April to June, October and November). They depart from the deluxe bus stand near Victory Tunnel. There are also four Himachal Road Transport Corporation (HRTC) Volvo buses to Delhi (₹785, nine hours) each day, along with three AC deluxe (₹550) and three semi-deluxe (₹312) rides. Deluxe/semi-deluxe buses head to Manali (₹455/325, 10 hours) in the morning and evening. All HRTC buses leave from the new bus station, 5km outside Shimla (a taxi here costs ₹200 to ₹300). Make reservations at the HRTC booth (⏰11am-2pm & 3-6.30pm) next to the HPTDC Tourist Office at Scandal Point.

ℹ️ Getting Around
The only way to get around central Shimla is on foot. Fortunately, there's a two-part lift (per person ₹8; ⏰8am-10pm, to 9pm Jul-Sep) connecting the east end of the Mall with Cart Rd. Taxis from the train station to the bottom of the lift cost about ₹150.

Manali
☎01902 / POP 4400 / ELEV 2050M
With super views of the Dhauladhar and Pir Panjal Ranges, and with mountain adventures beckoning from all directions, Manali is a year-round magnet for tourists. Backpackers come to hang out in the hippie villages around the main town; adventure tourists come for trekking, paragliding, rafting and skiing; and Indian

THE NORTHERN MOUNTAINS & AMRITSAR MANALI

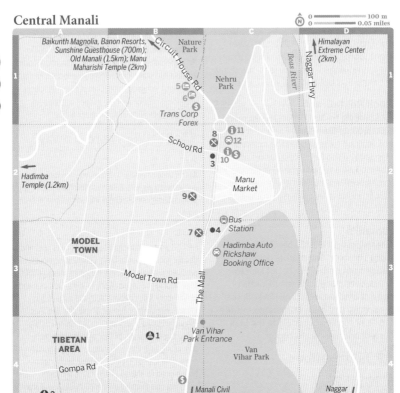

honeymoon couples or families come for the cool mountain air and their first taste of snow on a day trip to Rohtang La.

Most travellers stay in the villages of Vashisht or Old Manali, which have a laid-back vibe and plenty of services, but close for winter from sometime in October to May.

◉ Sights & Activities

Hadimba Temple   Hindu Temple

Also known as the Dhungri Temple, this ancient wood and stone mandir was erected in 1553. Pilgrims come here from across India to honour Hadimba, the wife of Bhima from the Mahabharata. Hadimba is a 20-minute walk northwest of Manali, or you can take an autorickshaw (₹50).

Buddhist Monasteries   Buddhist Temples

There's a small Tibetan community just south of the town centre. The **Himalayan Nyingmapa Buddhist Temple** (◷6am-6pm) contains a two-storey statue of Sakyamuni, the historical Buddha.

Just east is the more traditional **Panden Ngari Gompa** (◷6am-6pm), with an atmospheric juniper-scented prayer room crammed with statues of bodhisattvas, revered lamas and Buddhist deities. Chat with the Tibetan refugees over a bowl of *thukpa* noodles in the attached teashop.

Old Manali   Area

About 2.5km north of the Mall on the far side of the Manalsu Nala stream, Old Manali still has some of the feel of

Central Manali

an Indian mountain village once you get past the core backpacker zone. There are some remarkable old houses of wood and stone, and the towering **Manu Maharishi Temple** is built on the site where the Noah-like Manu meditated after surviving the great flood. A trail to Solang Nullah (11km) runs north from here through the village of Goshal (2km).

👉 Tours

In high season, the HPTDC offers day tours by bus to the Rohtang La (₹290), to Manikaran and the Parvati Valley (₹330) and to Naggar and Solang Nullah (₹240), if there are enough takers. Private travel agencies offer similar bus tours.

The **Him-Anchal Taxi Operators Union** (☎252120; The Mall) has fixed-price tours, including to Rohtang La (₹1900), Solang Nullah (₹600) and Naggar (₹650).

Adventure-tour operators include the following:

Himalayan Adventurers   Outdoor Adventure
(☎252750; www.himalayanadventurersindia. com; 44 The Mall) Trekking, skiing, mountain biking and mountaineering.

Himalayan Extreme Center   Outdoor Adventure
(☎9816174164; www.himalayan-extreme-center. com; Vashisht) With offices in Old Manali and Vashisht, this Swiss-run place is your one-stop shop for almost any adventure activity.

🛏 Sleeping

Peak-season rates (May to July and Christmas) are listed here but discounts of up to 50% are standard at other times, especially at top-end places. Heating is rare in budget places so be prepared to dive under a blanket to stay warm.

MANALI

Sunshine Guest House   Heritage Hotel $$
(☎252320; Circuit House Rd; r ₹1500) This ramshackle and rambling Raj-era mansion was due to be renovated in 2013, so you can expect the charming but neglected rooms to go upscale. Enormous suites with fireplaces, odd changing rooms and giant bathrooms may be a bit draughty, but the balconies, dining room and overgrown garden are full of colonial-era charm.

Johnson Hotel   Hotel $$$
(☎253764; www.johnsonhotel.in; Circuit House Rd; d ₹3757; ❄ @ 🛜) One of several places named in honour of the Raj-era landowner Jimmy Johnson. This is a classy wood-and-stone hotel that has nine snug rooms, a century-old lodge and lovely gardens, as well as an excellent garden restaurant (p363). Everything's in immaculate shape, making this one worth the price.

Baikunth Magnolia   Heritage Hotel $$$
(☎250118; www.baikunth.com; Circuit House Rd; r ₹6106; 🛜) Yet another gorgeous old heritage property, surrounded by pleasant

gardens and decked out with over-stuffed couches, old prints on the walls, an atmospheric bar and modern rooms, most of which have private balconies.

OLD MANALI

Veer Guest House   Guesthouse $
(📞252710; veerguesthouse@hotmail.com; r ₹440-1100, ste ₹1760-2350; @) Set in a pretty garden, long-running Veer is one of Old Manali's best-value hotels. Rooms in the quaint lime-green old block with wood-plank flooring have plenty of character, while new rooms at the front are bright and slick, with TVs and private balconies. There's a great little restaurant and an internet cafe.

Drifters' Inn   Hotel $
(📞9805033127; www.driftersinn.in; Old Manali Rd; r ₹660-1174, ste ₹1409; @ 🛜) The hipness of the ground-floor restaurant doesn't quite extend into the bland rooms but it's a spotless place with outdoor terraces on every floor. The loungey restaurant has great breakfasts, good espresso and

imaginative beverages such as a seabuckthorn fizz.

Mountain Dew Guesthouse   Hotel $
(📞9816446366; d ₹300-400; 🛜) This yellow three-storey hotel has good-sized rooms and nice balconies with an onsite coffee shop, though the quality of the mattresses varies. It's one of the best-value places in Old Manali.

Dragon Guest House   Hotel $$
(📞252290; www.dragontreks.com; Old Manali; r ₹550-1409, ste from ₹3288; ❄ @ 🛜) Dragon has a beautiful stone-and-wood facade and an orchard out front. All rooms are comfortable, though the better rooms are in the Swiss chalet–style upper floors. There's a great restaurant, an internet cafe, and a reliable travel agency for treks and tours.

🍴 Eating

Manali has some fine Indian and international restaurants, and there are lots of cheap travellers' cafes in Old Manali and Vashisht. Most restaurants serve trout sourced from local farms.

MANALI

Mayur   Indian, Multicuisine $$
(Mission Rd; dishes ₹90-210; 🕘9am-11pm) Locals rate Mayur highly for its well-prepared North and South Indian specialities. The decor downstairs is solidly old-school and classy, with impeccable uniformed waiters, while the upstairs is bright and contemporary. The Indian dishes are excellent and there are some refreshingly unusual Continental dishes including ratatouille, fish in coconut milk, and liver with onions and tomato.

Old Manali
ANDREW BAIN/GETTY IMAGES ©

Chopsticks
Asian $$

(The Mall; dishes ₹150-270; ⏱7.30am-10.30pm)
The most popular traveller choice in the
town centre, this intimate Tibetan-Chinese-
Japanese place has Tibetan lutes on the
walls and serves up good *momos* (dump-
lings) and *gyoza* (their Japanese equiva-
lent), plus sushi and lots of Chinese dishes.
Cold beers and fruit wines are also served.

Johnson's Cafe
Continental $$$

(Circuit House Rd; dishes ₹180-400; ⏱8am-
10.30pm) The restaurant at Johnson
Hotel is one of the best in town for
European food, with specialities such
as lamb and mint gravy, ravioli with
blue-cheese sauce, and fig and apple
crumble. The restaurant-bar is cosy
but the garden terrace is the place to
be, especially during afternoon happy
hours (2pm to 10pm).

OLD MANALI

All these places close by November.

Dylan's Toasted &
Roasted
Cafe $

(www.dylanscoffee.com; coffee ₹50-100;
⏱10am-8pm Mon-Sat) Manali's mel-
lowest hang-out, this hole-in-the-wall
coffeeshop serves the best espresso
in town, cinnamon tea, hearty breakfasts and wicked desserts including
choc-chip cookies and their version of
'Hello to the Queen', a local speciality
of ice cream and fried banana chunks
on a bed of broken biscuits. DVDs are
shown in an adjoining room.

People
Multicuisine $$

(mains ₹120-190) One of the best back-
packer places, serving up solid versions
of Thai curry, pizza, Israeli dishes,
fresh veggie salads and even sushi rolls
topped with grilled trout. The Russian
owner's roots are showing in the blinis
and *sirniki* fritters with condensed milk.
Get creative with the supplied crayons
and paper tablecloth and your artistic
expression will go up on the wall.

Pizza Olive
Italian $$

(pizza ₹170-190; ⏱9am-10pm) The aromas
wafting from the pizza oven give this
place an authentic Italian feel, and the

♥ **If You Like...**
Adventure
Activities

Manali is the adventure-sports capital of
Himachal Pradesh, and all sorts of outdoor
activities can be organised through tour
operators in town.

1 MOUNTAIN BIKING
Agencies offer bike hire for ₹500 to ₹850
per day (and can give current info on routes). One
audacious day trip is the freewheeling descent from
the Rohtang La – buses and taxis can transport you
and your bike to the pass. **Himalayan Extreme
Center** (☏9816174164; www.himalayan-extreme-
center.com; Manalsu Nala) offers this, as well as a
day's ride to Naggar and Kullu.

2 PARAGLIDING
Paragliding is popular at Solang Nullah and
at Gulaba (below the Rohtang Pass) from April
to October. Short flights start at ₹700 for a two-
minute flight, but adventure-tour operators can
organise longer flights from surrounding take-off
points for ₹1500 to ₹2500.

3 RAFTING
White-water rafting trips on the Beas River
start from Pirdi, 3km downriver from Kullu. There is
14km of Grade II and III white water between Pirdi
and the take-out point at Jhiri; trips cost between
₹350 and ₹550 per person, depending on the
duration. Book through travel agencies or directly
at Pirdi. May to July and late September are the
best times.

4 WALKING & TREKKING
Manali is a popular starting point for
organised mountain treks. Most agencies offer
multiday treks for around ₹2500 per day, all-
inclusive. Popular options include Beas Kund
(three days), the Pin-Parvati Trek from the Parvati
Valley to Spiti (eight days) and the Hamta Pass
(4270m) to Lahaul (four to five days). Plenty of
shorter walks are possible from Manali, though
the usual rules on safe trekking apply – tell
someone where you are going and never walk
alone.

pizzas and pasta dishes don't disappoint. You can eat in the sleek modern interior or out in the garden.

La Plage
French $$$

(☎9805340977; mains ₹280-450; ⊙noon-4pm & 7.30-10pm Tue-Sun) Head and shoulders above every other restaurant in town, dinner here is like being invited to the hip Paris apartment of your much, much cooler friend. Classic French standards such as liver pâté are joined by pumpkin ravioli and desserts including lime mousse and a chocolate thali selection, while the breakfasts are for serious aficionados. It's 1km from the old Manali bridge in an apple orchard, but call in advance and they'll pick you up in a customised tuk-tuk.

🍷 Drinking

Restaurants double as bars to form the centre of nightlife in Manali, and most serve alcohol. Himachal's bounteous orchards produce huge quantities of apples, pears, plums and apricots, some of which are fermented locally and made into alcoholic cider and perry (pear cider) and a wide range of strong fruit wines. In Manali town, the best places for a beer or fruit wine are **Khyber** (The Mall; dishes ₹80-280; ⊙8am-11pm) and Chopsticks (p363). The upmarket Johnson Hotel (p361), **Johnson Lodge** (☎251523; www.johnsonslodge.com; Circuit House Rd) and **Banon Resort** (☎253026; www.banonresortsmanali.com) also have good bars.

In Old Manali, **The Hangout** is popular for its outdoor firepits, though most traveller cafes serve beer.

ℹ️ Information

Banks in Manali don't offer foreign exchange but there are private moneychangers, and the State Bank of India has three international ATMs.

HPTDC Tourist Office (☎252116; The Mall; ⊙7am-8pm, 9am-5pm winter) Can book HPTDC buses and hotels.

Manali Civil Hospital (☎253385) Just south of town.

Tourist Office (☎253531; The Mall; ⊙8am-9pm, 10am-5pm Mon-Sat in winter) Helpful for brochures and local information. You can book

train tickets at the railway booking office (8am to 1.30pm Monday to Saturday) next door.

Trans Corp Forex (The Mall; ⊙10am-7pm) Changes cash and cheques.

ℹ️ Getting There & Away

Air

Manali's closest airport is 50km south at Bhuntar.

Bus

Government-run HRTC (www.hrtc.gov.in) buses are sold at the bus station. Luxury buses are run by the HPTDC and private operators. Tickets can be bought from their offices or from travel agencies thronging the Mall.

Delhi The most comfortable options for Delhi are the daily HPTDC buses; the AC Volvo coach leaves at 5.30pm (₹1220, 14 hours). Private travel agencies run similar overnight services starting at around ₹900. Government buses run regularly from the bus stand till midafternoon; the fare to Delhi is ₹512/880/1131 (ordinary/AC deluxe/AC Volvo). Deluxe buses depart at 5.45pm and 5.50pm; AC Volvos depart at 4pm.

Other Destinations In season, HPTDC runs a daily bus to Shimla (₹500, nine hours) at 8.30am and there are also early-morning and evening government buses (₹305 to ₹440). Private coaches run to Dharamsala/McLeod Ganj (₹450, 10 hours).

Taxi

A taxi to Bhuntar Airport, though the Him-Anchal Taxi Operators Union (☎252120; The Mall), costs ₹1100. To Dharamsala/McLeod Ganj expect to pay around ₹4000.

ℹ️ Getting Around

Autos run to Old Manali and Vashisht for ₹50. If you can't find an auto in the street, head to the Hadimba Auto Rickshaw Booking Office (☎253366; The Mall).

....

McLeod Ganj

☎01892 / ELEV 1770M

When travellers talk of heading up to Dharamsala (to see the Dalai Lama...), this is where they mean. Around 4km north of Dharamsala town – or 10km via the looping bus route – McLeod Ganj is the headquarters of the Tibetan govern-

McLeod Ganj

ment in exile and the residence of His Holiness the 14th Dalai Lama. Along with Manali, it's the big traveller hang-out in Himachal Pradesh, with many budget hotels, trekking companies, internet cafes, restaurants and shops selling Tibetan souvenirs crammed in just a couple of blocks, like a mini-Kathmandu. Naturally, there's a large Tibetan population here, many of whom are refugees, so you'll see plenty of maroon robes about, especially when the Dalai Lama is in residence.

◉ Sights

Tsuglagkhang Complex
Buddhist Temple

(Temple Rd, Central Chapel; ⏱5am-8pm) The main focus of visiting pilgrims, monks and many tourists is the Tsuglagkhang, comprising the *photrang* (official residence) of the Dalai Lama, the Namgyal Gompa,

Detour:
Norbulingka Institute

About 6km from Dharamsala, the wonderful **Norbulingka Institute** (☏01892-246405; www.norbulingka.org; ◷9am-5.30pm) FREE was established in 1988 to teach and preserve traditional Tibetan art forms, including woodcarving, statue-making, *thangka* painting and embroidery. The centre produces expensive but exquisite souvenirs, including embroidered clothes, cushions and wall hangings, and sales benefit refugee artists. Also here are delightful Japanese-influenced gardens and a central Buddhist temple with a 4m-high gilded statue of Sakyamuni.

Set in the gorgeous Norbulingka gardens, **Norling Guest House** (☏01892-246406; www.norbulingka.org; s/d ₹2220/2853, ste ₹3329-4280; ☏) offers fairy-tale rooms decked out with Buddhist murals and handicrafts from the Norbulingka Institute, and arranged around a sunny atrium. Meals are available at the institute's Norling Cafe.

Tibet Museum and the Tsuglagkhang itself.

The revered Tsuglagkhang is the exiles' concrete equivalent of the Jokhang Temple in Lhasa. Sacred to Avalokitesvara (Chenrezig in Tibetan), the Tibetan deity of compassion, it enshrines a 3m-high gilded statue of the Sakyamuni Buddha, flanked by Avalokitesvara and Padmasambhava, the Indian scholar who introduced Buddhism to Tibet. The Avalokitesvara statue contains several relics rescued from the Jokhang Temple during the Cultural Revolution.

Before visiting the main chapel, pilgrims first visit the **Kalachakra Temple** (Temple Rd), built in 1992, which contains mesmerising murals of the Kalachakra (Wheel of Time) mandala, specifically linked to Avalokitesvara, of whom the Dalai Lama is a manifestation.

The remaining buildings form the **Namgyal Gompa** (Namgyal Monastery; Temple Rd), where you can watch monks debate most afternoons (not Sunday), driving their points home with a theatrical clap of the hands.

Just inside the main entry gate is the **Tibet Museum** (admission ₹5; ◷9am-5pm Tue-Sun, closed 2nd and 4th Sat each month), telling the story of the Chinese occupation and the subsequent Tibetan exodus, through photographs, interviews and video clips. A visit here is a must. Documentaries (₹10) are shown daily at 3pm.

🏃 Activities

ALTERNATIVE THERAPIES, YOGA & MASSAGE

Holistic Ayurvedic Massage
Centre   Massage
(☏9418493871; Jogibara Rd, Ladies Venture Hotel; 30/60min ₹300/600; ◷9.30am-9pm) Resident masseur Shami gets rave reviews, so book ahead.

TREKKING

Regional Mountaineering
Centre   Trekking
(☏221787; ◷10am-5pm Mon-Sat) Uphill from the bus stand on the direct road to Dharamkot, this government-run organisation can arrange treks and adventure activities and offers courses and expeditions on set dates. It can also provide a list of registered guides and porters.

Walks   Walking
Short walks around McLeod include the 1.5km stroll to Bhagsu and the 2km uphill walk northeast to Dharamkot for uplifting

views south over the valley and north towards the Dhauladhar Ridge. Both walks follow the road but pass through lovely pine forest. You can do a loop to Bhagsu, visit the waterfall there, wind up and across to Dharamkot for lunch and then head back down to McLeod in a half-day walk.

About 4km northwest of McLeod Ganj on Mall Rd, the underwhelming Dal Lake is home to the **Tibetan Children's Village** (☏221348; www.tcv.org.in; ◷9.30am-5pm Mon-Fri), which provides free education for some 2000 refugee children. Visitors are welcome and there may be opportunities for volunteers. One good 45-minute hike is to walk above the school along forested hillside paths to the dirt road that runs from Galu Devi Temple back to Dharamkot.

🛏 Sleeping

Advance bookings are advised year-round, especially from April to June and October.

Om Hotel
Hotel **$**

(☏221313; omhotel@hotmail.com; Nowrojee Rd; d with/without bathroom ₹450/250) Conveniently located down a lane below the main square, the friendly family-run Om has simple but pleasing rooms with good views and the good Namgyal Restaurant, where the terrace catches the sunset over the valley. This might be the best deal in town; the main downside is that it's often full.

Green Hotel
Hotel **$$**

(☏221200; www.greenhotel.biz; Bhagsu Rd; r ₹880-2936; @ 🛜) A favourite with midrange travellers and groups, Green has a diverse range of sunny, stylish and super-clean rooms in two buildings, some with valley and mountain views. The pricier rooms have their own balconies. The busy lounge cafe feels like the hip place to be.

Hotel Tibet
Hotel **$$**

(☏221587; hoteltibetdasa@yahoo.com; Bhagsu Rd; r ₹660-1100; ✳) Bang in the centre of

Meeting the Dalai Lama

Meeting face to face with the Dalai Lama is a lifelong dream for many travellers and certainly for Buddhists, but private audiences are rarely granted. Tibetan refugees are automatically guaranteed an audience, but travellers must make do with the occasional public teachings held at the Tsuglagkhang during the monsoon (July/August), after Losar (Tibetan New Year) in February/March and on other occasions, depending on his schedule. For annual schedules and just about everything you need to know about His Holiness, check out www.dalailama.com. To attend, you have to register with your passport and two passport photographs, at the **Branch Security Office** (☏221560; Bhagsu Rd; ◷9am-1pm & 2-5pm Mon-Sat, closed 2nd & 4th Sat each month).

town, this place has the feel of an upmarket hotel yet it has almost budget prices. All rooms have TV and hot water and there's a cosy restaurant; credit cards accepted. Proceeds go to Tibetan settlements in India.

Chonor House
Boutique Hotel **$$$**

(☏221006; www.norbulingka.org; s/d from ₹3240/4086; ✳ @ 🛜) Hidden down a track off Hotel Bhagsu Rd, Chonor House is a real gem. It's run by the Norbulingka Institute, and rooms are decked out with its wonderful handicrafts and fabrics. Each of the bright and sunny 11 rooms has a Tibetan theme that runs from the bed-spreads to the murals on the walls. Even the cheapest rooms are spacious. There's also a lovely garden, with a reasonably priced terrace restaurant.

✖ Eating

Nick's Italian Kitchen   Italian $
(Bhagsu Rd; meals ₹50-100; ⏰7am-9pm; 📶)
At Kunga Guesthouse, Nick's is a well-run and unpretentious place has been serving up tasty vegetarian pizzas, lasagne and gnocchi for years. Follow up a ground coffee with a heavenly slice of lemon cheesecake – apparently Richard Gere's favourite when he stayed here. Eat inside or out on the sunny terrace.

Peace Cafe   Tibetan $
(Jogibara Rd; dishes ₹50-140; ⏰7.30am-9.30pm) This cosy little cafe below Takhyil Guest House is always full of monks chatting and dining on tasty Tibetan *momos*, *chow chow* (stir-fried noodles with vegetables or meat) and *thukpa*.

Tibet Kitchen   Tibetan $$
(Jogibara Rd; mains ₹90-150; ⏰noon-9.30pm) It's worth queueing here to get the opportunity to try spicy Bhutanese food including *kewa datse* (potatoes and cheese) and unusual Tibetan dishes like *shapta* (roasted lamb and onion) and *moktuk* (*momos* in soup). There are also Thai and Chinese flavours, from green curry to kung pao chicken. Even with three floors and a lounge on top, it's often full with a good mix of travellers, monks and locals.

McLlo Restaurant   Multicuisine $$
(Main Chowk; mains ₹150-250; ⏰10am-10pm)
Crowded nightly and justifiably popular, this big place above the noisy main square serves a mind-boggling menu of Indian, Chinese and international fare, including pizzas and grilled trout (₹320). It's also one of the best places to enjoy an icy cold beer (₹150) on the top-floor terrace.

Moonpeak Espresso
Multicuisine $

(www.moonpeak.org; Temple Rd; coffees & meals ₹50-170; ⏱7.30am-8pm; 🛜) A little chunk of Seattle, transported to India. Come for excellent coffee, cakes, imaginative sandwiches and dishes such as poached chicken with mango, lime and coriander sauce. Among the culinary highlights is the Himachali thali (₹200), a sampler of regional dishes.

⭐ Entertainment

Tibetan Music Trust Live Music
(☎9805661031; admission by donation) Performances of Tibetan folk music are held with varying regularity at Yongling School, off Jogibara Rd. The live shows feature demonstrations of traditional regional Tibetan instruments and song. It's a great cultural and educational experience.

ℹ️ Information

Medical Services

Delek Hospital (☎222053; Gangchen Kyishong; consultations ₹10; ⏱outpatient clinic 9am-1pm & 2-5pm)

Money

Several places around town offer Western Union money transfers.

State Bank of India (Temple Rd; ⏱10am-4pm Mon-Fri, to 1pm Sat) Has a busy international ATM.

Thomas Cook (Temple Rd; ⏱9.30am-6.30pm Mon-Fri, to 5pm Sat) Changes cash and travellers cheques for ₹60 commission and gives advance on credit cards for a 3% charge.

Tourist Information

HPTDC Tourist Office (☎221205; Hotel Bhagsu Rd; ⏱10am-5pm, closed Sun in Jul, Aug & Dec-Mar) Offers basic local information and can make bookings for HPTDC hotels and buses around Himachal.

Buses from McLeod Ganj

DESTINATION	FARE (₹)	DURATION (HR)	DEPARTURES
Dehra Dun	435	13	8pm
Delhi	450-1065	12	4am, 6pm & 7.30pm (ordinary); 5pm (semi-deluxe); 6.30pm & 7.45pm (deluxe); 7pm (Volvo)
Manali	300	11	4.30pm

Travel Agencies

Numerous travel agencies can book bus tickets, and can also arrange tours and treks.

Himachal Travels (☏221428; himachaltravels@sancharnet.in; Jogibara Rd)

Himalaya Tours & Travels (☏220714; www.himalayatravels.net; Bhagsu Rd)

ℹ Getting There & Around

Air

McLeod Ganj's nearest airport is at Gaggal, 15km southwest of Dharamsala. At the time of research no flights were operating but seasonal services to Delhi should resume eventually.

Autorickshaw

Autorickshaws are useful for getting around the immediate area – the autorickshaw stand is just north of the Main Chowk. Sample fares include Bhagsu (₹40), Dal Lake (₹80) and Dharamkot (₹60).

Bus

Book long-distance government buses in advance at the bus ticket office (◷10am-1.30pm & 2-4.30pm) in McLeod's Main Chowk. More frequent departures leave from lower Dharamsala bus station. Travel agencies can book seats on deluxe private buses to Delhi (₹700 to ₹1100, 12 hours, 6pm), Manali (₹550, 10 hours, 8pm) and other destinations.

Taxi

McLeod's taxi stand (☏221034) is on Mall Rd, north of the Main Chowk. To hire a taxi for the day, for a journey of less than 80km, expect to pay ₹2000.

One-way fares for short hops include Dharamsala bus station (₹200), Norbulingka Institute (₹400) and the airport at Gaggal (₹700).

Shawl stall, McLeod Ganj

PUNJAB

Amritsar

📞0183 / POP 1.13 MILLION

Founded in 1577 by the fourth Sikh guru, Ram Das, Amritsar is home to Sikhism's holiest shrine, the spectacular Golden Temple, one of India's most serene and humbling sights. Alas, the same can't be said for the hyperactive streets surrounding the temple – few places can compete with Amritsar when it comes to congestion, air pollution and traffic noise.

Sights

Jallianwala Bagh　　　Historic Site
(Golden Temple Rd; ⏱6am-9pm summer, 7am-8pm winter) Reached through a gatehouse on the road to the Golden Temple, this poignant park commemorates the 1500 Indians killed or wounded when a British officer ordered his soldiers to shoot on unarmed protesters in 1919.

🧭 Tours

The Grand Hotel runs good-value day tours of the main sights (₹350) and night tours to the Attari–Wagah border-closing ceremony, Mata Temple and Golden Temple from ₹580 per person.

The tourist office runs two-hour Heritage Walks (Indian/foreigner ₹25/75) starting from the old Town Hall at 8am daily (9am December to February). The tour visits gurdwaras, bazaars and historic buildings.

🛏 Sleeping

Grand Hotel　　　Hotel $$
(📞2562424; www.hotelgrand.in; Queen's Rd; r from ₹1426; ❄@🛜) Across the road from the train station, but far from grungy, the Grand is the top choice for budget travellers. Rooms are spacious, if not exactly grand, and the hotel has a recommended restaurant with seating overlooking the courtyard garden. Drop into the genuinely inviting bar – the cheerfully named Bot-

> ### Golden Temple Etiquette
>
> Before entering the compound, remove your shoes and socks – there are *chappal* (sandal) stands at the entrances – wash your feet in the shallow footbaths and cover your head; scarves can be borrowed (no charge) or hawkers sell souvenir scarves for ₹10. Tobacco and alcohol are strictly prohibited. If you want to sit beside the tank, sit cross-legged and do not dangle your feet in the water. Photography is only permitted from the walkway surrounding the pool. There's an information office near the main entrance.

toms Up. The owner runs recommended tours.

**Mrs Bhandari's
Guest House**　　　Guesthouse $$
(📞2228509; http://bhandari_guesthouse.tripod.com; 10 Cantonment; camping per person ₹200, s/d from ₹1846/2316, with AC ₹2424/2886; ❄@🛜🏊) Founded by the much-missed Mrs Bhandari (1906–2007), this friendly guesthouse is set in spacious grounds in the Amritsar cantonment, about 2km from the centre. The sprawling rooms have a hint of colonial bungalow about them, but the welcome is warm, and over-landers can set up camp in the gardens (₹100 per vehicle, plus camping fees). Pick-up is free from the train station and meals are available (breakfast/lunch/dinner ₹330/475/575).

Hotel Indus　　　Hotel $$
(📞2535900; www.hotelindus.com; 211-13 Sri Hamandir Sahib Marg; r from ₹1846; ❄@🛜) The dramatic million-dollar view of the Golden Temple from the rooftop is reason enough to stay at this modern-style hotel. Rooms are compact but comfy – book well ahead

Don't Miss
Golden Temple

Sikhism's holiest shrine, this gold-plated gurdwara glitters in the middle of its holy pool like a fantastical gold bullion bar; it's a sight some travellers rate as up there with seeing the Taj Mahal. And true to Sikhism's inclusive nature, all are welcome here, making the atmosphere incredibly friendly as well as genuinely spiritual.

information office 2553954

dawn-around 10pm, information office 8am-7pm

Amrit Sarovar

The Golden Temple is actually just a small part of this huge gurdwara complex, known to Sikhs as Harmandir Sahib (or Darbar Sahib).

Spiritually, the focus of attention is the tank – the **Amrit Sarovar** (Pool of Nectar), from which Amritsar takes its name, excavated by the fourth guru Ram Das in 1577. Ringed by a marble walkway, the tank is said to have healing powers, and pilgrims come from across the world to bathe in the sacred waters.

Golden Temple

Floating at the end of a long causeway, the Golden Temple itself is a mesmerising blend of Hindu and Islamic architectural styles, with an elegant marble lower level adorned with flower and animal motifs in pietra dura work (as seen on the Taj Mahal). Above this rises a shimmering second level, encased in intricately engraved gold panels, and topped by a dome gilded with 750kg of gold. In the gleaming inner sanctum (photos prohibited), priests and musicians keep up a continuous chant from the Guru Granth Sahib, the Sikh holy book, adding to the already intense atmosphere.

The Guru Granth Sahib is installed in the temple every morning and returned at night to the **Akal Takht** (Timeless Throne), the temporal seat of the Khalsa brotherhood. The building was heavily damaged when it was stormed by the Indian army during Operation Blue Star in 1984; it was repaired by the government but Sikhs refused to use the tainted building and rebuilt the tower from scratch.

More shrines and monuments are dotted around the edge of the compound. Inside the main entrance clock tower, the **Central Sikh Museum** (admission free; ⏱7am-7pm summer, 8am-6pm winter) shows the persecution suffered by the Sikhs at the hands of Mughals, the British and Indira Gandhi.

Golden Temple Don't Miss List

SHIREEN KUMAR IS A TEACHER, LOCAL CULTURE ENTHUSIAST AND UNOFFICIAL GUIDE TO THE TEMPLE

1 THE MAIN SHRINE
A confection of white marble, gilded frescoes and ornate domes, the main shrine has three storeys. Under a canopy studded with jewels on the ground floor is the Guru Granth Sahib, the holy book of the Sikhs. Beginning early in the morning and lasting until long past sunset, hymns are chanted to the exquisite accompaniment of flutes, drums and stringed instruments.

2 PALKI SAHIB
The Palki Sahib ceremony takes place twice a day where the Guru Granth Sahib is reverently brought to the temple in a decorative palanquin at around 4am, and is taken back to the Akal Takht at 9.30pm amid rousing devotion and thronging devotees. Check ahead regarding the timings, as these vary according to the season.

3 PILGRIMS' LUNCH
Langar (meal) preparation takes place in the community kitchen, where all persons, irrespective of race, religion or gender, perform a voluntary selfless service (*sewa*), serving food to the 35,000 pilgrims who visit the temple each day. The kitchen contains elaborate machines that make up to 6000 chapatis per hour. This is the busiest section of the temple and remains open 24/7. It symbolises the Sikh principle of inclusiveness and oneness of humankind.

4 AKAL TAKHT
Akal Takht is the highest Sikh religious authority, located in the Harmandir Sahib. It is decorated with inlaid marble, gold-leafed domes and wall paintings. The Guru Granth Sahib is kept in the Akal Takht at night. From around 6.30pm to 7.30pm every day, historic weapons are also on display here.

5 THE CENTRAL SIKH MUSEUM
The Central Sikh Museum is on the 2nd floor of the temple's main entrance, and has fascinating galleries displaying artefacts, coins, weapons, images and remembrances of Sikh gurus, warriors and saints. Details are also given in English.

Kulcha (filled parathas)

UNIQUELY INDIA/GETTY IMAGES ©

to secure one of the two rooms with temple vistas!

Country Inn & Suites   Hotel $$$
(☎5050555; www.countryinns.com; Queen's Rd; s/d from ₹5445/6655, ste ₹10,285; ❈@☎☎) A scent of lemongrass wafts around the lobby of this sleek new addition to the Amritsar skyline. Rooms are stylish and comfortable; the suites with water-spouting spa baths for two are positively opulent. The rooftop pool is a great place to watch the sunset.

🍴 Eating

Amritsar is famous for its *dhabas* (snack bars) serving such Punjabi treats as *kulcha* (filled parathas) and 'Amritsari' fish (deep-fried fish with lemon, chilli, garlic and ginger). Hotels and restaurants in the Golden Temple area don't serve alcohol.

Brothers' Dhaba   Punjabi $
(Town Hall Chowk; dishes ₹45-145; ☻7.30am-12.30pm) This fast and friendly *dhaba* serves Amritsar's tastiest *kulcha*, Punjabi-style *parathas* with herbs, potato and pomegranate seeds that pop in the mouth as tiny explosions of sweetness.

Kesar Da Dhaba   Punjabi $
(Chowk Passian; dishes ₹10-190; ☻11am-11pm) Devilishly hard to find (ask for directions in the old city), this takeway and *dhaba* serves delicious *paratha* thalis (₹140 to ₹190) and silver-leaf topped *firni* (ground rice pudding).

Crystal Restaurant   Multicuisine $$
(☎2225555; Crystal Chowk; mains ₹250-410; ☻11am-11.30pm) This ground-floor restaurant has a fin de siècle air, with mirror-lined walls and ornate stucco trim. The multicuisine menu is dominated by Mughlai favourites – the house speciality is delicious *mugh tawa frontier* (morsels of chicken in a dense onion gravy).

Thai Chi   Asian $$$
(☎2708888; Ista Hotel, GT Rd; mains ₹325-1150; ☻7.30-11.30pm Wed-Mon) A strong contender for the title of Amritsar's best restaurant, serving Chinese and Thai food in upmarket surroundings. Dishes are expertly spiced; dress to impress and make reservations for dinner.

ℹ️ Information

Internet Access

Wi-fi is widely available at Amritsar hotels.

Guru Arjun Dev Niwas Net Cafe (Guru Arjun Dev Niwas; per hr ₹25; ⊘24hr) Handy net cafe in the gurdwara complex.

Medical Services

Fortis Escorts Hospital (☑9915133330; www.fortishealthcare.com; Majitha Verka Bypass)

Money

Amritsar has an ever-mushrooming supply of ATMs, including one at the train station. Banks with foreign exchange facilities are scattered along the Mall and Queen's Rd.

HDFC Golden Temple branch (⊘9.30am-3.30pm Mon-Fri, to 12.30pm Sat) Exchanges travellers cheques and currencies; has an ATM.

Tourist Information

Tourist Office (☑2402452; www.punjabtourism.gov.in; Train station exit, Queen's Rd; ⊘9am-5pm Tue-Sun)

ℹ️ Getting There & Away

Air

About 11km northwest of the centre, Amritsar's Sri Guru Ram Dass Jee International Airport services domestic and international flights. One-way flights to Delhi/Mumbai cost around ₹3150/6170.

Bus

Private bus companies operate from near Gandhi Gate, and from Cooper Rd, near the train station.

Air-con buses run to Delhi (₹350 to ₹700, 10 hours) and Jaipur (₹600 to ₹700, 13 hours).

The main **Inter State Bus Terminal (ISBT)** is on GT Rd about 2km north of the Golden Temple near Mahan Singh Gate. There is at least one daily bus to Dharamsala (₹193, six hours) and Manali (₹456, 14 hours), plus frequent buses to Delhi (non-AC/AC ₹365/846, 10 hours).

Train

Apart from the train station, there's a less busy **train reservation office** (⊘8am-8pm, to 2pm Sun) at the Golden Temple.

The fastest train to Delhi is the twice-daily Shatabdi Express (chair car/executive ₹591/1305, 5¾ hours). Trains leave Amritsar at 5am and 4.55pm; from New Delhi railway station, trains leave at 7.20am and 4.30pm.

The daily Amritsar–Howrah Mail links Amritsar with Varanasi (sleeper/3AC/2AC ₹363/1028/1600, 22 hours) and Howrah (₹481/1370/2190, 37 hours).

ℹ️ Getting Around

Free (and jam-packed) yellow minibuses run from the train station and the bus stand to the Golden Temple from 4.30am to 9.30pm. Otherwise, from the train station to the Golden Temple, a rickshaw/autorickshaw will cost around ₹50/70 but you'll have to haggle like fury for a fair price. Taxis loiter around at the station, or there's a **prepaid booth** (☑9888561615) at the southeast entrance to the Golden Temple. To the airport, an autorickshaw costs ₹200 and a taxi ₹450 to ₹600.

India

In Focus

Women in colourful saris, Jaipur
ANDREW PEACOCK/GETTY IMAGES ©

India Today

belief systems
(% of population)

Chandni Chowk (p67), Delhi

> *With so many states, languages, cultures, religions, traditions, opinions and people, India always has a lot going on.*

belief systems
(% of population)

80	14	2	2	1	1
Hindu	Muslim	Christian	Sikh	Buddhist	Other

if India were 100 people

55 would speak one of 21 other official languages

41 would speak Hindi

4 would speak one of 400 other languages

population per sq km

👤 ≈ 30 people

India   China   USA

With so many states, languages, cultures, religions, traditions, opinions and people – so many people! – India always has a lot going on. The political, economic and social systems of the world's largest democracy are complex, and they don't always work. Conflicts with Pakistan have been obstacles to progress, as has violence at home, between religious groups and against women. But Indians are looking for change – and moving ever closer towards it.

The Kashmir Impasse

Recent border skirmishes, the worst in a decade, killed three Pakistanis and two Indian soldiers, one of whom was beheaded, but it was only the latest in a long series of tragic events in the Kashmir region. The predominantly Muslim Kashmir Valley is claimed by India and Pakistan (as well as the much less powerful Kashmiris themselves), and the impasse has plagued relations between the two countries since Partition in 1947. Three India–Pakistan wars – in 1947, 1965 and

Congress Today & the Economy

When the Congress Party regained power in 2004, it was under the leadership of Sonia Gandhi – the Italian-born wife of the late Rajiv Gandhi, who served as prime minister from 1984 to 1989. The BJP's planned national agitation campaign against Sonia Gandhi's foreign origins was subverted when she stepped aside to allow Manmohan Singh to be sworn in as prime minister.

In 1991, Singh, then finance minister, floated the rupee against a basket of 'hard' currencies. State subsidies were phased out and the economy was opened up to foreign investment. India became the world's second-fastest growing economy (after China). But in recent years, that growth has dropped off, the rupee has slumped and inflation has soared.

RICHARD I'ANSON/GETTY IMAGES ©

1971 – resolved little, and by 1989 Kashmir had its own Pakistan-backed armed insurgency.

Talks that might have created an autonomous region were derailed in 2008, when terrorists killed at least 163 people at 10 sites around Mumbai (Bombay) during three days of coordinated bombings and shootings.

Communal Tension

While Kashmir is the site of India's most persistent conflict, religion-based confrontation further south may be its most insidious. One of the most violent episodes occurred in 1992, when Hindu extremists destroyed a mosque, the Babri Masjid, in Ayodhya, Uttar Pradesh, revered by Hindus as the birthplace of Rama. The Hindu-revivalist BJP, then the main opposition party, did little to discourage the acts, and rioting in the north killed thousands.

Violence Against Women

In December 2012, a 23-year-old physiotherapy student and her male friend boarded a bus on their way home from the movies in Delhi only to find that it was a fake city bus, with blackened windows, where six men awaited them. The men beat the two friends, and raped the woman so brutally that she died 12 days later. The woman became known in India as Nirbhaya, or 'fearless one', and the event set off massive protests and soul-searching nationwide. Many in India are also now reflecting on other abuses of women (tens of thousands die over dowry disputes alone each year), widespread police and justice-system mishandling of cases (of the more than 600 reported rapes in Delhi in 2012, just one resulted in a conviction), and the larger problems of gender inequality. The situation for women's rights isn't good, but many are hopeful that, now that the issues are out in the open, change will follow.

379

History

Deities at a flower stand, Delhi

GRANT FAINT/GETTY IMA

Through thousands of years of great civilisations, invasions, the birth of religions and countless cataclysms, the irresistible story of India's long history has proved itself to be one of the world's great epics. From Brahmanical empires and Hindu-Buddhist dynasties through to Islamic sultanates, the British Raj and beyond, India's history has always been a work in progress; a constant process of reinvention and accumulation that is helping to shape one of the most vibrant, diverse and dynamic nations on earth.

Indus Valley Civilisation

The Indus Valley, straddling the modern India–Pakistan border, is the cradle of civilisation on the Indian subcontinent. The first inhabitants of this region were nomadic tribes who cultivated land and kept domestic animals. Over thousands of years, an urban culture began to emerge from these tribes, particularly from 3500 BC. By 2500 BC large cities were well established, the focal points

10,000 BC

Stone Age paintings first made in the Bhimbetka rock shelters, in what is now Madhya Pradesh.

of what became known as the Harappan culture, which would flourish for more than 1000 years.

Early Invasions & the Rise of Religions

The Harappan civilisation fell into decline from the beginning of the 2nd millennium BC. Some historians attribute the end of the empire to floods or decreased rainfall, which threatened the Harappans' agricultural base. The more enduring, if contentious, theory is that an Aryan invasion put paid to the Harappans, despite little archaeological proof or written reports in the ancient Indian texts to that effect. As a result, some nationalist historians argue that the Aryans (from a Sanskrit word meaning 'noble') were in fact the original inhabitants of India and that the invasion theory was actually invented by self-serving foreign conquerors. Others say that the arrival of Aryans was more of a gentle migration that gradually subsumed Harappan culture.

Those who defend the invasion theory believe that from around 1500 BC Aryan tribes from Afghanistan and Central Asia began to filter into northwest India. Many of the original inhabitants of northern India, the Dravidians, were pushed south.

The Hindu sacred scriptures, the Vedas, were written during this period of transition (1500–1200 BC), and the caste system became formalised.

As the Aryan tribes spread across the Ganges plain in the late 7th century BC, many were absorbed into 16 major kingdoms, which were, in turn, amalgamated into four large states.

The Best...
Ancient
Cities

1 Qutb Minar (p75)

2 Fatehpur Sikri (p101)

3 Old Delhi (p60)

The Mauryan Empire & its Aftermath

If the Harappan culture was the cradle of Indian civilisation, Chandragupta Maurya was the founder of the first great Indian empire. He came to power in 321 BC and soon expanded the empire to include the Indus Valley.

From its capital at Pataliputra (modern-day Patna), the Mauryan empire encompassed much of North and South India. The empire reached its peak under the emperor Ashoka. Such was Ashoka's power to lead and unite that after his death in 232 BC the empire rapidly disintegrated, collapsing altogether in 184 BC.

None of the empires that immediately followed could match the stability or enduring historical legacy of the Mauryans. Despite the multiplicity of ruling powers,

---

2600–1700 BC
The heyday of the Indus Valley civilisation, spanning parts of Rajasthan, Gujarat and the Sindh province in present-day Pakistan.

1000 BC
Indraprastha, Delhi's first incarnation, is founded. Archaeological excavations at the Purana Qila continue even today.

321–185 BC
The pan-Indian Maurya empire briefly adopts Buddhism during the reign of Emperor Ashoka.

this was a period of intense development. Trade with the Roman Empire (overland, and by sea through the southern ports) became substantial during the 1st century AD; there was also overland trade with China.

The Golden Age of the Guptas

Throughout the subcontinent, small tribes and kingdoms effectively controlled territory and dominated local affairs. In AD 319 Chandragupta I, the third king of one of these tribes, the little-known Guptas, came to prominence. Poetry, literature and the arts flourished, with some of the finest work done at Ajanta, Ellora and Sarnath. Towards the end of the Gupta period, Hinduism became the dominant religious force, and its revival eclipsed Jainism and Buddhism; the latter in particular went into decline in India and would never again be India's dominant religion. The invasions of the Huns at the beginning of the 6th century signalled the end of this era.

The Hindu South

Southern India has always laid claim to its own unique history. Insulated by distance from the political developments in the north, a separate set of powerful kingdoms emerged, among them the Satavahanas, who ruled over central India for about 400 years. But it was from the tribal territories on the fertile coastal plains that the greatest southern empires – the Cholas, Pandyas, Chalukyas, Cheras and Pallavas – came into their own.

The south's prosperity was based on long-established trading links with other civilisations, among them the Egyptians and Romans. In 850 the Cholas rose to power and superseded the Pallavas, who had ruled since the 4th century. They soon set about turning the south's far-reaching trade influence into territorial conquest.

The Muslim North

While South India guarded its resolutely Hindu character, North India was convulsed by Muslim armies invading from the northwest.

At the vanguard of Islamic expansion was Mahmud of Ghazni. Today, Ghazni is a nondescript little town between Kabul and Kandahar in Afghanistan. But in the early years of the 11th century, Mahmud turned it into one of the world's most glorious capital cities, which he largely funded by plundering his neighbours' territories. From 1001 to 1025, Mahmud conducted 17 raids into India, effectively shifting the balance of power in North India.

Following Mahmud's death in 1033, Ghazni was seized by the Seljuqs and then fell to the Ghurs of western Afghanistan, who similarly had their eyes on the great Indian prize. The Ghur style of warfare was brutal: the Ghur general Ala-ud-din was known as 'Burner of the World'.

AD 52
St Thomas the Apostle thought to have arrived in Kerala to bring Christianity to India through his preaching.

319–510
The golden era of the Gupta dynasty, marked by a creative surge in literature and the arts.

KAREN TRIST/GETTY IMAGES ©

In 1191 Mohammed of Ghur advanced into India. Although defeated in a major battle against a confederacy of Hindu rulers, he returned the following year and routed his enemies. One of his generals, Qutb ud-din Aibak, captured Delhi and was appointed governor; it was during his reign that the great Delhi landmark, the Qutb Minar complex, was built. A separate Islamic empire was established in Bengal and within a short time almost the whole of North India was under Muslim control.

The Best...
Mughal Sites

1 Taj Mahal (p95)

2 Fatehpur Sikri (p101)

3 Agra Fort (p93)

4 Red Fort (p60)

5 Humayun's tomb (p69)

IN FOCUS HISTORY

North Meets South

Mohammed Tughlaq ascended the throne in 1324. In 1328 Tughlaq took the southern strongholds of the Hoysala empire. India was Tughlaq's for the taking. However, while the empire of the pre-Mughal Muslims would achieve its greatest extent under Tughlaq's rule, his overreaching ambition also sowed the seeds of its disintegration.

The last of the great sultans of Delhi, Firoz Shah, died in 1388, and the fate of the sultanate was sealed when Timur (Tamerlane) made a devastating raid from Samarkand (in Central Asia) into India in 1398.

After Tughlaq's withdrawal from the south, several splinter kingdoms arose. The two most significant were the Islamic Bahmani sultanate, and the Hindu Vijayanagar empire, founded in 1336 with its capital at Hampi. The battles between the two were among the bloodiest communal violence in Indian history and ultimately resolved nothing in the two centuries before the Mughals rose to power.

The Mughals

Even as Vijayanagar was experiencing its last days, the next great Indian empire was being founded. The Mughal empire was massive, at its height covering almost the entire subcontinent. Its significance, however, lay not only in its size. Mughal emperors presided over a golden age of arts and literature and had a passion for building that resulted in some of the finest architecture in India.

The founder of the Mughal line, Babur, marched into Punjab in 1525 from his capital at Kabul. With technological superiority brought by firearms, and consummate skill in simultaneously employing artillery and cavalry, Babur defeated the numerically superior armies of the sultan of Delhi at the Battle of Panipat in 1526.

4th to 9th centuries
The Pallavas, known for their temple architecture, enter the shifting landscape of southern power centres.

7th century
The new religion of Islam spreads to India through Arab merchants and traders visiting the Keralan coast.

1192
Prithviraj Chauhan loses Delhi to Mohammed of Ghur. The defeat effectively ends Hindu supremacy in the region.

Jehangir (r 1605–27) ascended to the throne following Emperor Akbar's death. Despite several challenges to the authority of Jehangir himself, the now-mammoth empire remained more or less intact. He was succeeded by his son, Shah Jahan (r 1627–58), who secured his position as emperor by executing all male relatives who stood in his way. During his reign, some of the most vivid and permanent reminders of the Mughals' glory were constructed, including the Taj Mahal and Delhi's Red Fort.

The last of the great Mughals, Aurangzeb (r 1658–1707), imprisoned his father (Shah Jahan) and succeeded to the throne after a two-year struggle against his brothers. Aurangzeb devoted his resources to extending the empire's boundaries, and thus fell into much the same trap as that of Mohammed Tughlaq some 300 years earlier. He, too, tried moving his capital south (to Aurangabad) and imposed heavy taxes to fund his military. A combination of decaying court life and dissatisfaction among the Hindu population at inflated taxes and religious intolerance weakened the Mughal grip.

The empire was also facing serious challenges from the Marathas in central India and, more significantly, the British in Bengal. With Aurangzeb's death in 1707, the empire's fortunes rapidly declined.

Trinket sellers outside Jama Masjid (p101), Fatehpur Sikri

1325
Mohammed bin Tughlaq becomes sultan of Delhi, moves the capital to Daulatabad and creates forgery-prone currency.

1336
Foundation of the mighty Vijayanagar empire, named after its capital city, the ruins of which can be seen today close to Hampi.

1398
Timur (Tamerlane) invades Delhi with extreme violence, on the pretext that the Delhi sultans are too tolerant with their Hindu subjects.

The Rajputs & the Marathas

Throughout the Mughal period, there remained strong Hindu powers, most notably the Rajputs. Centred in Rajasthan, the Rajputs were a proud warrior caste with a passionate belief in the dictates of chivalry, both in battle and in state affairs. The Rajputs opposed every foreign incursion into their territory, but were never united or adequately organised to deal with stronger forces on a long-term basis. This eventually led to their territories becoming vassal states of the Mughal empire. Their prowess in battle, however, was acknowledged, and some of the best military men in the Mughal armies were Rajputs.

The Marathas were less swashbuckling but ultimately more effective. They gradually took over more of the weakening Mughal empire's powers, first by supplying troops and then actually taking control of Mughal land, but this expansion came to an abrupt halt in 1761 at Panipat, when they were defeated by Ahmad Shah Durani from Afghanistan.

The Rise of European Power

The British weren't the first European power to arrive in India, nor were they the last to leave – both of those 'honours' go to the Portuguese. In 1498 Vasco da Gama arrived on the coast of modern-day Kerala, having sailed around the Cape of Good Hope. Pioneering this route gave the Portuguese a century-long monopoly over Indian and far-eastern trade with Europe. In 1510 they captured Goa, which they controlled until 1961.

In 1600 Queen Elizabeth I granted a charter to a London trading company that gave it a monopoly on British trade with India. In 1613 representatives of the East India Company established their first trading post in northwest India.

By 1672 the French had established themselves at Pondicherry (now Puducherry), an enclave they held even after the British departed and where architectural traces of French elegance remain. But serious French aspirations effectively ended in 1750 when the directors of the French East India Company decided that their representatives were playing too much politics and doing too little trading. Key representatives were sacked, and a settlement designed to end all ongoing political disputes was made with the British. The decision effectively removed France as a serious influence on the subcontinent.

Britain's Surge to Power

The transformation of the British from traders to governors began almost by accident. Having been granted a licence to trade in Bengal by the Mughals, and following the establishment of a new trading post at Calcutta (now Kolkata) in 1690, business began to expand rapidly. Under the apprehensive gaze of the nawab (local ruler), British trading activities became extensive and the 'factories' took on an increasingly permanent (and fortified) appearance.

1498
Vasco da Gama, a Portuguese voyager, discovers the sea route from Europe to India.

1510
Portuguese forces capture Goa under the command of Alfonso de Albuquerque.

1526
Babur becomes the first Mughal emperor after conquering Delhi. He stuns Rajasthan by routing its confederate force.

Eventually the nawab decided that British power had grown large enough. In June 1756 he attacked Calcutta and, having taken the city, locked his British prisoners in a tiny cell. The space was so cramped and airless that many were dead by the following morning. The cell infamously became known as the 'Black Hole of Calcutta'.

Six months later, Robert Clive, an employee in the military service of the East India Company, led an expedition to retake Calcutta and entered into an agreement with one of the nawab's generals to overthrow the nawab himself. He did this in June 1757 at the Battle of Plassey (now called Palashi), and the general who had assisted him was placed on the throne.

The Best...
Colonial-era
Architecture

British India

By the early 19th century, India was effectively under British control, although there remained a patchwork of states who administered their own territories. However, a system of central government was developed. British bureaucratic models were replicated in the Indian government and civil service – a legacy that still exists.

Trade and profit continued to be the main focus of British rule in India, with far-reaching effects. Iron and coal mining were developed, and tea, coffee and cotton became key crops. A start was made on the vast rail network that's still in use today, irrigation projects were undertaken, and the zamindar (landowner) system was encouraged. These absentee landlords eased the burden of administration and tax collection for the British but contributed to the development of an impoverished and landless peasantry.

The Road to Independence

The desire among many Indians to be free from foreign rule remained. Opposition to the British increased at the turn of the 20th century, spearheaded by the Indian National Congress, the country's oldest political party.

It met for the first time in 1885 and soon began to push for participation in the government of India. A highly unpopular attempt by the British to partition Bengal in 1905 resulted in mass demonstrations and brought to light Hindu opposition to the division; the Muslim community formed its own league and campaigned for protected rights in any future political settlement.

1540
The Sur dynasty briefly captures Delhi from the Mughals, after Sher Shah Suri's Battle of Kanauj victory over Humayun.

1556
Hemu, a Hindu general in Adil Shah Suri's army, seizes Delhi after Humayun's death.

RICHARD I'ANSON/GETTY IMAGES ©

With the outbreak of WWI, the political situation eased. India contributed hugely to the war (more than one million Indian volunteers were enlisted and sent overseas, suffering more than 100,000 casualties). The contribution was sanctioned by Congress leaders, largely with the expectation that it would be rewarded after the war. No such rewards transpired. Disturbances were particularly persistent in Punjab, and in April 1919, following riots in Amritsar, a British army contingent was sent to quell the unrest. Under direct orders of the officer in charge, they ruthlessly fired into a crowd of unarmed protesters. News of the massacre spread rapidly throughout India, turning huge numbers of otherwise apolitical Indians into Congress supporters.

At this time, the Congress movement found a new leader in Mohandas Gandhi. As political power-sharing began to look more likely, and the mass movement led by Gandhi gained momentum, the Muslim community's reaction was to consider its own immediate future. The large Muslim minority realised that an independent India would be dominated by Hindus and that, while Gandhi's approach was fair-minded, others in the Congress Party might not be so willing to share power. By the 1930s Muslims were raising the possibility of a separate Islamic state.

Humayan's Tomb (p69), Delhi

1674
Shivaji establishes the Maratha kingdom, spanning western India and parts of the Deccan and North India.

1707
Death of Aurangzeb, the last of the Mughal greats. His demise triggers the gradual collapse of the Mughal empire.

1747
Afghan ruler Ahmad Shah Durani sweeps across northern India, capturing Lahore and Kashmir and sacking Delhi.

Independence & the Partition of India

The Labour Party victory in the British elections in July 1945 dramatically altered the political landscape. For the first time, Indian independence was accepted as a legitimate goal. This new goodwill did not, however, translate into any new wisdom as to how to reconcile the divergent wishes of the two major Indian parties. Mohammed Ali Jinnah, the leader of the Muslim League, championed a separate Islamic state, while the Congress Party, led by Jawaharlal Nehru, campaigned for an independent greater India.

In early 1946 a British mission failed to bring the two sides together, and the country slid closer towards civil war. In February 1947 the nervous British government made the momentous decision that independence would be effected by June 1948. In the meantime, the viceroy, Lord Wavell, was replaced by Lord Louis Mountbatten.

The new viceroy encouraged the rival factions to agree upon a united India, but to no avail. A decision was made to divide the country, with Gandhi the only staunch opponent. Faced with increasing civil violence, Mountbatten made the precipitous decision to bring forward Independence to 15 August 1947.

Dividing the country into separate Hindu and Muslim territories was immensely difficult; the dividing line proved almost impossible to draw. Some areas were clearly Hindu or Muslim, but others had evenly mixed populations, and there were 'islands' of communities in areas predominantly settled by other religions. Moreover, the two overwhelmingly Muslim regions were on opposite sides of the country and, therefore, Pakistan would inevitably have an eastern and western half, divided by India. The instability of this arrangement was self-evident, but it was 25 years before the split finally came and East Pakistan became Bangladesh.

The problem was worse in Punjab, where intercommunity antagonisms were already running at fever pitch. Punjab, one of the most fertile and affluent regions of the country, had large Muslim, Hindu and Sikh communities. The Sikhs had already campaigned unsuccessfully for their own state and now saw their homeland divided down the middle. The new border ran straight between Punjab's two major cities, Lahore and Amritsar.

Punjab contained all the ingredients for an epic disaster, but the resulting bloodshed was far worse than anticipated. Huge population exchanges took place. Trains full of Muslims, fleeing westward, were held up and slaughtered by Hindu and Sikh mobs. Hindus and Sikhs fleeing to the east suffered the same fate at Muslim hands. The army that was sent to maintain order proved inadequate and, at times, all too ready to join the sectarian carnage. By the time the Punjab chaos had run its course, more than 10 million people had changed sides and at least 500,000 had been killed.

India and Pakistan became sovereign nations under the British Commonwealth in August 1947 as planned, but the violence, migrations and the integration of a few states, especially Kashmir, continued. The Constitution of India was at last adopted

1757
The East India Company registers its first military victory on Indian soil in the Battle of Plassey.

1857
First War of Independence against the British; freedom fighters coerce the Mughal king to proclaim himself emperor of India.

1858
The British government assumes control over India, beginning the period known as the British Raj.

The Kashmir Conflict

Kashmir is the most enduring symbol of the turbulent partition of India. In the lead-up to Independence, local rulers were asked which country they wished to belong to. Kashmir was a predominantly Muslim state with a Hindu maharaja, Hari Singh, who tried to delay his decision. A ragtag Pashtun (Pakistani) army crossed the border, intent on annexing Kashmir for Pakistan, whereupon the maharaja panicked and requested armed assistance from India. The Indian army arrived only just in time to prevent the fall of Srinagar, and the maharaja signed the Instrument of Accession, tying Kashmir to India, in October 1947. The legality of the document was immediately contested by Pakistan, and the two nations went to war, just two months after Independence.

In 1948 the fledgling UN Security Council called for a referendum to decide the status of Kashmir. A UN-brokered ceasefire in 1949 kept the countries on either side of a demarcation line, called the Cease-Fire Line (later to become the Line of Control, or LOC), with little else resolved. Two-thirds of Kashmir fell on the Indian side of the LOC, which remains the frontier, but neither side accepts this as the official border.

in November 1949 and came into effect on 26 January 1950. After untold struggles, independent India had officially become a republic.

After Independence

Jawaharlal Nehru tried to steer India towards a policy of nonalignment, balancing cordial relations with Britain and Commonwealth membership with moves towards the former USSR. The latter was due partly to conflicts with China, and US support for its arch-enemy Pakistan.

The 1960s and 1970s were tumultuous times for India. A border war with China in what was then known as the North-East Frontier Area (NEFA; now the Northeast States) and Ladakh, resulted in the loss of Aksai Chin (Ladakh) and smaller NEFA areas. Wars with Pakistan in 1965 (over Kashmir) and 1971 (over Bangladesh) also contributed to a sense among many Indians of having enemies on all sides.

In the midst of it all, the hugely popular Nehru died in 1964 and his daughter Indira Gandhi (no relation to Mahatma Gandhi) was elected as prime minister in 1966. Indira Gandhi, like Nehru before her, loomed large over the country she governed. Unlike

1869
Suez Canal opens; journey from England reduced from three months to three weeks. Bombay's economic importance skyrockets.

1919
On 13 April, unarmed Indian protesters are massacred at Jallianwala Bagh in Amritsar (Punjab).

1947
India gains independence on 15 August. Pakistan is formed a day earlier. Partition is followed by mass cross-border exodus.

Nehru, however, she was always a profoundly controversial figure whose historical legacy remains hotly disputed.

In 1975, facing serious opposition and unrest, she declared a state of emergency (which later became known as the Emergency). Freed of parliamentary constraints, Gandhi was able to boost the economy, control inflation remarkably well and decisively increase efficiency. On the negative side, political opponents often found themselves in prison, India's judicial system was turned into a puppet theatre and the press was fettered.

Gandhi's government was bundled out of office in the 1977 elections, but the 1980 election brought Indira Gandhi back to power with a larger majority than ever before, firmly laying the foundation for the Nehru-Gandhi family dynasty that would continue to dominate Indian politics to the present day.

1948
Mahatma Gandhi is assassinated in New Delhi by Nathuram Godse on 30 January.

26 January 1950
India becomes a republic. Date commemorates Declaration of Independence proposed by Congress in 1930.

Family Travel

Sikh boy at the Golden Temple (p372), Amritsar

SARA-JANE CLELAND /GETTY IMAGES ©

Travel with children in India can be a delight, and warm welcomes are frequent. Locals will thrill at taking a photograph or two beside your bouncing baby and while this may prove disconcerting for some, remember that the attention your children will inevitably receive is almost always good natured. Kids are the centre of life in many Indian households, and your own will be treated just the same.

Food

India's fabulous food offerings are usually fresh, fragrant, colourful and healthy. The most common problem for families is trying to avoid overly spicy dishes. Safe bets for steering clear of chillies are steamed rice, plain *papad* (crispy chickpea-flour wafer), flat breads (such as naan, chapati or roti), Tibetan *momos* (dumplings) and south Indian specialities like dosa (paper-thin lentil-flour pancake), *idly* (spongy, round, fermented rice cake) and *vada* (doughnut-shaped deep-fried lentil savoury). Fresh fruit is widely available, as is plain yogurt (or curd) - great for cooling spicy mouths. Lassis (yogurt drinks) also go down very well with kids. Traveller-friendly restaurants and cafes usually do Western dishes too, meaning you're rarely too far from pasta and pizza.

Accommodation

India offers such an array of accommodation, from beach huts to five-star fantasies, that you're bound to find something that will appeal. Most places don't mind cramming several children into a regular-sized double room along with their parents. If your budget can stretch a bit, a good way to maintain familial energy levels is to mix in a few top-end stays.

Health

The availability of a decent standard of health care varies widely in India. Talk to your doctor about where you will be travelling to get advice on vaccinations and what to include in your first-aid kit. Access to health care is certainly better in traveller-frequented parts of the country where it's almost always easy to track down a doctor at short notice (most hotels will be able to recommend a reliable one). Prescriptions are quickly and cheaply filled over the counter at numerous pharmacies, often congregating near hospitals. Diarrhoea can be very serious in young children; rehydration is essential and seek medical help if it's persistent or accompanied by fever. Heat rash, skin complaints such as impetigo, insect bites or stings can be treated with the help of a well-equipped first aid kit.

The Best...
Adventures
for Kids

1 Tiger Spotting

2 Trekking & Rafting

3 Camel Safaris

4 Elephant Rides

5 Beaches

Need to Know

Changing facilities Not usually available – take a portable changing mat and plenty of wipes.

Cots Bring the lightest fold-up baby bed you can find.

Health Bring a first-aid kit, plus insect repellent, sun lotion and – for those with younger children – nappy-rash (diaper-rash) cream. Calendula cream works well against heat rash, too.

Highchairs Available in some upmarket restaurants.

Kids' menus Found at occasional big-city restaurants, but otherwise there's plenty of cuisine to please all palates.

Nappies (diapers) Available in India, but relatively expensive and may not be your preferred brand.

Pushchairs (strollers) Forget them. Pavements, if they exist, are usually rough, making them a bane rather than a boon. Baby-carrier rucksacks are the way forward.

Transport Book seats in advance if possible, and pack diversions – books, music and movie-loaded iPads.

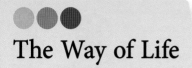

The Way of Life

Bangle seller, Delhi

PAUL BEINSSEN/GETTY IMAGES ©

Spirituality is the common thread in the richly diverse tapestry that is India. And for travellers, one of the most enduring impressions of India is the way everyday life is intimately intertwined with the sacred.

Along with religion, family lies at the heart of society – for most Indians, the idea of being unmarried by their mid-30s is somewhat unpalatable. Despite the rising number of nuclear families – primarily in the larger, more cosmopolitan cities – the extended family remains a cornerstone in both urban and rural India, with males – usually the breadwinners – generally considered the head of the household.

Marriage, Birth & Death

Marriage is an exceptionally auspicious event for Indians and although 'love marriages' have spiralled upwards in recent times (mainly in urban hubs), most Hindu and many Muslim marriages are arranged.

Dowry, although illegal, is still a key issue in many arranged marriages, with some families plunging into debt to raise the required cash and gifts. Health workers claim that India's high rate of abortion of female foetuses (though sex-identification tests are banned in India, they still clandestinely occur in some clinics) is predominantly due to the financial burden of providing a daughter's dowry.

Divorce and remarriage is becoming more common (primarily in India's bigger cities), but divorce is still not granted by courts as a matter of routine and is generally not looked upon favourably by society.

The birth of a child, in Hindu-majority India, is another momentous occasion, with its own set of ceremonies taking place at various auspicious times – the child's first horoscope, name-giving, feeding the first solid food and the first hair-cutting.

Hindus cremate their dead, and funeral ceremonies are designed to purify and console both the living and the deceased.

The Best... Places for Spiritual Fervour

1 Varanasi (p316)

2 Pushkar (p158)

3 Hazrat Nizam-ud-din Dargah, Delhi (p73)

4 McLeod Ganj (p364)

The Caste System

Although the Indian constitution does not recognise the caste system, it still wields considerable influence, especially in rural India, where your family's caste largely determines your social standing in the community, and can influence one's vocational and marriage prospects. Traditionally, caste is the basic social structure of Hindu society. Living a righteous life and fulfilling your dharma (moral duty) raises your chances of being reborn into a higher caste and thus into better circumstances. Hindus are born into one of four varnas (castes): Brahmin (priests and scholars), Kshatriya (soldiers), Vaishya (merchants) and Shudra (labourers).

Beneath the four main castes are the Dalits (once known as Untouchables), who hold menial jobs such as latrine cleaners.

Women in India

Women in India are entitled to vote and own property. While the percentage of women in politics has risen over the past decade, they're still notably underrepresented in the national parliament, accounting for around 10% of parliamentary members.

Professions are still male-dominated, but women are steadily making inroads, especially in urban centres.

For the urban middle-class woman, life is materially much more comfortable, but pressures still exist. Broadly speaking, she is far more likely to receive a tertiary education, but once married is still usually expected to 'fit in' with her in-laws and be a homemaker above all else. Like her village counterpart, if she fails to live up to expectations – even just not being able to produce a grandson – the consequences can sometimes be dire, as demonstrated by the extreme practice of 'bride burning', wherein a wife is doused with flammable liquid and set alight. Reliable statistics are unavailable, but some women's groups claim that for every reported case, roughly 300 go unreported, and that less than 10% of the reported cases are pursued through the legal system.

Following the highly publicised brutal gang rape (and subsequent death) of a 23-year-old Indian physiotherapy student in Delhi in December 2012, tens of thousands of people protested in the capital, and beyond, demanding swift government action to address the country's escalating gender-based violence. The government introduced harsher, but somewhat controversial punishments (including possible death penalty) for sex offenders. Time will tell how effective such new reforms are.

Cricket

Cutting across all echelons of society, cricket is more than just a national sporting obsession – it's a matter of enormous patriotism (especially evident when India plays Pakistan!). And travellers who show even the slightest interest in the game can expect to strike up passionate conversations with people of all types.

The most celebrated contemporary Indian cricketer is Sachin Tendulkar – fondly dubbed the 'Little Master' – who, in 2012, became the world's only player to score one hundred international centuries.

India's first recorded cricket match was in 1721, and it won its first Test series in 1952 in Chennai against England. Today cricket – especially the Twenty20 format (the jewel in its crown is the Indian Premier League, or IPL; www.iplt20.com) – is big business in India, attracting lucrative sponsorship deals and celebrity status for its players. The sport has not been without its murky side though, with IPL teams and Indian cricketers among those embroiled in match-fixing scandals over past years.

Internationals and IPL matches are played at various venues throughout the country – see Indian newspapers and/or cricket websites (www.espncricinfo.com is the best) for details about matches that coincide with your visit.

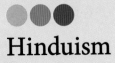

Hinduism

Spices and the goddess Durga, Udaipur

GREG ELMS/GETTY IMAGE

Hinduism has no founder or central authority and it isn't a proselytising religion. Essentially, Hindus believe in Brahman, who is eternal, uncreated and infinite. Everything that exists emanates from Brahman and will ultimately return to it. The multitude of gods and goddesses – the Hindu pantheon is said to have a staggering 330 million deities – are merely manifestations; knowable aspects of this formless phenomenon. Brahman has three main representations, the Trimurti: Brahma, Vishnu and Shiva.

Brahman

The One; the ultimate reality. Brahman is formless, eternal and the source of all existence. Brahman is *nirguna* (without attributes), as opposed to all the other gods and goddesses, which are manifestations of Brahman and therefore *saguna* (with attributes).

Brahma

Only during the creation of the universe does Brahma play an active role. At other times he is in meditation. His consort is Saraswati, the goddess of learning, and his vehicle is a swan. He is sometimes shown sitting on a lotus that rises from Vishnu's navel, symbolising the interdependence of the gods. Brahma is generally depicted with four (crowned and bearded) heads, each turned towards a point of the compass.

Vishnu

The preserver or sustainer, Vishnu is associated with 'right action'. He protects and sustains all that is good in the world. He is usually depicted with four arms, holding a lotus, a conch shell (it can be blown like a trumpet so symbolises the cosmic vibration from which existence emanates), a discus and a mace. His consort is Lakshmi, the goddess of wealth, and his vehicle is Garuda, the man-bird creature. The Ganges is said to flow from his feet.

Shiva

Shiva is the destroyer – to deliver salvation – without whom creation couldn't occur. Shiva's creative role is phallically symbolised by his representation as the frequently worshipped lingam. With 1008 names, Shiva takes many forms, including Nataraja, lord of the *tandava* (cosmic victory dance), who paces out the creation and destruction of the cosmos.

Sometimes Shiva has snakes draped around his neck and is shown holding a trident (representative of the Trimurti) as a weapon while riding Nandi, his bull. Nandi symbolises power and potency, justice and moral order. Shiva's consort, Parvati, is capable of taking many forms.

The Best...
Hindu Temples

1 Meenakshi Amman Temple, Madurai (p282)

2 Kandariya-Mahadev Temple, Khajuraho (p328)

3 Kailasa Temple, Ellora (p134)

4 Vittala Temple, Hampi (p217)

5 Shore Temple, Mamallapuram (p272)

Other Prominent Hindu Deities

Elephant-headed **Ganesh** is the god of good fortune, remover of obstacles, and patron of scribes (the broken tusk he holds was used to write sections of the Mahabharata).

Krishna is an incarnation of Vishnu sent to earth to fight for good and combat evil. Depicted with blue-hued skin, Krishna is often seen playing the flute.

Hanuman is the hero of the Ramayana and loyal ally of Rama. He embodies the concept of bhakti (devotion). He's the king of the monkeys, but is capable of taking on other forms.

Among the Shaivite (followers of the Shiva movement), **Shakti**, the goddess as mother and creator, is worshipped as a force in her own right. The concept of *shakti* is embodied in the ancient goddess **Devi** (divine mother), who is also manifested as **Durga** and, in a fiercer evil-destroying incarnation, **Kali**.

Delicious India

Spices for sale, Goa

HUW JONES/GETTY IMAC

India's phenomenal culinary terrain – with its especially glorious patchwork of vegetarian cuisine – is not only intensely delectable, it's also richly steeped in history. From the flavoursome meaty preparations of the Mughals and Punjabis to the deep-sea delights of former southern colonies, Indian kitchens continue to whip up traditional favourites as part of a national cuisine that combines fresh local produce with an extraordinary amalgam of regional and global influences.

Land of Spices

Christopher Columbus was looking for the black pepper of Kerala's Malabar Coast when he stumbled upon America. The region still grows the world's finest pepper, and it's integral to most savoury Indian dishes. Turmeric and coriander seeds are other essentials, while most Indian 'wet' dishes begin with the crackle of cumin seeds in hot oil. The green cardamom of Kerala's Western Ghats scents and flavours savouries, desserts and chai (tea).

Rice Paradise

Rice is a staple, especially in South India. Long-grain white rice varieties are the most popular, served with just about any 'wet' cooked dish. Rice is often cooked up in a pilau (or pilaf; spiced rice dish) or biryani.

Flippin' Fantastic Bread

While rice is paramount in the south, wheat is the mainstay in the north. Roti, the generic term for Indian-style bread, is a name used interchangeably with chapati to describe the most common variety, the unleavened round bread made with whole-wheat flour.

Puri is deep-fried dough puffed up like a crispy balloon. Flaky, unleavened *paratha* can be eaten as is or jazzed up with fillings such as *paneer* (soft, unfermented cheese). The thick, teardrop-shaped *naan* is cooked in a tandoor.

Dhal-icious!

While the staple of preference divides north and south, the whole of India is melodiously united in its love for *dhal* (curried lentils or pulses). You may encounter up to 60 different pulses. Common varieties include: *channa,* a sweeter version of the yellow split pea; tiny yellow or green ovals called *moong* (mung beans); salmon-coloured *masoor* (red lentils); and the ochre-coloured southern favourite, *tuvar* (yellow lentils; also known as *arhar*).

Meaty Matters

Chicken, lamb and mutton (sometimes goat) are the mainstays; religious taboos make beef forbidden to devout Hindus and pork to Muslims.

In northern India you'll come across meat-dominated Mughlai cuisine, which includes rich curries, kebabs, koftas and biryanis.

Tandoori meat dishes are another North Indian favourite. The name is derived from the clay oven, or tandoor, in which the marinated meat is cooked.

The Best...
Dishes to Try

1 Masala dosa (curried-vegetables pancake), Chennai (p266)

2 Bhelpuri (fried dough with lentils and spices), Mumbai (p118)

3 Rasgulla (cream-cheese balls flavoured with rose-water), Kolkata (p296)

4 Paratha (stuffed bread), Delhi (p60)

5 Bebinca (coconut cake), Panaji, Goa (p196)

Street Food

Tucking into street food is one of the joys of travelling in India – here are some tips to help avoid tummy troubles:

- If the locals are avoiding a vendor, you should too.
- Unless a place is reputable (and busy), avoid eating meat from the street.
- Be wary of juice stalls. Fresh fruit juices are often mixed with tap water (not good for fragile foreign bellies).
- Likewise, don't be tempted by glistening pre-sliced fruit, which keeps its luscious veneer with the regular dousing of water.

Deep-Sea Delights

With around 7500km of coastline, it's no surprise that seafood is an important staple, especially from Mumbai (Bombay) down to Kerala. Kerala is the biggest fishing state, while Goa boasts particularly succulent prawns and fiery fish curries.

Fruit & Veg

Sabzi (vegetables) is a word recognised in every Indian vernacular. They're generally cooked *sukhi* (dry) or *tari* (in a sauce).

Potatoes are ubiquitous, often cooked with various masalas and other vegetables, or mashed and fried for *aloo tikki* (potato patties), or cooked with cauliflower to make *aloo gobi* (potato-and-cauliflower curry). Fresh green peas are stir-fried with other vegetables in pilaus and biryanis and in the magnificent *mattar paneer* (unfermented cheese and pea curry). *Baigan* (eggplant/aubergine) can be curried or sliced and deep-fried. Also popular is *saag* (a generic term for leafy greens), which can include mustard, spinach and fenugreek.

India's fruit basket is a bountiful one. Along the southern coast are super-luscious tropical fruits such as pineapples and papayas. Citrus fruits are widely grown, and mangoes abound during the summer months (especially April and May).

Vegetarians & Vegans

India is king when it comes to vegetarian fare. However, there's little understanding of veganism (the term 'pure vegetarian' means without eggs), and animal products such as milk, butter, ghee and curd are included in most Indian dishes.

Dear Dairy

Dahi (curd/yogurt) is commonly served with meals and is great for subduing heat; *paneer* is a godsend for vegetarians; *lassi* is one in a host of sweet and savoury beverages; *ghee* is the traditional cooking medium; and some of the finest *mithai* (Indian sweets) are made with milk.

Sweet at Heart

India has an incredible kaleidoscope of *mithai* (sweets), usually sinfully sugary. The main categories are *barfi* (a fudgelike milk-based sweet), soft *halwa* (made with vegetables, cereals, lentils, nuts or fruit), *ladoos* (sweet balls made of gram flour and semolina), and those made from *chhana* (unpressed paneer) such as *rasgullas* (cream-cheese balls flavoured with rose water).

Feasting Indian-Style

Most people in India eat with their right hand – the left hand is reserved for unsanitary actions such as removing shoes. Before and after a meal, it's good manners to wash your hands.

Architecture & the Arts

ANDERS BLOMQVIST/GETTY IMAGES ©

Over the centuries India's many ethnic and religious groups have spawned a vivid artistic heritage that is both inventive and spiritually significant. Today, artistic beauty lies around almost every corner, manifesting itself in everything from poetry and paintings to temples and tombs.

Music

Indian classical music traces its roots back to Vedic times, when religious poems chanted by priests were first collated in an anthology called the Rig-Veda. Over the millennia classical music has been shaped by many influences. The legacy today is Carnatic (characteristic of South India) and Hindustani (the classical style of North India) music.

Both styles use the raga (the melodic shape of the music) and *tala* (the rhythmic meter characterised by the number of beats); tintal, for example, has a *tala* of 16 beats. The audience follows the *tala* by clapping at the appropriate beat, which in tintal is at beats one, five and 13. There's no clap at the beat of nine; that's the *khali* (empty section), which is indicated by a wave of the hand. Both the raga and the *tala* are used as a basis for composition and improvisation.

Both Carnatic and Hindustani music are performed by small ensembles, generally comprising three to six musicians, and both have many instruments in common. The most striking difference, to the uninitiated, is Carnatic's greater use of voice.

Literature

Bengalis are credited with producing some of India's most celebrated litera-ture, a movement often referred to as the Indian or Bengal Renaissance, which flourished from the 19th century with works by Bankim Chandra Chatterjee. But the man mostly credited with first propelling India's cultural richness onto the world stage is the Nobel Prize-winning poet Rabindranath Tagore.

India has an ever-growing list of internationally acclaimed contemporary authors. Particularly prominent writers include Vikram Seth, best known for his epic novel *A Suitable Boy*, and Amitav Ghosh, whose *Sea of Poppies* was shortlisted for the 2008 Man Booker Prize.

Indian-born Booker Prize winners include Salman Rushdie (*Midnight's Children*, 1981), Arundhati Roy (*The God of Small Things*, 1997), Kiran Desai (*The Inheritance of Loss*, 2006) and Aravind Adiga (*The White Tiger*, 2008).

Traditional Musical Instruments

One of the best-known Indian instruments is the **sitar** (large stringed instrument), with which the soloist plays the *raga*. Other stringed instruments include the **sarod** (which is plucked) and the **sarangi** (which is played with a bow).

Also popular is the **tabla** (twin drums), which provides the *tala*. The drone, which runs on two basic notes, is provided by the oboe-like **shehnai** or the stringed **tampura** (also spelt tamboura). The hand-pumped keyboard harmonium is used as a secondary melody instrument for vocal music.

Painting

Primitive cave paintings, thought to be around 12,000 years old, still survive in Bhimbetka, just outside the city of Bhopal. Fast forward to around 1500 years ago and artists were covering the walls and ceilings of the Ajanta caves in Maharashtra, not far from Mumbai, with scenes from the Buddha's past lives. The figures are endowed with an unusual freedom and grace, and contrast with other styles that later emerged from this part of India.

The 1526 victory by Babur at the Battle of Panipat ushered in the era of the Mughals in India. Although Babur and his son Humayun were both patrons of the arts, it's Humayun's son Akbar who is generally credited with developing the characteristic Mughal style. This painting style, often in colourful miniature form, largely depicts court life, architecture, battle and hunting scenes, as well as detailed portraits.

Various schools of miniature painting emerged in Rajasthan from around the 17th century. The subject matter ranged from royal processions to shikhar (hunting expeditions), with many artists influenced by Mughal styles.

By the 19th century, painting in North India was notably influenced by Western styles (especially English watercolours), giving rise to what has been dubbed the Company School, which had its centre in Delhi.

Religious Architecture

Complex rules govern the location, design and building of each Hindu temple, based on numerology, astrology, astronomy, religious principles and the concept of the square as a perfect shape. Essentially, a temple represents a map of the universe. At the centre is an unadorned space, the *garbhagriha* (inner sanctum), which is symbolic of the 'womb-cave' from which the universe is said to have emerged. This provides a residence for the deity to whom the temple is dedicated. Above the shrine rises a superstructure known as a *vimana* in South India, and a *sikhara* in North India.

From the outside, Jain temples can resemble Hindu ones, but inside they're often a riot of sculptural ornamentation, the very opposite of ascetic austerity. Meanwhile, gurdwaras (Sikh temples) can usually be identified by a *nishan sahib* (flagpole flying a triangular flag with the Sikh insignia). Amritsar's sublime Golden Temple is Sikhism's holiest shrine.

Stupas, which characterise Buddhist places of worship, essentially evolved from burial mounds. They served as repositories for relics of the Buddha and, later, other venerated souls.

India's Muslim rulers contributed their own architectural conventions, including arched cloisters and domes. The Mughals uniquely melded Persian, Indian and provincial styles. Examples include the tomb of Humayun in Delhi and Agra Fort. Emperor Shah Jahan was responsible for some of India's most spectacular architectural creations, most notably the milky-white Taj Mahal.

The Best...
Revered
Buildings

1 Taj Mahal (p95)

2 Golden Temple, Amritsar (p373)

3 Meenakshi Amman Temple (p282)

4 Temples at Khajuraho (p328)

5 Kailasa Temple, Ellora (p134)

IN FOCUS ARCHITECTURE & THE ARTS

Landscape & Wildlife

Tourists and elephant, Corbett Tiger Reserve (p352)

HIRA PUNJABI/GETTY IMAGE

Vast and incredibly diverse, India's landscape encompasses everything from steamy jungles and tropical rainforest to arid deserts and immense Himalayan peaks. Such variety supports an extraordinary array of wildlife, including elephants, tigers, lions, monkeys, leopards, antelope, rhinos, crocodiles, many different species of reptiles and a kaleidoscopic quantity of birdlife.

The Land

At 3,287,263 sq km, India is the world's seventh-largest country. It forms the vast bulk of the South Asian subcontinent – an ancient block of earth crust that carried a wealth of unique plants and animals like a lifeboat across a prehistoric ocean before slamming into Asia about 40 million years ago.

Plants

Once upon a time India was almost entirely covered in forest; now the total forest cover is estimated to be around 22%. Despite widespread clearing of native habitats, the country still boasts 49,219 plant species, of which some 5200 are endemic. Species on the southern peninsula show Malaysian ancestry, while desert plants in Rajasthan are more clearly allied with the Middle East, and conifer forests of the Himalaya derive from European and Siberian origins.

Environmental Issues

With over a billion people, ever-expanding industrial and urban centres, and an expansive growth in chemical-intensive farming, India's environment is under tremendous threat. An estimated 65% of India's land is degraded in some way, and nearly all of that land is seriously degraded, with the government consistently falling short on most of its environmental protection goals due to lack of enforcement or will power.

Animals

Big sprawling India harbours some of the richest biodiversity in the world, with 397 species of mammals, 1250 bird species, 460 reptile species, 240 species of amphibians and 2546 kinds of fish – among the highest counts for any country in the world. Understandably, wildlife-watching has become one of the country's prime tourist activities and there are dozens of national parks and wildlife sanctuaries offering opportunities to spot rare and unusual creatures.

The Big Ones

Elephants (now classified as endangered despite being revered for centuries in Hindu custom) and rhinos (classified as vulnerable, and found mostly in the

The Best... Wildlife & Birdwatching Experiences

1 Ranthambhore National Park (p161)

2 Kerala Backwaters (p241)

3 Periyar Wildlife Sanctuary (p242)

4 Sunderbans Tiger Reserve (p306)

5 Jaisalmer Camel Safaris (p182)

IN FOCUS LANDSCAPE & WILDLIFE

Project Tiger

When naturalist Jim Corbett first raised the alarm in the 1930s nobody believed that tigers would ever be threatened. At the time it was believed there were 40,000 tigers in India, although nobody had ever conducted a census. Then came Independence, which put guns into the hands of villagers who pushed into formerly off-limits hunting reserves to hunt for highly profitable tiger skins. By the time an official census was conducted in 1972, there were only 1800 tigers left and an international outcry prompted Indira Gandhi to make the tiger the national symbol of India and set up **Project Tiger** (http://projecttiger. nic.in). The project has since established 39 tiger reserves that aim to protect this top predator as well as all other animals that live in the same habitats. After an initial round of successes, tiger numbers in India plummeted from 3600 in 2002 to a low of 1400 in 2008 due to relentless poaching, although numbers are thought to have risen again to around 1700.

Tiger conservationist Valmik Thapar has analysed the perceived failure of Project Tiger, drawing attention to what he calls mismanagement by a forest bureaucracy that is largely not scientifically trained. He criticises the Ministry of Environment and Forests' unwillingness to curb poaching through armed patrols and its refusal to open forests to scholarly scientific enquiry.

northeastern state of Assam) are the two heavyweights of India's big game. Undoubtedly, though, the star of the show here is the tiger.

Also classified as endangered, wild tigers number around 3500 worldwide. Around half of these are found in India, with the population spread across three dozen tiger reserves spanning nine different states. Your chances of seeing a tiger are decent in some reserves; slim in others. In October 2012 a temporary ban on tiger tourism was lifted on the proviso that no more than 20% of each tiger reserve could be open to tourists.

Hoofed & Handed

By far the most abundant forms of wildlife you'll see in India are deer (nine species), antelope (six species), goats and sheep (10 species) and primates (15 species). In the open grasslands of many parks, look for the stocky nilgai, India's largest antelope, or elegantly horned blackbucks. If you're heading for the mountains, keep your eyes open in the Himalaya for blue sheep with their partially curled horns or the rare argali with its fully curled horns that can be found in Ladakh. The deserts of Rajasthan are home to desert-adapted species such as chinkaras (Indian gazelles).

India's primates range from the extremely rare hoolock gibbon and golden langur of the northeast, to species that are so common as to be a pest – most notably the stocky and aggressive rhesus macaque and the elegant grey langur.

Birds

With well over one thousand species of birds, India is a birdwatcher's dream. Winter can be a particularly good time because northern migrants arrive to kick back in the lush subtropical warmth of the Indian peninsula. In the breeding season look for colourful barbets, sunbirds, parakeets and magpies everywhere you travel.

Survival
Guide

Pilgrims at Dashashwamedh Ghat (p318), Varanasi
RICHARD I'ANSON/GETTY IMAGES ©

A-Z

Directory

Sample Accommodation Costs

CATEGORY	DELHI	RAJASTHAN	KERALA
budget $	<₹1000	<₹500	<₹1000
midrange $$	₹1000-5000	₹500-1500	₹1000-3500
top end $$$	>₹5000	>₹1500	>₹3500

Accommodation

Accommodation in India ranges from grim hostels to opulent palaces converted into five-star hotels. In this guide, we've not included anywhere grim, and we've listed reviews by author preference within each of the three price brackets we use.

Price Icons

The price indicators in this book refer to the cost of a double room, including private bathroom, unless otherwise noted. The sample costs table you see here is based on price indicators for Delhi, Rajasthan and Kerala and gives an example of what these price indicators stand for, but note that the price bands we use for these price icons will vary from state to state.

Seasons

Rates in this guide are full price in high season. High season usually coincides with the best weather for the area's sights and activities – normally summertime in the mountains (around June to October), and the cooler months in the plains (around October to mid-February).

In areas popular with foreign tourists there's an additional peak period over Christmas and New Year; make reservations well in advance.

At other times you may find significant discounts; if the hotel seems quiet, ask for one.

Some hotels in places like Goa shut during the monsoon period.

Many temple towns have additional peak seasons around major festivals and pilgrimages; for festival details see the Month by Month chapter.

Taxes & Service Charges

State governments slap a variety of taxes on hotel accommodation (except at the cheaper hotels), and these are added to the cost of your room.

Taxes vary from state to state and are detailed in the regional chapters.

Many upmarket hotels also levy an additional 'service charge' (usually around 10%).

Rates quoted in this book's regional chapters include taxes.

Budget & Midrange Hotels

If you're planning on staying in budget places, bring your own sheet or sleeping-bag liner. Sheets and bedcovers at cheap hotels can be stained, well worn and in need of a wash.

Sound pollution can be irksome (especially in urban hubs); pack good-quality earplugs and request a room that doesn't face a busy road.

It's wise to keep your door locked, as some staff (particularly in budget accommodation) may knock and automatically walk in without awaiting your permission.

Blackouts are common (especially during summer and the monsoon) so double-check that the hotel has a backup generator if you're paying for electric 'extras' such as air-conditioners and TVs.

Note that some hotels lock their doors at night. Members of staff might sleep in the lobby but waking them up can be a challenge. Let the hotel know in advance if you'll be arriving or returning to your room late in the evening.

Book Your Stay Online

For more accommodation reviews by Lonely Planet authors, check out http://hotels.lonelyplanet.com. You'll find independent reviews, as well as recommendations on the best places to stay. Best of all, you can book online.

Activities

India covers every terrain imaginable, from sun-baked deserts and moist rainforests to snow-dusted mountains and plunging ravines. With all this to play with, the opportunities for outdoor activities are endless. Choose from trekking, paragliding, mountaineering, jungle safaris, scuba diving, surfing and elephant rides as well as yoga, meditation and much, much more. See individual listings in each chapter for more information.

Business Hours

Official business hours are from 10am to 5pm Monday to Friday but many offices open later and close earlier.

Most offices have an official lunch hour from around 1pm.

Bank opening hours vary from town to town so check locally; foreign-exchange offices may open longer and operate daily.

Some larger post offices have a full day on Saturday and a half-day on Sunday.

All timings vary regionally; exceptions are noted in the regional chapters.

Customs Regulations

Travellers are supposed to declare any amount of cash/travellers cheques over US$5000/10,000 on arrival.

Indian rupees shouldn't be taken out of India; however, this is rarely policed.

Officials occasionally ask tourists to enter expensive

Practicalities

o **Newspapers & Magazines** Major English-language dailies include the *Hindustan Times,* the *Times of India, Indian Express, Hindu, Statesman, Telegraph, Daily News & Analysis (DNA)* and *Economic Times.* Regional English-language and local-vernacular publications are found nationwide. Incisive current-affairs magazines include *Frontline, India Today, The Week, Tehelka* and *Outlook.*

o **Radio** Government-controlled All India Radio (AIR), India's national broadcaster, has over 220 stations broadcasting local and international news. Private FM channels broadcast music, current affairs, talkback and more.

o **Television** The national (government) TV broadcaster is Doordarshan. More people watch satellite and cable TV; English-language channels include BBC, CNN, Star World, HBO and Discovery.

o **Weights & Measures** Officially India is metric. Terms you're likely to hear are lakhs (one lakh = 100,000) and crores (one crore = 10 million).

items such as video cameras and laptops on a 'Tourist Baggage Re-export' form to ensure they're taken out of India at the time of departure.

Electricity

220V/50Hz

220V/50Hz

Gay & Lesbian Travellers

Homosexuality is legal in India, although the country remains largely conservative.

Public displays of affection are generally frowned upon for gay and lesbian couples (and even for heterosexual couples).

There are gay scenes in a number of cities including Mumbai, Delhi, Kolkata, Chennai and Bengaluru – Gay Pride marches are held annually at some of these centres.

Publications

Time Out Delhi (www.timeoutdelhi.net) Fortnightly listing of gay events in Delhi.

Time Out Mumbai (www.timeoutmumbai.net) Gay events in Mumbai.

Websites

Delhi Frontrunners & Walkers (www.delhifrontrunners.org) Weekly running and walking club for Delhi's LGBT crowd.

Gay Bombay (www.gaybombay.org) Lists gay events as well as offering support and advice.

Gay Delhi (www.gaydelhi.org) LGBT support group, organising social events in Delhi. Register for more details.

Indian Dost (www.indiandost.com/gay.php) News and information including contact groups in India.

India Pink (www.indiapink.co.in) India's first 'gay travel boutique' founded by a well-known Indian fashion designer.

A number of Indian cities have support groups, including the following:

Chennai

Chennai Dost (www.chennaidost.blogspot.com) Organises varied events, including parties, exhibitions, campaigns and the Chennai Rainbow Pride march every June.

Delhi

Nigah (http://nigahdelhi.blogspot.com) Autonomous collective that holds monthly queer events and organises the annual Nigah Queerfest.

Kolkata

Sappho (www.sapphokolkata.org) operates as a support group for lesbian, bisexual and transgender women.

Mumbai

Humsafar Trust (☎022-26673800; www.humsafar.org) Runs gay and transgender support groups and advocacy programs. The drop-in centre in Santa Cruz East hosts workshops and has a library – pick up a copy of the pioneering gay-and-lesbian magazine *Bombay Dost*.

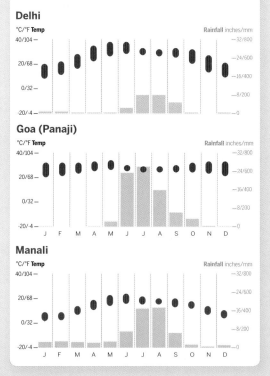

Climate

Delhi

Goa (Panaji)

Manali

Standard Hours

We've only listed business hours where they differ from the following standards.

BUSINESS	OPENING HOURS
Airline offices	9.30am-5.30pm Mon-Sat
Banks	10am-2pm or 4pm Mon-Fri, until noon or 1pm Sat
Government offices	9.30am-1pm & 2-5.30pm Mon-Fri, closed alternate Sat (usually 2nd & 4th)
Post offices	9am-6pm Mon-Fri, to noon Sat
Museums	10am-5pm Tue-Sun
Restaurants	lunch noon-2.30pm or 3pm, dinner 7-10pm or 11pm
Sights	10am-5pm or dawn-dusk
Shops	10am-7pm or 8pm, some closed Sun

Health

India's huge geographical variation can present environmental issues that cause health problems, and hygiene is poor in most regions, so food and water-borne illnesses are common. Insect-borne diseases are present in tropical areas. Medical care is basic in many areas (especially beyond the larger cities) so it's essential to be well prepared.

Becoming ill in some way is very common, but fortunately most travellers' illnesses can be prevented with some common-sense behaviour or treated with a well-stocked medical kit. However, never hesitate to consult a doctor while on the road: self-diagnosis can be hazardous.

Insurance

Don't travel without health insurance. Emergency evacuation is expensive – bills of over US$100,000 are not uncommon. Consider the following when buying insurance:

o You may require extra cover for adventure activities such as rock climbing and scuba diving.

o In India, doctors usually require immediate payment in cash. If you do have to claim later, make sure you keep all relevant documentation.

Medical Care

Medical care is hugely variable in India. Some cities now have clinics catering specifically to travellers and expatriates; they're usually more expensive than local medical facilities and offer a higher standard of care. They also know the local system, including reputable local hospitals and specialists, and can liaise with insurance companies should you require evacuation. It's usually difficult to find reliable medical care in rural areas.

Infectious Diseases

Malaria

This is a serious and potentially deadly disease, caused by a parasite transmitted by the bite of an infected mosquito. Before you travel, seek expert advice according to your itinerary (rural areas are especially risky) and on medication and side effects.

The most important symptom of malaria is fever, but general symptoms, such as headache, diarrhoea, cough or chills, may also occur. Diagnosis can only be properly made by taking a blood sample.

To prevent malaria, you need to avoid mosquito bites *and* take antimalarial medications. Most people who catch malaria are taking inadequate or no antimalarial medication.

To prevent mosquito bites:

o Use a DEET-containing insect repellent on exposed skin. Wash this off at night, as long as you are sleeping under a mosquito net. Natural repellents such as citronella can be effective, but must be applied more frequently than products containing DEET.

o Sleep under a mosquito net impregnated with pyrethrin.

411

Vaccinations

The only vaccine required by international regulations is **yellow fever**. Proof of vaccination will only be required if you have visited a country in the yellow-fever zone within the six days prior to entering India.

The World Health Organization (WHO) recommends the following vaccinations for travellers going to India (as well as being up to date with measles, mumps and rubella vaccinations):

○ **Adult diphtheria & tetanus** Single booster recommended if none in the previous 10 years. Side effects include sore arm and fever.

○ **Hepatitis A** Provides almost 100% protection for up to a year; a booster after 12 months provides at least another 20 years' protection. Mild side effects such as headache and sore arm occur in 5% to 10% of people.

○ **Hepatitis B** Now considered routine for most travellers. Given as three shots over six months. A rapid schedule is also available, as is a combined vaccination with Hepatitis A. Side effects are mild and uncommon, usually headache and sore arm. In 95% of people lifetime protection results.

○ **Typhoid** Recommended for all travellers to India, even those only visiting urban areas. The vaccine offers around 70% protection, lasts for two to three years and comes as a single shot. Tablets are also available, but the injection is usually recommended as it has fewer side effects. Sore arm and fever may occur.

○ **Varicella** If you haven't had chicken pox, discuss this vaccination with your doctor.

as it increases the likelihood of haemorrhaging. Make sure you see a doctor to be diagnosed and monitored.

Hepatitis A This food- and water-borne virus infects the liver, causing jaundice (yellow skin and eyes), nausea and lethargy. There is no specific treatment for hepatitis A; the liver simply needs time to heal. All travellers to India should be vaccinated against hepatitis A.

Hepatitis B This sexually transmitted disease is spread by body fluids and can be prevented by vaccination. The long-term consequences can include liver cancer and cirrhosis.

Hepatitis E Transmitted through contaminated food and water, hepatitis E has similar symptoms to hepatitis A, but is far less common. It is a severe problem in pregnant women and can result in the death of both mother and baby. There is no commercially available vaccine, and prevention is by following safe eating and drinking guidelines.

○ Choose accommodation with proper screens and fans (if not air-conditioned).

○ Impregnate clothing with pyrethrin in high-risk areas.

○ Wear long sleeves and trousers in light colours.

○ Use mosquito coils.

○ Spray your room with insect repellent before going out for dinner.

Other diseases

Dengue Fever This mosquito-borne disease is becoming increasingly problematic, especially in cities. There's no vaccine available, so it can be prevented only by avoiding mosquito bites at all times. Symptoms include high fever, severe headache and body ache, and sometimes a rash and diarrhoea. Treatment is rest and paracetamol – do not take aspirin or ibuprofen

Other Hazards

Traveller's Diarrhoea By far the most common problem affecting travellers in India. Treatment consists of staying well hydrated; rehydration solutions like Gastrolyte are the best for this. Antibiotics such as ciprofloxacin or azithromycin should kill the bacteria quickly. Seek medical attention quickly if you do not respond to an appropriate antibiotic. Loperamide is just a 'stopper' and doesn't get to the cause of the problem. It can be helpful, though (eg for long bus rides). Don't take loperamide if you have a fever or blood in your stools.

Giardiasis Giardia is a parasite that is relatively common in travellers. Symptoms include nausea, bloating, excess gas, fatigue and intermittent diarrhoea. The parasite will eventually go away if left untreated but this can take months; the best advice is to seek medical treatment. The treatment of choice is tinidazole, with metronidazole being a second-line option.

Food

Eating in restaurants is a big risk for contracting diarrhoea. Ways to avoid it include:
- eat only freshly cooked food
- avoid shellfish and buffets
- peel fruit
- cook vegetables
- eat in busy restaurants with a high turnover of customers

Heat

Many parts of India, especially down south, are hot and humid throughout the year. For people not accustomed to this climate, swelling of the feet and ankles is common, as are muscle cramps caused by excessive sweating. Prevent these by avoiding dehydration and excessive activity in the heat. Don't eat salt tablets (they aggravate the gut); drinking rehydration solution or eating salty food helps. Treat cramps by resting, rehydrating with double-strength rehydration solution and gently stretching.

Dehydration is the main contributor to heat exhaustion. Recovery is usually rapid and it is common to feel weak for some days afterwards. Symptoms include:
- feeling weak
- headache
- irritability
- nausea or vomiting
- sweaty skin
- a fast, weak pulse
- normal or slightly elevated body temperature.

Treatment for dehydration:
- get out of the heat
- fan the sufferer
- apply cool, wet cloths to the skin
- lay the sufferer flat with their legs raised
- rehydrate with water containing one-quarter of a teaspoon of salt per litre

Heat stroke is a serious medical emergency. Symptoms include:
- weakness
- nausea
- a hot dry body
- temperature of over 41°C
- dizziness
- confusion
- loss of coordination
- seizures
- eventual collapse

Treatment for heat stroke:
- get out of the heat
- fan the sufferer
- apply cool, wet cloths to the skin or ice to the body, especially to the groin and armpits

Prickly heat is a common skin rash in the tropics, caused by sweat trapped under the skin. Treat it by moving out of the heat for a few hours and by having cool showers. Creams

Drinking Water

- Never drink tap water.
- Bottled water is generally safe – check that the seal is intact at purchase.
- Avoid ice unless you know it has been safely made.
- Be particularly careful of fresh juices served at street stalls – they may have been watered down or be served in unhygienic jugs/glasses.
- Boiling water is usually the most efficient method of purifying it.
- The best chemical purifier is iodine. It should not be used by pregnant women or those with thyroid problems.
- Water filters should also filter out viruses. Ensure your filter has a chemical barrier such as iodine and a small pore size (less than four microns).

and ointments clog the skin so they should be avoided. Locally bought prickly-heat powder can be helpful.

Insurance

o Comprehensive travel insurance to cover theft, loss and medical problems (as well as air evacuation) is strongly recommended.

o Some policies specifically exclude potentially dangerous activities such as scuba diving, skiing, motorcycling, paragliding and even trekking: read the fine print.

o Some trekking agents may only accept customers who have cover for emergency helicopter evacuation.

o If you plan to hire a motorcycle in India, make sure the rental policy includes at least third-party insurance.

o Check in advance whether your insurance policy will pay doctors and hospitals directly or reimburse you later for overseas health expenditure (keep all documentation for your claim).

o It's crucial to get a police report in India if you've had anything stolen; insurance companies may refuse to reimburse you without one.

o Worldwide travel insurance is available at www. lonelyplanet.com/travel_services. You can buy, extend and claim online anytime – even if you're already on the road.

Internet Access

Internet cafes are widespread and connections are usually reasonably fast, except in more remote areas. Wireless (wi-fi) access is available in an increasing number of hotels and some coffee shops in larger cities. In this book, hotels offering internet access are marked by @.

Practicalities

o Internet charges vary by area (see regional chapters); charges fall anywhere between ₹15 and ₹100 per hour and often with a 15- to 30-minute minimum.

o Power cuts are not uncommon; avoid losing your email by writing and saving messages in a text application before pasting them into your browser.

o Bandwidth load tends to be lowest in the early morning and early afternoon.

o Some internet cafes may ask to see your passport.

Security

o Be wary of sending sensitive financial information from internet cafes; some places are able to use keystroke-capturing technology to access passwords and emails.

o Avoid sending credit-card details or other personal data over a wireless connection; using online banking on any nonsecure system is generally unwise.

Laptops

o Many internet cafes can supply laptop users with internet access through wi-fi or over a LAN Ethernet cable; alternatively take out an account with a local Internet Service Provider (ISP).

o Companies that offer prepaid wireless 2G and 3G modem sticks (called dongles) include Reliance, Airtel, Tata Docomo and Vodafone. Just plug it into into the USB port of your laptop and you can access the internet.

o To subscribe for a connection, you have to submit your proof of identity and address in India – usually, a letter or receipt from your hotel will suffice. A nonrefundable activation fee (around ₹1200) has to be paid, which includes the price of the dongle.

o Tariffs for broadband internet start from ₹150 per month for 4GB up to ₹1000 per month for 11GB.

o Make sure the areas you will be travelling to are covered by your service provider.

o Consider purchasing a fuse-protected universal AC adaptor to protect your circuit board from power surges.

o Plug adaptors are widely available throughout India.

Legal Matters

If you're in a sticky legal situation, contact your embassy as quickly as possible. However, be aware that all your embassy may be able to do is monitor your treatment in custody and arrange a lawyer. In the Indian justice system, the burden of proof can often be on the accused and stints in prison before trial are not unheard of.

Antisocial Behaviour

- Smoking in public places is illegal throughout India but this is very rarely enforced; if caught you'll be fined ₹200.

- People can smoke inside their homes and in most open spaces such as streets (heed any signs stating otherwise).

- A number of Indian cities have banned spitting and littering, but this is also variably enforced.

Drugs

- Indian law does not distinguish between 'hard' and 'soft' drugs; possession of any illegal drug is regarded as a criminal offence.

- If convicted, the *minimum* sentence is 10 years, with very little chance of remission or parole.

- Cases can take months, even several years, to appear before a court while the accused may have to wait in prison. There's also usually a hefty monetary fine on top of any custodial sentence.

- Marijuana grows wild in various parts of India, but consuming it is still an offence, except in towns where bhang is legally sold for religious rituals.

- Police have been getting particularly tough on foreigners who use drugs, so you should take this risk very seriously.

Police

- You should always carry your passport; police are entitled to ask you for identification at any time.

- Corruption is rife so the less you have to do with local police the better; try to avoid all potentially risky situations.

Money

The Indian rupee (₹) is divided into 100 paise (p) coins, which are becoming increasingly rare. Coins come in denominations of ₹1, ₹2 and ₹5; notes come in ₹5, ₹10, ₹20, ₹50, ₹100, ₹500 and ₹1000 (this last is handy for paying large bills but can pose problems in getting change for small services). The Indian rupee is linked to a basket of currencies and has been subject to fluctuations in recent years.

ATMs

- ATMs are found in most urban centres.

The Art of Haggling

Government emporiums, fair-trade cooperatives, department stores and modern shopping centres in India almost always charge fixed prices. Anywhere else, you'll need to bargain. Shopkeepers in tourist hubs are accustomed to travellers who have lots of money and little time to spend it, so you can often expect to be charged double or triple the 'real' price (souvenir shops are the most notorious for this).

The first rule of haggling is to never show too much interest in the item you've got your heart set upon. Also, resist buying the first thing that takes your fancy. Wander around and price items at different shops, but don't make it too obvious – if you return to the first shop the vendor will know it's because they're the cheapest, resulting in less haggling leeway for you.

Decide how much you'd be happy to pay, and then express a *casual* interest in buying. If you have absolutely no idea of what something should really cost, start by slashing the price by half. The vendor will (most likely) look utterly aghast, but you can now work up and down respectively in small increments until you reach a mutually agreeable price. You'll find that many shopkeepers will lower their 'final price' once you start to leave and say you'll 'think about it'. If a vendor seems to be charging an unreasonably high price, simply look elsewhere.

Haggling is a way of life in India and is usually taken in good spirit – it should never turn ugly. Remember to always keep in mind exactly how much a rupee is worth in your home currency to put things in perspective.

Prohibited Exports

To protect India's cultural heritage, the export of certain antiques is prohibited. Many 'old' objects are fine, but the difficulties begin if something is verifiably more than 100 years old. Reputable antique dealers know the laws and can make arrangements for an export-clearance certificate for any old items that you're permitted to export. Detailed information on prohibited items can be found on the government webpage www.asi.nic.in/pdf_data/8.pdf. The rules may seem stringent but the loss of artworks and traditional buildings in places such as Ladakh, Himachal Pradesh, Gujarat and Rajasthan, due to the international trade in antiques and carved windows and doorframes, has been alarming. Look for quality reproductions instead.

The Indian Wildlife Protection Act bans any form of wildlife trade. Don't buy any products that endanger threatened species and habitats – doing so can result in heavy fines and even imprisonment. This includes ivory, shahtoosh shawls (made from the down of chirus, rare Tibetan antelopes), and anything made from the fur, skin, horns or shell of any endangered species. Products made from certain rare plants are also banned.

◦ Visa, MasterCard, Cirrus, Maestro and Plus are the most commonly accepted cards.

◦ The ATMs listed in this book accept foreign cards (but not necessarily all types of cards).

◦ Banks in India that accept foreign cards include Citibank, HDFC, ICICI, HSBC and the State Bank of India.

◦ Before your trip, check whether your card can reliably access banking networks in India and ask for details of extra charges.

◦ Notify your bank that you'll be using your card in India (provide dates) to avoid having your card blocked; take along your bank's phone number just in case.

◦ Always keep the emergency lost-and-stolen numbers for your credit cards in a safe place, separate from your cards, and report any loss or theft immediately.

◦ Away from major towns, always carry cash or travellers cheques as back-up.

Black Market

Black-market moneychangers exist but legal moneychangers are so common that there's no reason to use them, except perhaps to change small amounts of cash at border crossings. If someone approaches you on the street and offers to change money, you're probably being set up for a scam.

Cash

◦ Major currencies such as US dollars, British pounds and euros are easy to change throughout India, although some bank branches insist on travellers cheques only.

◦ Some banks also accept other currencies such as Australian and Canadian dollars, and Swiss francs.

◦ Private moneychangers deal with a wider range of currencies, but Pakistani, Nepali and Bangladeshi currency can be harder to change away from the border.

◦ When travelling off the beaten track, always carry an adequate stock of rupees.

◦ Whenever changing money, check every note. Don't accept any filthy, ripped or disintegrating notes, as these may be difficult to use.

◦ It can be tough getting change in India so keep a stock of smaller currency; ₹10, ₹20 and ₹50 notes are helpful.

◦ Officially you cannot take rupees out of India, but this is laxly enforced. You can change any leftover rupees back into foreign currency, most easily at the airport (some banks have a ₹1000 minimum). You may have to present encashment certificates or credit-card/ATM receipts, and show your passport and airline ticket.

Credit Cards

◦ Credit cards are accepted at a growing number of shops, upmarket restaurants and midrange and top-end hotels, and they can usually be used to pay for flights and train tickets.

- Cash advances on major credit cards are also possible at some banks.

- MasterCard and Visa are the most widely accepted cards.

Encashment Certificates

- Indian law states that all foreign currency must be changed at official moneychangers or banks.

- For every (official) foreign-exchange transaction, you'll receive an encashment certificate (receipt), which will allow you to change rupees back into foreign currency when departing India.

- Encashment certificates should cover the amount of rupees you intend to change back to foreign currency.

- Printed receipts from ATMs are also accepted as evidence of an international transaction at most banks.

International Transfers

If you run out of money, someone back home can wire you cash via moneychangers affiliated with **Moneygram** (www. moneygram.com) or **Western Union** (www.westernunion. com). A fee is added to the transaction.

To collect cash, bring your passport and the name and reference number of the person who sent the funds.

Moneychangers

Private moneychangers are usually open for longer hours than banks, and are found almost everywhere (many also double as internet cafes and travel agencies).

Upmarket hotels may also change money, but their rates are usually not as competitive.

Tipping, Baksheesh & Bargaining

- In tourist restaurants or hotels, a service fee is usually already added to your bill and tipping is optional. Elsewhere, a tip is appreciated.

- It's not mandatory to tip taxi or rickshaw drivers, but it's good to tip drivers who are honest about the fare.

- If you hire a car with driver for more than a couple of days, a tip is recommended for good service.

- Baksheesh can loosely be defined as a 'tip'; but it covers everything from alms for beggars to bribes.

- Some people prefer not to hand out sweets, pens or money to children, believing it encourages them to beg. To make a lasting difference, consider donating to a reputable school or charitable organisation.

- Except in fixed-price shops (such as government emporiums and fair-trade cooperatives), bargaining is the norm.

Travellers Cheques

- All major brands are accepted, but some banks may only accept cheques from American Express (Amex) and Thomas Cook.

- Pounds sterling and US dollars are the safest currencies, especially in smaller towns.

- Keep a record of the cheques' serial numbers separate from your cheques, along with the proof-of-purchase slips, encashment vouchers and photocopied passport details. If you lose your cheques, contact the American Express or Thomas Cook office in Delhi.

Public Holidays

There are officially three national public holidays. Every state celebrates its own official holidays, which cover bank holidays for government workers as well as major religious festivals. Most businesses (offices, shops etc) and tourist sites close on public holidays, but transport is usually unaffected. It's wise to make transport and hotel reservations well in advance if you intend visiting during major festivals.

Public Holidays

Republic Day 26 January

Independence Day 15 August

Gandhi Jayanti 2 October

Major Religious Festivals

Mahavir Jayanti (Jain) February

Holi (Hindu) March

Easter (Christian) March/ April

Buddha Jayanti (Buddhist) April/May

Eid al-Fitr (Muslim) August/ September

Dussehra (Hindu) October

Diwali (Hindu) October/ November

Nanak Jayanti (Sikh) November

Christmas (Christian) 25 December

Safe Travel

Travellers to India's major cities may fall prey to petty and opportunistic crime but most problems can be avoided with a bit of common sense and an appropriate amount of caution. Also have a look at the India branch of Lonely Planet's **Thorn Tree Travel Forum** (www. lonelyplanet.com/thorntree), where travellers often post timely warnings about problems they've encountered on the road. Always check your government's travel advisory warnings.

Female Solo Travellers

The following tips will hopefully help women who are travelling alone avoid uncomfortable situations during their trip:

o Keep conversations with unknown men short – getting involved in an inane conversation with someone you barely know can be misinterpreted as a sign of sexual interest.

o Questions and comments such as 'Do you have a boyfriend?' or 'You're very beautiful' are indicators that the conversation may be taking a steamy tangent.

o Some women wear a pseudo wedding ring, or announce early on in the conversation that they're married or engaged (regardless of the reality).

o If you feel that a guy is encroaching on your space, he probably is. A firm request to keep away usually does the trick, especially if your tone is loud and curt enough to draw the attention of passers-by.

o Follow local women's cues and instead of shaking hands say namaste – the traditional, respectful Hindu greeting.

o Check the reputation of any teacher or therapist before going to a solo session (get recommendations from travellers). Some women have reported being molested by masseurs and other therapists. If you feel uneasy at any time, leave.

o Arrive in towns before dark. Don't walk alone at night and avoid wandering alone in isolated areas even during daylight.

o If arriving after dark, prearrange an airport or train-station pick-up from your hotel.

o Delhi and some other cities have prepaid radio cab services such as Easycabs – they're more expensive than the regular prepaid taxis, but promote themselves as being safe, with drivers who have been vetted as part of their recruitment.

o Avoid taking taxis or auto-rickshaws alone late at night and never agree to have more than one man (the driver) in the car – ignore claims that this is 'just my brother' etc.

o Solo women have reported less hassle by opting for the more expensive classes on trains.

Telephone

o There are few payphones in India (apart from in airports), but private PCO/STD/ISD call booths do the same job, offering inexpensive local, interstate and international calls at lower prices than calls made from hotel rooms.

o These booths are found around the country. A digital meter displays how much the call is costing and usually provides a printed receipt when the call is finished.

o Costs vary depending on the operator and destination but can be from ₹1 per minute for local calls and between ₹5 and ₹10 for international calls.

o Some booths also offer a 'call-back' service – you ring home, provide the phone number of the booth and wait for people at home to call you back, for a fee of around ₹20 on top of the cost of the preliminary call.

o Getting a line can be difficult in remote country and mountain areas – an engaged signal may just mean that the exchange is overloaded, so keep trying.

o Useful online resources include the **Yellow Pages** (www. indiayellowpages.com) and **Justdial** (www.justdial.com).

Mobile Phones

o Indian mobile phone numbers usually have 10 digits, typically beginning with 7, 8 or 9.

- There's roaming coverage for international GSM phones in most cities and large towns.

- To avoid expensive roaming costs (often highest for incoming calls), get hooked up to the local mobile-phone network.

- Mobiles bought in some countries may be locked to a particular network; you'll have to get the phone unlocked, or buy a local phone (available from ₹2000) to use an Indian SIM card.

Getting Connected

- Getting connected is inexpensive but complicated, owing to security concerns, and involves some amount of paperwork.

- Foreigners must supply between one and five passport photos, their passport, and photocopies of their passport identity and visa pages.

- You must also supply a residential address, which can be the address of your hotel (ask the management for a letter confirming this).

- Some phone companies send representatives to the listed address; others call to verify that you are actually staying there. Some travellers have reported their SIM cards being 'blocked' once the company realised they had moved from the hotel where they registered their phone. Others have been luckier for the entire duration of their travels.

- Another option is to get a friendly local to obtain a connection in their name.

- Prepaid mobile phone kits (SIM card and phone number, plus an allocation of calls) are available in most towns for about ₹200 from a phone shop, local STD/ISD/PCO booth or grocery store. You must then purchase more credit, sold as direct credit. You pay the vendor and the credit is deposited straight into your account, minus some taxes and service charges.

Charges

- Calls made within the state or city in which you bought the SIM card are cheap – ₹1 per minute – and you can call internationally for less than ₹10 per minute.

- SMS messaging is even cheaper. International outgoing messages cost ₹5. Incoming calls and messages are free.

- Most SIM cards are state specific. If you use them in another state, you have to pay (nominal) roaming charges for both incoming and outgoing communications.

- The government could do away with roaming charges altogether by the near future, making calls on the move cheaper.

- Unreliable signals and problems with international texting (messages or replies not coming through or being delayed) are not uncommon.

- The leading service providers are Airtel, Vodafone, Reliance, Idea and BSNL.

Phone Codes

Calling India from abroad

See above; for mobile phones, the area code and initial zero are not required.

Important Numbers

From outside India, dial your international access code, India's country code then the number (minus '0', which is used when dialling domestically).

Country code	91
International access code	00
Ambulance	102
Fire	101
Police	100

Calling internationally from India Dial 00 (the international access code), then the country code of the country you're calling, then the area code (without the initial zero if there is one) and the local number.

- Landline phone numbers have an area code followed by up to eight digits.

- Toll-free numbers begin with 1800.

- To call a landline from a mobile phone, you always have to add the area code (with the initial zero).

- Some call centre numbers might require the initial zero (eg calling an airline ticketing service based in Delhi from Karnataka).

- A Home Country Direct service, which gives you access to the international operator in your home country, exists for the US (📞 000 117) and the UK (📞 000 4417). To access an international operator elsewhere, dial ✆ 000 127. The operator can place a call to anywhere in the world and allow you to make collect calls.

Time

India uses the 12-hour clock and the local standard time is known as IST (Indian Standard Time). IST is 5½ hours ahead of GMT.

CITY	NOON IN DELHI
Beijing	2.30pm
Dhaka	12.30pm
Islamabad	11.30am
Kathmandu	12.15pm
London	6.30am
New York	1.30am
San Francisco	10.30pm
Sydney	4.30pm
Tokyo	3.30pm

Tourist Information

In addition to the Government of India tourist offices (also known as 'India Tourism'), each state maintains its own network of tourist offices. These vary in their efficiency and usefulness – some are run by enthusiastic souls who go out of their way to help, others are little more than a means of drumming up business for State Tourism Development Corporation tours. Most of the tourist offices have free brochures and often a free (or inexpensive) local map.

See regional chapters for contact details of relevant tourist offices.

Travellers with Disabilities

India's crowded public transport, crush of humanity and variable infrastructure can test even the hardiest able-bodied traveller. If you have a physical disability or you are vision impaired, these can pose even more of a challenge. If your mobility is considerably restricted you may like to ease the stress by travelling with an able-bodied companion.

Accommodation Wheelchair-friendly hotels are almost exclusively top end. Make pre-trip enquiries and book ground-floor rooms at hotels that lack adequate facilities.

Accessibility Some restaurants and offices have ramps but most tend to have at least one step. Staircases are often steep; lifts frequently stop at mezzanines between floors.

Footpaths Where pavements exist, they can be riddled with holes, littered with debris and packed with pedestrians. If using crutches, bring along spare rubber caps.

Transport Hiring a car with driver will make moving around a lot easier; if you use a wheelchair, make sure the car-hire company can provide an appropriate vehicle to carry it.

For further advice pertaining to your specific requirements, consult your doctor before heading to India.

The following organisations may be able to offer further information or at least point you in the right direction.

Mobility International USA (MIUSA; www.miusa.org)

Access-Able Travel Source (www.access-able.com)

Global Access News (www.globalaccessnews.com)

Royal Association for Disability & Rehabilitation (RADAR; www.radar.org.uk)

Accessible Journeys (www.disabilitytravel.com)

Visas

Citizens of Finland, Japan, Luxembourg, New Zealand, Singapore, Cambodia, Vietnam, Phillipines, Laos, Myanmar and Indonesia are currently granted a 30-day single-entry visa on arrival at Mumbai, Chennai, Kolkata and New Delhi airports. All other nationals – except Nepal and Bhutan – must get a visa before arriving in India. These are available at Indian missions worldwide.

Note that your passport needs to be valid for at least six months beyond your intended stay in India, with at least two blank pages.

Entry Requirements

Most people travel on the standard six-month tourist visa.

Tourist visas are valid from the date of issue, not the date you arrive in India. You can spend a total of 180 days in the country.

An onward travel ticket is a requirement for most visas, but this isn't always enforced (check in advance).

Additional restrictions apply to travellers from Bangladesh and Pakistan, as well as certain Eastern European, African and Central Asian countries. Check any special conditions for your nationality with the Indian embassy in your country.

Visas are priced in the local currency and may have an added service fee (contact your country's Indian embassy for current prices).

Passport

To enter India you need a valid passport, visa and an onward/return ticket. Your passport should be valid for at least six months beyond your intended stay in India. If your passport is lost or stolen, immediately contact your country's embassy or consulate. Keep photocopies of your airline ticket and the identity and visa pages of your passport in case of emergency. Better yet, scan and email copies to yourself. Check with the Indian embassy in your home country for any special conditions that may exist for your nationality.

Airports

As India is a big country, it makes sense to fly into the airport that's nearest to the area you'll be visiting. India has six main gateways for international flights: Bengaluru (Bangalore), Chennai (Madras), Delhi, Hyderabad, Kolkata (Calcutta) and Mumbai (Bombay).

Transport

⬤⬤⬤
Getting There & Away

Getting to India is increasingly easy, with plenty of international airlines servicing the country. Flights, tours and other tickets may also be booked online at www.lonelyplanet.com/bookings.

Entering India

Entering India by air or land is relatively straightforward, with standard immigration and customs procedures.

⬤⬤⬤
Getting Around

 **Air**

Airlines in India

Apart from airline websites (see right), bookings can be made through reliable ticketing portals such as **Cleartrip** (www.cleartrip.com), **Make My Trip** (www.makemytrip.com) and **Yatra** (www.yatra.com).

Keeping peak-hour congestion in mind, the recommended check-in time for domestic flights is two hours before departure – the

Climate Change & Travel

Every form of transport that relies on carbon-based fuel generates CO_2, the main cause of human-induced climate change. Modern travel is dependent on aeroplanes, which might use less fuel per kilometre per person than most cars but travel much greater distances. The altitude at which aircraft emit gases (including CO_2) and particles also contributes to their climate change impact. Many websites offer 'carbon calculators' that allow people to estimate the carbon emissions generated by their journey and, for those who wish to do so, to offset the impact of the greenhouse gases emitted with contributions to portfolios of climate-friendly initiatives throughout the world. Lonely Planet offsets the carbon footprint of all staff and author travel.

deadline is 45 minutes. The usual baggage allowance is 20kg (10kg for smaller aircraft) in economy class.

Air India (☎1800 1801407; www.airindia.com) India's national carrier operates many domestic and international flights.

GoAir (☎1800 222111; www.goair.in) Reliable low-cost carrier servicing Goa, Kochi, Jaipur, Delhi and Bagdogra among other destinations.

IndiGo (☎09910383838; www.goindigo.in) The best and trendiest of the lot, with plenty of flights across India and to select overseas destinations. Has an untarnished reputation for being on time.

Jet Airways (☎1800-225522; www.jetairways.com) Operates flights across India and to select overseas destinations.

JetKonnect (☎1800-223020; www.jetkonnect.com) Jet Airways' budget carrier flies to numerous destinations including Amritsar, Dehradun, Chennai and Jodhpur.

Spicejet (☎1800-1803333; www.spicejet.com) Destinations include Bengaluru (Bangalore), Varanasi, Srinagar, Colombo (Sri Lanka) and Kathmandu (Nepal).

🚌 Bus

Buses go almost everywhere in India and are the only way to get around many mountainous areas. They tend to be the cheapest way to travel; services are fast and frequent.

Roads in curvaceous terrain can be especially perilous; buses are often driven with willful abandon, and accidents are always a risk.

Avoid night buses unless there's no alternative: driving conditions are more hazardous and drivers may be suffering from lack of sleep.

Classes

State-owned and private bus companies both offer several types of buses, graded loosely as 'ordinary', 'semi-deluxe', 'deluxe' or 'super deluxe'. These are usually open to interpretation, and the exact grade of luxury offered in a particular class can vary from place to place.

In general, ordinary buses tend to be ageing rattletraps while the deluxe grades range from less decrepit versions of ordinary buses to flashy Volvo buses with AC and reclining (locally called 'push-back') two-by-two seating.

Luggage

Oversized luggage is stored in compartments underneath the bus (sometimes for a small fee) or carried on the roof.

If your bags go on the roof, make sure they're securely locked, and tied to the metal baggage rack – unsecured bags can fall off on rough roads.

Theft is a (minor) risk: watch your bags at snack and toilet stops; *never* leave day-packs or valuables unattended inside the bus.

Reservations

Most deluxe buses can be booked in advance – government buses usually a month ahead – at the bus station or local travel agencies.

Online bookings are now possible in select states such as Karnataka and Rajasthan, or at the excellent portal **Redbus** (☎1800-300-10101; www.redbus.in).

Reservations are rarely possible on 'ordinary' buses; travellers can be left behind in the mad rush for a seat.

🚗 Car

Few people bother with self-drive car hire – not only because of the hair-raising driving conditions, but also because hiring a car with driver is wonderfully affordable in India, particularly if several people share the cost. Seatbelts are either nonexistent or of variable quality.

Hertz (www.hertz.com) is one of the few international rental companies with representatives in India.

Hiring a Car & Driver

○ Most towns have taxi stands or car-hire companies where you can arrange short or long tours (see regional chapters).

○ Not all hire cars are licensed to travel beyond their home state. Those that are will pay extra state taxes, added to the hire charge.

○ Ask for a driver who speaks some English and knows the region you intend visiting, and try to see the car and meet the driver before paying anything.

○ A wide range of cars now ply as taxis. From a proletarian Tata Indica hatchback to a comfy Toyota Innova SUV, there's a model to suit every pocket.

○ For multiday trips, the charge should cover the driver's meals and accommodation. Drivers should make their own sleeping and eating arrangements.

○ It is *essential* to set the ground rules from day one; politely but firmly let the driver know that you're boss in order to avoid anguish later.

Costs

○ The price depends on the distance and the terrain (driving on mountain roads uses more petrol, hence the higher cost).

○ One-way trips usually cost the same as return ones (to

cover the petrol and driver charges for getting back).

○ Hire charges vary from state to state. Some taxi unions set a time limit or a maximum kilometre distance for day trips. If you go over, you'll have to pay extra.

○ Prices also vary according to the make, model and size of the taxi.

○ To avoid potential misunderstandings, get *in writing* what you've been promised (quotes should include petrol, sightseeing stops, all your chosen destinations, and meals and accommodation for the driver). If a driver asks you for money for petrol en route because he is short of cash, get receipts for reimbursement later.

○ For sightseeing day trips around a single city, expect to pay upwards of ₹1000/1200 for a non-AC/AC car with an eight-hour, 80km limit per day (extra charges apply). For multi-day trips, operators usually peg a 250km minimum running distance per day and charge around ₹8/10 per km for a non-AC/AC car. If you overshoot, you pay extra.

○ A tip is customary at the end of your journey; ₹100 per day is fair (more if you're really pleased with the driver's service).

Local Transport

○ Buses, cycle-rickshaws, autorickshaws, taxis, boats and urban trains provide transport around India's cities.

○ Costs for public transport vary from town to town (consult regional chapters).

○ For any transport without a fixed fare, agree on the price *before* you start your journey and make sure that it covers your luggage and every passenger.

○ Don't pay the agreed fare until *after* you've reached your destination.

○ Even where meters exist, drivers may refuse to use them, demanding an elevated 'fixed' fare.

○ Fares usually increase at night (by up to 100%) and some drivers charge a few rupees extra for luggage.

○ Carry plenty of small bills for taxi and rickshaw fares as drivers rarely have change.

○ Some taxi/autorickshaw drivers are involved in the commission racket.

Autorickshaw, Tempo & Vikram

○ The Indian autorickshaw is a three-wheeled motorised contraption with tin or canvas roof and sides, with room for two passengers (although you'll often see many more squeezed in) and limited luggage.

○ They are also referred to as autos, scooters, riks or tuk-tuks.

○ They are mostly cheaper than taxis and usually have a meter, although getting it turned on can be a challenge.

○ Travelling by auto is great fun but, thanks to the open windows, can be smelly, noisy and hot!

○ Tempos and *vikrams* (large tempos) are outsized autorickshaws with room for more passengers, running on fixed routes for a fixed fare.

○ In country areas, you may also see the fearsome-looking 'three-wheeler' – a crude tractorlike tempo with a front wheel on an articulated arm.

Cycle-Rickshaw

○ A cycle-rickshaw is a pedal cycle with two rear wheels, supporting a bench seat

Prepaid Taxis & Radio Cabs

Most Indian airports and many train stations have a prepaid-taxi booth, normally just outside the terminal building. Here, you can book a taxi for a fixed price (which will include baggage) and thus avoid commission scams. However, officials advise holding onto the payment coupon until you reach your chosen destination, in case the driver has any other ideas! Smaller airports and stations may have prepaid autorickshaw booths instead.

Radio cabs cost marginally more than prepaid taxis, but are air-conditioned and manned by the company's chauffeurs. Cabs have electronic, receipt-generating fare meters and are fitted with GPS units, so the company can monitor the vehicle's movement around town. These minimise chances of errant driving or unreasonable demands for extra cash by the driver afterward.

Manning the Meter

Getting a metered ride is only half the battle. Meters are almost always outdated, so fares are calculated using a combination of the meter reading and a complicated 'fare adjustment card'. Predictably, this system is open to abuse.

To get a rough estimate of fares in advance, try www.taxiautofare.com.

for passengers. Most have a canopy that can be raised in wet weather, or lowered to provide extra space for luggage.

o Many of the big cities have phased out (or reduced) the number of cycle-rickshaws, but they are still a major means of local transport in many smaller towns.

o Fares must be agreed upon in advance – speak to locals to get an idea of what is a fair price for the distance you intend to travel. Tips are always appreciated, given the slog involved.

o Kolkata is the last bastion of the hand-pulled rickshaw, known as the tana rickshaw. This is a hand-cart on two wheels pulled directly by the rickshaw-wallah.

Taxi

o Most towns have taxis, and these are usually metered, but getting drivers to use the meter can be a major hassle. If drivers refuse to use the meter for any reason, find another cab.

o To avoid fare-setting shenanigans, use prepaid taxis where possible (regional chapters contain details). These are most commonly found outside major train stations.

o Be aware that many taxi drivers supplement their earnings with commissions from hotels or shops that they may try to take you to.

Other Local Transport

In some towns, tongas (horse-drawn two-wheelers) and victorias (horse-drawn carriages) still operate. Kolkata has a tram network, and both Delhi and Kolkata have efficient underground train systems. Mumbai, Delhi and Chennai, among other centres, have suburban trains that leave from ordinary train stations. See regional chapters for comprehensive details.

Tours

Tours are available all over India, run by tourist offices, local transport companies and travel agencies. Organised tours can be an inexpensive way to see several places on one trip, although you rarely get much time at each place. If you arrange a tailor-made tour, you'll have more freedom about where you go and how long you stay.

Drivers may double as guides, or you can hire a qualified local guide for a fee. In tourist towns, be wary of touts claiming to be professional guides. See the

Tours sections in the regional chapters for details about local tours.

International Tour Agencies

Many international companies offer tours to India, from straightforward sightseeing trips to adventure tours and activity-based holidays. To find current tours that match your interests, quiz travel agents and surf the web. Some good places to start your tour hunt:

Dragoman (www.dragoman. com) One of several reputable overland tour companies offering trips in customised vehicles.

Exodus (www.exodustravels. co.uk) A wide array of specialist trips, including tours with a holistic, wildlife and adventure focus.

India Wildlife Tours (www. india-wildlife-tours.com) All sorts of wildlife tours, plus jeep, horse or camel safaris and birdwatching.

Indian Encounter (www. indianencounters.com) Special-interest tours that include wildlife spotting, river-rafting and ayurvedic treatments.

Intrepid Travel (www. intrepidtravel.com) Endless possibilities, from wildlife tours to sacred rambles.

Peregrine Adventures (www. peregrine.net.au) Popular cultural and trekking tours.

Sacred India Tours (www. sacredindiatours.com) Includes tours with a holistic focus such as yoga and ayurveda, as well as architectural and cultural tours.

Shanti Travel (www.shantitravel.com) A range of family and adventure tours run by a Franco-Indian team.

World Expeditions (www.worldexpeditions.com.au) An array of options, including trekking and cycling tours.

Train

Travelling by train is a quintessential Indian experience. Trains offer a smoother ride than buses and are especially recommended for long journeys that include overnight travel. India's rail network is one of the largest and busiest in the world and Indian Railways is the largest utility employer on earth, with roughly 1.5 million workers. There are around 6900 train stations scattered across the country.

We've listed useful trains but there are hundreds more. The best way of sourcing updated railway information is to use relevant internet sites such as **Indian Railways** (www.indianrail.gov.in) and the excellent **India Rail Info** (www.indiarailinfo.com), with added offline browsing support.

There's also *Trains at a Glance* (₹45), available at many train station bookstands and better bookshops/newsstands, but it's published annually so it's not as up to date as websites. Nevertheless, it offers comprehensive timetables covering all the main lines.

Train Classes

There is a range of classes on Indian trains, though not all are offered on all trains. Air-Conditioned 1st Class (1AC) is most expensive, with two- or four-berth compartments. The next level down is Air-Conditioned 2-Tier (2AC), with two-tier berths, while 3AC has three-tier berths. AC Executive Chair and AC Chair offer comfortable, reclining chairs and plenty of space. Sleeper Class features open-plan carriages with three-tier bunks and no air-con (but the open windows afford great views, and a breeze). Unreserved 2nd Class is extremely cheap and involves wooden or plastic seats and a lot of people.

Booking Tickets in India

You can either book tickets through a travel agency or hotel (for a commission) or in person at the train station. You can also book online through **IRCTC** (www.irctc.co.in), the e-ticketing division of Indian Railways, or portals such as **Make My Trip** (www.makemytrip.com) and **Yatra** (www.yatra.com). Remember, however, that online booking of train tickets has its share of glitches: travellers have reported problems with registering themselves on some portals and using certain overseas credit cards. Big stations often have English-speaking staff who can help with reservations; at smaller stations, the stationmaster and his deputy usually speak English. It's also worth approaching tourist-office staff at train stations if you need advice.

At the Station

Get a reservation slip from the information window, fill in the name of the departure station, destination station, the class you want to travel and the name and number of the train. Join the long queue for the ticket window where your ticket will be printed. Women should take advantage of the separate women's queue – if there isn't one, go to the front of the regular queue.

Tourist Reservation Bureau

Larger cities and major tourist centres have an International Tourist Bureau, which allows you to book tickets in relative peace – check www.indianrail.gov.in for a list of these stations.

Reservations

• Bookings open 120 days before departure and you must make a reservation for all chair-car, sleeper, and 1AC, 2AC and 3AC carriages. No reservations are required for general (2nd class) compartments.

• Trains are always busy so it's wise to book as far in advance as possible, especially for overnight trains. There may be additional services to certain destinations during major festivals but it's still worth booking well in advance.

• Reserved tickets show your seat/berth and carriage number. Carriage numbers are written on the side of the train (station staff and porters can point you in the right direction). A list of names and berths is posted on the side of each reserved carriage.

o Refunds are available on any ticket, even after departure, with a penalty – rules are complicated, so check when you book.

o Trains can be delayed at any stage of the journey; to avoid stress, factor some leeway into your plans.

o Be mindful of potential drugging and theft.

o If the train you want to travel on is sold out, make sure to enquire about the following.

Tourist Quota

A special (albeit small) tourist quota is set aside for foreign tourists travelling between popular stations. These seats can only be booked at dedicated reservation offices in major cities (see regional chapters for details), and you need to show your passport and visa as ID. Tickets can be paid for in rupees (some offices may ask to see foreign exchange certificates – ATM receipts will suffice), British pounds, US dollars or euros, in cash or Thomas Cook and American Express travellers cheques.

Taktal Tickets

Indian Railways holds back a (very) small number of tickets on key trains and releases them at 10am one day before the train is due to depart. A charge of ₹10 to ₹300 is added to each ticket price. First AC and Executive Chair tickets are excluded from the scheme.

Reservation Against Cancellation (RAC)

Even when a train is fully booked, Indian Railways sells a handful of seats in each class as 'Reservation Against Cancellation' (RAC). This means that if you have an RAC ticket and someone cancels before the departure date, you will get his or her seat (or berth). You'll have to check the reservation list at the station on the day of travel to see where you've been allocated to sit. Even if no one cancels, as an RAC ticket holder you can still board the train and, even if you don't get a seat, you can still travel.

Waitlist (WL)

If the RAC quota is maxed out as well, you will be handed a waitlisted ticket. This means that if there are enough cancellations, you may eventually move up the order to land a confirmed berth, or at least an RAC seat. Check your booking status at www.indian rail.gov.in/pnr_stat.html by entering your ticket's PNR number. A refund is available if you fail to get a seat – ask the ticket office about your chances.

Costs

Fares are calculated by distance and class of travel; Rajdhani and Shatabdi trains are slightly more expensive, but the price includes meals. Most air-conditioned carriages have a catering service (meals are brought to your seat). In unreserved classes it's a good idea to carry portable snacks. Seniors (those over 60) get 30% off all fares in all classes on all types of train. Children below the age of five travel free, those aged between five and 12 are charged half price.

a b c
Language

HINDI

Hindi has about 180 million speakers in India, and it has official status along with English and 21 other languages.

If you read our pronunciation guides as if they were English, you'll be understood. The length of vowels is important (eg 'a' and 'aa'), and 'ng' after a vowel indicates nasalisation (ie the vowel is pronounced 'through the nose'). The stressed syllables are marked with italics. The abbreviations 'm' and 'f' indicate the options for male and female speakers respectively.

Basics

Hello./Goodbye.
नमस्ते ।   na·ma·*ste*
Yes.
जी हाँ ।   jee haang
No.
जी नहीं ।   jee na·*heeng*
Excuse me.
सुनिये ।   su·ni·*ye*
Sorry.
माफ़ कीजिये ।   maaf *kee*·ji·ye
Please ...
कृपया ...   kri·pa·*yaa* ...
Thank you.
थैंक्यू ।   *thayn*·kyoo
How are you?
आप कैसे/कैसी   aap *kay*·se/*kay*·see
हैं?   hayng (m/f)
Fine. And you?
मैं ठीक हूँ ।   mayng teek hoong
आप सुनाइये ।   aap su·*naa*·i·ye
Do you speak English?
क्या आपको अंग्रेज़ी   kyaa aap ko an·*gre*·zee
आती है?   *aa*·tee hay
How much is this?
कितने का है?   *kit*·ne kaa hay

I don't understand.
मैं नहीं समझा/   mayng na·*heeng* sam·jaa/
समझी ।   *sam*·jee (m/f)

Accommodation

Do you have a single/double room?
क्या सिंगल/डबल   kyaa *sin*·gal/da·*bal*
कमरा है?   *kam*·raa hay
How much is it (per night/per person)?
(एक रात/हर व्यक्ति)   (ek raat/har *vyak*·ti)
के लिय कितने   ke li·*ye kit*·ne
पैसे लगते हैं?   *pay*·se *lag*·te hayng

Eating & Drinking

I'd like ..., please.
मुझे ... दीजिये ।   mu·*je* ... *dee*·ji·ye
That was delicious.
बहुत मज़ेदार हुआ ।   ba·*hut* ma·ze·*daar* hu·*aa*
Please bring the menu/bill.
मेन्यू/बिल लाइये ।   *men*·yoo/bil *laa*·i·ye

I don't eat ...
मैं ... नहीं   mayng ... na·*heeng*
खाता/खाती ।   *kaa*·taa/*kaa*·tee (m/f)
   fish   मछली   *mach*·lee
   meat   गोश्त   gosht
   poultry   मुर्गी   *mur*·gee

Emergencies

I'm ill.
मैं बीमार हूँ ।   mayng *bee*·maar hoong
Help!
मदद कीजिये!   ma·*dad kee*·ji·ye
Call the doctor/police!
डॉक्टर/पुलिस   *daak*·tar/pu·*lis*
को बुलाओ!   ko bu·*laa*·o

Directions

Where's a/the ...?
... कहाँ है?   ... ka·*haang* hay
   bank
   बैंक   baynk
   market
   बाज़ार   *baa*·zaar
   post office
   डाक ख़ाना   daak *kaa*·naa
   restaurant
   रेस्टोरेंट   *res*·to·rent
   toilet
   टॉइलेट   *taa*·i·let
   tourist office
   पर्यटन ऑफ़िस   *par*·ya·tan *aa*·fis

TAMIL

Tamil is the official language in the state of Tamil Nadu and one of the major languages of South India, with about 62 million speakers.

Note that in our pronunciation guides, the symbol 'aw' is pronounced as in 'law' while 'ow' is pronounced as in 'how'.

Basics

Hello.
வணக்கம்.   va·*nak*·kam

Goodbye.
போய் வருகிறேன்.   *po*·i va·*ru*·ki·reyn

Yes./No.
ஆமாம்./இல்லை.   *aa*·maam/*il*·lai

Excuse me.
தயவு செய்து.   ta·ya·*vu* sei·*du*

Sorry.
மன்னிக்கவும.   *man*·nik·ka·vum

Please ...
தயவு செய்து ...   ta·ya·*vu* chey·*tu* ...

Thank you.
நன்றி.   *nan*·dri

How are you?
நீங்கள் நலமா?   *neeng*·kal na·*la*·maa

Fine, thanks. And you?
நலம், நன்றி.   na·*lam nan*·dri
நீங்கள்?   *neeng*·kal

Do you speak English?
நீங்கள் ஆங்கிலம்   *neeng*·kal *aang*·ki·lam
பேசுவீர்களா?   *pey*·chu·*veer*·ka·la

How much is this?
இது என்ன வீலை?   i·*tu* en·na vi·*lai*

I don't understand.
எனக்கு   e·*nak*·ku
வீளங்கவில்லை.   vi·*lang*·ka·vil·*lai*

Accommodation

Do you have a single/double room?
உங்களிடம் ஓர்   *ung*·ka·li·tam awr
தன/இரட்டை   ta·*ni*/i·rat·*tai*
அறை உள்ளதா?   a·*rai* ul·la·taa

How much is it per night/person?
ஓர் இரவுக்கு/   awr i·ra·*vuk*·ku/
ஒருவருக்கு   o·ru·va·*ruk*·ku
என்னவீலை?   en·na·vi·lai

Eating & Drinking

I'd like the ..., please.
எனக்கு தயவு   e·*nak*·ku ta·ya·*vu*
செய்து ...   chey·*tu* ...
கொடுங்கள்.   ko·*tung*·kal

  bill   வீலைச்சீட்டு   vi·*laich*·cheet·tu
  menu   உணவுப்–   u·na·*vup*·
     பட்டியல   pat·ti·yal

I'm allergic to ...
எனக்கு ... உணவு   e·*nak*·ku ... u·na·*vu*
சேராது.   *chey*·raa·tu

  dairy   பால்   paal
  products   சார்ந்த   *chaarn*·ta
  meat   இறைச்சி   i·*raich*·chi
  stock   வகை   va·*kai*
  nuts   பருப்பு வகை   pa·*rup*·pu va·*kai*
  seafood   கடல்   ka·*tal*
     சார்ந்த   *chaarn*·ta

Emergencies

Help!
உதவு!   u·ta·*vi*

Call a doctor!
ஐ அழைக்கவும்   i a·*zai*·ka·vum
ஒரு மருத்துவர்!   o·*ru* ma·*rut*·tu·var

Call the police!
ஐ அழைக்கவும்   i a·*zai*·ka·vum
போலிஸ!   pow·*lees*

Directions

Where's a/the ...?
... எங்கே   ... *eng*·key
இருக்கிறது?   i·*ruk*·ki·ra·tu

  bank
  வங்கி   *vang*·ki
  market
  சந்தை   *chan*·tai
  post office
  தபால் நிலையம்   ta·*paal* ni·*lai*·yam
  restaurant
  உணவகம   u·na·va·*kam*
  toilet
  கழிவறை   ka·*zi*·va·rai
  tourist office
  சுற்றுப்பயண   chut·*rup*·pa·ya·na
  அலுவலகம்   a·lu·va·la·*kam*

To enhance your trip with a phrasebook, visit **lonelyplanet.com**. Lonely Planet iPhone phrasebooks are available through the Apple App store.

Behind the Scenes

Our Readers

Many thanks to the travellers who used the last edition and wrote to us with helpful hints, useful advice and interesting anecdotes: Andrew Dunlop, Daniel Costa-Roberts, Delphine Percipalle, Hsiao Yang, Jordan McGregor, Paul Reeder

Author Thanks

Daniel McCrohan

Thanks to Abigail Hole for her fabulous work on the 1st edition of this book, and to my coauthors for bringing so much India expertise to the table. On the ground in Rajasthan, special thanks to Satinder Pal Singh in Jaipur and Sunny Gaur in Jodhpur. Closer to home, thank you to my wonderful mum, my darling wife and our incredible children for being brave enough to join me on this latest adventure.

Acknowledgements

Climate map data adapted from Peel MC, Finlayson BL & McMahon TA (2007) 'Updated World Map of the Köppen-Geiger Climate Classification', Hydrology and Earth System Sciences, 11, 1633-44.

Illustrations p102, p260 by Michael Weldon; p62, p96, p330 by Javier Zarracina.

Cover photographs: Front: Taj Mahal, Gavin Hellier/AWL; Back: Making offerings in Uttarakhand, Ignacio Palacios/Getty Images.

This Book

This 2nd edition of Lonely Planet's *Discover India* guidebook was researched, and compiled or written, by Daniel McCrohan, based on his research and that of Michael Benanav, Joe Bindloss, Lindsay Brown, Mark Elliott, Paul Harding, Trent Holden, Amy Karafin, Bradley Mayhew, Kate Morgan, John Noble, Kevin Raub and Sarina Singh. The previous edition was coordinated by Abigail Hole. This guidebook was commissioned in Lonely Planet's Melbourne office, and produced by the following:

Commissioning Editor Suzannah Shwer
Coordinating Editors Samantha Forge, Kate James
Senior Cartographer David Kemp
Coordinating Layout Designer Clara Monitto
Managing Editors Brigitte Ellemor, Annelies Mertens
Senior Editor Catherine Naghten
Managing Layout Designer Jane Hart
Assisting Editor Elizabeth Jones
Cover Research Naomi Parker
Internal Image Research Kylie McLaughlin
Language Content Branislava Vladisavljevic

Thanks to Ryan Evans, Larissa Frost, Genesys India, Jouve India, Wayne Murphy, Trent Paton, Kerrianne Southway, Gina Tsarouhas, Gerard Walker, Amanda Williamson

SEND US YOUR FEEDBACK

Things change – prices go up, schedules change, good places go bad and bad places go bankrupt. So if you find things better or worse, recently opened or long since closed, or you just want to tell us what you loved or loathed about this book, please get in touch and help make the next edition even more accurate and useful. We love to hear from travellers – your comments keep us on our toes and our well-travelled team reads every word. Although we can't reply individually to postal submissions, we always guarantee that your feedback goes straight to the appropriate authors, in time for the next edition. Each person who sends us information is thanked in the next edition – the most useful submissions are rewarded with a selection of digital PDF chapters.

Visit lonelyplanet.com/contact to submit your updates and suggestions or to ask for help. Our award-winning website also features inspirational travel stories, news and discussions.

Note: We may edit, reproduce and incorporate your comments in Lonely Planet products such as guidebooks, websites and digital products, so let us know if you don't want your comments reproduced or your name acknowledged. For a copy of our privacy policy visit lonelyplanet.com/privacy.

Index

How to Use This Book

These symbols give you the vital information for each listing:

☏ Telephone Numbers	☎ Wi-Fi Access	🚌 Bus
☺ Opening Hours	☒ Swimming Pool	⛴ Ferry
Ⓟ Parking	🌶 Vegetarian Selection	Ⓜ Metro
⊖ Nonsmoking	📖 English-Language Menu	Ⓢ Subway
❄ Air-Conditioning	🚼 Family-Friendly	🚊 Tram
@ Internet Access	🐾 Pet-Friendly	

Look out for these icons:

 No payment required

🍃 A green or sustainable option

Our authors have nominated these places as demonstrating a strong commitment to sustainability – for example by supporting local communities and producers, operating in an environmentally friendly way, or supporting conservation projects.

All reviews are ordered in our authors' preference, starting with their most preferred option. Additionally:

Sights are arranged in the geographic order that we suggest you visit them, and within this order, by author preference.

Eating and Sleeping reviews are ordered by price range (budget, midrange, top end) and within these ranges, by author preference.

Map Legend

Sights
- 🏖 Beach
- ☸ Buddhist
- 🏰 Castle
- ✝ Christian
- 🕉 Hindu
- ☪ Islamic
- ✡ Jewish
- ❗ Monument
- 🏛 Museum/Gallery
- 🏚 Ruin
- 🍇 Winery/Vineyard
- 🐾 Zoo
- ● Other Sight

Activities, Courses & Tours
- 🤿 Diving/Snorkelling
- 🛶 Canoeing/Kayaking
- ⛷ Skiing
- 🏄 Surfing
- 🏊 Swimming/Pool
- 🚶 Walking
- 🏄 Windsurfing
- ● Other Activity/ Course/Tour

Sleeping
- 🛏 Sleeping
- ⛺ Camping

Eating
- 🍴 Eating

Drinking
- ☕ Drinking
- ☕ Cafe

Entertainment
- 🎭 Entertainment

Shopping
- 🛍 Shopping

Information
- 🏦 Bank
- 🏛 Embassy/ Consulate
- ➕ Hospital/Medical
- @ Internet
- 👮 Police
- ✉ Post Office
- ☎ Telephone
- 🚻 Toilet
- ⓘ Tourist Information
- ● Other Information

Transport
- ✈ Airport
- ⊗ Border Crossing
- 🚌 Bus
- ⊷⊕⊶ Cable Car/ Funicular
- 🚲 Cycling
- ⛴ Ferry
- 🚝 Monorail
- Ⓟ Parking
- ⛽ Petrol Station
- 🚕 Taxi
- 🚉 Train/Railway
- 🚊 Tram
- Ⓜ Underground Train Station
- ● Other Transport

Routes
- ═══ Tollway
- ═══ Freeway
- ═══ Primary
- ═══ Secondary
- ─── Tertiary
- ─── Lane
- ═══ Unsealed Road
- ▨▨ Plaza/Mall
- ⊪⊪⊪ Steps
-)═(Tunnel
- ═══ Pedestrian Overpass
- ▬▬▬ Walking Tour
- ▬ ▬ Walking Tour Detour
- ─── Path

Geographic
- 🏠 Hut/Shelter
- 🗼 Lighthouse
- 👁 Lookout
- ▲ Mountain/Volcano
- 🌴 Oasis
- 🅿 Park
-)(Pass
- 🏞 Picnic Area
- 💧 Waterfall

Population
- 🟊 Capital (National)
- ◉ Capital (State/Province)
- ● City/Large Town
- ○ Town/Village

Boundaries
- ─ ─ ─ International
- ─ ─ ─ State/Province
- ─ ─ Disputed
- ─ ─ Regional/Suburb
- 〰 Marine Park
- ⌐⌐ Cliff
- ▬▬ Wall

Hydrography
- 〰 River/Creek
- 〰 Intermittent River
- 〰 Swamp/Mangrove
- 〰 Reef
- 〰 Canal
- ◯ Water
- ◯ Dry/Salt/ Intermittent Lake
- ◯ Glacier

Areas
- ▨▨ Beach/Desert
- ▨▨ Cemetery (Christian)
- ▨▨ Cemetery (Other)
- ▨▨ Park/Forest
- ◖◗ Sportsground
- ▨▨ Sight (Building)
- ▨▨ Top Sight (Building)

John Noble

Kerala & South India John, from England, lives in Spain and has written about 20-odd countries for Lonely Planet. He first experienced Tamil Nadu in the 1980s when Chennai's Triplicane High Rd was clogged with bullock carts and families milked their buffaloes beside it. Autorickshaws have replaced bullock carts now, but the bustle of Tamil cities remains as exhilarating and exhausting as ever. John wrote the Tamil Nadu section of the Kerala & South India chapter.

Read more about John at:
lonelyplanet.com/members/ewoodrover

Kevin Raub

Delhi & the Taj Mahal; Darjeeling, Varanasi & the Northeast Kevin grew up in Atlanta and started his career as a music journalist in New York, working for *Men's Journal* and *Rolling Stone* magazines. He ditched the rock 'n' roll lifestyle for travel writing and moved to Brazil. On his seventh trip to India, a cow threw sand at him and he was nearly attacked by a monkey – but he persevered. This is Kevin's 23rd Lonely Planet guide. He wrote the Uttar Pradesh & the Taj Mahal section of the Delhi & the Taj Mahal chapter, and the Varanasi section of the Darjeeling, Varanasi & the Northeast chapter. Find him at www.kevinraub.net.

Read more about Kevin at:
lonelyplanet.com/members/kraub

Sarina Singh

Plan Your Trip; In Focus After finishing a business degree in Melbourne, Sarina travelled to India where she pursued a hotel corporate traineeship before working as a journalist. After five years she returned to Australia and completed postgraduate journalism qualifications before coauthoring Lonely Planet's first edition of *Rajasthan*. Apart from numerous Lonely Planet books, she has written for a raft of newspapers and magazines, and has been a high-profile travel columnist. She is also the author of two books – *Polo in India* and *India: Essential Encounters*. Her award-nominated documentary film premiered at the Melbourne International Film Festival before being screened internationally.

Mark Elliott

Darjeeling, Varanasi & the Northeast Mark has been making forays to the subcontinent since a 1984 adventure that lined his stomach for all eventualities. When not writing guidebooks Mark is studying geopolitics in Sussex while rediscovering the England of his birth after living abroad for over 20 years. Mark wrote the Kolkata (Calcutta) section of the Darjeeling, Varanasi & the Northeast chapter.

Paul Harding

Goa & Around; Kerala & South India Paul has explored India and all its mayhem many times over the past 15 years, frequently writing about it. He still has a soft spot for the south, where the pace of life is that little bit slower. For this trip he investigated Kerala's backwaters at close range, was charged by wild elephants in Wayanad, and carefully inspected all of Goa's beautiful beaches while taste-testing fresh seafood. Tough life! This was Paul's seventh assignment on *India* and he has also authored the *Goa* guidebook. Paul wrote the Goa section of the Goa & Around chapter, and the Kerala section of the Kerala & South India chapter.

Trent Holden & Kate Morgan

Goa & Around; Kerala & South India Having worked together on books from Zimbabwe to Japan, Trent and Kate were thrilled to be assigned to India again for Lonely Planet, this time working as coauthors. Based in Melbourne, in between travels they write about food and music. Trent and Kate wrote the Karnataka section of the Goa & Around chapter, and the Southern Karnataka section of the Kerala & South India chapter.

Amy Karafin

Mumbai (Bombay) & Around Indian in several former lives, Amy first fell for the country in 1996, when she discovered *idlis* (spongy round fermented rice cakes), meditation and endless train rides. In many visits since, she has written about everything from Bollywood to *mithai* (sweets), contemporary art to ancient religions, and yoga ghettoes to nizams' palaces; read more at www.amykarafin.com. When not on the road, she can be found watching Guru Dutt movies or singing filmi in Brooklyn, where she mostly lives. Amy has coauthored five editions of Lonely Planet's *India*. She wrote the Mumbai (Bombay) section of the Mumbai (Bombay) & Around chapter.

Read more about Amy at:
lonelyplanet.com/members/amykarafin

Bradley Mayhew

Northern Mountains & Amritsar; Darjeeling, Varanasi & the Northeast A self-professed mountain junkie, Bradley has been travelling to the Indian Himalaya for almost 20 years. He is the coordinating author of Lonely Planet guides to Tibet, Bhutan and Nepal, and recently completed a five-part Arte TV documentary retracing the route of Marco Polo. He wrote the Himachal Pradesh section of the Northern Mountains & Amritsar chapter, and the Darjeeling section of the Darjeeling, Varanasi & the Northeast chapter. See what he's up to at www.bradleymayhew.blogspot.com.

Read more about Bradley at:
lonelyplanet.com/members/nepalibrad

Our Story

A beat-up old car, a few dollars in the pocket and a sense of adventure. In 1972 that's all Tony and Maureen Wheeler needed for the trip of a lifetime – across Europe and Asia overland to Australia. It took several months, and at the end – broke but inspired – they sat at their kitchen table writing and stapling together their first travel guide, *Across Asia on the Cheap*. Within a week they'd sold 1500 copies. Lonely Planet was born.

Today, Lonely Planet has offices in Melbourne, London, Oakland and Delhi, with more than 600 staff and writers. We share Tony's belief that 'a great guidebook should do three things: inform, educate and amuse'.

Our Writers

Daniel McCrohan
Coordinating Author; Rajasthan; Plan Your Trip; In Focus; Survival Guide

Originally from the UK, Daniel lives in China these days, but has been travelling to India on and off for more than 20 years. An experienced travel writer, Daniel has worked on close to 20 Lonely Planet guidebooks, including seven India titles. This latest India assignment – exploring the realms of royal Rajasthan – was as incident-packed as ever. Scariest moment: being chased through the crowded streets of Jodhpur by crazed hotel touts on mopeds. Highlight: looking out from a rampart on top of Jaisalmer Fort to see the sun sinking into the Thar Desert. You can follow Daniel's travels round Asia on his website, daniel mccrohan.com, and he's always happy to chat to travellers on Twitter (@danielmccrohan).

Michael Benanav
Northern Mountains & Amritsar A writer and photojournalist who covers issues affecting traditional cultures, Michael has migrated with nomadic water buffalo herders into the Himalayas and joined religious worshippers on mountainous pilgrimage trails. The abundance of fascinating stories – and the friendships he's formed in these places – keep drawing him back. Michael wrote the Uttarakhand section of the Northern Mountains & Amritsar chapter.

Joe Bindloss
Delhi & the Taj Mahal; Northern Mountains & Amritsar Joe has been writing about India for more than a decade, covering everywhere from Delhi to the high Himalaya. He has written more than 40 guides for Lonely Planet, trotting the globe from Australia and Asia to Africa and Europe. If pushed, he would say his favourite spot in the world was somewhere in India, ideally with a clear mountain view. Between projects, Joe is based in London, with his growing collection of Indian musical instruments. Joe wrote the Delhi section of the Delhi & the Taj Mahal chapter, and the Punjab section of the Northern Mountains & Amritsar chapter.

Lindsay Brown
Darjeeling, Varanasi & the Northeast; Mumbai (Bombay) & Around Lindsay, a former conservation biologist and publishing manager at Lonely Planet, has been a frequent visitor to India for more than 25 years. Lindsay has trekked, jeeped, ridden and stumbled across many a mountain pass and contributed to Lonely Planet's *Bhutan, Nepal, South India, Rajasthan, Delhi & Agra* and *Pakistan & the Karakoram Highway* guides, among others. Linsday wrote the Madhya Pradesh section of the Darjeeling, Varanasi & the Northeast chapter, and the Maharashtra section of the Mumbai (Bombay) & Around chapter.

← More Writers ....

Published by Lonely Planet Publications Pty Ltd
ABN 36 005 607 983
2nd edition – December 2013
ISBN 978 1 74220 566 3
© Lonely Planet 2013   Photographs © as indicated 2013
10 9 8 7 6 5 4 3 2 1
Printed in Singapore